We, The People

OF EARTH AND ELDERS – VOLUME II

ALSO BY SERLE CHAPMAN

The Trail of Many Spirits:
Paws-Wings-Hooves-Moccasins

Of Earth and Elders:
Visions and Voices from Native America

Blood, Sweat and Tears:
Inside the American Indian Movement

For my teachers, Henri Mann and Fern Mathias, with much love and respect.

In memory of Antonio Wayne Good Plume –
in the all too brief time I knew him, Tony reminded me of why it is that I do this.

WE, THE PEOPLE

OF EARTH AND ELDERS – VOLUME II

Photographed, Edited and Compiled by

SERLE L. CHAPMAN

preface by

KAREN L. TESTERMAN

postscript by

LORI LEA POURIER

With foreword remarks by the former President of the United States

WILLIAM JEFFERSON CLINTON

Buffy Sainte-Marie image adapted from a photograph by Simon Fuller from her album *Coincidence and Likely Stories.*
Photograph of Chief Gall by D.F. Barry – Smithsonian Institution, National Anthropological Archives.

Design and artwork by Serle Chapman.

Gwich'in art by Lawrence Dean Charlie (Vuntut Gwich'in Nation).
Reproduction Manager and Creative Consultant: John Parker.
Project manager and International Coordinator: Sarah Gilbertson.
Transcriptions Administrator: Mary Hunwicks.
Proofreader: Ken Blower.
Photographic Printer: Jon Frost.

Graphic Reproduction: Colour Concept Precision House Leeds LS14 1NH United Kingdom.
Printed in Hong Kong by MANTEC.

Photographs of Serle Chapman by Karen Testerman (Pine Ridge) and Steve Dutton (studio).

Produced by Bear Print International Limited.
bearprint@bun.com
bpiltd@hotmail.com
www.gonativeamerica.com

Mountain Press Publishing Company 1301 S. Third Street W. PO Box 2399 Missoula Montana 59806 USA. Toll Free 1-800-234-5308.
mtnpress@montana.com
www.mountainpresspublish.com

Cover shots: AJ McDonald (Salish/San Felipe Pueblo) photographed at Nine Pipes on the Flathead Indian Reservation. Marley Shebala (Navajo/Zuni) photographed at Window Rock on the Navajo Nation.

FIRST EDITION 2001.

ISBN 0-9528607-5-9
Library of Congress Catalog Card Number: 2001132522

Acknowledgements

People who know about these things have told me that, in most instances, the bulk of the author's acknowledgements is disproportionate to the interest of the reader. That being the case, I'll ditch the concept of Julia Roberts reciting the Gettysburg Address and simply say that this is a book of, by and for The People, and quickly make mention of the following before Elvis leaves the building . . . As with *Of Earth and Elders* – Volume I, this book would not exist were it not for the knowledge, passion and patience of those who appear in the following pages and those behind the scenes who kept the wheels on the wagon and the author off Prozac. I am indebted to all of those who have welcomed me into their communities and homes during this process and for now being able to call many of them friends. I'd particularly like to offer sincere thanks and appreciation to: Rob Williams, John Rimel and all at Mountain Press for their continued interest and support; my longtime colleagues and friends John Parker and Eric Tomlinson who manage to keep straight faces no matter how bizarre the circumstances or requests I confront them with; Sarah Gilbertson who among myriad kindnesses even tries to break it gently down transatlantic phone lines when Leeds United lose; Mary Hunwicks for her friendship, time and tolerance; my bro. Steve Reevis; and Johnnie Walker who called out and listened to the bears. My sincere thanks to you all and to the following:

Marlene Anguilla (Indian Pueblo Cultural Center). Jack and Carol Bailey. Luci Beach (Gwich'In Steering Committee). Raphael Begay. Vernon Bellecourt (AIM Grand Governing Council/American Indian OIC). Wilbur Between Lodges. Big Mountain resistors and supporters; Dixie, Francine Little, Sarah Begay and Willie Begay, Jr. Ken Blower. Leslie Caye (The People's Center). The Chato Family. Patricia Cochrane. Cree Clover @ Donald Miller. David Cournoyer. Michael Darrow. Paul DeMain. Kitty Deernose (Little Bighorn Battlefield NM). Janice Denny (AIM Grand Governing Council). John Doerner (Little Bighorn Battlefield NM). Faith Gemmill (Gwich'in Steering Committee). Kent Gordon (Barnes and Noble, Oklahoma). John Gritts (American Indian College Fund). Rachel Hamilton. Steve Hitchcock. Jim and Lisa Hogan. Mary Hunwicks. Micheal Van Leeston (Mashantucket Pequot Tribal Nation). Henrietta Mann. Kaneeta Red Star Harris. Jill Johnson. Elsie Kahn. Linda Turnbull-Lewis. Wenda Livingston (The People's Center). Rubert Lupe. James Marienthal (Silverwave). Fern Mathias (AIM Southern California). Pearl Means (Treaty Productions). Wilmer Mesteth. Trace De Meyer (*The Pequot Times*). Merida Miller. Cheryl and Manny Morales. Julia Payne (Clinton Transition Office). Darlene Pearl. Betty Price (Oklahoma State Arts Council). Curly and Lila Reevis. Ellen Big Rope (Mescalero Apache Culture Center). Gayle Ross. Harold Salway. Margaret Sanchez. Marley Shebala (*The Navajo Times*). Lisa Standing Elk. Arigon Starr. Herb Stevens (San Carlos Apache Cultural Center). Karen Testerman. Andrew Thomas (Indian Pueblo Cultural Center). Guy and Kathy Tillett. Charles Towers. Montoya Whiteman (Native American Rights Fund). Debbie and Alex White Plume. Ricki @ Donald Buchwald Agency. Armstrong Victor. Willie Lone Wolf. Tribal Offices of: Oglala Lakota Sioux; Franklin and Bernadine @ San Carlos Apache Nation; Felicia Olaya @ Cherokee Nation; Nez Perce; Crow Nation; Sandra Newman and Chief Joe Linklater @ Old Crow Vuntut Gwich'in.

In closing, I would like to recognize all of those people in the book trade who never get mentioned but without whom there would not be such freedom for words.

And mum, you're right as usual – we haven't much money but we do see life; as always my greatest debt is to you and dad.

CONTENTS

WE, THE PEOPLE

GOVERNMENT BY, OF AND FOR THE PEOPLE?

AMERICAN INDIAN MOVEMENT

VOICES FROM NATIVE AMERICA

Serle L. Chapman

First Amendment

TRULY, MADLY, DEEPLY: WHAT LIES BETWEEN BLACK AND WHITE?

I'm back in a coffee shop in Phoenix on Friday 13, October, 2000, waiting for my friend, Marley Shebala. Marley has taught me much about the fiber of words and the sacrifice given that brings meaning and the freedom to speak them and the sacred layers of silence that fall in between and are suddenly revealed, those moments being the wings of a flock of small birds bursting in a plume from roadside mesquite. As I wait I remember another Native woman who in my mind is synonymous with Phoenix. I do not know this woman but I stood a few feet away from her once a number of years ago and although I would struggle to recognize her, I will never forget her. A park ranger at Casa Grande, a few miles south of here, asked her if she would sign the center's visitors' book. She started crying. "Mam", he asked. "What's wrong?" "These are my people", was all she said. That sunburnt grid of walls blown shallow and smooth by sand and time and peppered in caliche dust was constructed by hands that moulded one hope on top of another's dream and beginnings passed, renewed and fulfilled slipped through their fingers as happens in any home. I don't know what that woman saw there but it wasn't a ruin, maybe she had just found her way home. In the visitors' center it says that the people who lived there were the Hohokam and that in the O'odham language that translates to 'All used up', but that woman couldn't have been more alive. It's 110 degrees outside and hundreds of years later the anthropologists are still asking 'Where and why did they go?' Phoenix might have forgotten it's a Hohokam town but it will remember when the outside air-conditioning fails and everybody realizes why the Hohokam left and they follow them up and over the bajadas.

Marley is making her way from a rally across town after marching through the streets against the 'English-Only Initiative', Proposition 203. As I wait there's an odd juxtaposition, the synthetic view from this window and the window in which a man is standing with blood on his hands in the photograph on the front page of today's paper. I take a mouthful of coffee and think how he looks like he's just filled some hungry mouths with a piece of steak but he hasn't, he's just participated in killing a man and throwing him out of that window. I put my coffee down. I wish I didn't understand but I think I do. We're hostages, even here in this plaza:

The world passed by or at least the parts that were owned by the separatists in the privacy of their oblivion, hostages passing by an oasis of hostages. Feather down palms held hostage to the sun in concrete, held firm to provide shade for sidewalks, shade for the artificial and shade for their fellow hostages – the water spouting from an architect's mind consigned to a fate there would never be because there never was green concrete or concrete green. Women with tans real or imagined in spray-on orange pants and peel-here-to-reveal white vests quench the parched from thirst with promise real or imagined. So goes the ownership of land, then body, then soul, hovering around the needy, the consumers of want, they make this wilderness bloom for some where once it always bloomed for all and the concept of creation and the after from birth was beautiful, not a mess to be wiped from a floor, or paved over or ignored. A parade is muffled by this cafe window, a protest for the after from birth, the tongues of this land. These hostages to the cross and the sword and this idea called progress expend a moment they can ill afford from their life expectancy and then meld into the museums that display their lives and make this city cosmopolitan, and become a footnote in tomorrow's edition that may survive the coffee stains at breakfast and Columbus. The print's not good in this USA Today, *the color's are faded. A young man with spray-on orange gloves stands exultant at another window, but if this was real life and not a picture that orange would be red and those wouldn't be gloves, and the world passed by or at least the parts that were owned by the separatists in the privacy of their own oblivion. And the bloody hands and the life and death and the after from birth will blow around this oasis until a hostage in half-light will pick up yesterday's trash so the streets and concrete green are clean, tomorrow.*

I put the newspaper down as you always can when it's not your life or death. And then I wonder about this book: this isn't my life or death either but I haven't put it down. So what does that make me – an inside outsider, an outside insider, or a man searching for a tribe who in the process believes he has produced some kind of 'definitive work'? Or as improbable as it might seem am I none of those things, and I'm just following through on a commitment? Other than these in this introduction, the words in this book aren't mine and between the times that they were shared until now the only shift has been in the movement from the spoken to the written word, and so it's for you to decide. Do I care what you think? Maybe. Maybe on the good days or the bad days or the days without rain. But then reality intervenes. I've always liked rain. Beneath this concrete there is earth and the slightest touch of rain brings a reminder, a second in which the famine of disconnect ends. I recognize the smell of fresh rain. I recognize it but I don't know it, just as I recognize a kiva but have only seen the interior of my own imagination where that smell of rain is a prayer and the rain falls as chants that are songs to the memory's ear, but out upon the mesas where I have been they are corn, they are sacred, they are alive in the memory of the here and now. Footsteps rise and fall to them, voices are painted in that rhythm and from below looking up I've seen those mesas canopied by a swarm of stars, each dappling the immortal violet frayed at the edges where clouds slide into the contour of belief and the silt of the day's passage is poured over the landscape so each feature becomes a shape quieted by shadow in the desert basin, in the distance, in the mind. I remember sounds are colors and I look for the color of rain. Marley arrives and we share another part of the eternal procession from birth to death. We remember one whose journey was interrupted, then a couple more, and like rain I recall that death has its own perfume. In the course of my work I've talked to killers, natural born and otherwise, and I've tried to discern if all that each has in common is a fear of the lie and not the truth. *I've been told*, 'She loves me'. *But I think she loves you not.* Maybe there's freedom in a creed guarded by others and in the conviction of those others that it didn't happen that way there lies that belief in just cause, but I can't imagine there is because if there was your lips wouldn't belie what the rest of you says. They did it, it happened and in that stillness it's there in arterial brown not an onlooker's red, coagulating without the lie. 'Say I slew them not.' Then say they were not slain – but dead they are.

Now it is today and again it starts to rain and once more I remember that sounds have colors and if I can recognize this one, if I can dredge it up from where it has long since been buried in the useless importance constricting my senses, then who knows where it will lead? I might even rid myself of the beliefs of believers and ask, 'Show me a beautiful picture, a picture so I can imagine how life began'. The world I mean, not human existence. And not me. So where was before? Just where. I'm afraid to know because probably I've seen it. Probably we all have and it's safer in here where never before has so much been said by people who say so little. So little to believe but we're told to. These are strange days. Twenty-odd years ago I remember the collective sharp in-take of breath when, in some parts of the world, a man who was best known for starring in a movie alongside a chimp was elected President of the United States. Now it's happened, I suppose we have to accept that there was an inevitability to us one day ending up with the chimp, and monkey sees. The Makah held ceremony and asked a whale for forgiveness and its blessing to revitalize and sustain them and then hundreds of protestors demonstrated. "Hell, they're just pissed-off with us because they found out that Chief Seattle's speech was phony", an Indian man in Tacoma told me as far-right extremists and environmentalists mingled, and I think of that and wonder if some of those greens might be moved to protect the Gwich'in or the caribou from monkey does.

Do we create our holy men behind bars or are the bars full of men who claim to be, each sanctified by the distance from our touch and reach beneath this blindfold of good intentions and dissatisfaction in which we stumble for belief? So whose Indians are they anyway, said the look on the face of the right-on white radical, indignant that ownership of their greater cause and weekly issue had been threatened by a contrary opinion. You have to watch that T-shirt, it can be on your back before you've even tried it on and I can tell you that it isn't pre-shrunk or colorfast. Why did I put this person in? How could I put that person in? Maybe I didn't choose and maybe it just happened because I don't believe that all the real Indians are on postcards. Is there much difference between ignoring history, inventing history or reinventing history? And if we only listen to the people we like and ignore all the others where do we go or have we already arrived, resplendent in T-shirts and soundbites to preserve what's precious to our strand of identity or to protect a cult of personality it's easy to believe in? If we disagree with something somebody says should we dismiss it as a lie for that greater cause of political blackjack, suppress it for the sake of misplaced belief, or just deny it exists because it's easier to get through the night on that Appaloosa riding unburdened by thought? Who cares about balance or the truth when you've got a horse as good as that to ride? But who put you in the saddle anyway?

If you don't like some of the people in this book or you disagree with what they say, comfort yourself with this thought: It has probably taken you thirty seconds to pick this book up and about three minutes to reach this page but these are people's lives, lived and breathed, blood and sinew, and it's the book that's easy to pick up and put down. It took about three years of my life to put this book together and there are people in it I love, people I admire, and one or two who wouldn't be at the top of my list of dinner dates. Do I agree with and believe everything that is expressed in these pages? That's irrelevant because this book isn't about what I think or feel, only this essay is from me. I have observed some of the events and moments recounted in *We, The People* and played a part in others, but I haven't necessarily lived any of them and to borrow a phrase from Johnson Holy Rock, 'Therein lies the difference'.

Peace,

A NOTE ABOUT WE, THE PEOPLE

In addition to the photography in We, The People, *Serle Chapman conducted the interviews with the book's contributors. The interviews were recorded, transcribed and then edited for syntax and morphology in the transition from an oral to a written expression. In an effort to avoid any misinterpretation or misrepresentation of the interviewees or their statements, the text includes some colloquialisms. With the exception of the preface, foreword, introduction, postscript and 'First Amendment', 91 per cent of the pieces in* We, The People *are derived from that interview process, the other 9 per cent being written submissions. In the main, American-English is used throughout the book.*

Eagle Dance: *Laguna Pueblo.*

'Now is the time for more words . . .
The hour of the Indian has come.'

Subcomandante Marcos,
Zapatista National Liberation Army (EZLN)

An Indirect Descendant

THE TIMES AND LIFE OF ONE WOMAN

This is my life, or a part in this time. My grandmother, Sister Margaret Two Bulls-Hawk, was born in 1913 and passed away in 1993. Two Bulls was my grandmother's maiden name, her father being Tatanka Nupa, or Two Bulls, who also had the English name 'Fred'. Zintkala Cikala Win, or Little Bird Woman, was her mother who in English became known as Alice White Plume-Two Bulls. Their communion produced twelve children, so you can imagine how many aunts, uncles, cousins and nieces and nephews I have through the Two Bulls name alone. The Two Bulls family resides on the Pine Ridge Reservation and became enrolled as Oglala Sioux (Lakota) but my grandfather, Enoch Hawk, was from the Standing Rock Reservation and was enrolled as Hunkpapa Sioux (Lakota). My great-grandfather's name was William Hawk and he was the son of Chief Gall's sister, so I'm probably what they call an 'indirect descendant' of Gall. I'm proud to be related to Gall but I think too many people are hung up on having a direct bloodline with a famous Indian name, and somehow I feel that isn't what our ancestors' teachings reflect. Each leader had to earn their place of honor in the respect of their people; Gall was a War Chief, but that didn't mean his title and deeds

Photograph of Chief Gall by D.F. Barry from the Smithsonian Institution, National Anthropological Archives.

were handed down to the next male or female child, that child had to earn their own place of respect. I think colonialism and assimilation has damaged a lot of Indian people's thinking. It created a loss of identity and I'm reminded of that when I hear an Indian person continuously telling others that they are a 'direct descendant' of whomever, as if they yearn the stature of their ancestor rather than seeking to earn their own. It is honorable to be a direct descendant of great chiefs. It is also honorable to be a direct descendant of those whose names aren't mentioned in history books. Just knowing who came before you is honorable.

I'm a simple woman. I don't have a grandiose education, in fact I dropped out of school when I was seventeen. I was transferred from Chilocco Indian High School to a public school in Oklahoma City and I dropped out because I couldn't handle the culture shock. I didn't fit in. So far, through my thirty-eight years on this earth, I've walked on both sides of the fence and even balanced on the top when I couldn't fit on either side. I've seen the alcohol and drug scene, abandonment scenes; physical, mental and sexual abuse; and I've seen racism rear its ugly head in many forms. I've been to poor people's homes and rich people's homes, so I've slept on a pallet in a one-room shack with a wood stove on the reservation, and on a queen-sized bed in an ocean side mansion in California. And either way, I slept. I've eaten hardcore commodities, which I enjoy, and tasted caviar, which I didn't like. I've walked miles through blizzards to fetch water and food and I've flown in the finest airplanes to go to places I couldn't afford. I've been blessed to have experienced the things I have in this life, whether good or bad.

I learned how to survive and how to provide for my children in honorable ways, working as a printer, roofer, painter, waitress, cashier and writer. I've worked on movies. I've made crafts to sell. I've even sold my plasma – a pint of plasma put food on the table. I'm not rich nor am I poor, although I've been pretty close to living on the streets a few times. But, through it all, I remain proud of who I am and this is what I have worked hard at to instill in my children. Life isn't about how much money you can earn or having an abundance of material things. Life is about living it the best way you can in an honorable way. This is something I learned at a very young age; as the oldest of four sisters and one brother I didn't have time to worry about my wants because my worries were less than my siblings' needs. I tried to look out for them and as small as the deeds I managed were, they suffered less for it. I survived so they could live. We are all grown now.

My grandmother used to tell me how important it is to give something when you go to someone's house. And "Feed those who come to visit", she would say of those who may come to our own home. My grandmother told me a lot of things about life. I remember asking her why there were men who had several wives back in the old days and she told me that back then, a man would marry a woman and they would make a family together but when the woman could no longer bear children, she would allow her husband to choose a second wife, and that is how it went. She said it was all done in the greatest of respect with the consent of all involved. "Not like it is today", she would say. "No one really respects the other these days", she said. Grandmother was right, it is crazy. As a Lakota woman I find it hard to have a relationship, I'm always told that I'm stubborn or bull-headed. And I often question whether there are still honorable Lakota men in this world; there are, no doubt, but they are all married – which they should be.

I have much to look forward to in my children. When I am a grandmother I hope that I will be able to teach my grandchildren what I have learned in this life, and if I'm really lucky, I'll even get to teach my great-grandchildren a thing or two. I find it interesting when things happen the way they do. When, as a journalist, I went to interview the author of *Of Earth and Elders,* Serle Chapman, I couldn't have predicted the changes in my life that would result from that meeting. His work is important, as I found out during that interview, and we discovered that we shared a desire to tell the real history of the Indigenous Peoples of America. What I admire most about Serle is his respect for Indigenous People and through his previous books he is the first and only non-Indian author who has ever truly portrayed the Indigenous Peoples of America accurately. Never have I worked with anyone who understands us and our history the way he does; he may know more about us than many of our own people, but instead of promoting himself as the 'all knowing' he has taken these empty pages to *the people* and allowed them to tell *their* stories. Never in my life had I expected to be a part of this book and I feel honored to have contributed.

I hope an understanding of who we are as individuals and as nations will come to all of you who are reading this book. I think those who sit in the United States Congress should join with you in reading this book and then maybe they too will get an understanding. Maybe they will? In life you never know, and in these pages we share our lives. This was a time in mine.

Karen Testerman (Oglala/Hunkpapa Lakota) has served as editor for Indian Country Today, The Lakota Times, The Lakota Nation Journal *and* The Black Hills People's News. *Her work as a features writer for all of the aforementioned has been reproduced in publications throughout the United States. In 2001 the Oglala Sioux Tribe engaged her to lead a research effort into treaty and land issues, focusing on the Mitigation Act.*

"In this work, we celebrate the culture and contributions of the first Americans. We also remember with sorrow the suffering they endured because of past Federal actions and policies that had long-term and often devastating consequences for Native Americans and their culture."

President Clinton receiving the 1868 Fort Laramie Treaty Pipe from Millie Horn Cloud – Oglala Lakota Nation, July 7, 1999.

FORMER PRESIDENT OF THE UNITED STATES

WILLIAM J. CLINTON

native america – a proclamation

American Indians, Alaska Natives, and Native Hawaiians are a special part of the tapestry of our Nation's history. As keepers of a rich and ancient cultural heritage, Native Americans share with all of us the beauty of their art, the power of their songs, and the grace of their people. As individuals, they have distinguished themselves in virtually every field, from the arts to the sciences, from the world of sports to the world of commerce.

In this work, we celebrate the culture and contributions of the first Americans. We also remember with sorrow the suffering they endured because of past Federal actions and policies that had long-term and often devastating consequences for Native Americans and their culture. But, as the new millennium dawns, there is reason for optimism. During my 1999 New Markets tour of the Pine Ridge Reservation in South Dakota, and my visit to the Navajo Nation in New Mexico in April 2000, I saw first-hand a strength of spirit and hope sweeping through Indian Country. The Vice-President and I worked with tribes to foster this hope – through economic development initiatives and improved education and health care.

We still have much to accomplish, however. While my Administration worked hard to bridge the digital divide and bring the Information Superhighway to Indian Country, some areas still do not have telephone and power lines. We must continue striving to provide American Indians with the tools they need to strengthen family and community life by fighting poverty, crime, alcohol and drug abuse, and domestic violence, and work with tribes to improve academic achievement and strengthen tribal colleges.

We must also seek to ensure that tribal leaders have a voice equal to that of Federal and State officials in addressing issues of concern to all our citizens. I reaffirmed that commitment to tribal sovereignty and self-determination in November of 2000 by issuing a revised Executive Order on Consultation and Coordination with Indian Tribal Governments. The order builds on prior actions, and strengthens the government-to-government relationship with Indian tribes by ensuring that all Executive departments and agencies consult with Indian tribes and respect tribal sovereignty as the agencies consider policy initiatives that affect Indian communities.

My Administration proposed the largest budget increase ever for a comprehensive Native American initiative for health care, education, infrastructure, and economic development. As part of the Department of the Interior appropriations legislation, I signed into law one segment of that budget, including significant investments for school construction in Indian Country and the largest funding increase ever for the Indian Health Service. These are the kinds of investments that will empower tribal communities to address an array of needs and, ultimately, to achieve a better standard of living.

Back in 1994, when I first met with the tribal leaders of more than 500 Indian nations at the White House, I saw the strength and determination that has enabled Native Americans to overcome extraordinary barriers and protect their hard-won civil and political rights. Since then, by working together, we established a new standard for Federal Indian policy – one that promoted an effective government-to-government relationship between the Federal Government and the tribes, and that sought to ensure greater prosperity, self-reliance, and hope for all Native Americans. While we cannot erase the tragedies of the past, we can create a future where all of our country's people share in America's great promise.

Harold Salway, the then Oglala Sioux Tribal President, said former President Clinton was the only sitting US President in history to travel to an Indian reservation for a 'nation-to-nation' meeting. Prior to that, Franklin D. Roosevelt had been the last sitting US President to visit an Indian reservation when he called in on the Cherokees of North Carolina during his 1936 vacation. Former President Clinton was the first US President since James Monroe in the 1820s to host a meeting of tribal leaders from all of the federally recognized tribes at the White House, and throughout his administration he opposed oil exploration in the Arctic National Wildlife Refuge.

Introduction

Commentary by Faith Gemmill · Gwich'in Steering Committee

Creator speak through me and walk with me

K'eegwadhat Sheenjit ginhii Tsa' sha hinhaii

Gwich'in Niintsyaa

"My people, the Gwich'in, are currently resisting substantial efforts by multinational oil companies, corporations, the state of Alaska and the current President of the United States, to allow oil development in the Arctic National Wildlife Refuge. I would like to share our story with you . . ."

Grizzly Bear.

I am of Neets'aii Gwich'in, Pit River and Wintu descent. I was raised in a small village about 110 miles above the Arctic Circle called *Vashraii K'oo* in our traditional language, now known as Arctic Village. My hometown is very small, and we are a close-knit community. We live a land-based lifestyle and our culture is still quite strong, in spite of modern times.

The Gwich'in live in fifteen villages in Northeast Alaska and Northwest Canada, and our population numbers about 10,000. We are a people who rely heavily on the Porcupine Caribou Herd: The caribou provides us with our physical, cultural, spiritual and social needs.

Our creation story tells of the time when there were only animals. The animals became people and when that happened, the Gwich'in came from the caribou. So it was that a pact was made between us that still stands today; the Gwich'in will forever retain a piece of the caribou heart, and the caribou will always retain a piece of the Gwich'in heart. We are as one. Whatever befalls the caribou will befall the Gwich'in.

We became aware of this threat to our culture and way of life in 1988. Major oil companies, profit driven corporations, and the state of Alaska were trying to gain access to the coastal plain of the Arctic National Wildlife Refuge for oil development. This is the area known to the Gwich'in as the birthplace of the caribou and in our language we call it *Vadzaii googii vi dehk'it gwanlii* which translates to, 'The sacred place where life begins'. Beyond being the core birthplace and nursery for the Porcupine Caribou Herd, the Arctic National Wildlife Refuge is a nesting area for over 100 species of migratory birds, an on land denning area for polar bears, and year round home for the musk oxen. From a traditional perspective, as people reliant upon the land we believe that a birthplace is sacred and should not be intruded upon. We must allow the animals that time to replenish themselves.

The sacred place where life begins

Vadzaii googii vi dehk'it gwanlii

In the summer of 1988, our people held a traditional meeting to address our concerns over oil development in the Arctic Refuge, 'Gwich'in Niintsyaa'. During the meeting we spoke of the importance of the caribou in our culture and maintaining our way of life for our future generations. The meeting resulted in a united position among the Gwich'in people; that we could not allow oil and gas development in the birthplace of the caribou. We steadfastly maintain this position; without compromise we are united with one voice against oil development of the coastal plain of the Arctic National Wildlife Refuge. This political position is at the direction of our elders, and this struggle born from a spiritual foundation. Our elders had a vision that we would be successful in our effort if we educated the public about our way of life in a good way. We took this position for the benefit of our future generations. For us, this is a human rights issue. We only ask that our basic inherent fundamental human rights to live our own way of life be recognized and respected.

We have lived in the Arctic for thousands of years and we understand our environment, we know if oil development is allowed in the birthplace, the caribou will be adversely impacted and our way of life will be devastated. We want to teach all people the lessons the land has taught us. My elders instilled in me some of our traditional beliefs, and our reverence for our lands – and now I share them with you.

We, as Native Americans, have always maintained a close relationship to the land, and through this relationship we are respectful of all forms of life. The beauty in our way of life is the foundation of our spirituality. The Creator has Blessed the Gwich'in with the beauty of our home and our way of life. The values of the land and our way of life are hospitality, sharing, loving, and respect. To walk in beauty we must remember to carry ourselves in love and unity. The land must be kept clean and pure for our future generations. We gain a sense of peace from the land, the beauty that surrounds us.

When the caribou come to our village, my people prepare before their arrival. Our community is filled with excitement, united in our anticipation of this annual event. When we move up on *Dachanlee*, the hunt itself is an ancient ritual and the ritual brings our people closer together and to the land. The hunt includes many prayers and spiritual aspects in itself: the hunter offers prayers of thanks and gratitude for once again providing us with food; the women are thankful and are working in the camps together drying the meat, choosing choicest parts for our elders, and sharing in the food. Once again, a tradition that is thousands of years old is passed on to the younger generation. The young men learn the skills of hunters; the young women learn the skills of the women. Unity.

Bull Moose.

Dall's Ram.

"Our creation story tells of the time when there were only animals. The animals became people and when that happened, the Gwich'in came from the caribou. So it was that a pact was made between us that still stands today; the Gwich'in will forever retain a piece of the caribou heart, and the caribou will always retain a piece of the Gwich'in heart. We are as one. Whatever befalls the caribou will befall the Gwich'in."

Lynx.

Gray Wolf.

". . . all trying to gain access to the coastal plain of the Arctic National Wildlife Refuge for oil development. This is the area known to the Gwich'in as the birthplace of the caribou . . . We know if oil development is allowed in the birthplace, the caribou will be adversely impacted and our way of life will be devastated."

When we are out there on the land we gain a sense of peace, a oneness with all creation and the Creator. The land, and the beauty that surrounds us, gives us this sense. The wind, the air, the birds, the plants, the animals; all life forms have a purpose in the circle of life. If we break a strand of the web of life, we destroy the whole web. You see, all things are interconnected, and interdependent. When you are on the land you have time to contemplate all of these elements and take notice, you are at one with yourself and your total environment. The quietness of the land teaches you to walk in Respect. That is true spirituality. You learn that you are only a small part of this circle and that in turn teaches you humility. As you see, the environment has many gifts to offer people if only they would realize and take notice. Mother Earth is crying, we must do what we can to protect her, she needs to heal and replenish herself. Then later on in time our grandchildren will learn the true gift of spirituality from the Creator through the land.

The vision and hope of the Gwich'in is that our values will teach the policy makers that all life deserves respect and we should honor life, not destroy it. The Arctic National Wildlife Refuge is public land. We are asking for the support of all people to help us maintain our way of life and protect this fragile ecosystem – not just for the Gwich'in, but for all humankind.

Thank You All My Relations

Masi' choh shalak naii

"*When* our children are hungry, we *cannot feed* them oil . . . *We* have a *spiritual connection* with the caribou. If the *caribou are gone*, we will lose our *spirits* one by one."

Sandra Newman: Tribal Government Councilor – Vuntut Gwich'in First Nation

ELDERS
IN THEIR OWN WORDS

Semu Huaute

Joseph Medicine Crow

Location: *Lodge Grass, Crow Indian Reservation, Montana.*

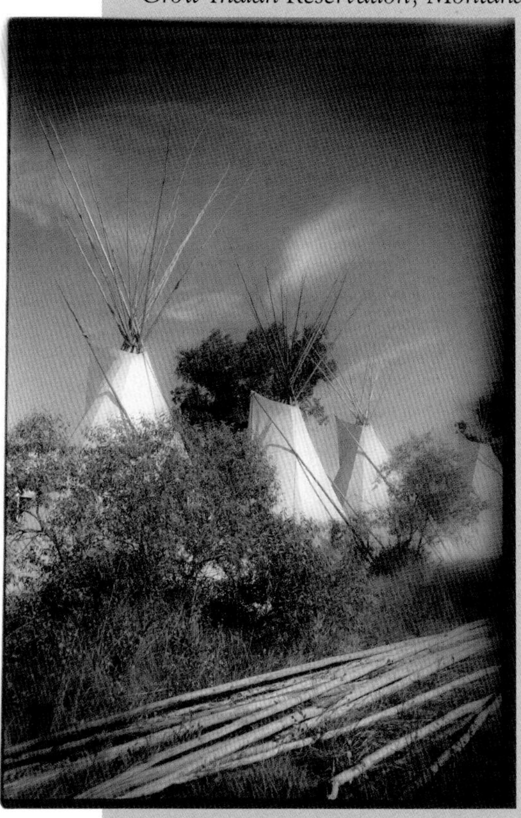

Above: *Running free - mustangs on the reservation.*
Far right: *Tipis at Crow Fair, the annual Crow Nation celebration.*
Right: *Overlooking Custer's fall.*

Joseph Medicine Crow

Long before the white men showed up over here, our Indian prophets knew they were coming. A long time ago one of them said, "There are people with light eyes and bushy faces who are coming from across the big water. A lot of them are already on this side. They are coming fast and before long they'll be here. They are going to take our land. They will take everything but when they show up," the old prophet continued, "my advice is to work with them because there will be too many for you to resist them. They'll be like ants, at first you can tread on them but more will follow. When they come, sit and work with them. Take them to other tribes and give your daughters to them for their wives. Some day their children will have the blood of two people and they'll be strong people." So in a way, that philosophy has

Joe Medicine Crow is affectionately referred to as 'living history'. A World War II combat veteran himself, Joe's grandfather, the revered Crow leader Medicine Crow, fought alongside General Crook at Rosebud Creek on June 17, 1876. Eight days later, another of his grandfathers, White Man Runs Him, was among the Crow warriors who advised General Custer not to enter the valley of the Little Bighorn. One of the most respected tribal historians in North America, Joe authored *From the Heart of Crow Country* and co-authored *White Man Runs Him*. He has contributed to several texts and documentaries about Crow history and the Battle of the Little Bighorn.

Apsáalooke

carried from chief to chief up to this present day. The La Vérendrye brothers were the first whites to appear in Crow country sometime around 1743, near present day Hardin. So we Crows have always worked with non-Indians but sometimes we use them, like in the Custer deal.

The Sioux were going to take over our land back then, when our country was still open and had lots of buffalo. It was getting dangerous for us, so when this campaign of 1876 took place, our leaders talked it over and said, "Let's go in with the white men. We'll use them and let them fight our enemies, the Sioux and Cheyenne", and that's what they did. General Crook came from Fort Fetterman, Wyoming with a big army and the Crows sent one hundred and seventy-six top warriors to help him. My grandfather, Medicine Crow, and his friend, Plenty Coups, were the young chiefs in charge. They were at the Rosebud as allies, not just as mere scouts. For the Battle of the Little Bighorn, it was more or less left up to the individuals to go where they wanted to on a volunteer basis. No group

". . . in the Custer deal, when this campaign of 1876 took place, our leaders talked it over and said, 'Let's go in with the white men. We'll use them and let them fight our enemies, the Sioux and Cheyenne', and that's what they did. General Crook came with a big army and

was ordered to go because there was no telling when and where the Sioux might catch us and if our good fighters would be around. So twenty-nine Crows signed up from here and six were involved in the battle as scouts for Custer, Benteen and Reno. The Crows always felt that way, that we used the government, and the government must have thought they used us because they called us 'Indian scouts'. White Man Runs Him was one of those scouts who told Custer not to go down into the valley. In the Crow kinship system, White Man Runs Him is also my grandfather. He was my mother's full brother. After my biological father, Leo Medicine Crow, died they gave his wife to his cousin, John White Man Runs Him, which was customary. He was White Man Runs Him's son so there's a kinship relationship and a blood relationship. Today, those Sioux and Cheyenne guys are always joking with me but at one time it was serious. Now some of my best friends are Cheyenne.

People like to travel. Human-beings can eat anything and that's why we are able to travel. The Crows travelled a lot. Our migration to where we are now began about AD 1200. There are a lot of theories about this, particularly among non-Indian historians and those who write books about the Crows, but this is what happened according to Crow historians: Way back in the 1500s, what might be called our ancestral tribe, lived east of the Mississippi in a land of forests and lakes, possibly present day Wisconsin. They began migrating westward around 1580 until they crossed the Mississippi to follow the buffalo. As far as the Crows are concerned, they separated from this main band in about 1600-1625. The two head chiefs of the group were brothers, one was called No Vitals, the other Red Scout. On their journey they decided to seek guidance from the Great Spirit and so they fasted at what is now called Devil's Lake. Well, they travelled on and were in the Dakotas by this time. Then they reached a point along the Knife and Missouri Rivers in what is now North Dakota and Red Scout decided that it was the place the Great Spirit had guided him to, and so his followers settled there and became known as the Hidatsa. No Vitals and about 400 others carried on and they just travelled round and round, to Canada, Utah, Oklahoma, and eventually back up the Missouri River until they arrived here in about AD 1700. At one time ancestors of the Crows travelled as far as South Carolina. It took them about 100 years of travelling after that separation and then, after another 100 years, they divided again. This group that had been led by No Vitals

the Crows sent one hundred and seventy-six top warriors to help him. My grandfather, Medicine Crow, and his friend, Plenty Coups, were the young chiefs in charge. They were at the Rosebud as allies, not just as mere scouts."

were now known as *Apsáalooké*, which in the Hidatsa language means 'Children of the Large Beaked Bird', and the white-men decided that bird was a crow. By the early part of the 1800s the tribe had grown quite large, maybe 8,000 people, and it had become difficult to move around and so they decided to separate again. So, because of that and I think some rivalry between the chiefs, one group travelled along the rivers and streams, the *Binnéessiippeele* – They Travel Along the Riverbanks or 'River Crow', and the main band here, the *Ashalahó* – The Many Lodges or Mountain Crow. The Mountain Crows sub-divided later and so a third group, the *Eelalapíio* – The Kicked in the Bellies, appeared. In the mid-1800s the Crows were hit by smallpox and the population went down to about 2,000.

About 1825, some of the so-called Mountain Crow went back to North Dakota to visit their relatives and when they got there they found a United States Treaty Commission talking with the Hidatsas. The commission had travelled up the Missouri River to make treaties with the tribes around there but as the Crows were visiting, the commission met with them and made a treaty with them right there. White historians call the guy who signed that 1825 Treaty, Chief Long Hair. It was just a treaty of friendship, recognition that they would help each other in times of war and such because the United States was worried that the British were going to come back and take this part of the country. Chief Long Hair died in the early 1840s and then the responsibility for making treaties went to Chief

Sits-in-the-Middle-of-the-Land. Sits-in-the-Middle-of-the-Land died in Wyoming one year after the Battle of the Little Bighorn, but he was the man who signed the Fort Laramie Treaty of 1868 for the Crows, which established our reservation boundaries and title. It was a pretty big area, 8,400,000 acres, but there have been reductions since. The first Fort Laramie Treaty of 1851 set Crow country at over 35 million acres.

Around 1600, before the separation, there was already an important clan system in place. Those people brought it along with them and the clan system that is so important to the Crows – even today – is a continuation of that. It is a good system that kind of subdivides the tribe into family groups. I belong to the Whistling Water Clan. A clan is a grouping of individuals who claim some relationship to a remote ancestor, sometimes it's an animal, which will be reflected in the clan's name. When No Vitals' people got here they drew out about ten or twelve clans; now we're around ten. A person is born into a clan through their mother, so the Crow clan system is matrilineal whereas some tribes are patrilineal.

". . . the US Secretary of the Interior issued what we called 'Secretary's Orders', which amounted to several pages of prohibitions. For example, if Medicine Men conducted ceremonies they were thrown in jail.

Although you become a clan member through your mother, you also retain a good connection with your father's clan. For young people, it teaches them to respect the older clan members, their clan fathers and their father's clan members. When I see an older member of my father's clan I say 'father', and I'm good to him. Your clan relatives pray for you and give you support if you have a problem; clan members look after each other. Same with the women. When tribes lose their clan system they lose a real connection. Clans are extended families and the Crows still have them in place and that along with our language is what keeps us going as a tribe. Our language helps to keep us together but we are losing it fast. Our children go off to school and get away from the Crow language and when they do, they lose that good connection with their clan uncles and clan aunts. When the language goes the culture deteriorates. We are working to preserve our language by recording it. We have it in book form now and teach it to our children through bilingual classes. It might be a losing battle but we are trying.

When the reservations were first established there was a direct attempt by the United States government to turn the 'Red Man' into a 'White Man' unilaterally. Every effort was made to 'de-tribalize' Indian people and here that included prohibiting the use of the Crow language. The government boarding schools came to Crow Agency with the missionaries and church groups in an attempt to kill Crow culture. The Catholics were here by 1887 and the Baptists by 1904 and they worked with the government to destroy our Indian ways, our sayings, practising our medicine and so forth. They worked hard on us Crow Indians and, of course, the other tribes. I think it was 1887 when the US Secretary of the Interior issued what we called 'Secretary's Orders', which amounted to several pages of prohibitions. For example, if Medicine Men conducted healing ceremonies they were thrown in jail. The Secretary's Orders were harsh and attacked Crow tribal culture in every way, be it language, customs or religion, but the Crows are what you might call 'culturally persistent' and hung on. They would hide in the mountains, like the Shoshones in Wyoming, when they performed the Ghost Dance. It was the same with the Sun Dance but the Crows quit Sun Dancing before 1900 and didn't come back to it until 1938 when they followed the Shoshone version. We were also hit with the Homestead Act during that period. This reservation was first opened to allotment in the 1890s when the government created two classes of Indians; those they considered competent enough to take care of their own business, and those they

The orders attacked Crow tribal culture in every way but the Crows hung on and would hide in the mountains like the Shoshones when they performed the Ghost Dance or the Sun Dance . . ."

didn't. That last group received trust payments for the land that was allotted to them, or alternatively, their land could be held in trust by the government. A lot chose the payment because at least they would receive *something*. So we lost a lot of land that way and also the other way, which was, if they considered you competent, you made an application to sell your land. When those applications were approved that land was advertised to non-Indians and that's how non-Indians acquired almost half of the land on this reservation.

In the 1930s things changed some. The US government brought in what they called Indian self-government, which was actually the Indian Reorganization Act. They brought it to our tribal council but we turned it down because we already had a form of self-government through the Crow Act, which was a Congressional Act from June 1920 that permitted us to set up our own government on our reservation. We didn't want to get involved in the Indian Reorganization Act because we didn't know what it would bring. Now we do know, a lot of tribes who signed up to it find themselves in the tight grip of the US government. Of course, on most reservations the Bureau of Indian Affairs comes in for a lot of criticism and in the early days they deserved it. Here, the BIA government agent let non-Indian stockmen use our land for 3 cents an acre! It went up to 10 cents an acre but that's how big cattle companies controlled our reservation range at one time and why non-Indian millionaires were made right here from our land. After World War II the BIA Agent became known as

Apsáalooke

'Superintendent' and today most BIA Superintendents are Indian boys but it wasn't like that when I started work for the BIA in 1948, there were only three of us Indians on the payroll and we were all at the bottom. We blame everything on the BIA but I think that without the BIA on this reservation the non-Indians would have taken over long ago.

There are a lot of reasons why we have to watch non-Indians here. One of them is Water Rights and we have to watch the State of Montana all the time. Water is survival out in Western country and in the old treaties the Crows made with the United States, we were given a lot of assurances about water. Then a big question came up when they wanted to build a dam – who owns the water in the Big Horn River? Crow treaty rights state that everything within our reservation area belongs to us, timber, game, water, everything, but then they started building the dam and the question was taken to court. It went through the High Court and the Supreme Court and they ruled that the river bed and the shores belonged to the Crow Indians but the water belonged to the State of Montana – well, if

"I belong to an organization called the Circle of Elders and the purpose of the group is to keep our tribal religious traditions and spiritual values alive. Now, about ten years ago this 'Wannabe Medicine Man' thing started

that's not our water why can't they take it off our reservation? We have to fight them in the courts but we usually lose, just as we lost over this issue and gaming, because these judges here are all politicians.

On an ordinary day here, most tourists won't recognize that we're Indians. We live in houses here now, not tipis. In the last twenty-five years the US government's urban housing program has put up some pretty good houses but before that a lot of Indians here lived in shacks and sometimes tents. I think the Crow Indians are better off than a lot of tribes. Here our natural resources and location helps us but on poorer reservations they don't have those advantages. You don't see the levels of poverty here that you do on some of the reservations in the Dakotas. We still have all kinds of problems though, mainly due to alcohol and drugs. Even our young kids are vulnerable and it's the same on most reservations. But drinking alcohol and using drugs is a world-wide trap and isn't just confined to Indian reservations and I think that's where we got it, through our white neighbors who used to come in here and sell drugs up by our school. Now we have drug peddlers from within our own people. Years ago we had all kinds of generals who came out here and killed Indians; Generals Crook, Carrington, Sheridan and of course General Custer, although he didn't quite make it. And there's one general still doing it – General Motors. We lose a lot of young people on the highways and that's exacerbated by this drug and alcohol situation. Among older people we have two main health problems, cancer and diabetes. Years ago we never had cancer but it's on the rampage and everybody here seems to have diabetes. I think it has to do with the food we have now and our diets compared to what we used to eat years ago.

Our neighbors, the Northern Cheyenne, have a rough time because of the lack of resources and opportunities on their reservation. They have also rejected coal mining even though it would bring them a good income because they'd rather have clean air and be free from the negative impacts of mining. However, coal mining hasn't hurt us Crow Indians. Our coal fields are up in the Wolf Mountains and nobody lives there. The eastern part of our reservation is underlaid with coal and because there's money it, coal development is allowed here. The pollution issue hasn't affected us yet. You can't stop commercialism, like the lumber companies destroying the rain-forests in the Amazon. That destruction has wide ranging consequences but where there is money in it from lumber or minerals they'll go for it and it's hard to stop them. 'A lot of horses have already been stolen', as the saying goes.

coming up . . . These guys also write a lot of books, 'Chief So and So on Indian Religion', that kind of thing . . . They charge hundreds, sometimes thousands, of dollars to Sun Dance or for sweatlodges. It's terrible . . ."

I belong to an organization called the Circle of Elders that consists of very old people and Medicine Men. The purpose of the group is to keep our tribal religious traditions and spiritual values alive. Now, about ten years ago this 'Wannabe Medicine Man' thing started coming up and these 'Wannabe Indians'. Because of our concern we felt we needed to do something and so we went after one of the notorious ones. We told him, "What you are doing is wrong, absolutely wrong, and you should stop it", to which he said, "Is there a law against it? No. So take your people and leave." And that's the way they operate, they're mean, sometimes dangerous, forward and brazen, not at all like us regular Indians. These guys also write a lot of books, 'Chief So and So on Indian Religion', that kind of thing, and it's a big problem throughout Indian country. They either give themselves Indian names or become buddies with an Indian who they use as a front man and then charge hundreds, sometimes thousands, of dollars to Sun Dance or to hold sweatlodges. It's terrible and what's happening is non-Indians are taking away our cultural activities, starting with our tribal ceremonies and even powwows. A lot of these Wannabe Medicine Men go off to Europe and get involved with these Wannabe's groups. In the Circle of Elders we're trying to influence our non-Indian brothers to respect our tribal religious systems in the hope that one day we might also influence them to treat our Mother Earth with a little more respect. That's our mission.

Above: *Elbys Naiche Huger.* Far right: *Bowie rail junction, Arizona.* Right: *The rock pile in Skeleton Canyon, Arizona, where Naiche and Geronimo finally acquiesced to the demands of the US Army.*

Elbys Naiche Huger's great-grandfather is the legendary Chiricahua Apache Chief, Cochise. Her grandfather, Naiche, inherited the leadership of Cochise's Chokonene band and was the pre-eminent chief among the last group of Chiricahuas to accept the terms of the United States in return for the cessation of hostilities. Accompanying Naiche was the Bidánku holy man Geronimo, who along with other illustrious figures from Chiricahua history such as Lozen, Dahteste, Asa Daklugie and Jasper Kanseah, feature in Elbys's first-hand recollections, or those passed on by her father. Elby's is actively involved with the preservation of Chiricahua history through the Mescalero Apache Culture Center and she has compiled a Chiricahua/English dictionary. Elbys was featured in Henrietta Stockel's *Women of the Apache Nation* and she has appeared in various TV documentaries.

Elbys Naiche Huger

Cochise is my great-grandfather. He had two sons, the first was Taza and the second was my grandfather, Naiche. My grandfather became known as Christian Naiche Senior, and my late father was Christian Naiche Junior. All of my people at Mescalero, the Chiricahua Apaches, came here from Oklahoma after 27 years' imprisonment. They're the ones that were sent to prison along with Geronimo and my grandfather Naiche. My father told me that Cochise's name was *Chish*, which means 'wood'. My grandfather's name, *Naiche*, means 'digging around', like somebody who is searching or looking for something. From what I heard from my father, Cochise was a great man. He was a tall husky man with great strength who was both respected and respectful. He was a great leader for his people, the Chiricahua Apaches.

Cochise was the kind of person who never wanted to lie or steal, it was against his beliefs. Nowadays people will kill to rob and steal money, but we don't care for money. A whole lot of money is not good for one person. If you happen to win a lottery or something, you should share it and give it to those that are poor. If you help others with it something good will come back to you. If you keep it all to yourself you're not a rich person, you only think you have everything, but it's nothing – you've got to have love and give to those that need it – that is the way Cochise was. Cochise was always

Location: *Mescalero, Mescalero Apache Reservation, New Mexico.*

"Jeffords told the story about Cochise dying from cancer but that's not true. What happened was once, when they were trying to fight off the army at the Stronghold in the Dragoon Mountains; Cochise got shot. He did not die from cancer, he was shot and killed by the cavalry. When his people saw that happen they laid his body to rest and threw rocks on top of him so that the cavalry wouldn't find him. The people who covered Cochise with rocks were the only ones that knew where Cochise's remains were and they told my father where that was."

thinking for his people, directing them to areas where they might be safer. He led them in that way, thinking more of his people than himself. That was the kind of love Cochise had for his people. He didn't lie because that's as low as a person can get. What are you if you're the kind that lies? What would your people think about you? Would they trust you again? If you're their leader and you're lying to them, they're not going to respect you as their leader anymore. This is one reason why the people believed in him because everything he promised, he tried to get done. In the Indian way of thinking, when you're a leader of your people you help all of them, every last one of them, and that is the way Cochise led his people. I'm glad I have his blood inside of me. Sometimes I don't even like the hospital here to take that blood from my arm.

Many things happened with Cochise at Apache Pass but most of the books that are written speak of when Geronimo and Naiche were around there instead of the times of Cochise. That part when Cochise cut the tent on Apache Pass is true. My father told us about that little boy that had been taken and that the army blamed Cochise. Lieutenant Bascomb accused Cochise of taking that little boy but he didn't. Cochise never had the boy but they didn't believe him so they tried to take him by force while he was sat in Bascomb's tent and that's why he cut that tent and took off. Cochise said, "I'm telling the truth and these people don't believe me! Where is the little boy? I don't have him! If I did I'd be loving him but he's not with me." I know that is true because my father told me. After that the trouble started. They killed some of Cochise's relatives there and it was hard for Cochise to trust any of them again.

I guess the only one Cochise ever trusted was Tom Jeffords. In our language, Cochise called him 'The Man with Red Whiskers'. They got along well together because Jeffords made a promise to Cochise one time, that he would do something for him, and he did it. He kept his word and that's why Cochise trusted him but there are still some things that Jeffords said about Cochise that are not true. Jeffords told the story about Cochise dying from cancer but that's not true. What happened was once, when they were trying to fight off the army at the Stronghold in the Dragoon Mountains, Cochise got shot. He did not die from cancer, he was shot and killed by the cavalry. When his people saw that happen they laid his body to rest and threw rocks on top of him so that the cavalry wouldn't find him. The people who covered Cochise with rocks were the only ones that knew where Cochise's remains were and they told my father where that was. Cochise's remains are still there in the Stronghold where they threw rocks on top of him, between the east and the west side, right in the middle.

I don't know what to think sometimes about the kind of life my people went through. They were always trying to escape from the cavalry. My father used to tell us how it became that little kids would have to run barefooted in the rocks and the cactus until it got to where the soles of their feet became hard like brick. It's very sad about my people. My

"Geronimo was the type of man who wouldn't let things go and did to others what they did to him. He wanted to defend his people that way and that's why he became the way he was. He fought fire with

grandfather, Naiche, surrendered because he was told that his mother, his wife and their children had already been captured and shipped off to Fort Marion, Florida. After he heard this, he told Geronimo what he felt he had to do, and that is what caused Geronimo to go with him. They went into Skeleton Canyon together and made an agreement with General Miles but the only part of that agreement the US government and General Miles kept was that Geronimo, Naiche and their people would be spending some time out of Arizona. Our people were all treated badly. When they took them from Arizona they loaded them into box cars like animals and they were sent on that train from Bowie all the way to Florida. They were imprisoned at Fort Marion and Fort Pickens in Florida, Mount Vernon barracks in Alabama and then Fort Sill, Oklahoma. It was meant for them all to die while they were in prison but some of them survived. While they were imprisoned many contracted smallpox and a lot of them went down with tuberculosis. It's very sad to think about and every time I talk about this it's hard for me. Before they were taken, when they were free and living in our country in Arizona, they knew all of their herbs and their uses. When they needed herbs for curing they knew where to find them and they always knew where to find fresh water and where the springs were. Our country was hot and dry but the people lived well there. But after they were taken to Florida as Prisoners of War, the government put them on islands where it was very humid and, of course, they weren't used to that and a lot of them became ill.

I went to Fort Marion, Fort Pickens and Mount Vernon with my husband to see where my people had been kept. I remember going across a bridge which was about three miles long, with the ocean on both sides. We got to where they had kept our people at one end of this island. The walls and floors of that fort are bare concrete. There was one fireplace and they had a few hard wood frames to sleep on. At Mount Vernon they had to move the first camp because so many of our people just died. My father was among the eight boys who were born at Mount Vernon, Alabama. He was nearly 90 years old when he died. He was a great man who was full of wisdom. He was a great medicine man and he passed that on to two of his grandsons and both of them are hanging on to the medicine.

When my father was still living we used to take him to see Cochise's Stronghold and the Dragoon Mountains. He felt good when he was in that area again and the places where Geronimo and Naiche fought for the people. Geronimo was the type of man who wouldn't let things go and did to others what they did to him. He wanted to defend his people

fire. I can remember listening to his last wife. She would make strong coffee and mix it with her finger. Once she made us coffee that way and told us that Geronimo always regretted surrendering."

that way and that's why he became the way he was. He fought fire with fire. I can remember listening to his last wife. She would make strong coffee and mix it with her finger. Once she made us coffee that way and told us that Geronimo always regretted surrendering. Geronimo died in 1909 at Fort Sill, Oklahoma. Four years later, in 1913, they finally released the Chiricahua Apaches. When they were released they had a choice to make, whether they wanted to join the Mescalero Apaches in New Mexico or remain over there in Oklahoma and 127 of them stayed there

Chiricahua Apache

I was born in the camp our people established here at Mescalero. In those days they didn't have doctors and nurses so my grandmother and my aunt helped deliver me. I grew up with my two sisters and brother but before us there were two boys and a girl who died before my oldest sister was born. We lived near the Mescalero Agency in tents and tipis, even in the winter. I can recall many times that I watched as my father went outside to sweep the snow off the tepee. Later the authorities moved all of the Chiricahuas to a small community east of Mescalero called White Tail, where we lived in two-room shacks until around 1936 when they built framed homes for us. Of course, we didn't have electricity so we used oil lamps and I remember many nights when I sat at the table with my brother doing homework by a kerosene lamp. Our water was outside so we had to haul it inside in buckets for drinking, cooking and bathing – we had to bring a lot of water in and heat it up on the stove to take a bath in those galvanised tubs.

It was a hard life. We had to get the wood for our stoves from the mountains; we had a heating stove in the living room and a cooking stove in the kitchen. We were all very poor in those days. At White Tail my grandfather, Naiche, became a Christian man which is how he got the name 'Christian'. He joined the Dutch Reformed Church and so did my father. My grandfather taught my father about our Apache medicines and he used it to heal many sick people. My father learned a lot of our Indian medicine songs and I still have those, our spiritual songs. Naiche died in 1921 and he is buried here at Mescalero as is my grandmother, Haozinne, my father and his grandmother. Taza is buried in the Congressional Cemetery in Washington, DC. Some say that Taza died of food poisoning but he didn't, it was pneumonia and the reason he was buried out there is because back then they didn't embalm bodies. They also say that Taza was married and had a child – he wasn't and he didn't have a child.

When we were at White Tail we used to be asked, "What are you all called in Apache?" And we always answered that we were Chokonene,

"In those days I used to see Asa Daklugie and Jasper Kanseah in White Tail. They had both been with my grandfather Naiche and Geronimo at times during those final days . . . When I went

the people of Cochise or Cochise's band. In those days I used to see Asa Daklugie and Jasper Kanseah in White Tail. They had both been with my grandfather Naiche and Geronimo at times during those final days. They were boys when they were sent away with the others to Florida. Daklugie was the son of Juh, a chief of the Ndé'ndaí, and Kanseah was a nephew of Geronimo. When I went into town, I would sometimes see Dahteste. With Lozen, she carried messages back and forth for Geronimo and my grandfather right before they came in for the last time. In Ruidoso I would see her in the passenger seat of an old blue pick-up that a young girl drove. Dahteste never had an English name.

It's very hard to change. When I started school I didn't know a word of English and I had a rough time learning. Like many others, I went through a lot in the 1930s trying to learn this different or modern way of life. I still believe that our old Apache ways were better. Look at it today, all the things that are happening and what they show on TV – it's not surprising that our children are picking up bad habits. When I was growing up we didn't have TV or these fancy toys. We learned the ways of our people. We made our own Indian food that was better for our bodies than what we have today. A lot of us eat junk food now and I can remember once crying for a hamburger when I was small. We were at a 'July 4th' celebration and it was the first time I'd seen a hamburger and I just wanted to taste one. They only cost 25 cents but we didn't have the money and my father said they were bad for us anyway. We would eat a good meal for breakfast to take us throughout the day but not eggs or bacon, we had stews, rice, beans, deer meat – there's a lot of ways we use deer meat; we dry it and pound it, make stews or just boil it with white corn meal. We were poor but we tried to stay healthy.

It wasn't just my family, it was all of us here, we were all poor. We used to go to school with torn clothes and shoes but we never laughed at one another because it was nothing to us to see that, that's just how it always was. I didn't have anything but I was happy. I could feel the love within our home. Everyday when I came home from school I could feel the love that we had for one another. The way your parents raise you, how much love they give you, you feel this within yourself and when they hold you, you can feel the warmth and the love from their bodies. When you're taken away from that it's very hard. When I was leaving home to go to a boarding school it was like leaving all of that behind, and I remember feeling that I would never come back to it and I was right, it was never the same again. My parents suffered from the separation as much as I did and

into town, I would sometimes see Dahteste. With Lozen, she carried messages back and forth for Geronimo and my grandfather right before they came in for the last time."

the closeness that we shared seemed to fade a little. Then I felt some of what my people went through. While they were at Fort Marion some of the children were taken from their parents and sent to Carlisle boarding school. I was told that some hung on to their mother's aprons and they had to be pulled off to separate them from their mothers. Some of these children never came back, they died there in Carlisle, Pennsylvania, while they were trying to learn English and to live the modern way.

Our Chiricahua traditions are different to other Apaches. The Chiricahuas are closer to the Mescalero Apaches on this reservation but to me, the only thing that all Indians have in common is the feather. When we see these movies that are supposed to be about us we try to laugh about them because the way they portray us is not true. They might have Indians in them, sometimes even Apaches, but they are not our people, they will be Apaches from San Carlos or White River. It's always the Western Apaches they show singing and dancing even though the movies are supposed to be about us. We have our own songs, dances and ceremonies; even our language is different to theirs. I've seen movies where they have Navajo people playing Apaches because they think their language and songs are like ours. If they want to make movies about Cochise or Geronimo or Naiche, this is where they should come.

Our ceremonies are very powerful. I have seen people cured from diseases, even cancer, by our medicine people here. I believe in our Indian medicine and rituals and I myself have been healed with it many times.

Elbys Naiche Huger

When our ancestors first came to this reservation, they put medicine in each direction of this land so no harm would be done to our people. We believe in our Crown Dancers, the Mountain Spirits, and we believe in White Painted Woman. Our girls go through the ritual of White Painted Woman, as I did. Here we say White Painted Woman, other Apaches might say Changing Woman or call this a Sunrise Ceremony. When a girl comes of age and first becomes a woman she is blessed and the preparations begin. It will take a year from that point because you have to gather Indian medicine, Indian foods, Indian paint and the deer hides which have to be tanned before you make the suit with them that the girl is going to wear. Each fringe on the suit, each jingle and bead, will be blessed. It has to be pure when the girl puts it on. Her Godmother will bless it at that time and with her Godfather, will support her through the four nights and four days of the ritual. Everything within her, inside her body and mind, will be cleansed and purified. Sometimes the girl will fast and by the time the fourth day comes around she has to dance all that last night. That's when her Godfather gets rid of anything bad from the girl and the Medicine Man will sing and use the deer rattle to help cleanse her so she will be set for a long life that will be lived in a good way. In the same vein, for a long life, she is taught to look into the fire inside that medicine tipi and not at the doorway or the people. Everything that is expected of her throughout her life, the standards we live by in our way, are taught during this ceremony.

"I would be glad to go back and live in the areas where my great-grandfather Cochise lived. I would do anything to live that way again, the way my people lived years ago when there was no fighting and they were free in the land they loved so much."

Our medicine is very strong and if you believe in it, it will heal you. It is important that some of our young people learn to speak Indian, our Apache language, because when they learn about our traditions and rituals they will need the language. There are a lot of things said in our language, especially prayers, ceremonies and rituals, that you can't say in English. Some are hard to say but we're not allowed to say them in English, we have to keep these sacred things in our own language. I have helped compile a dictionary here on the reservation for my people, something to help them learn our language that can be kept for the tribe. We're coming out with a medical dictionary next. A lot of our old people don't understand English and it is very uncomfortable for them if they are taken to a hospital and they can't understand what they are being told. With this dictionary the nurses and doctors will be able to speak to them in our language. As it is, a lot of the elderly won't be seen by a nurse or doctor, they prefer to use our traditional herbs and Indian medicines. Many of our elderly didn't agree to change to this modern way of living.

I would be glad to go back and live in the areas where my great-grandfather Cochise lived. I would do anything to live that way again, the way my people lived years ago when there was no fighting and they were free in the land they loved so much. I want to be strong for my people and my family. I'm the last one left from Christian Naiche Junior's family; my mother, my father, my brother, my sisters, they're all gone.

Location: *Indian Pueblo Cultural Center, Albuquerque, New Mexico.*

Joe Sando was born into the Sun Clan at Jémez Pueblo. He is widely respected as an authority on Pueblo culture and history, as evidenced by his position as Director of Archives of the Pueblo Indian Study and Research Center at the Indian Pueblo Cultural Center in Albuquerque, New Mexico. Joe has a principal role in the Center's museum presentations and he has taught Pueblo history at the University of New Mexico and Ethnohistory at the Institute of American Indian Arts. He has compiled numerous articles and papers on Pueblo history, culture and contemporary perspectives, and he is the author of *Pueblo Profiles: Cultural Identity Through Centuries of Change, A book about Jemez* and *Pueblo Nations – Eight Centuries of Pueblo Indian History,* described by the *New York Times* as '. . . an excellent book'.

JOE S. SANDO

Traditional Pueblo history tells of how the Pueblos arrived at their present areas of residence. At their place of origin, *Shibapu*, they emerged from the underworld by way of a lake. During their journey they were led by the War Chief and his War Captains. With them came the Great Spirit and He it was who guided the ancient ones, many of them finally settling in what is now called the Four Corners area. For unknown ages the ancient ones had travelled from place to place before they developed their civilization in the Four Corners and it was the Great Spirit who impelled them to migrate once more, this time to their present homeland; a journey they undertook to save their people from annihilation. Over a long period of time, they were brought to a land where they would be safe from natural disasters and this is the Pueblo homeland, land that was given to the ancestors of the Pueblo people by a divine being at the beginning of time. Here the One Above gave them their final instructions; the necessity to plant and harvest crops for survival – more especially, corn. The systematic raising of corn shaped Pueblo religion, rituals, prayers and dances that are practiced to this day. After the final divine instructions were given, the Great One returned to His home beyond the clouds and the people were left under the leadership of the *cacique* and his appointed leaders.

When we talk about the ancient ones we don't use the word 'Anasazi'. We try to tell the teachers not to use it in the Pueblo classroom because it is a corruption of a Navajo term that means 'Enemy of our ancestors' and we don't want Pueblo students calling Pueblo ancestors enemies. The word Ana means enemy or war enmity; and the second part of the term was supposed to be *saja* but the guy who documented it forgot that and wrote *sazi* – *'Anasazi'* – so Anasazi actually has no meaning at all but anthropologists picked it up and archeologists use it commonly. The Navajos who originally applied this term did not know the ones they were describing. The ancient ones who lived in the Four Corners region left that area between 1250 and 1275, and by 1300 they were living along the Rio Grande where the Pueblos are today. Many believe that the Navajos didn't arrive in the Four Corners until about 1400, one hundred years after the ancient ones had vacated their pueblos there, so how could the Navajos apply such a term to the ancient ones when they had never known them? The term that they should have used is *Kiisáannii*, which means 'People that live in four-square houses', which is what the Navajos call the Pueblos today.

The Hopis call their ancient ones Hisatsinom and although the Hopis might correctly be considered separate from the Pueblos, the *Hisatsinom* probably wandered to either or both Chaco Canyon and Mesa Verde and intermarried with the Keresan and Tanoan Pueblos there, which might explain the existence of the Sun Clan among the three groups. The Hopis themselves are two peoples, originating from the basin area of Nevada and Idaho. With the exception of the Comanches who went farther east and the Hopis who settled on their mesas, all of the other tribes that speak a similar language to the Hopis are still around those areas – like the Utes, Paiutes and Shoshones. Some who travelled through eastern Utah to

"Were there Libyans at Zuni? Because there were many others in the ancient world who did come to this area . . . On the Northeast coast and down in South America, there are also signs that others were here in those early days . . . the Olmecs carved huge sculptures of heads [and] one of the most striking aspects of these sculptures is that they have Negroid features and these are depictions of the people who intermarried with the indigenous people of that area and developed the Olmec civilization. It was the Phoenicians who brought those people . . . how the Olmecs developed is the kind of thing we forget because the New World tries to talk about history from 1492 and not before that."

the Four Corners even speak Hopi, but in Hopi country the Hopis call them Utes. They are all separate tribes of people but they all speak the language of Uto-Aztecan and whereas the Utes, Shoshones and Comanches developed and followed a horse culture, the Hopis picked up the Pueblo culture.

I can also see where the Hopis were influenced by a group of West Africans who had a trade route through southern New Mexico. A culture developed in the Mogollon area of New Mexico and the group of people there who were influenced by the West Africans are known as the Mimbres. They eventually moved on to Casa Grande in northern Mexico but today you can still see those West African influences on the pottery they make down there. Many of the Pueblo ruins on the Mogollon Rim are only known by Zuni names and this group of West Africans who came across the Atlantic influenced the Hopis and Zunis more than the Rio Grande Pueblos, but some of these things are hardly talked about because the American mind-set is 'Prove it before I'll accept it'. But this is the story that they talk about and there are other indications of that influence on the Hopis and Zunis; when we do our ceremonial dances we each dress differently, but the Hopis and Zunis both dance and wear their clothing differently.

". . . based upon linguistics, the Keresans may have come from the Caribbean but I haven't proved that yet . . . When Columbus arrived on Hispaniola one of the leaders of the Arawakan-speaking Taino

Our ties to the old people are our languages and our religion – they are still the same. There are three different kinds of Pueblos here which are distinguished and categorized by language families: Tanoan, Keresan and Zunian. The Tanoan language includes the three dialects of Tiwa, Tewa and Towa: The Tiwa speakers are the Taos, Picuris, Sandia and Isleta pueblos; the Tewa speakers are the San Juan, Santa Clara, San Ildefonso, Nambé, Tesuque and Pojoaque pueblos; Towa is only spoken by the Jémez. The Keresan language is spoken by the Ácoma, Cochiti, Laguna, San Felipe, Santa Ana, Santo Domingo and Zia pueblos. The Zuni language is spoken only by the Zunis. Collectively, these nineteen pueblos are referred to as the Rio Grande Pueblos. The Tanoans were probably here first, settling in the Cortez area of present day Colorado before moving on to Mesa Verde. The Keresans were next and they settled in Chaco Canyon. What I've found through my research is the likelihood that the Tanoans started out from the Tehuacan Valley in Mexico and began to migrate when corn was domesticated and became the food source that sustained them and enabled them to move up this way. Then, based upon linguistics, it is possible that the Keresans may have come from the Caribbean but I haven't proved that yet.

So far as I'm aware, up until now there hasn't been a Native speaker involved in the kind of work I'm doing and I have found a lot of similarities between the Keresan language and the Arawak language in the Caribbean area. There are several similar words but as an example I'll use *Hatuéy*. When Columbus arrived on Hispaniola one of the leaders of the Arawakan-speaking Taino people there was called Hatuéy; the Spaniards referred to him as the *cacique* but his Indian name was Hatuéy. Now over five-hundred years later, Hatuéy is still a common name around here among the Keresans; it means 'Corn Pollen' and boys are frequently given that name. I will probably go down there and to Brazil where I understand some of the forest people speak Arawak and I'll be interested to hear if any of it is still around.

The Zunis were the last of the three groups to arrive. Up until now, linguists haven't been able to classify the Zuni language but studies exist that talk about 'The Libyans at Zuni' and discuss the similarity of languages. Were there Libyans at Zuni? Because there were many others in

people there was called Hatuéy; the Spaniards referred to him as the cacique but his Indian name was Hatuéy. Now over five-hundred years later, Hatuéy is still a common name among the Keresans . . ."

the ancient world who did come to this area. About twenty miles south of Albuquerque, west of Los Lunas, is a big stone which used to be called the Mystery Stone and on it have been deciphered the Ten Commandments in Hebrew – and they're still there today. On the Northeast coast and down in South America, there are also signs that others were here in those early days. It's a well known fact that the Olmec culture created the first great civilization on this continent. The Olmec civilization flourished from around 1400 BC and included writing, a complex calendar and an elaborate religion. They carved huge eight to ten feet sculptures of heads out of basalt and these figures are wearing headdresses that look almost like football helmets. But one of the most striking aspects of these sculptures is that they have Negroid features and these are depictions of the people who intermarried with the indigenous people of that area and developed the Olmec civilization. It was the Phoenicians who brought those people across the Atlantic to southern Mexico.

The Phoenicians travelled a lot and how the Olmecs developed is the kind of thing we forget because the New World tries to talk about history from 1492 and not before that. But those are the kinds of things that happened because there was so much trafficking going on; some Near East people came across the Mediterranean until the Romans closed the Gates of Hercules, after which the Vikings were the main group to come across to the New World. All of these are important parts of history which are ignored because of the concentration upon 1492.

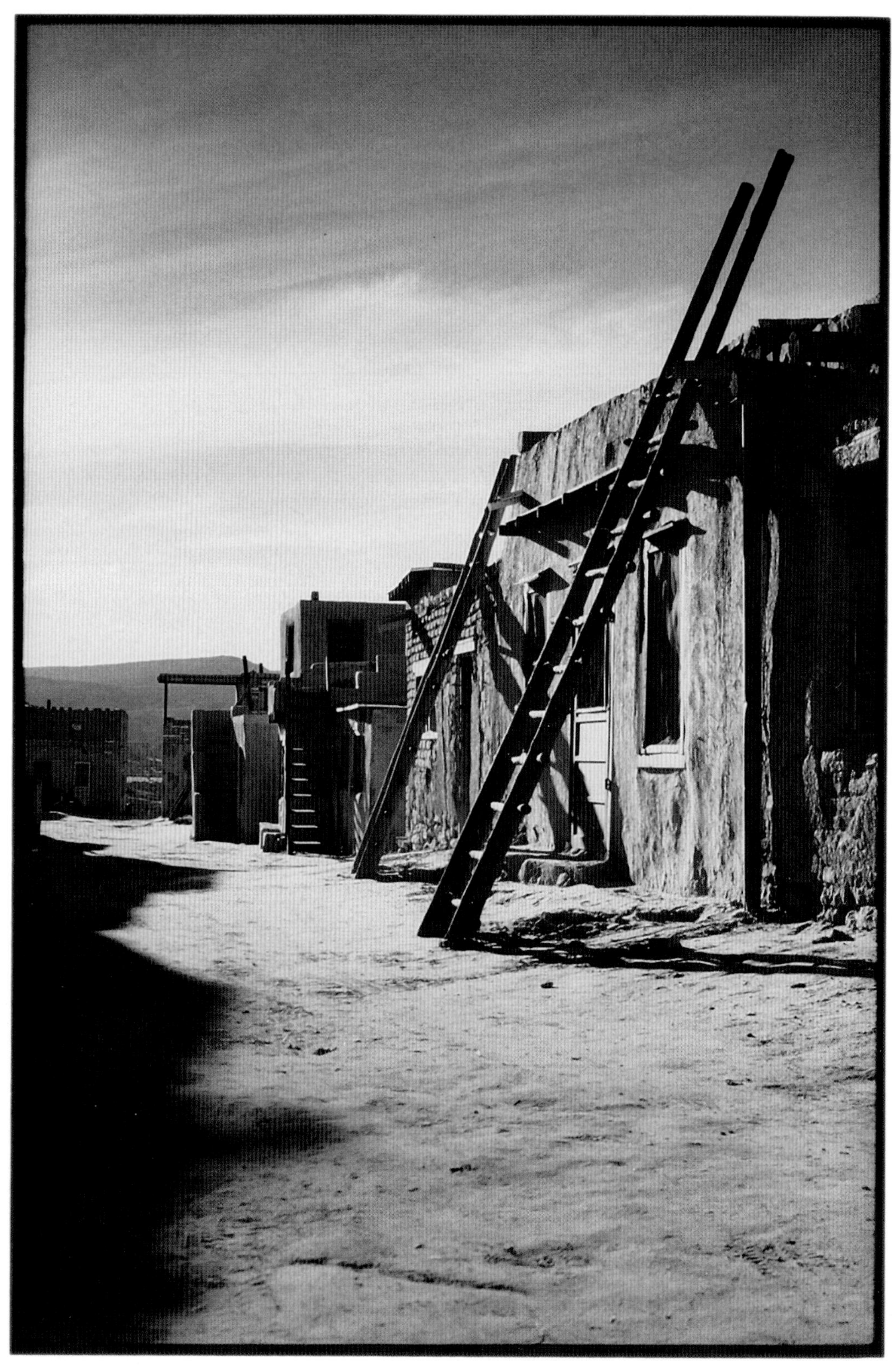

". . . the Pueblos went underground with their religion which is the reason why it's still alive. To this day, when the Pueblos have a ceremonial dance they are private – there are no cameras or sketching, and non-Indians are not allowed to observe them. This is what keeps us practicing our culture without losing any part of it . . ."

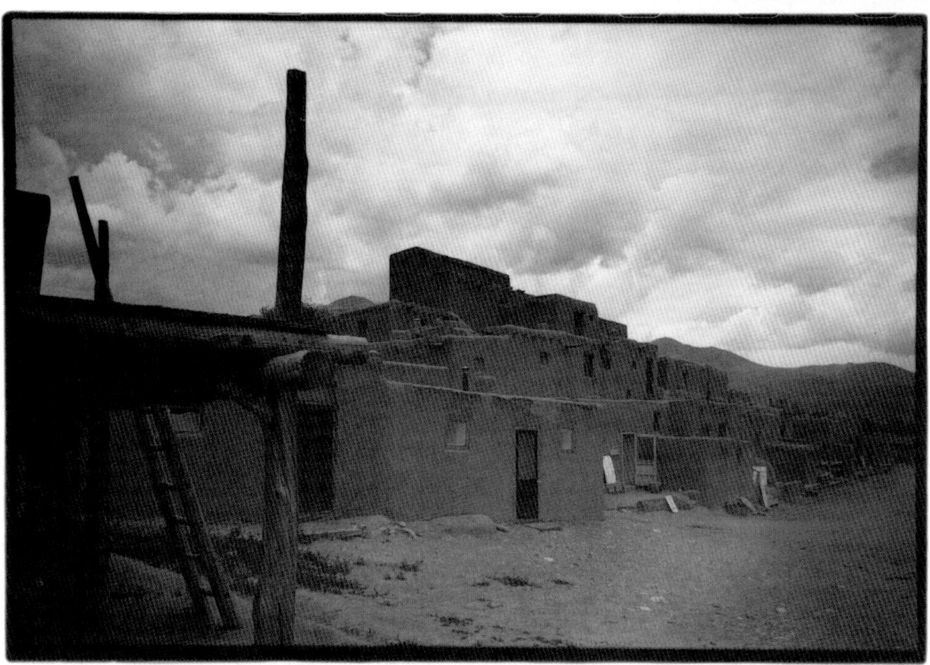

Left: *'Sky City' – Ácoma Pueblo.* **Top right:** *Inside Pueblo Bonito, Chaco Canyon.* **Above:** *Tua-Tah – Taos Pueblo.*

Hemish

With 1492 came the Spanish and the Portuguese, the Catholic faith and the papal bulls. They were the power at that time and whoever is in power determines what happens and it's hard to argue with that, but in 1680 the Pueblos expelled the Spanish. After coexisting for eighty-two years with the Spaniards under an odious system their patience was exhausted. The economic system, the forced religious practices and the cruelty, harassment and punishment for infraction of Spanish religious and secular rules, or for the failure to provide tithes under the *encomienda* and *repartimiento* systems became heavy burdens. Fray Alonso de Posada outlawed the Pueblos' Kachina Dances and ordered the missionaries to take every mask, prayer stick and effigy they could find and burn them. Just as it would be today, to the Pueblos giving up their religion would be like giving up life itself. They were often ordered to do one thing by the Church and another in the name of the Crown, so indignity was heaped upon indignity and then during the reign of Governor Juan Francisco de Trevino, a number of Pueblos were accused of 'sorcery'. The accused were

"Fray Alonso de Posada outlawed the Pueblos' Kachina Dances and ordered the missionaries to take every mask, prayer stick and effigy they could find and burn them. Just as it would be today, to the

either hung or whipped in public and one of those was a man from San Juan Pueblo by the name of Popé and tradition has it that he was the one who united the Pueblos and began the revolt – the first American revolution. August 10, 1680 is the date when Pueblo tribal and religious leaders united to expel the Spaniards.

The Pueblos remained free and independent of the Spanish for twelve years, until Diego de Vargas led the re-conquest of Pueblo lands. Initially there was some bloodshed but mostly the Spaniards had changed their attitude; they no longer applied the systems or tried to force their religion upon us. However, the Pueblos went underground with their religion which is the reason why it's still alive. To this day, when the Pueblos have a ceremonial dance they are private – there are no cameras or sketching, and non-Indians are not allowed to observe them. This is what keeps us practicing our culture without losing any part of it; our children are born into it and they accept it throughout their lives. In our culture, our religious activities can only be performed using our Native languages which also helps us to maintain our religion.

One of the reasons that the Pueblos became closer to the Spaniards when they returned was the raiding tribes; the Navajos and the Apaches. The Pueblos had taken the brunt of their raids after they expelled the Spanish, but after they returned the Pueblos joined with them to fight the raiders. They were forced to work together to fight the Navajos and Apaches until eventually they became *compadres*, and through being *compadres* they became neighbors and to this day each Pueblo community has a neighboring Spanish community. So this helped the Spanish and Pueblos develop what we call the culture of New Mexico.

I guess there are things that we have in common with other Indian tribes. One is the Bureau of Indian Affairs. Prior to 1849, what became the Bureau of Indian Affairs was originally known under the Trade and Intercourse Act, a bill that required the early colonists to be licensed to trade with Indians. For various reasons, we were placed under the protection of the BIA even though, in a way, we didn't really qualify. By that time we were already considered 'civilized' because of how we lived with the Spanish and through a body of law passed by the Mexican revolutionary government following their independence. Known as the Plan of Iguala, it was proclaimed to be a doctrine of equal rights when it was adopted on February 23, 1821 due to the following statement: ". . . all inhabitants of New Spain without distinction, whether Europeans, Africans, or Indians, are citizens of this monarchy, with the right to be

Pueblos giving up their religion would be like giving up life itself. They were often ordered to do one thing by the Church and another in the name of the Crown, so indignity was heaped upon indignity . . ."

Jémez Pueblo

employed in any post according to their merit and virtues and that the person and property of every citizen will be respected and protected by law." However, this doctrine of equal rights soon became the right for all equally to take Pueblo land, but even so, we were still considered citizens when the United States took control following the Mexican-American War of 1846 and the execution of the Treaty of Guadalupe Hidalgo in 1848 that officially ended the war and set forth the terms.

Articles of that treaty provided for the recognition and protection of the rights to private property established under the Spanish and Mexican regimes. However, in 1876 the Pueblos were denied such protection through the Indian Trade and Intercourse Act when the Act was adjudged to be inapplicable to the Pueblos and consequently some 15,000 immigrants settled on Pueblo lands. Later, in the form of *United States v. Sandoval*, the opinion issued by the US Supreme Court superseded that 1876 ruling and those 15,000 settlers became trespassers. Therefore, in 1913 we became recognized as Native American Indians like tribes throughout the country, because we were losing our land to squatters and only the US government could provide us with a remedy.

I don't say that the Spanish were particularly violent compared to what was happening in Europe at that time; they just brought European culture, such as it was. Eventually the Spanish followed Vitoria's Principles, based upon the philosophy of Professor Francisco de Vitoria, and only when those rules were broken on the other side did they respond militarily. Vitoria's Principles established that when the Spaniards went into an area they would offer their culture four times, but if the people of that area refused it and instead wanted war, then the rules of war would apply, which included slavery. The Navajos and Apaches very plainly came under that and were taken as slaves. But here again is a misconception; when people say 'Indians were enslaved', it would suggest that the Pueblos were included but they were not because they accepted Christianity.

Early on, some of the Ácoma Pueblos were enslaved after they challenged the Spanish. The Ácomas couldn't tolerate how they were being treated and in December 1598 they killed Juan de Zaldivar, the nephew of Juan de Oñate, who had been awarded the contract to colonize New Spain. In January 1599 Vicente de Zaldivar's forces defeated the Ácomas and all Ácoma men over twenty had one hand and one foot cut off, and those under twenty were sold into slavery. That's the only instance I know of Pueblos being enslaved. Pueblos like other Indians were forced to help build churches and a lot of Indian people thought that was enslavement,

"Many of the Pueblo ruins on the Mogollon Rim are only known by Zuni names and this group of West Africans who came across the Atlantic influenced the Hopis and Zunis more than the Rio

but once those churches were built they began to use them.

The Roman Catholic Church is so deeply involved in the Pueblo culture that it's hard to separate them. Half of our culture comes out of the Catholic Church today, like our governing system; every year on January 6th, the feast day of the Three Kings – Epiphany Sunday, all the new officials for the coming year take their canes – the sign of authority – to the church where the priest blesses them. We were 98 per cent Catholic until World War II and then a handful of the veterans changed their religion but usually it's the members of the Catholic Church that are the ones who become officials among the Pueblos. I know from my village that all the traditionalists are also Catholics; they would go to church on Sunday morning and in the afternoon participate in traditional Pueblo religion, but in the end they will be buried by a Catholic priest in a cemetery alongside a Catholic church.

It is said, but without definite proof, that Juan de Oñate established the system of civil government among the Pueblos and introduced the Spanish canes that the Pueblo governors possess today. Others say that the canes were issued by royal decree. However they came to be, following the institution of the Spanish form of government among the Pueblos, each governor received a silver crowned cane of office that is a symbol of justice and leadership. A Christian cross is engraved on the head of the cane to indicate the blessing of the Catholic Church and the support of the Spanish Crown. Franciscan priests apparently originated the giving of the canes, influenced by the passage from Exodus, 'The cane and staff to be their comfort and strength, and their token against all enemies.' When Mexico won independence from Spain, new silver crowned canes were presented to the Pueblos and those staffs are held by the Pueblo lieutenant governors. Another cane held by each Pueblo governor is the Abraham Lincoln cane which was presented in 1863 in recognition of the authority of the Pueblo form of government under the United States. In 1981 a third cane was presented to each Pueblo governor by the New Mexico State Governor to reaffirm Pueblo sovereignty, and in 1987 King Juan Carlos of Spain gave a second Spanish cane to the governors. So for over three hundred years this form of Native American government has been recognized; and the canes are symbols of the Pueblo governments' responsibilities to the people, and the people's recognition that all power and authority exist in their own form of government.

The Pueblo people are in control of their lands and I'm sure we'll keep it that way providing no coal or gold turns up in the earth. The valuable resource we have is water and consequently we have had a water rights suit going for over thirty years. We also face the challenge of bringing economic development and then retaining a balance between that and our traditional way of life. In the last census the Pueblos were identified as the Indian group in North America who have retained the greatest majority of their culture; although the term 'Indian' perplexes a lot of Pueblo people because when journalists use it as a generalization, in something like 'Indian Uprising' or 'Indian Gangs', non-Natives assume those headlines refer to all 'Indians', including Pueblos, and yet we weren't and aren't involved in those kinds of things.

Grande Pueblos, but some of these things are hardly talked about because the American mind-set is 'Prove it before I'll accept it'. But this is the story that they talk about . . ."

The nineteen Rio Grande pueblos have retained their identities because we never signed treaties with the Spanish, Mexican or American governments because they always recognized us as a people they could talk to on a government to government basis. We are sovereign people at each pueblo, each pueblo has a governor and that governor is a member of the All Indian Pueblo Council. The All Indian Pueblo Council was formed around 1400 in response to the raids of the Navajos and Apaches and today it is our third branch of government alongside the traditional system from the time beginning and the secular form introduced by the Spanish. The Council brings the ancient groups together in a modern governmental body that allows the two systems – traditional and modern – to work together to preserve Pueblo cultural values and handle the business of today in meetings with the state and federal governments.

Location: *Pine Ridge, Pine Ridge Indian Reservation, South Dakota.*

Johnson Holy Rock is one of the most respected elders in Native America. As an eleven-year-old boy, his father witnessed the Battle of the Little Bighorn and his family travelled with the band of the great Oglala Lakota leader, Crazy Horse. Johnson Holy Rock is an esteemed tribal historian who has appeared in several TV documentaries, including the award winning *Last Stand at Little Bighorn.* Johnson served as Oglala Sioux Tribal President during the US Presidential administration of John F. Kennedy, and latterly on the tribal council as Fifth Member. He is a voice of contemplative reason and wisdom through sometimes turbulent and challenging times on Pine Ridge. A statesman of the highest calibre, Johnson Holy Rock secured federal housing programs for the Oglala Lakota Nation, and remains committed to the Great Sioux Nation's struggle for the return of the Black Hills.

Johnson Holy Rock

Around the land of many lakes, we were known collectively as the Seven Camp Fires, of which the seventh is the Tetonwan – the Lakota. The other bands are recognised by their own names and respective territories. The Tetonwan drifted west, crossing the Missouri River onto the plains. With the acquisition of the horse they changed their lifestyle. They became more aggressive and with that mobility they moved quickly from one area to another so the horse made them a stronger people. Naturally, when they moved into these areas they encountered other tribes but because of their aggression and mobility they were able to pressurise the occupying tribes to the outer fringes of the territory and in so doing, acquire their hunting grounds, which in turn, helped to sustain their lifestyle. The Crows on the western fringe disliked the Tetonwan because they were so aggressive but for some strange reason the Cheyennes and the Tetonwan always got along. Maybe they recognised their similarities and built a mutual respect but other tribes, like the Poncas, were pushed out. That established the reputation of the Tetonwans as a people to be reckoned with and so other tribes, not wishing to come into conflict with them, kept moving away. Our reputation went before us and some tribes still don't have much use for us!

It is believed that amongst our band of the Tetonwan, the Oglala Lakotas, one particular event was a source of trouble. Over the years I've learned of two or three different

Far left: *Wounded Knee Massacre monument, Pine Ridge Indian Reservation, Oglala Lakota Nation.* **Above:** *Badlands – a Pine Ridge landscape.* **Left:** *Bull Buffalo in the Black Hills.*

versions of this, when Red Cloud clashed with Bull Bear. At that time the 'Smoke people' were the predominant group among the Oglalas and seemingly Chief Smoke had many wives and one version indicated that Bull Bear absconded with one of his wives. She must have been a good woman because Smoke was persistent in his efforts to have her returned, sending horses and other gifts to Bull Bear to achieve this. Bull Bear just laughed at him. Bull Bear had a reputation for being an aggressive individual and Smoke was old so he didn't want to openly clash with him. After a while, Red Cloud felt indignantly for Smoke, so he went to the camp of Bull Bear and told him that he should have more respect for a fellow chief and asked him to give Smoke's woman back. Bull Bear was a real powerful individual – and he knew it – so he would dare anyone to challenge his position, regardless of the reason or the excuse, and on this occasion he openly laughed at Red Cloud before turning his back on him and walking away. Red Cloud then left but he was very disgruntled about the way Bull Bear had treated him so he prepared himself and went back. He rode up to Bull Bear's tipi and told him that now he'd come to take Smoke's woman back. The story goes that Bull Bear said 'alright' and then went into his tipi, but when he came out, Red Cloud saw the barrel of a gun, so as Bull Bear emerged he shot him. That settled the issue as far as Red Cloud was concerned but Bull Bear's people, the 'Bear people', were very unhappy and very angry but instead of retaliation they just moved away and Little Wound took over the range of responsibilities for the Bear people.

Another version has it that Bull Bear openly challenged Smoke to physical combat because he wanted to humiliate Smoke in the eyes of his people. Being long in years, there was no way Smoke could stand up against Bull Bear and Red Cloud watched this unfolding from a distance. Being part of Smoke's band, Red Cloud went over and told Bull Bear to leave but Bull Bear insulted Red Cloud as before. Red Cloud then rode over to the Bear people's camp and challenged Bull

"I am the last of the tipi of Holy Rock, a descendant of Holy Bull. My grandfather conveyed to my father what his vision was, after which he was named Holy Buffalo or Holy Bull . . . Those involved with the Battle of the Little Bighorn were mostly the northern bands of the Lakotas; Sitting Bull, Crazy Horse and my grandfathers . . . Crazy Horse said, 'Custer was a foolish man. He came to make war – it wasn't me', and that about told it. I believe that because my grandfathers were involved in it and those ancestors of mine believed in telling the truth."

Bear. Of course, Bull Bear wasn't about to take that laying down so he called out from inside his tepee, "Just wait, I'll be right out with you", and as he came out of his tepee Red Cloud could see that he was armed, so he didn't waste any time and shot him down right in front of his tepee. There are one or two other versions but I can't say which one is actually true because I don't know. It stands that way even today, nobody really knows. The Bear people have their own version of what caused it and say it didn't involve a woman. I would like to know who is telling the truth but I'm afraid I probably won't know even when I'm ready to take the long journey on the spirit trail. But I heard that there was a woman involved, just as there was a woman involved when Crazy Horse got shot. So evidently women were held in high esteem.

In a way it is true to say that the United States government encouraged traders to court favor with the leaders of bands, the results of which are the historic difficulties between full bloods and mixed bloods, but in another way it was culturally recognised that if a trader found an Indian woman fair to look upon, then the best of what he had would be given up for her. In that sense, the more that was offered for a woman by the one who desired her, the greater the prestige for her father. At that time, the woman went to live with the trader, the non-Indian, and their children were not to be a part of the Indian people. I used to hear the elders say that when an Indian woman marries a white man she is then under the protection of his wing and therefore cannot stay with her people; consequently, her children were not viewed as Lakota. Of course, this thing has been kicked around back and forth, upstairs, downstairs and every place over the years, but that's the way it was viewed.

"I used to hear the elders say that when an Indian woman marries a white man she is then under the protection of his wing and therefore cannot stay with her people; consequently, her

After the different bands were confined on reservations, the US government came out and asked the chiefs the question, "We know that you have children and grandchildren that are not full-blood; they are not white and they are not Indian, so how do you wish the Great White Father to see these grandchildren?" And that was a tough question because even though these were mixed marriages, the mothers, fathers and grandfathers valued their non-Indian son-in-laws because of their daughters. I don't know how the other chiefs answered that question on the other reservations but I used to hear my father-in-law say that when they came here and asked Red Cloud, "Which way do you want them to swing, they are like the pendulum of a clock. They can't stay one or the other and they can't swing back and forth all their lives. How do you want to see your grandchildren and your daughters?" The only answer Red Cloud gave them was, "They're my relatives". His response didn't directly answer the question and they're still swinging back and forth. But since 1879, when Red Cloud's band came here from the Red Cloud Agency they had near Fort Robinson, the white men that were married to Indian women came back to the Indian reservation. Today it's still unsettled but if we went by the concept of our grandfathers, the offspring of a white man who took an Indian wife would not be considered Indian. Once on a trip to Washington, DC, when I was chairman of the tribe, the question was put to me by one of the Bureau officials and I was hard put to come up with a quick answer. I said, "Let me put it to you this way. Suppose, as an example, I had a bottle of whisky and when I took a drink out of it I replaced it with water. Each time I took a nip I kept replacing it with water. At what point would I have a bottle of water?" He laughed and said it was an interesting analogy but that the Bureau worked it out mathematically. I never was good at maths.

From what I understand of Indian culture in the nineteenth century, the leaders were very jealous about their station in life. Chiefs disliked each other because they felt threatened when another chief came into the neighborhood who had a better reputation than they did; likewise, other leaders who might be considered chiefs in the future and thereby be in a position to depose the incumbents. Crazy Horse lost his chance to become a

children were not viewed as Lakota. Of course, this thing has been kicked around back and forth, upstairs, downstairs and every place over the years, but that's the way it was viewed."

chief when he ran off with No Water's wife because that was a 'No No'. A leader aspiring to be a chief must have a clean record; he can't be accused of having run off with someone's wife, thereby violating the cultural requirement that they don't engage in that kind of behavior. But still, his reputation as a warrior and a leader couldn't be denied. Of course, when No Water found out that Crazy Horse had left with his wife he located them and just walked into his tepee and shot him. He thought he'd killed Crazy Horse and as he came out of Crazy Horse's tepee he announced that to anybody who was listening. However, he was afraid because he was still among Crazy Horse's people, so he got out of their camp while he could. He had gone there on a racing mule – I don't know how he came by it but he had a racing mule – but in his haste to get away he missed his mule and got on somebody else's horse. Believing Crazy Horse was dead, his people were very angry and they chased No Water for a while but whether it was luck, a bad aim or whatever, No Water hadn't killed Crazy Horse and a messenger left with that news and asked them to come back. When they returned they were still very angry so they killed No Water's mule.

I received this information from my father. When they finally took a pipe to Crazy Horse they told him that if he came into Fort Robinson the Great White Father would receive him in Washington, DC and agree to give him his own Agency on Beaver Creek. I used to believe that was the creek between Chadron and Hay Springs, Nebraska, but it was actually a different Beaver Creek; what he was talking about was another Beaver Creek, west of the Black Hills. By this time both Red Cloud and Crazy Horse's uncle, Spotted Tail, felt threatened by him and suspected that they might be deposed

by Crazy Horse as chief of all the Tetonwans. The story has it that when Crazy Horse finally agreed a lot of the wise elders told him not to go to Fort Robinson because they didn't like the look of things and that some, through Holy Ceremonies, had learned that Crazy Horse was going to die because there was a conspiracy. But by then Crazy Horse was tired of fighting and he was tired of running. The military was constantly harassing him because they were afraid of him and feared that if they let up on him and he recovered some strength, more followers would gather to his standard. They wanted to get rid of him, so they conspired to get him into Fort Robinson, where he was killed.

It was designed to happen that way. His people were becoming sick. They were being decimated by death. When the band fled after the Battle of the Little Bighorn, my grandfather's twin brother died as they headed toward Canada. When Crazy Horse agreed to go to Fort Robinson, my grandfather's group angled off from that main band so he could visit his brother's grave. He was completely healthy when he went up there to visit his twin brother's grave but when he returned he was deathly ill. The medicine man did the best

"Crazy Horse once said, 'Out there,' and he spread his arms in a wide circle, 'out there lie my people. One does not sell where his people lie.' I believe I would have taken the same view as my

he could to bring him out of it but didn't take long, so they took him back into the mountains and buried him by the side of his twin brother. Then my grandmother and the remnants of the group went on to Fort Robinson but by that time Crazy Horse was dead. His people took his body and left and no one knows where he is today. He was harassed all his life, hounded here and there, and if he lived today he would still be hounded.

My father was approximately ten or eleven years old at the Battle of the Little Bighorn and the first thing he recalled of that day was the commotion outside the tipi and the sound of horses' hooves pounding. He heard shouts that the Long Knives were coming so, curiosity getting the better of him, he ran out of the tipi. It was then that he saw the image that was stamped indelibly on his mind, of a long line of horsemen, the soldiers, coming along the ridge. Pretty soon the gunfire started and he said the sound of the bullets whipping by his head was like a swarm of angry bees. One of his uncles was going to take him to the battlefield but my grandmother cried and carried on, so in the end he didn't. Those involved at the Little Bighorn were mostly the northern bands of the Lakotas; Sitting Bull, Crazy Horse and my grandfathers, the Northern Cheyenne and even some survivors and leaders of the Dakota uprising in Minnesota, such as Inkpaduta. Of course, they were all described as 'wild Indians' but they were just living the life they had chosen – one of freedom – but the government didn't want that. As long as they were free the government believed they would be a pain in the you know where and they kept asking them to come back onto the Great Sioux Reservation but they didn't feel compelled to 'come back' because they had never signed the treaty that established the Great Sioux Reservation. That's when they sent the military forces out there to drive them back like a bunch of cattle and strangely, two days before Custer arrived in the vicinity, the chiefs and headmen took council and said if the army came peacefully and asked them to go to the reservation, they'd go. They were prepared to do it and they weren't going to fight but the mistake Custer made was that he attacked without formality and they weren't going to take that. They were forced to defend themselves because they had their women and children there and what little else they had left, and so history tells and re-tells what happened at the Little Bighorn depending on who's writing the story. Following the battle, Crazy Horse said, "Custer was a foolish man. He came to make war, it wasn't me", and that about told it. I believe that because my grandfathers were involved in it and those ancestors of mine believed in telling the truth. When they said something, it was so. If they committed themselves to something, they committed themselves without condition, so when they said they were prepared to come back under peaceful conditions I believe that. But the time and the place didn't permit that because the man who searched for them was intent on building a great reputation as an Indian

grandfathers. This was their land, this was the land of their ancestors. If I had been living then, I'd probably have been one of the 'wild Indians' and I would have lived and died accordingly."

fighter. From what I can find out about the man he was a glory hunter and he was impetuous in his behaviour, so in a way he found whatever it was that he was looking for. He was told to go and scout, to locate the Indians, but not to do anything – to wait for his compatriots – but he didn't want to let the others get in on a job he could do all by himself. His Crow scouts told him that the valley of the Little Bighorn was 'crawling with Indians', but he told them, "I brought you along to find them. The job is done and you can leave. The rest is mine." And I guess it was. I believe I would have taken the same view as my grandfathers. This was their land, this was the land of their ancestors. Crazy Horse once said, "Out there," and he spread his arms in a wide circle, "out there lie my people. One does not sell where his people lie." I have the same view. If I had been living then, I'd probably have been one of the 'wild Indians' and I would have lived and died accordingly. In the end, did anyone else gain anything? The Crows who scouted for the military – are they free to roam? No. They're on the same type of land that has been parceled out to all other such people, so they didn't gain anything. There may have been a little favorable treatment but as far as a place of occupation and life, it's no better than ours.

The location of our reservation was located based upon the viewpoint of Red Cloud, with the exception of the Black Hills. Red Cloud considered the Black Hills to be his storage bag, the place where he went for sustenance, "If a sick man goes into the Black Hills in the fall he will return fat and healthy in spring. So I want to live close to my storage place", he explained. The western boundary of this reservation was to have been the 104th parallel but when they surveyed it they pulled it back to the 103rd, so although Red Cloud's intentions were good he didn't get the cooperation he anticipated because he wanted his reservation butting up against the southern part of the Black Hills and it didn't happen. We were placed out here in the most barren part of the Dakotas and he didn't receive what he thought he would in accordance with the [Fort Laramie] Treaty of 1868 because to the north of where he wanted to be gold was discovered and it is doubtful that he could have held on to that land. In a way he was one of the last chiefs to sign the Treaty of 1868. The foremost chief at that time was an old chief, Man Afraid of His Horses, whose name is the first in the list of signers. Red Cloud didn't sign on April 29th as most did, he waited until November. I suppose he wanted to be seen as a hold-out but he wasn't very strong about it, he wasn't like Sitting Bull or Crazy Horse because the Government knew they could pretty well control Red Cloud but with Sitting Bull and Crazy Horse they weren't so sure, that's why they had to get rid of them. They killed both of them which left the 'aggressive band' of the Sioux Nation without a leader, or at least the type of leader they needed.

The treaties that were signed are still alive and I'm ready to debate

". . . the Oglalas were assigned to Pine Ridge. When they finally realized that they no longer had freedom of movement they had already become slaves. They had to live under the concepts of this

the issue with anyone, anywhere, even the smartest attorneys. I'm guided by the findings of the Supreme Court that the treaties were made with a people that were unlettered. Therefore it is only right and proper that the treaties should be interpreted according to the way the Indians themselves understood them, so I have my own interpretation as compared to the way the Supreme Court interprets it. They're just as valid as in 1868 and 1851. That's why when a reporter approached me from the *Wall Street Journal* and asked me if I believed that the Lakotas would get the Black Hills back, I said, "Of course we will". And he said, "How do you believe they will do it?" I said, "Tell me this. If you were involved in a game of poker and you held a winning hand, would you show it to your opponent?"

It is true that Hitler based the model of his concentration camps on early reservations. As our land mass was diminished, the Oglalas were assigned to the Pine Ridge reservation. When they finally realized that they no longer had freedom of movement they had already become slaves. They had to live under the concepts of this other civilisation and they found it very hard. They could see then that this was a vast prison where they were concentrated and that's when they knew that they were enslaved to a system that was not theirs. But it was too late then to do anything. All the great leaders and warriors were gone and today that type of strong aggressive leadership is gone. A few might rise up every now and then but it's not the true way of Lakota leadership. The aggressiveness is gone. If they are told that they have to negotiate for whatever they can get and the pressure becomes too great, they fold. They do not act like their grandfathers did. They don't show that degree of aggression to their opponents and impart to them that they have a right to behave as their grandfathers. We have lost that, where Lakota ancestors were proud to point their fingers and let everyone know who their descendants were. I am the last of the tepee of Holy Rock, a descendant of Holy Bull. The one thing I still believe is that with the right set of principles, an amount of aggressiveness can be followed. We still have the opportunity – I saw that in my vision. Consider the fall of the Berlin Wall and the reunification of a people who were also divided and conquered. They were restored and the US was very prominent in that restoration. They did have a selfish reason for doing it, to create a buffer between the western nations and the big Russian bear but regardless of self-interests, Germany was restored and the same principles should apply to the Sioux Nation. We should have our land restored to us just like they restored the former German empire. They still might and that's what I told the *Wall Street Journal* reporter when I told him we would get our Black Hills back.

I remember that the traditional people in our neighborhood always came to our house to confer with my father and make a determination as to which way they were going to jump when the thorny questions were raised.

other civilisation and they found it very hard. They could see then that this was a vast prison where they were concentrated and that's when they knew that they were enslaved to a system that was not theirs."

At the time that the Indian Reorganization Act came about I was in junior high and I didn't understand much about politics or legislative activity but I remember my father saying that he would not go to the voting place because our traditional people did not want it. When the result of the vote was made public the traditional people were unhappy and they could not understand why it had happened; mainly because they didn't understand the voting system. Up to then, the leadership had always been determined for them by the elders, whereby the retired chiefs and headmen were depended upon to advise with their wisdom and knowledge, and so this voting was completely unfamiliar to them. Had they known what the requirements were and why it was necessary to vote, they would not have had the Indian Reorganization Act, but no one advised them and therein lies the reason as to why we have the Indian Reorganization Act. However, the situation was partially retrieved by the constitution; the Act was adopted and the constitution was adopted by a real narrow vote, but by the time the US authorities came back and suggested the people vote on a charter, the traditional leaders understood what was happening and they went to the polls and knocked it in the creek by almost two to one. So we are not chartered – we are organized as a tribe under the Indian Reorganization Act. Even today our tribal council has a constitution and is organized but still retains a hold on the treaties – basically we still retain our rights and privileges under treaty law. So the tribal council are often caught in the middle and when difficult issues arise there is a lot of confusion because young people see things differently to us who are longer in years. We tend to have a division of thought and viewpoint but usually, over the long haul, the young people listen to us.

One thing we flounder over is money and that usually ends up being our Waterloo. We do not know how to handle money. We never did and never have. I have lived this long and a lot of money has passed through my hands. The meaning of it took me a long time to understand and even today, when they analyze money and discern that one group has progressed successfully whereas another group is almost on the rocks, I have a lack of knowledge. I can sympathise with those who don't know how, because after all these years, I don't know any better than when I got my first pay check. It's at this stage, the use of money, where our present type of government falters and sometimes fails. There are some tribes that are very successful but while we are the descendants of 'wild Indians' maybe we have an excuse!

There are significant differences between the IRA system of government and the traditional Lakota form of government. The Indian Reorganization Act governments are based constitutionally in their structure, whereas I believe traditionally orientated people lean more to tribal law as governance; so it's two different concepts. Under traditional law, if the chief system was restored, the chief would be the cure all and all the rights of the

"Consider the fall of the Berlin Wall and the reunification of a people who were also divided and conquered. They were restored and the US was very prominent in that restoration

people would be vested in that one man. He is the chief negotiator for the people. They don't have to go out there and argue and fuss about different issues, it's up to the Chief and he will listen patiently and help to interpret the terms or whatever but if he says no, that's it. There is no room for negotiation because he has a whole parcel of people that he is responsible for. So when he says no, the people accept it, good or bad, because he is their leader. Under IRA constitutional government, you have very different offices. You have a governmental structure which sets forth the powers of the legislative bodies, the executive officers and the courts, and those are supposed to provide the checks and balances for that democratic form of government – and therein lies the difference in the understanding.

Under the traditional form of tribal government the people feel comfortable, especially if they have a wise, strong, fearless, aggressive chief. They are comfortable because he is looking out for their best interests and they accept that and support him. There could be a few headmen that would disagree with some of his interpretations and policies regarding how his people should live, but not much beyond that. There would be no open opposition but by the same standard that he has total authority to make decisions for his people, if he did something wrong and injured the lives of his people, the council of chiefs and headmen would call a meeting in a council tipi. In there would sit the council circle with the chief's place in the center. If he was going to be impeached or removed no one would openly charge him with wrongdoing. There would be no articles of impeachment, nobody would prosecute him or question him before the council; instead, a large bowl of liquid fat would be set in front of his chosen place as Chief, and every chief knew what that bowl of liquid fat meant. Nobody would accuse him but it would be there and he had to either drink all of it, or remove his symbol of authority, his war bonnet, and walk out of the council tipi with as much dignity as he could muster if he wanted to be a living ex-chief! I used to believe that it was just symbolic, that if he chose to drink the big bowl of liquid fat that the worst that could come of it would be a month of having the runs and an upset system. So I casually asked a medical officer what would happen if a man drank a large bowl of liquid fat and he said that if he had nothing in his stomach and drank it all, he would probably be dead in two hours or close thereby, because the liquid fat would permeate his whole system and get into his blood stream and it would be just a matter of time. So it was a very drastic impeachment but the choice was not the council's, it was the chief's – whether he wanted to be a dead chief or a live ex-chief. If he drank it he died and they had to choose another chief. If he took off his symbol in recognition of his impeachment they still had to choose another leader. I mentioned this to a man a while back. I said, "If you don't behave, we'll make you drink a big bowl of liquid fat." He said, "What

. . . the same principles should apply to the Sioux Nation. We should have our land restored to us just like they restored the former German empire."

for?" I told him that was the traditional impeachment, to which he said, "I don't know anything about that." That's the difference. They don't understand the traditional form of government enough to fall back to it and live comfortably under the rules of tribal law. They still don't know enough about modern concepts – the government constitution, or a democratic way of operating tribal government – to demonstrate an ability to uphold a successful form of government. They are in the middle again. Some talk real aggressive, saying we can do it, that we have enough education and we can make it work, but I have been around long enough to know and I have seen them come and go. Very few of them carry out tribal government that I would term as being successful in nature. So I never commit myself as to what I would favor because I know that we are caught in the middle. Over a long passage of time we will probably become more familiar with the constitutional form of government and be successful at it, and it would probably take much longer to fall back to the traditional way and make it as successful. We aspire to it. We wish and we dream of it, but in my experience when it's placed in our lap we don't know what to do with it or how to handle it.

Uniting the different factions here seems almost impossible. It would take great wisdom and although unity is very desirable, I have seen those who aspire come and go. They are strong in one department but weak in another. The one thing they all have in common is a lack of patience. They want to move, move, move and yet they don't know how to move, move, move, or in what direction and for what reason and what that move would accomplish. They don't know and yet they are still impatient about changing and, as they say, to move and live with the changes. I can't buy that because my understanding of being Lakota is to be patient and that comes from way back. For example, back in the days when there were no guns, if I was a young man and I wanted to prove my prowess as a hunter I would have been given one arrow. I used to wonder how that would feel. There were no horses then and in the winter travel became even harder. So faced with that, I concluded that I would have picked a very good vantage point at a watering place that was open during the winter, where I would have found the tracks of animals going to drink. There I would have waited. One arrow and I would live or die by it to support my reputation as a hunter. Maybe I would have to lay there and freeze for hours and by the time my fingers are numb here would come a deer. I have only one shot and it has to hit the vital spot, but if I wanted to prove my prowess as a hunter I would have to endure that freezing cold and lay there for hours waiting for the game to come. So I have learned to develop patience. I am not spontaneous in revealing my feelings, but that is what makes a leader. You can't be spontaneous in your feelings, actions, thoughts and behavior because you are not acting and behaving for yourself, you are representing a lot of people who depend on your ability. So that's the difference between those who have traditional thoughts and feelings and those who exhibit a high degree of intelligence but also a high degree of impatience.

"When the result of the vote was made public the traditional people were unhappy and they could not understand why it had happened; mainly because they didn't understand the voting system. Had they

Of course, the future of our young people lies in how they are going to survive in this world as it is; their capacity to operate and feel comfortable in the field of technology and the latest practices as well as the field that deals with humanity – relating to other people. After I became involved with people and got on the board as a freshman council member and then one year later tried for the chief's war bonnet and won, a wise old leader visited me and said, "Young man, you are now the leader for the tribe, for the people. We're going to look to you. Don't get impatient. Take one step at a time. If you get impatient and try to run with the affairs of the people, they are heavy like water and it will be like running with a barrel of water. And if you run with it, the weight of the water will swing back and forth and pull you off balance and you will drop the barrel and lose the faith of your people." He was right. Over a period of time, sometimes my impatience would make me recall the words of that wise old leader. So therein lies the future of the people. Wise, sure, strong and patient leadership is necessary for the survival of the Lakota people. Today for some reason our people wish to choose younger and younger leadership. But the young leadership, even though it may be aggressive, intelligent and have a desire to move quickly, takes me back to that wise old leader's advice. I see clearly what the results of going against that advice are and it happens just as he said. That's what's happening now – our young people think they have sufficient education and knowledge about the things required to operate and promote self government and do it successfully. However, in the past they've moved so fast that they have lost sight of the goals that they should have set for themselves. They have a short period of time; two years is the term of office in which they are required to achieve something for the benefit of the people. This is a very short period but when I was in office I applied the principles of that old leader and pulled it off to some degree. By comparison, these last two or three administrations have spent anywhere from $30 to 45 million annually. I don't know where it went, where it goes or what it has accomplished, except that we seem to have become mired down in financial debt. How they got there they can't explain and it's hard to determine why they got our people so overburdened with debt. Right now we're too busy trying to find our way out of that mess, so I don't know how successful they can be. They try to justify themselves but very unsuccessfully because spending all of that money should have at least showed some visible signs of accomplishment, but there are none that I have seen.

When I was tribal chairman I set a goal for myself that, in my two years, I would try and find the best source of housing possibilities. We had a lot of young people growing up, and young families having families themselves. They had no jobs and very little money to be doing the things for themselves that they should have been doing. I was fortunate in finding out about a housing program for poor people. It was practiced in the urban areas of the southern states and so I made a trip to Washington, DC to find out more about it. I found there was such a program, but there was nothing in it for Indians. There were housing programs for Spanish, Mexicans, blacks and whites, but no provision for Indians – I don't know how we got lost in the shuffle – so I told our lawyers to analyze the law from cover to cover and they found a loophole which we worked on. John F. Kennedy was president at the time and we put a paper together which I presented and they accepted it. Then you started to see houses a little better than what we used to have. Before, we just had little tin shacks or old log houses chinked with mud plaster, dirt roofs and dirt floors, that were without heat or running water. In two years I changed that. The tribe had benefited and yet there was still dissatisfaction – there were not enough houses to go round, but what did they expect in two years? After all, we had come well over a century with no houses, poor houses or tents. But I did not feel upset about it. When I drive down the road and see those nice houses that young people are living in I still feel proud – I did something and it's here. I have never revealed that publicly before because I was just doing my job. I never brag about it because in Indian culture if you brag about your accomplishments you have to have a giveaway every time you open your mouth and I am not about to brag myself into the poor house!

known what the requirements were, they would not have had the Indian Reorganization Act, but no one advised them and therein lies the reason as to why we have the Indian Reorganization Act."

"They don't understand the traditional form of government enough to fall back to it and live comfortably under the rules of tribal law . . . Some talk real aggressive, but I have been around long enough to know and I have seen them come and go . . . We aspire to it. We wish and we dream of it, but in my experience when it's placed in our lap we don't know what to do with it or how to handle it."

Addressing what might be called our social and economic crisis on this reservation could be real difficult because this is something that has developed over almost a century and a half. These things cannot be changed with the flick of a wand and it doesn't make any difference how strong the magic is, but it can be done with a lot of dedication and involvement. The leadership have to be role models and they have to speak intelligently and appeal to the disturbed, confused nature of our young people and even some of our elders who have depressive conditions. I have been there and I have been back but unfortunately it's pretty hard to try to help a person stand up when he wants to fall down. You can't make him stand up when he does not want to stand up. The people have to recognise the need and respond to it. But every time people get down they tend to fall off the wagon and lose patience, so that's where patience comes in again. You have to be a patient person if you want to bring about a positive achievement. Naturally, one thing that would help considerably is work opportunities. We have to develop them and we have to do it positively and aggressively.

When President Clinton came here I think it was pretty much show. When I heard his slogan, 'shared vision', I asked myself, "When did he go on a vision quest?" Did he want us to share our visions with him or did he want to share his with us? It was very general and the concept was lost in the manner it was delivered it was very clear that it was delivered for media consumption. I did not attend because if something is going to be done I want to see it visibly. If a leader comes out here and says that something is going to be done within a period of time and makes it happen then I will believe that man. I will believe that he is sincere and is being truthful when he has visibly made it happen. So far I have heard a lot of rhetoric in one form or another but like I say, I'm patient – it hasn't happened yet, but I'm patient. I'm still looking for that leader here who is going to get up there and make things happen – that's the bottom line – but I am afraid I don't see that leader yet. Maybe he will appear after I have gone, but I am patient. I'm waiting. Maybe he will still appear before I go on the long journey.

My grandfather's vision was the same vision that my father had and I used to wonder what the meaning was. My grandfather conveyed to my father what his vision was, after which he was named Holy Buffalo or Holy Bull. My father had the same vision, the very same thing, and I used to wonder if it was the vision in which my grandfather manifested himself to my father. I don't know. In his dream he saw a buffalo mired down in a quagmire of quicksand and the buffalo was trying to extricate himself from the mire. He was very powerful and as he struggled to free himself he shook the entire world. The whole earth around him moved with his struggles. I once told my daughter that my father failed to fulfill the vision of my grandfather and maybe my life had been prolonged for some reason, as I should have died three times already; once as a baby, once as a young man when a horse rolled over on me, and once as an old man when I had a heart attack while I was all alone. Maybe I have lived this long to fulfill the legacy of Holy Bull. If that happens it's not me who's going to do it, but perhaps it can be done through me.

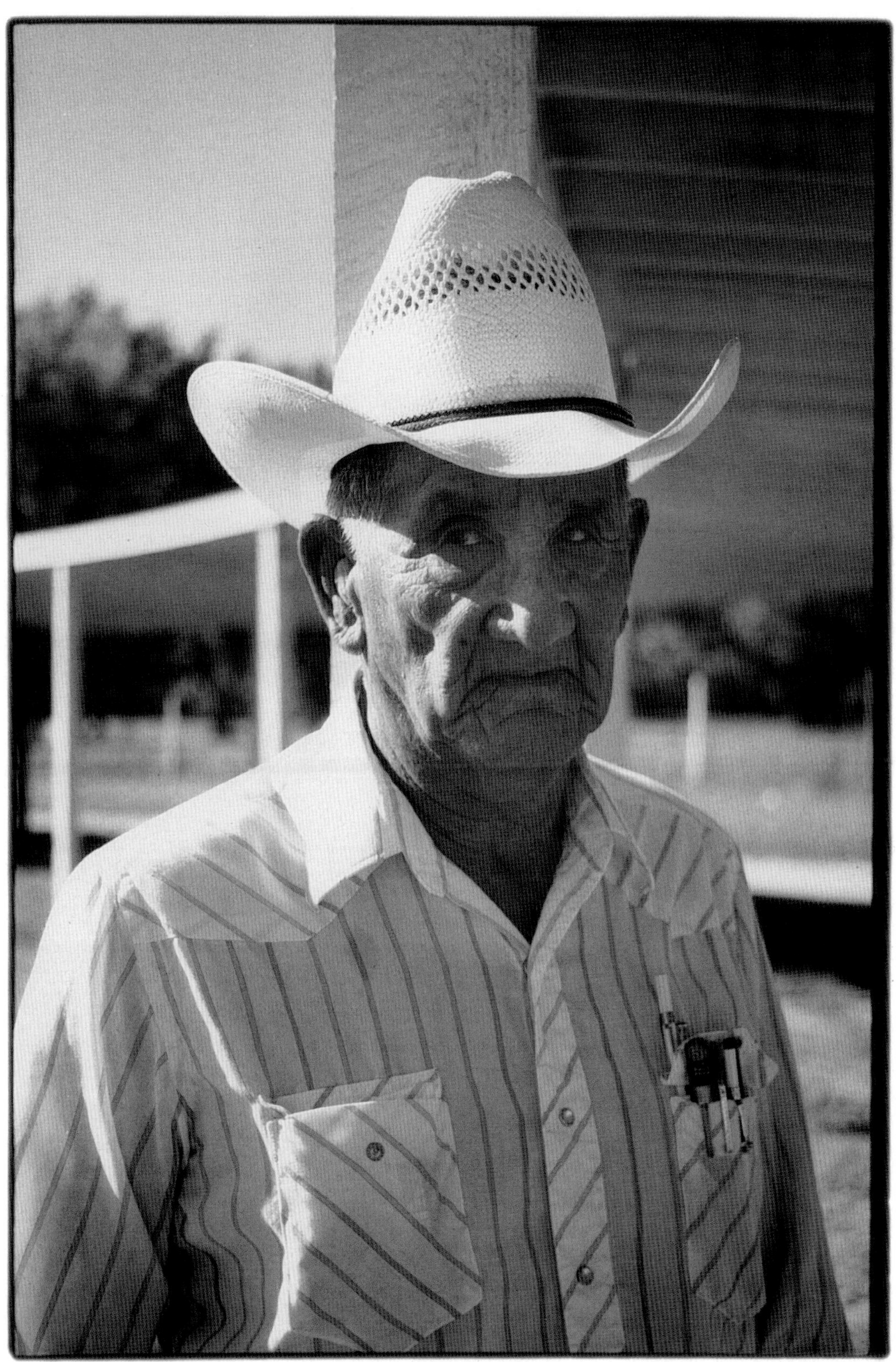

Johnson Holy Rock

"I hope to God you will not ask me to go to any other country except my own", Barboncito implored General Sherman during the Navajo/US treaty negotiations of 1868. Barboncito was a leader of the Navajo refugees who had somehow survived four years of General James Carleton's 'Great Experiment' at Bosque Redondo, a model that would later inspire the Third Reich. Some 9,000 Navajos had been forced to undertake the infamous Long Walk away from Diné Bikéyah, the Sacred Navajo Homeland that lies within the boundaries of the Four Sacred Mountains, between which the Navajo, or Diné, relate every aspect of their physical and spiritual existence. During the treaty conference, Barboncito referred to an area called Black Mesa that was sacred to the Diné. At the heart of Black Mesa is Big Mountain. There, a female deity blesses the land with rain and purifies the waters through what might be called her liver – a vast coal seam. In the 1940s corporate interests 'discovered' that coal and filed their applications to exploit one of the richest energy resources on the continent. In doing so, they escalated what became known as 'The Navajo-Hopi Land Dispute', which had been framed by US President Chester Arthur's 1882 Executive Order that created the Hopi Indian Reservation; a 57-by-70 mile tract containing Big Mountain, demarcated from the surrounding Navajo Reservation and declared a 'joint occupation' area. In the interim period, the federally mandated Hopi and Navajo Tribal governments were established and the Peabody Coal Company solicited the Hopi Tribal government to

Pauline Whitesinger

Above: *The traditional Diné way of life under threat on Big Mountain: Huck Grey-eyes tends to his livestock.*

Location: *Big Mountain, Black Mesa, Arizona.*

"I was born on the other side of Big Mountain. I want to be around this area with this land that I love. At first we didn't realize that this mine would change our lives and that we would no longer be able to live the way we always have . . . Now the officials from the Relocation Commission tell me that it is time for them to move me off the land, to relocate me. I think of the day when they're going to come for me and what might happen then, when they take me away."

secure mining leases. In the landmark *Healing v. Jones*, the Hopi Tribal government successfully litigated against the Navajo Tribal government for exclusive control of a land parcel from the 'joint occupation' area designated as District 6. *Healing v. Jones* established the basis upon which partition and relocation could be promoted as a solution to the problem, and in 1974 the US Congress enacted the Relocation Act which divided the surface area into Hopi Partition Lands (HPL) and Navajo Partition Lands (NPL) that required each tribe's respective members to relocate from the other's partitioned land, the vast majority of those affected being Diné, many of whom resided on Black Mesa where, since 1970, Peabody Coal had expanded its operation and begun strip mining. The Diné on Black Mesa were to be relocated to 'New Lands'; an area unacceptable to most because it is located outside of Diné Bikéyah; plus concerns regarding uranium contamination. Thousands were made refugees, leaving a pocket of elderly resistors, one of whom is Pauline Whitesinger. The fabric of Diné history and culture embraces Big Mountain as a sacred area; the 1991 Kelley, Francis and Scott Report identified some 222 Diné sacred sites on the HPL. Big Mountain gave sanctuary to those Diné who escaped the Long Walk and the crisis submerging their descendants has been called the Second Long Walk. The deadline for relocation passed on February 1, 2000. "There is no word in Diné for relocation. To relocate is to disappear and never be seen again", says Pauline Whitesinger. This is her story.

I don't know the English words to speak so I speak in my language. In the Diné language, the way you go about it is to speak with your heart. I speak with my heart because that's who I am and my mind is how I express myself. I was born and raised here and now I'm over seventy years old. My mother stayed here with this land before me. I'm used to this land. When I go to Gallup or Flagstaff, or wherever I go away from here, I think about this land. This land is my home and I always think about how I just want to return to it. My great-grandfather had land out here and in the canyons. It seems like yesterday when they started the mine here and it seems like it was just yesterday that I was a small child and we used to go and take the sheep up that way. I remember that and it doesn't seem that long ago.

At first we didn't really notice, or realize, that this mine would change our lives and that we might not be able to live as we always had. We didn't really react until we discovered something was wrong. We used to pick pinons up where they have built the mine and then one day as we approached that area we saw that everything was being cleared away. The land was being cleared away. Then we heard that the mine was being built because they had discovered ore and all of this coal. Suddenly there was a police presence there and it was like the place was

run by this security. As more coal was discovered they would clear away more of the land up there. People who lived over there were affected by it right away because when they began clearing away the land they began clearing away the people too. They had to move but over here it didn't really affect us in the beginning. We looked at it from a distance. People now talk about this being a land dispute between tribes, the Hopis and the Diné, but what about the politicians and the mining operators? The way I look at it is that I don't know what pressures they are under and why they are doing this or what their plans are, and it's the same thing over here. They probably don't know what I'm going through, or why. But I know this, as far as I'm concerned, what was happened has affected me and what happens still affects me today. As for politicians, what they're doing and how their laws are affecting us, well we're paying for that right here and now.

When this whole thing started I believe that the Hopi government officials and the United States government worked together and that, back

"As more coal was discovered they would clear away more of the land up there. People who lived over there were affected by it right away because when they began clearing away the land they began

then, the Hopis didn't really want all of this land but they did want the coal and so, because of the coal, the United States government ordered this land to be split in two – the HPL [Hopi Partition Lands] and the NPL [Navajo Partition Lands]. That's how come we are fighting today. This is where we have always lived but they are saying that this land is now the Hopis share under that order. Not only that but our own Navajo Nation Tribal Council appears to have turned against us because they want the coal as well and the mine employs a lot of Navajos. When they go to Window Rock and sit in the council chambers there are so many who think that they are leaders, but why would we need so many leaders? So these governments are against us. That's why the Hopi Rangers come over here giving me notices and harassing me to leave my home. It's not like when they come over I tell them, "Okay, that's your part of the land, your share, so stay over that line on your part of your land". I don't tell them that but that's what they tell me. They'll tell me that I can't have my livestock on a certain part of the land, or that I can't cut wood again over here on this part. I get harassed a lot. I'm sure they all recognise me now. Even when I put a blanket over my face they still recognise me because it's been going on for so long.

When I was a young girl I remember how they started to take our sheep and cows away. Now the Hopi officials and representatives from the Relocation Commission come here to tell me that it is time for them to move me off the land, to relocate me, and now others come and tell me the same thing. Two men, an Anglo and a Diné from Window Rock, came here saying that they'd given me official notice and that I was to move to the New Lands. When I said that I wouldn't go they told me, "If we can't move you we're going to have to kill you here". My response was, "Go ahead, I'm not going to move. I'm not going to leave." Even now I don't have a firearm but if they start shooting at me, I'm going to find a way to shoot back. I recognize them by their uniforms, that's how I know whether they are from the Hopi Tribal government, the Navajo Tribal government, the United States government or from Peabody Western Mining. If they come here in a suit it means they're from the United States government. Every time something happens out here the Navajo Tribal government say it's up to the rangers and the BIA police to handle it. Sometimes I am frightened for my life.

Some people have signed the relocation agreements. It's been proposed to me twice, right here. I had officials walk into my home and place a big book on my table which they told me to sign but my son was

clearing away the people too. They had to move . . . People now talk about this being a land dispute between tribes, the Hopis and the Diné, but what about the politicians and the mining operators?"

here then and he read the entire thing. He told me that it was not a good proposal and so I did not sign. They were offering me a small house away from here. I couldn't have kept any livestock so what would I have done? Just sit and be isolated in a small construction away from my home – this land? I think about the people who sign. They don't know where they're going or where they're heading. It just seems like they want you to sign your life away but you don't know where you're going to move to and you don't know where or how you're going to start a new life. It seems that if and when people get those houses built in the New Lands they distance themselves from those of us who resist. They seem to change and support what the governments want and what they are doing to us out here. They start supporting the officials who try to move us off. They say we should just move and get this thing over with but I refuse to sign because I have been to many places before, many towns, and I always think of home when I am away and here on this land is my home. That is why I keep coming back here. I also have my livestock. My lifestyle includes my cattle, my sheep and goats. I feel really close with them and I'm trying to protect them as well. That is what made me realise that I'll never sign and agree to be relocated.

The officials keep taking my livestock. They took away my cattle. They impounded them and haven't given them back to me. So now I have to look out for my livestock as well as myself because they might take more. But I'm here by myself, alone with my medicine and my corn and all of my other sacred items. I don't really remember the first time they impounded my livestock but it was probably about fourteen years ago. Back then when they took my livestock the Navajo Tribal government would pay the fine and get my livestock back but they won't do that anymore. They say I've resisted all of these different agencies, the Hopi Rangers, the monitors and the BIA, right through to the US Congress, for twenty-five years now. Are they afraid of me? If they are it's only because I make my point. At first they used to intimidate me. They used to come here and try to harass me but then all of their talk didn't scare me anymore. What I'm afraid of is their guns. They always carry guns. One time they came here and I told them they shouldn't be carrying their guns over here so they parked away. Then I noticed there was a gun – the barrel was sticking out of the car when the guy came in here so I kept an eye on it. One of these guys had a flash light and he was trying to push me around while another guy was calling in on a radio, saying that I was arguing with them. Then it happened. I took off but they started running beside me.

"They say I've resisted all of these agencies, the Hopi Rangers, the monitors and the BIA, right through to the US Congress, for twenty-five years now. At first they used to intimidate me but

I was going to try and grab that gun but right when I was reaching for it, the other guy grabbed it and said, "What you gonna do with that gun?" After that it seemed that they became wary of me.

One day I was planting over in my cornfield. I had two volunteer couples there helping me. We were all planting corn when I heard a noise coming from the north east. I waited and took a few steps in that direction and then I saw helicopters coming towards me. The people helping me just took off running. Then I heard a radio transmission and there was a ranger looking for me. I heard that transmission and then I noticed a vehicle, and there was the ranger. I want people to see my situation out here and get an understanding of it, that I'm living in fear, that every day I fear for my life. I look at this life, the way that I'm living right now, and it's hard. When I look back on my childhood years it was a better life, those were good years. Sometimes I think about that, how that was a better time than what I am experiencing now. I look back on the good years. I look back on my childhood and wish that it could be that way again but life is hard now and I'm getting older. I'm not as young as I used to be. I feel sick at times and sometimes I can't eat or sleep because I live this every day. I think of the day when they're going to come for me and what might happen then, when they take me away.

Look around here. The livestock know that something is going on. They're not as they used to be because of what's happening out here. Maybe this is why we don't get any rain. Maybe this is the reason why there's a lot of fighting, even amongst ourselves. This is why nature's out of balance and I think that if it was restored, none of this would be happening and people would live in harmony again. This land is like my mind and my body and how I conduct myself on this land is like a child. When a child comes to you for help, or when they're in trouble, you try to help them. That's how I learned from this land. I learned everything that way – by myself with the land – from 'hands-on' experience. When I'm facing a task today, I look back to see how I learned and that is what's made me a strong woman today. I look at our young people today and see how they're distracted and brainwashed because of modern technology. They tend to disrespect the land and our traditional ways and lifestyle. I remember when I was a child. I was born on the other side of Big Mountain. I didn't know of anyone at that time who couldn't ride a horse or take care of livestock. My great-grandmother used to ride horses around this area but now I'm the only one that rides horses here. I want to be around this area, this land that I love. I used to be married many years

then all of their talk didn't scare me anymore. What I'm afraid of is their guns . . . When I said that I wouldn't go they told me, 'If we can't move you we're going to have to kill you here' . . ."

ago but my husband died and he's buried not too far from here, so that's another reason why I don't intend to go anywhere else. I look back to my grass roots, to where I was born, and they are in this land. I don't know what the unexpected is but I think I'm capable and strong enough to face it. I feel like we're up against a wall now, or tied by a leash, but I have my prayers and my medicine bundle with me. We'll have to see what happens.

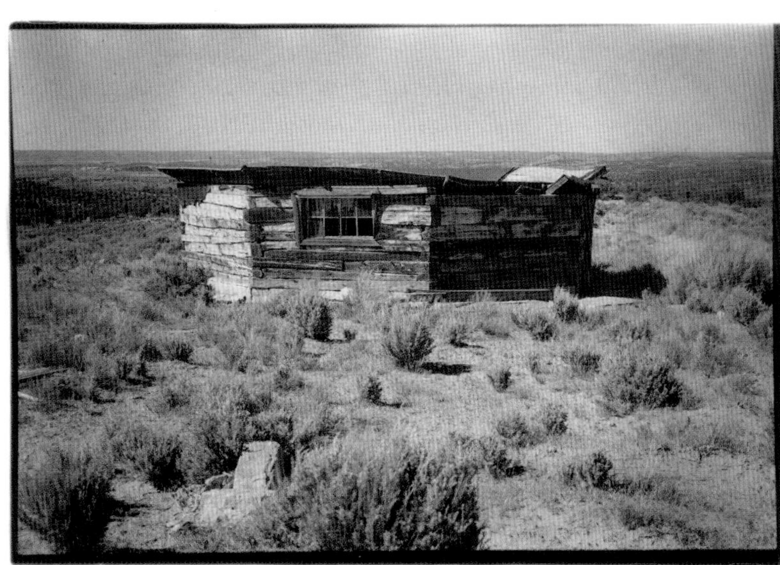

Above: *The devastation – an abandoned hogan on Big Mountain with the coal mine in the distance.*

Location: *Prague, Oklahoma.*

Grace's father, the legendary 'Athlete of the Twentieth Century', Jim Thorpe, is the only athlete in history ever to win Olympic gold in both the pentathlon and decathlon at the same Olympiad when, in 1912, he represented both the Sac and Fox Nation and the USA. Arbitrarily stripped of his gold medals a year later, Thorpe was finally exonerated and reinstated in 1983, following an exhaustive campaign led by Grace and other Thorpe family members. Grace is respected throughout Native America for her forthright yet even-handed leadership – her Sac and Fox name, *No Tenoquah*, means 'Woman With the Power of the Wind that Blows Up Before a Storm'. She is at the vanguard of the fight to stop nuclear waste disposal on Indian lands and is President of the National Environmental Coalition of Native Americans, and the author of *Our Homes are not Dumps: Creating Nuclear Free Zones.* A veteran of the Indians of All Tribes occupation of Alcatraz, Grace became Director of the Return Surplus Lands to Indians Project, and she has held positions with the US House of Representatives-American Indian Policy Review Commission, the US Senate-Indian Affairs, and the National Congress of American Indians. Grace has served as a Sac and Fox tribal judge, and as the tribe's Health Commissioner.

GRACE THORPE

Above: *Carlisle Indian School, Pennsylvani*

One of my very first memories of Dad is from when I was about six or seven years old. Dad was visiting Haskell Indian Boarding School in Lawrence, Kansas where they were opening a new football stadium. It was kind of a homecoming for him. I remember that he put me in a blue jersey before he walked out into the middle of the football field. Then he drop-kicked a football through one goal post and turned around in the center of the field and did it the other way. As he left the field he put me on his shoulders, just before he was mobbed by people who all wanted his autograph. I remember becoming upset with them because Dad had promised me that after the exhibition he was going to buy me an ice cream cone and after a while I started grumbling, "Come on, let's go, let's go, you promised me an ice cream cone". One of my very last memories of him came when I lived in Pearl River, New York. When Dad came to visit me I would drive him to where the bus stopped for New York City, which was around the Main Street in Pearl River near the movie theatre. On this occasion, I dropped Dad off

Grace Thorpe

Meshkwahkihaki

on the corner and then turned to wave and there, right above him, I saw '*Jim Thorpe, All American*'. The Burt Lancaster movie about Dad was playing there, and there was Dad stood below the hoarding with his suede fringed jacket and his big round leather suitcase. That movie premiered in 1951 and Dad passed on in 1953.

Both Dad and my mother attended Indian Boarding Schools. My dad went off to Indian School when he was six years old. He grew up in Indian School and reached his fame in sports in Indian School. That was just the way it was then. When kids reached six years old they went off to Indian Boarding Schools. That was the policy then and it was an assimilation policy. They felt that if they kept Indian kids there for such long periods of time, away from their language, away from their families and everything, it would be easier to assimilate them. Dad went to Carlisle from 1904 to 1909. Then, like many others, when he finished his five straight years, he went to school part of the year and in the summer worked out on the farms. The girls worked in the kitchens on a lot of those

". . . in the summer of 1912 he went to Stockholm, Sweden where he won the Pentathlon and the Decathlon. Dad is the only one in history that has ever won both events . . . One time I asked Dad how

Asakiwaki

Pennsylvanian farms. After he left there he went to North Carolina where he played semi-pro baseball in the summers of 1909 and 1910. Soon after, Pop Warner, who was the coach at Carlisle, was looking for athletes for the 1912 Olympics and that's how Albert Exendine, who was a Player-Coach when Dad first started in football at Carlisle, was sent to look for Dad because he was also from Oklahoma. When he found Dad he talked him into going back to Carlisle to train for track and field in the Olympics, and in the summer of 1912 he went to Stockholm, Sweden where he won the Pentathlon and the Decathlon. Dad is the only one in history that has ever won both of those events.

Prior to the Olympics, when Dad played semi-pro baseball in North Carolina, he registered under his own name and he wasn't aware that he was doing anything wrong. However, a reporter there remembered his name because he recalled that he was a good player, and this guy reported that he was not an amateur and you were supposed to be an amateur to compete in the Olympics. At that, the American Olympic Association voted that Dad's records were to be stricken from the books and his medals returned to the International Olympic Committee. Dad returned the medals that were then given to the runners-up but at first they said, "No way, we didn't win – Thorpe did". The organisation that made the decision against Dad was not the International Olympic Committee, it was the American Olympic Association. The modern day Olympics didn't start until 1896 and so by 1912 they were not very far along in terms of the rules and they used Dad as a guinea pig. Avery Brundage, who also competed in the 1912 Olympics, took charge of the American Olympic Association and then he was a representative to the International Olympic Committee for years and years and years and years. Mother always said that Brundage was jealous of Dad. He was in his 80s when he retired from the IOC and it was only after that, that we were able to get Dad reinstated. I remember getting Senator Cranston to introduce a Bill into Congress for Dad to be reinstated. I was also able to get the then US President, Gerald Ford, to intercede on behalf of the Jim Thorpe family at the Montreal Olympics in 1976. But in order to make this whole thing happen Dad's status had to be changed from professional back to amateur by the Amateur Athletic Union, so I called Jack Kelly, the brother of Grace Kelly, and asked him if he would represent the Thorpe family at the Annual Meeting of the Amateur Athletic Union as he was active in that organization. He did and they voted unanimously to change Dad's status from professional back to amateur. That happened in 1972 but with

he felt about having those medals taken away and he said, 'I never once wrote a letter or asked the International Olympic Committee to return those medals', and then he went on reading his newspaper."

politics being what they are it still took about ten years after that. Ultimately it was a grass roots effort by individuals from all over the world. One time I asked Dad how he felt about having those medals taken away and he looked at me and said, "I never once wrote a letter or asked the International Olympic Committee to return those medals", and then he shut up and went on reading his newspaper. He didn't like talking about it, or himself.

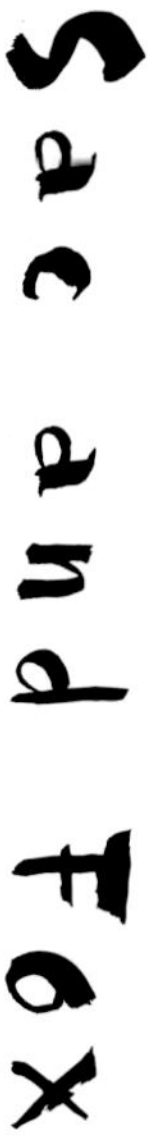

I think people consider Dad to be America's greatest all round male athlete because no other male athlete has achieved more, or competed and excelled in more than two sports – much less three. Dad was, as an amateur, an All American football player at Carlisle Indian School. He became the first President of what was then the American Football Association, which is now the National Football League, so he is considered a 'founding father' of professional football. In 1950, Dad was proclaimed both America's greatest all round male athlete in an associated press poll, and greatest football player. He also made his living for twenty years in the Major and Minor Leagues in baseball! And that's probably why he deserved the title of America's Greatest Male Athlete.

A book where a present-day athlete competes against the ghost of Jim Thorpe is being made into a movie. I've seen a copy of the script and they got Dad's tribe wrong so they were happy when I corrected it! Dad's Sac and Fox name was Wa Tha Huck, 'Bright Path'. The Sac and Fox were Woodland Indians from the Great Lakes area. We were finally pushed out

Sac and Fox

of Illinois when, amongst others, Abraham Lincoln and Jefferson Davis, prosecuted a war against us, known as the 'Black Hawk War'. The Sac and Fox were practically all killed off and the survivors pushed out of Illinois and Wisconsin across the Mississippi River over into Iowa. Then the next generation was pushed out of Iowa and down into Kansas. Then the next generation was pushed out of Kansas into Oklahoma and that's the group that I come from. My grandfather and my grandmother came down from Kansas and Dad was born here in Oklahoma. Dad was in the same clan as Black Hawk. In some books it says that he was a direct descendent of Black Hawk but he wasn't. We belong to the same Thunder Clan as Black Hawk. I do resent that today Black Hawk's name is used in all kinds of ways, from sports mascots to helicopters. If he was my ancestor and I was a direct blood descendent, I'd probably go after them for it. Dad respected the Indian traditions although he was not really 'traditional'. He did speak the Sac and Fox language though. I remember visitors coming who were Sac and Fox and they all talked in our language. I never really learned it.

"In January 1993 I read in the paper that the Sac and Fox had put in for a nuclear waste study grant. I didn't think that was the kind of thing our tribe should be doing, after all, the Sac and Fox

Again, I left here and then left the Indian Boarding Schools when I was 13. Even in recent times many of our best have been lost after they've gone off to colleges. It's a terrible situation to be in. You want your kids to be educated and have a good life, yet you want them here to keep the traditions alive and that's difficult. So the traditions are threatened but we do have several groups that are traditional and we still have naming ceremonies that take place, and our births and our deaths.

In January 1993 I read in the paper that the Sac and Fox had put in for a nuclear waste study grant. I didn't think that was the kind of thing our tribe should be doing, after all, the Sac and Fox were the last tribe to fight for their lands east of the Mississippi River and I thought, 'Here we are with the few acres we have left and we're going to put nuclear waste on them!' I worked in Japan after World War II and I saw the horrors of radio activity after Hiroshima. With that first-hand experience, I thought, 'Oh my gosh, this isn't something we want to get involved in', and so I got our tribe to withdraw which was achieved in accordance with our Constitution. The only ones who voted for the MRS [Monitored Retrievable Storage Program] – the temporary storage of nuclear waste – were the elected tribal officials. After that I received an invitation to be a keynote speaker for the Indigenous Environmental Network and from there I met a guy from A Nuclear Free America and I thought, 'That's a good way to go – nuclear free tribes and so we started setting up nuclear free tribes. The Sac and Fox were the first and now we have seventy-five in Canada, Alaska and the United States.

When they close down these nuclear reactors in the east, the people that live around them don't want anything to do with nuclear waste. But the commercial industry needs some place to get rid of it so they give notice to all the States and all the tribes, stating that there's $100,000 grants for anybody willing to undertake a feasibility study toward putting nuclear waste on their land. They target Indian tribes because they have land, which in many cases is isolated, and because they believe that Indian tribes struggle to fight off the pressure and the politics, and because of the poverty levels among many tribes, the need for finance that putting nuclear waste on their land would bring. I think it was in 1992 that some guy who had been a Lieutenant Governor of Idaho addressed the tribes at the National Congress of American Indians. In his motivational speaking style he said that infrastructures with streets, sewers, health clinics, new housing, community centers and wonderful schools would be theirs if they took nuclear waste. Some of them fell for it and put in for the grants but the only ones who have gone for it are the Goshutes in Utah. All of the other seventeen tribes who sought nuclear waste zoning withdrew.

AsaKiwaKi

were the last tribe to fight for their lands east of the Mississippi River and I thought, 'Here we are with the few acres we have left and we're going to put nuclear waste on them!'"

When I was in better health I used to go out on protests, especially over to Ward Valley and Yucca Mountain. Yucca Mountain is Shoshone land by the Treaty of Ruby Valley. The Federal Government offered to buy it but the tribe voted not to accept the money. Even so, Yucca Mountain is being considered by the Federal Government for permanent waste disposal of radio active materials. There is a bill, the National Nuclear Waste Policy Act, that we were able to get the President to veto for five consecutive years but the Federal Government is all set and ready to go as far as where they are going to ship the waste, what roads they are going to use, what transportation, and what railroads will go into Yucca Mountain. It looks like they're planning on sending it to the Goshutes temporarily for above ground storage until Yucca Mountain is ready, which apparently will not be until 2010. My goodness, we are talking about an earthquake zone here! More of our Government money should be spent on alternative sources of energy – the wind's there, the sun's there for heaven's sake but they haven't explored these alternatives because how would the utilities make any money from them? And that's what it all comes down to. They can make money from nuclear power plants. Our homes are not nuclear waste dumps. We've lost so much of our land why should we stand for this? There's also human waste, the pig farms they are wanting to open on reservations and the way they mine uranium by just throwing it in open ditches. That's how it got into the watersheds which contributed to the suffering of the Laguna Pueblos and Navajos.

Meshkwahkihaki Asakiwaki

To some degree my activism period started in 1969 when I'd just finished working for the National Congress of American Indians in Washington, DC. I was selling real estate in Arizona when I became aware of a surplus airforce site near Roswell, New Mexico. At the time, Nixon's administration had a lot of these surplus military properties that they were giving away to states and municipalities and it occurred to me that Indian tribes could also get these properties. I looked into it and part of the criteria to receive a surplus property entailed establishing a non-profit educational corporation. This was all mulling through my mind when Alcatraz hit. It was late November 1969 and they just plain needed somebody there that knew how to work with the media, VIPs and in public relations. I'm not trying to make myself out to be a big deal because there's no big deal about it and that's how I became Public Relations Director of Alcatraz. I was probably one of the luckier ones. I had some money, though not much, and a car which I parked over at Fisherman's Wharf. A lady by the name of Dr Dorothy Miller, who had an organisation called the Scientific Analysis Corporation, let us have one of her offices there so I would work there everyday and take the boat back over to Alcatraz at night. She also had something to do with Adam Nordwall and the group who first tried to occupy Alcatraz before Richard Oakes and the students actually did. Even before that, in 1964, some relocatees, mostly Sioux out of the Bay Area, went over to Alcatraz and claimed it as Sioux territory based upon treaty and land claims. Among them was Russell Means and his father, and Nordwall was also there for that to organize the publicity. I don't think the press took it seriously then, but I guess Russell and that bunch could be called the forerunners for the main occupation.

". . . just about every celebrity that came into San Francisco wanted to visit Alcatraz. Buffy Sainte-Marie used to come, Merv Griffin and Marlon Brando supported us, and I remember making the arrangements for Jane Fonda to stay the weekend on Alcatraz. I was

When I arrived in late 1969 the publicity was not as good as it could have been, there were stories about drug running and all kinds of things. I was there about three months during which time just about every celebrity that came into San Francisco wanted to visit Alcatraz. Buffy Sainte-Marie used to come, Merv Griffin and Marlon Brando supported us, and I remember making the arrangements for Jane Fonda to stay the weekend on Alcatraz. One time I think the rock group Creedence Clearwater Revival performed on a ship near Alcatraz and then gave us the boat to use.

There were a lot of power plays between people who were there but I purposely didn't get involved in any of them. If they elected officials or had meetings I'd maybe do a news story on it afterwards. I was there to represent the 'Indians of All Tribes' to the general public and secure as much good publicity as we possibly could. John Trudell did a lot of that too. John operated the radio station, 'Radio Free Alcatraz', and I was the first person he ever interviewed on the station. John and his wife Lou were always around and I think they had a son who was born on the island, maybe the only baby born on Alcatraz during the occupation. Others who became prominent in AIM were also there. I remember Dennis Banks and Clyde Bellecourt showing up for a couple of weeks before they had long hair and braids.

I don't know whether it's Mother Nature or what, but in order for you to survive you remember the funny things. How Alcatraz stayed occupied for 18 months I'll never know because the water had to be piped in there, the food and everything else had to be brought over by ship – sometimes there wasn't any money to get food in the first place let alone people to collect it until donations started coming in from all over the United States. The media coverage was unbelievable but we had problems from the lack of food, to worrying about drinking the water, to no sewage. Even finding people to clean up messes was an organisational disaster! In remembering things that make you laugh you also recall the sadder things, and certainly Alcatraz was sad and cold – oh my, how cold it was. When Richard Oakes' daughter Yvonne fell down a stairwell and was killed, I remember giving a pair of yellow beaded earrings for her to be buried in. After that Richard Oakes didn't seem to be around. Richard himself nearly died during the occupation when he left the island and ended up in an 'Indian bar' on Mission Street. A Samoan guy, who he had had an altercation with some months before, cracked his skull with a billiard cue. Richard was in a coma for many days after that. I can remember visiting him and he was absolutely out. Then some Iroquois people came from the Six Nations; Mad Bear Anderson – who is Tuscarora, and Peter Mitten. They asked the doctors if they could give Richard something – Richard himself being Mohawk. The doctors said they'd done everything they could to bring him out of the coma so what harm could it do? So they gave him this medicine. I didn't see them do it but I was in the hospital when it happened and darned if a few minutes later he didn't start waking up after that Indian medicine. He was never the same after the coma, he just lost his spark. Richard was a leader and the first spokesman for Alcatraz. He eventually got shot and killed a couple of years later at a YMCA camp in Northern California, while defending some Indian boys in an argument.

there to secure as much good publicity as possible. John Trudell did a lot of that too, operating 'Radio Free Alcatraz'. How Alcatraz stayed occupied for 18 months I'll never know – we had problems from the lack of food, to worrying about drinking the water, to no sewage."

Fighting to preserve traditions: *Red Earth, Oklahoma.*

". . . I left here and then left the Indian Boarding Schools when I was 13. Even in recent times many of our best have been lost after they've gone off to colleges. It's a terrible situation to be in. You want your kids to be educated and have a good life, yet you want them here to keep the traditions alive and that's difficult. So the traditions are threatened . . ."

Conditions certainly improved after Alcatraz and after the Indians started revolting against conditions on reservations. I believe Alcatraz did a lot of good in bringing attention to Indian problems. In 1969 we didn't have housing as we do today. I live in an Indian house right here, which was built by HUD [Housing and Urban Development]. Today an Indian with a 'C' average can get in college on a scholarship – before you had to be an 'A' student and try to get a loan from the BIA. The Bureau of Indian Affairs has also come under greater scrutiny. These changes happened after Alcatraz and after the American Indian Movement. Fort Lawton was another surplus property protest I became involved with. About 27 years later, on a visit to Seattle, I went back to see Fort Lawton and met up with Bernie White Bear who had been at Alcatraz and pretty much led the Fort Lawton take over. Bernie helps operate the tribal facility they have there now. After Fort Lawton I had various Indian people coming to me for help in securing surplus property. I worked with a group of California Indians and some people from Davis, California, who were trying to get a surplus communications site there. Some of these people were highly qualified educators, both Chicano and Indian, that ran the minority programs at the university there. They hired me and we got the property, which is now known as D~Q University.

When I worked as an intern with Senator Abourezk on the Senate Sub Committee on Indian Affairs I saw the statutes of the Surplus Property Act – that Indians get first crack at surplus property within their relevant territorial boundary lines – so I followed that all the way through. Being an intern was actually a nightmare, I don't know when else I've ever been so busy. They told me to just prioritize and work on what I wanted to and to just throw the rest out and I thought, 'You don't pay any attention to what doesn't interest you? So that's how Senate offices and committees work!' During this period AIM had the Trail of Broken Treaties and took over the Bureau of Indian Affairs in Washington, DC. I used to go there everyday after work to see what was going on and I remember seeing Carter Camp a lot and also many of the Washington State Indians – I guess I could also have been called a Washington State Indian then. When that was over I went to work for Ernie Stevens on the American Indian Policy Review Commission and I acted as liaison between congressional officers and the commission. This was a 2½ year study of American Indian problems on reservations and we had people like Hank Adams working on it and heading up taskforces on education, health, housing and all, at hearings scattered throughout the United States. The findings of that commission are still available through Congress. There really hadn't been a comparable study done since the Meriam Report in 1928 and it was much needed.

I came back here to Oklahoma in 1976 with hopes of trying to get a museum dedicated to Dad but it hasn't worked out that way yet.

"In some books it says that Dad was a direct descendent of Black Hawk but he wasn't. We belong to the same Thunder Clan as Black Hawk. I do resent that today Black Hawk's name is used in all kinds of ways, from sports mascots to helicopters. If he was my ancestor and I was a direct blood descendent, I'd probably go after them for it."

Location: *Anchorage, Alaska.*

PAUL THEODORE

Paul Theodore is a traditional Chief of the Athabascan peoples of Alaska. Embraced by elders at an early age, tribal leaders impressed upon his parents the significance of the role they believed he would serve in later years. 'He will be the one to save the people. He will be the one to lead the people out. He is going to be the last Chief here, so take care of him', they advised. In his lifetime Chief Theodore has seen the influx of non-Natives to Alaska, oil exploration in his people's territory, and he has contested legislative maneouvers by the federal and state governments to justify the effects of both on Alaska Natives. He has the capacity to validate the oral history and explanations of his people not only through the grasp of cultural tradition, but the ability to define artifacts, and structural relics in geographic locations, which challenge much of Western academia's entrenched hypotheses regarding the continent's indigenous peoples.

Top left: *Russian Orthodox influence over Eklutna village.* **Above:** *Alaskan monarch – Dall ram.*

It started when I was a small boy, when the elders would come to visit my dad. The old people stopped at our fish camp and they would say, 'He will be the one to save the people. He will be the one to lead the people out. He is going to be the last Chief here, so take care of him.' They kept telling my mom and dad that and then when I started travelling with my dad the elders started to take care of me. They treated me like an old person, not as a child. They took me into the steam baths and in there they began training me by singing, by teaching me all of the songs. At the time I didn't realize that I was being trained but they were preparing me because soon after they started to pass on and we were at their funerals. The elders who were left saw me there with my dad and so then we travelled around the country with them. They taught me the stories and significance of different places and I learned each of their songs. They told me how my dad was the Chief and that one day I would follow him.

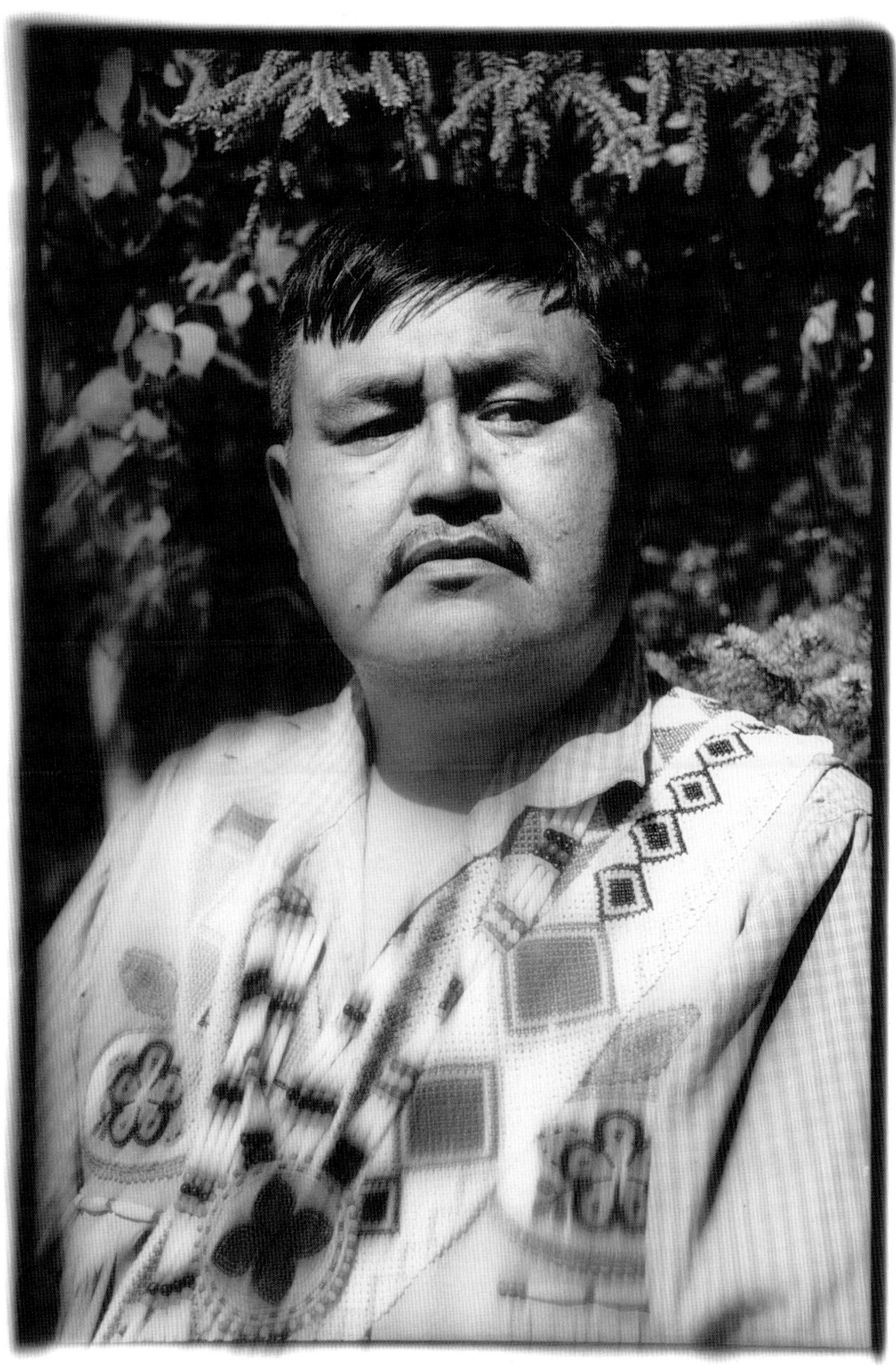

Chief Paul B. Theodore

Athabascan

I went to school but it was after I got out of school that I started to learn. I learned even more from the elders then and so that period of time became like my college, a college education taught by elders who each had eight or nine hundred years of knowledge that they passed on to me. They taught me all of the trails and the traditions from their bands and where their Chiefs came from. They shared most everything that they had done in their entire lives. It was good that they did because soon, like I said, they started burying my people and their people. A lot were lost during the epidemics of the 1920s and before that, in 1918. There was a lot of death during their times and so they trained me to cope with that too, so I learned from that place in the human condition.

Our people are known by the name 'Athabascan' and we have always been here in Alaska. My dad's tribe are the Chesyee and my mom's tribe are the Kalahee. My mom was the daughter of the Chief of Knik and Knik means 'the people'. We were here long before the Russians arrived and long before what the white man might call the 'bible times'. One of

"The old people stopped at our fish camp and they would say, 'He will be the one to save the people. He will be the one to lead the people out. He is going to be the last Chief here, so take care of him' . . .

our sacred sites dates back to that period, the time when the earth was flooded. Our people had to climb a mountain and live upon it until the water level subsided and then they came back down and resettled on this land here that had been their home before. They had to stay up there for a long time during the flood of all the land and they lived in a dwelling that was like a yurt, a house covered with skins that they built out of dinosaur bones. Our people were saved on that mountain and survived there and although I won't name it, I can say that it's near Anchorage. I'm trying to build a monument there so that Native people can learn about that place and truly understand that we were here before the Russians, Americans or anybody else.

On the rare occasions that we talk about our history to outsiders, the white man usually brings up the Bering Strait land bridge theory and how all of the Indians are supposed to have crossed that to get to where we are now. I sat down with two or three other Chiefs to discuss this and when we had finished talking about it all we could say was 'Baloney!' We know where those stone houses are and those sacred places to the southeast, just as we know where that skin house is on the mountain that saved us from the flood. Their Bering Strait idea is just another way of trying to lift us off the land and remove us from our traditional places and to sever us from our places of origin. It's something they use to justify taking over here. Whatever they want to make-up and call 'history' is their problem, not ours!

We know their history here and we know ours. In this area, the Russians arrived near Kenai in a ship. They tried to go ashore in a boat but some Indians caught sight of them and when they were close enough, they shot arrows at them. There were probably about ten Indians; first one would stick his head out and shoot and then the next one would and so on, back and forth, in and out of the cover. They managed to hit one or two of the Russians at which point they jumped back in their boat and headed for their ship. The Russians thought there were thousands of Indians but there were only about ten moving in and out of the trees! The Americans didn't really start to settle here until the 1950s, so they're just like babies to us. They've been here fifty or sixty years and now they claim this land as their own. Our history proves that we've been here since the beginning of time, before the earth was flooded, and yet it's like they've just come over on a little boat, jumped out and made a big mess and are now trying to tell us what to do in our own land!

As far as I know our people weren't aware that the United States

I learned even more from the elders and so that period of time became like my college, a college education taught by elders who each had eight or nine hundred years of knowledge that they passed on to me."

Government had supposedly bought Alaska from Russia but I think they probably had a feeling about it. These newcomers knew Alaska belonged to the Indians and they weren't as mouthy back then as they are now because if they had been they would have got rubbed out! That's why they brought an army with them in 1935 to settle here, because they were so scared that they might be killed by the last of the Natives who had survived the epidemics. They didn't go out of the towns or go out in boats to fish because 'there were Indians out there' and they were afraid that we'd kill them, so they stayed around the military bases they built near their towns.

We had prophecies about the coming of the whites. Going back nearly three hundred years, one elder described aeroplanes amongst everything he saw from that time to this. They journeyed into dying by drinking certain herbs that would kill them and then they would travel to our final resting place before they would return. After they were revived they would tell everybody what they saw. There are very few people that know anything about that any more and those who are looking for it need to be warned that it's something you can't mess with. A lot of people come to me who have spirits bothering them and ask me to relieve them but I don't do that anymore and I'm not going to be going back into that business for these 'New Age spiritual seekers'!

We were the first people here and we have always been here but gradually we had to adapt to accommodate others but at first we didn't get along too well. Our ancestors had troubles that were of their time and then

Kalahce

they also had their common problems, like getting through the winters. To make a living our people traded with other Natives to the southeast and up North, but as the white men came they took over all of our trade routes so we had little choice but to work with them. Our elders did what they had to do to exist all through time; like they both fought and traded with the Russians, but it wasn't easy and it still isn't. They had their troubles and inequalities to fight and now we have to do it in the modern day.

Outsiders say that we are related to others they call 'Athabascan' or 'Athapaskan', the Navajos and Apaches in the southwest of the Lower 48, but based upon what I've seen and heard I don't believe that. They say that we talk the same language but I've never seen the similarity in some of the things they say and so I always go back the point that it's the white people's college professors who are trying to push us to fit into their theories, whether we like it or not and irrespective of what we say from our perspective and knowledge of the truth. As near as I can tell we might have some connections in Canada. We speak three different Athabascan

"We know where those stone houses are and those sacred places to the southeast, just as we know where that skin house is on the mountain that saved us from the flood. Their Bering Strait idea is just another

languages here; Southern Athabascan, Interior, and ours which is spoken around the Cook Inlet area. From those three, Interior Athabascan is the closest to what is spoken in Canada but those people have their own distinct ways. With my father, I listened to them at potlatches and we would say that their language might be easy to learn because it sounds similar – but it's not – it's different and there are words that may sound the same but they have totally different meanings and so you have to watch what you say!

Our people lived off the land and took care of it. Our ancestors were good stewards of the land long before we had to fight for it. They never destroyed any other species; they took care of their food sources and only in recent 'date' years, since the coming of the white man, has there been those problems. It's hard to explain to others that each one of our elders was like a human library. They each specialized in specific aspects of our lifeway to the smallest detail, be it plants, water, animals, treating skins, medicines; whatever their role was, they learned everything about it. They were the scholars of their generations and we would be considered babies compared to them. Their knowledge of astrology, ocean currents, the animals, and different types of land were vast. Theirs was a living study of their lifestyle and nowadays it's all coming out of books and those books don't have anything to do with our ancestors' knowledge. That information was passed from father to son, mother to daughter, and through aunts, uncles, medicine people and storytellers.

Sacred knowledge was brought to people here in teachings and that's how traditional values evolved and then they were passed from generation to generation. Everything evolves from one generation that dies out, to the next that may take time to cover the knowledge of the last, so history builds over time and then one person carries it on. It's like oral history that goes from generation to generation, where some have to learn it over and over again but regardless of who knows what, that history is still there. Every hill, battle site and sacred place is known and those who are chosen by the elders – the storytellers – are the ones that knowledge is left with. There are many stories. Once, I heard an elder explaining how man first figured out how to make the canoe. He said an old guy observed ducks for a long time, particularly how a duck's breast was formed, and so he made a craft based upon the shape of a duck's breast and that's how the brow of the canoe came into being. That's one example of how birds and animals taught us and how everything has a meaning. Others followed the caribou and moose and learned how they could clothe and feed us and

way of trying to lift us off the land and remove us from our traditional places and to sever us from our places of origin. It's something they use to justify taking over here."

provide us with weapons and tools. It is told that because of certain world conditions, like volcanoes and ash, earthquakes and fires from lightning flashes, many of them were destroyed but they came back to us and there were stories that compared moose before and after that time. They didn't return here until the 1920s and when the people saw the first one, they killed it and fed it to an orphan child. They did that to see if the moose had changed, because if anything had happened to the orphan they would have know but nothing happened, the orphan grew stronger and so the moose gave its life to the orphan, and in turn the orphan was prepared to give his life for the people – had he died from eating the moose, he would have saved all of the people but he survived and from then on the people returned to the moose and the nutrition it gives us.

Athabascan

This knowledge is gifted to us. I have an arrowhead dating back thousands and thousands of years that I found where I thought I would find something from my ancestors and it was gifted to me because I believed it would come to me and it did. They used the ribs of the moose to carve arrowheads and spears which they used to hunt belugas, seals and king salmon. One of our main ceremonies here in the summer time was the potlatch to celebrate the king salmon and the gathering of the fish. They'd come back to us spring after spring and our people would invite one another to their potlatches where they'd share their songs and trade.

When I was learning from the old people it was hard because they were dying and they could see the future. The main chiefs would always say, 'Stand up for yourself, stand up for the people and stand up for doing your part'. I think that's what all of our younger generations need to do – stand up for their people and take charge. Don't worry about what might hold them back, just go from where they are and don't look back and that will get them further than worrying about it. A lot of action, working for the people, is better than not working at all. Mostly, in the old days, we were a happy people here. There weren't any sorrow or death songs then, those songs are of these recent times. Anger and jealousy were unfamiliar emotions to us, unlike today when some of our own people don't give a damn about anything and don't help each other. They need to learn that our people weren't selfish, they were a giving people who shared, but today some won't even give a helping hand and that's really sad as many in the non-Indian community here are anti-Native.

This society and its institutions in these towns and cities like Anchorage, has little or no respect for the original people of this land.

"The churches have been replaced by the corporations and oil companies – they are now the killing machines of the Native people here . . . I remember when they first hit oil and gas in our country. My dad was part of the Kenai River community and they came

Their ideas and practices are the same as those who took over in the Lower 48 and here, in this modern day and age, I don't think they will ever change unless they themselves are overpowered by an invading force or some kind of disaster makes them change and I haven't seen any on the horizon that are going to come soon. I don't think it's down to the whites being in a form of historical denial as to what they've done, I think the number one reason with many is greed. They are after money and only push their own causes so that they can take control of everything. They are not willing to share anything and throughout history I think that has been their policy of managing people. Here the Americans inherited what the Russian Orthodox Church started and that's how I think they rubbed us out – they didn't deny their own history, they denied us ours so they could wipe us from the records and if we aren't on their records, in their way, we don't exist. They deny our history that tells of how their church did more to destroy us than anything else I have seen. They turned the people against our Chiefs and Shamans by calling them 'sinners' and instilling a fear about our own beliefs being 'evil' and then when they got our people into their churches they made them kiss the cross, knowing that epidemics like tuberculosis were around, and that each who kissed the cross would pass the germs from one to the next. Their religion is something that they believe in and ours is what we have always lived.

The churches have been replaced by the corporations and oil companies – they are now the killing machines of the Native people here.

At first it's almost invisible, then comes the financial destruction that makes you sell your land because they want to develop your land to make their living off it, which destroys it and leaves no way to get it back or even buy anything back. I remember when they first hit oil and gas in our country. My dad was part of the Kenai River community and they came over and asked him to invest in it because the Kenai River was going to be developed. They said, "Everybody's gonna get rich", but nobody got rich except the white men and oil companies! So we're still sitting here in Third World conditions in our own land but they keep coming and it's all for development. Soon after my dad told them he didn't want anything to do with it a Cadillac pulled up and picked up our neighbor!

This is how the oil discovery happened: The neighbor was a white guy who came here straight out of college. He had a family to support and he would ask my dad to help him. One time he came down and told my dad that they were hungry and didn't have anything to eat and so my dad

over and asked him to invest in it because the Kenai River was going to be developed. They said, 'Everybody's gonna get rich', but nobody got rich except the white men and oil companies! So we're still sitting here in Third World conditions in our own land . . ."

went out and shot him a moose. A few days later the game warden came by and asked the college kid where he got the moose meat and so he told him and then the warden showed up at my dad's and took his gun and the rest of the meat away from him. A couple of days later the neighbor came down and said he was hungry again, so as my dad didn't have a gun anymore he went out and caught a king salmon and gave it to him. Now the white guy took it but didn't eat it, he cut it up and threw it in his garden! His family were still hungry but he told my dad, 'Oh, this is good fertiliser'. My dad left it and went fishing and on that occasion he earned a lot of money, over $10,000. Then the neighbor came by again and said, "Hey, I've found oil on the Kenai River! Do you want to invest in it?" And my dad said, "Hell no, I don't want to invest with nobody who throws my meat away or uses salmon as fertilizer. Get out of here!" So he went home and pretty soon the Cadillac came. They drove up and asked where the neighbor was, went over there and pulled him out of his house, took his family, and went back to town – and that's how they started the oil company!

We're still at the bottom of the list and everybody else is getting rich off us and it's all about development. The concept of the Alaska Native Claims Settlement is just the development of land and resources. The Native people put in a claim for about three hundred and eighty million acres of land and ended up with forty-four million acres, but to have any rights we had to organize ourselves into corporations. That

"We were here in Alaska long before the Russians arrived and long before what the white man might call the 'bible times'. One of our sacred sites dates back to that period, the time when the earth was flooded. Our people had to climb a mountain and live upon it until the water level subsided and then they came back down and resettled on this land here that had been their home before. They had to stay up there for a long time during the flood of all the land and they lived in a dwelling that was like a yurt, a house covered with skins that they built out of dinosaur bones."

imposed a whole different philosophy upon our people. These so-called Native corporations were created with boards of directors, so the Natives can now make money developing their land from the claim and then pay everything back in taxes to the United States government! When this was first proposed I sat in that meeting with my father for about forty-five minutes and it felt like we were being raped, so he said, "Let's get out of here, this aint the place to be. Let's not join this, let's just stay by ourselves", and I agreed. We want to be independent. When the white man first came that's how our people survived, we stayed away from them so we wouldn't get diseases or anything; in those times, if our people saw them coming down a trail they'd move away from them. We just stayed out in the woods by ourselves and that's how our people survived through the generations.

It all comes down to money but even though the rich people are taking over America, buying up everything including these corporations, I don't think it will continue indefinitely. The rich have taken over the poor but the poor can eventually take over the rich, but to do that Native people have to take control of one concept – that we are the landowners. Native people in Alaska need to be prepared to fight for their rights because we'll never attain anything unless we fight for it and then hang on to it and make it work for the good of the people. Right now it seems that we haven't got enough direction and so the white man will never turn it over, which comes back to the development of land and leads to the subsistence issues we now face. But the key to it is to keep pushing for self-determination and get together to build a strong Nation. It might take two or three generations of Native people to realize that before anything happens because this white man's way is new to us here and we're slow to learn it. In the meantime we are falling further behind because of the advantages whites have over us with modern technology.

Today our priorities as Native people start with having food, then come jobs, training and health. After that we can worry about trying to keep up with computers, telecommunications and technology. Everybody else seems to be prepared and trained for it but our younger generations aren't. If it isn't addressed it will create a further divide and add to the catastrophe here because the way it looks is that if our young people can't keep up with technology through being trained, then they won't be able to support their families. Our young people are already suffering from an identity crisis due to the clash in education between the white way and the Native way – they don't know which to believe. It started with the white man's boarding schools and it has carried on. We will lose a generation here and there, whole cycles of people that then can't be relied upon to return to their villages which leaves big gaps in our cultures. In some of the smaller communities we do have some Native teachers but overall it is a big test and the education provision has deteriorated. We're stuck in two

"The subsistence struggle is having a big impact in our communities. Some of them are barely making it and quite a few are starving, which is the cumulative effect of what's been imposed upon us . . . We have a lot of mass suicides around our villages because of these conditions and government policies that have resulted in the decline of our societies through these social problems that were alien to us . . . Most of these problems are short term but our people are long term."

worlds and the white culture appears to keep advancing through technology beyond our teachings and that's the divide between the corporate and traditional. Having said that, our people built all the railroads and the roads here, we built all of the canneries, we hauled the mail for years and delivered the coal to the boats rather than shipping it from Seattle – we built the economy of this State but we're still called bums in our own land.

The subsistence issue is a fight over food and resources on our part, a struggle to retain the way we have always fed and clothed ourselves according to our teachings. On the white man's part it's just something else that they want to take away from us and control to make money out of, but we've never said that we wouldn't share! We've never said the white man can't hunt here but I think they're scared of that and fear they would lose financial opportunities if they agreed to share. They destroyed the Lower 48 in the same way and that's the direction they're taking this. Part of the problem is down to philosophy; for Native people there's ceremony and spiritual aspects to hunting and living the subsistence lifestyle off the land, whereas for a lot of white people it's about trophy hunting and the money hunters from out of state pay to come here. We share our tomorrow with our people and we take care of our people and we have always done that through the subsistence way. I've been fighting this for over twenty-five years.

The subsistence struggle is having a big impact in our communities. Some of them are barely making it and quite a few are starving, which is the cumulative effect of what's been imposed upon us and taken from us. In future generations, more Native people will have to move to towns and cities here which will separate us from our traditions and scatter us further, but that's the state and federal government's policy – to take over all of our lands. We have a lot of mass suicides around our villages because of these conditions and government policies that have resulted in the decline of our societies through these social problems that were alien to us; broken families, drugs and alcohol, mental illness, Fetal-Alcohol-Syndrome babies and so on. When we leave this cycle we have to look forward to our future generation doing better than the last. Our grandfathers and fathers had their problems to get through and these are ours.

We tend to focus on everything that's bad and we ignore the good, the changes we have made as Native people and that we have survived. Occasionally we should say, 'Hey, we did make a change and there is hope', because hope gives us courage and energy to carry on. Our grandfathers and the old chiefs always said pray to the Creator and that prayer and our spirituality was the answer. That's the only reason people exist, even in the white man's culture! Most of these problems are short term but our people are long term.

Location: *Arlee, Flathead Indian Reservation, Montana.*

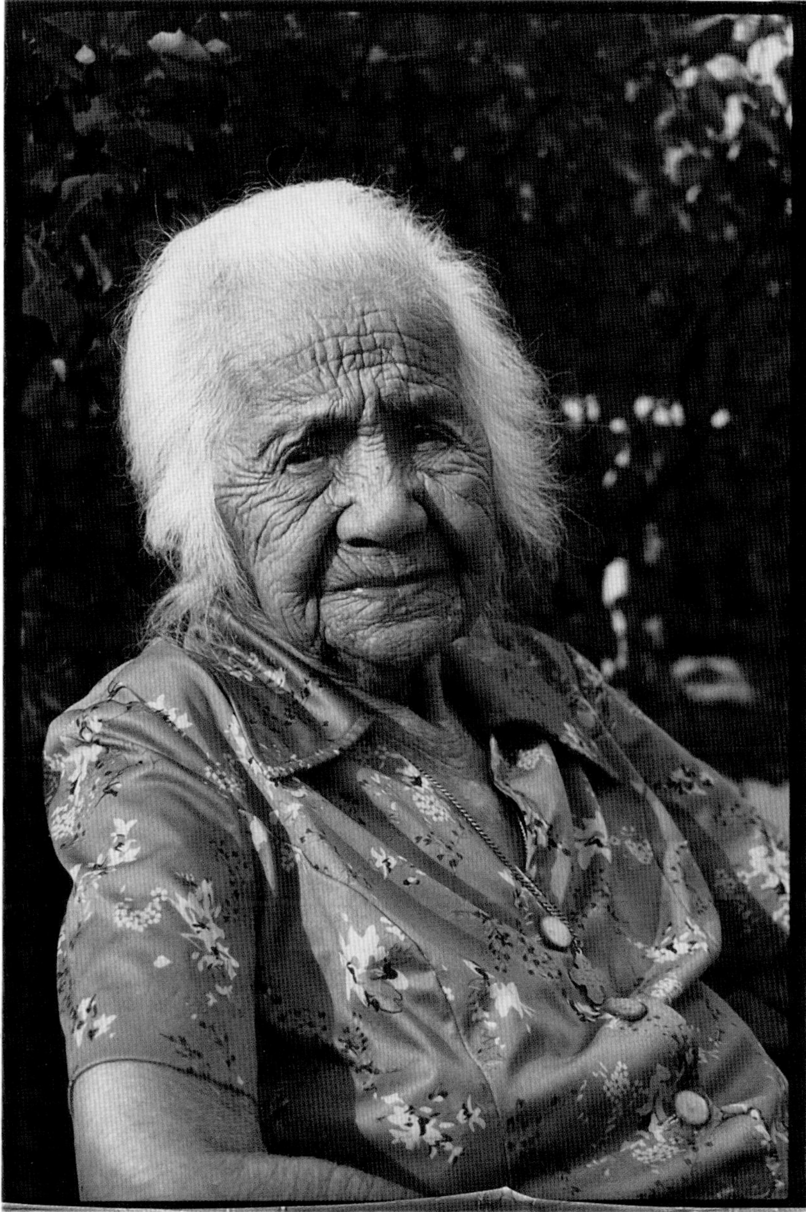

LOUISE COMBS

"I'm Salish from the Bitterroot and proud of it", said the tribe's senior member, Louise Combs, a witness to over a century of change in the Bitterroot Valley and on the Flathead Indian Reservation. Louise's grandfather was among the Salish delegations who, having being intrigued by stories of Black Robes, in the 1830s established the connections that brought the eminent Jesuit Father, Pierre Jean DeSmet, to the Bitterroot Valley in 1841. At over 100 years old, Louise's recollections include experiences of some of the most prominent tribal leaders in the history of the Flathead's confederated tribes – Antoine Moiese became her neighbor, and as a child there were visits to the home of Chief Charlo when he convened the Bitterroot Salish's weekly gatherings upon their relocation to the reservation. A bridge to the past two centuries and the historic events that forged the present, in 2001 Louise continued to withstand the sands of time.

I don't have too many regrets when I look back on my life. There are places where I could have done better if I'd used my head but a lot of times you don't do that! After it's too late, you know that you should have done this or you should have done that, but you can't correct it once it's done. You can't turn back. As far back as I can remember; which is from when I was old enough to recognize my surroundings; I was with my grandparents and my dad and mom, at the bottom of the hill here, just outside of Arlee. We lived there with the rattlesnakes but they never bothered us and we didn't bother them. We never had any trouble with them but when it was strawberry time my grandma never stopped scolding us, 'Take a stick with you and hit all round before you kneel down so there won't be any snakes waiting for you!' she'd say. That was in the days when there were a lot of wild berries and roots; so many that they were easy to pick here and around the Mission Mountains, but it's not like that now. In those days the old Indians knew how you were supposed to pick these foods, that you should give thanks and pray, but today a lot of young ones don't care much about that and that's why a lot of this is gone.

I am Salish from the Bitterroot. That's where we lived before the Agency and the white people, in the Bitterroot Valley. When they say Flatheads, they mean us. On this Flathead Reservation there are Indians who talk different kinds of Salish – Flathead and Kalispel. The Pend d'Oreilles around St Ignatius and the Spokanes are Salish. There are a lot of other Salish tribes all over the Northwest and Columbia River. The Kootenais from here lived up around Flathead Lake, near where Elmo is today. They speak a different language and are related to other Kootenai tribes in Canada but we have always got along together in this area.

> *"I remember Chief Charlo and when I get to thinking about it most of his ideas were good. His father, Chief Victor, signed the Treaty of Hellgate for the Bitterroot Salish . . . Chief Charlo was always*

Our chief, Charlo, never took up arms against the United States because his father who was chief before him didn't, but he fought in every other way he knew how to stay in the Bitterroot. When the Nez Perce came through [1877] with Chief Joseph they asked him to fight with them but he wouldn't, he stayed out of it; he wouldn't fight with them or against them. I remember Martin – that's what they called the Chief, Martin Charlo – and when I get to thinking about it most of his ideas were good. He made little mistakes once in a while, but not too often. His father, Chief Victor, signed the Treaty of Hellgate [1855] for the Bitterroot Salish. He didn't agree to live on what they called the Jocko Reservation made by that treaty, but Alexander of the Pend d'Oreille and Michel for the Kootenai signed on that – Victor signed to stay in the Bitterroot. Later they made another treaty because the settlers wanted the Salish moved out of the Bitterroot but Charlo refused to go. The other leading men, Arlee and Joseph Nine Pipes, agreed to move onto the Jocko Reservation but Charlo wouldn't and so his signature was forged on that treaty. President Grant ordered him to move [an Executive Order, signed by President Grant in November 1871] but he stuck it out with the people and stayed there for another twenty years. They were poor by then. The railroad had come and there was a lot of pressure on him to move – which he did, after he was made all kinds of promises that were never kept.

Chief Charlo was always striving to tell the people what to do for the best and what not to do. The Chief used to gather the people in and around his own house on Sundays. He had quite a large house up at the Agency and he would give his ideas as what to do and what not to do, and he punished some people that didn't do right. He used to put a blanket on the floor and then he'd get the 'Indian Whip'. They'd get another guy to use it, to give whoever had done wrong one or two strikes on the back. That was the punishment in them days, there wasn't the law there is today but if somebody did wrong they were taken to the Chief's house. When the sub-agent arrived at Dixon he put a stop to that though; he said that anybody who needed punishment must be sent to him and he'd lay the law down to them.

Charlo used to get help from Antoine Moiese and a guy by the name of Louie John who used to live at the old Agency. Having fought to stay in the Bitterroot, when they finally came to this reservation Charlo and Antoine Moiese tried to stop the Allotment of Flathead land along with the Kootenai's Chief, Isaac. Charlo fought against it until he died because he knew it would

striving to tell the people what to do for the best. He used to gather the people around his own house on Sundays up at the Agency and he would give his ideas as what to do and what not to do . . ."

mean that we would lose more land if it was allotted and that settlers would come in and take it. He was right you know, the Indians lost about half of this Flathead Reservation because of Allotment and today there are more white people on this reservation than Indians. I think the Mourns, the Grants and the Downeys were the first white people to settle in this valley and after them, others came in and made their homes here. At the time we didn't know anything was being said, I thought the Chief was just letting them go where they chose! In a way Allotment was one of the worst things that ever happened. We either received eighty acres of agricultural land or one hundred and sixty acres to run livestock on. I remember a couple who were pretty well satisfied but most weren't satisfied at all. You had to stay where you were allotted and it wasn't your choice. My sister Helen should have been allotted near us but she was allotted at Post Creek, where years before the McDonalds first came in here for the Hudson's Bay traders [Angus McDonald was born in Craig, Scotland and arrived at the Fort Connah trading post on Post Creek in 1847; McDonald Peak in the Mission Mountains is named for him].

Before they allotted us, the Salish and Kootenai lived pretty nearly all over the reservation. When the Agency allotted me, Antoine Moiese asked the agent to put me next to him across the Jocko River. Antoine Moiese said, "If I die first my place will go to you, but if you die first your place goes to me". Well, that was written down at the Agency and we thought that's the way it would be but it didn't happen the way it was written down and I still don't know why not.

Sometimes when I begin to wonder about when we lost control of our lives I think back to when we got our first sub-agent – and that's when we first had to do what they said. We had to do just what the agent said. I don't like to say it but it's a fact, after that we really didn't have our own say about our lives anymore. They wanted us to become farmers. The Indians here were told that if they put in reclamation ditches and planted their crops they could use all the water they wanted for free. A lot of them plowed up their land and put in wheat, oats or barley because of that, but two years later it changed and we suddenly had to pay for the water! I remember Louie Demerse saying that he saw the day that Indians were told to pay for water and so they put their plows away.

They put us to school at St Ignatius and left us there most of the year. We weren't scholars, we had to stay there and we didn't have any choice because it was a boarding school; they'd bring us over in September and go after us in June. When we got there most talked Indian but it was English only there and they scolded you if they heard you talk Indian. The Sisters of Charity were the schoolmistresses there at St Ignatius. It's supposed to be named after an Iroquois Indian from the east called Big Ignace who came out here with traders and encouraged the Salish to go to St Louis and ask the Catholics to send a priest here, which they did [Father DeSmet established St Mary's Mission in 1841]. Father DeSmet came. I had relatives involved in that and DeSmet came and started St Mary's Mission in Stevensville and then St Ignatius. DeSmet didn't stay here, I think he went on to the Coeur d'Alenes.

I left St Ignatius when I was in the 6th Grade and went to Cushman. Cushman Indian School was a big industrial boarding school on the Puyallup Indian Reservation. The Puyallup are also Salish, sometimes they were called the South Coast or Puget Sound Salish. There are a lot of Salish tribes over there. Then white people built the city of Tacoma on the Puyallup's land – which is where Cushman was – and the Skokomish Salish are also near there and they had an Indian school on their land before Cushman took its place. Indian children from around the Northwest and Alaska went to Cushman and I spent three years of my life there. My sister Helen didn't like it and after that first summer we went home, she wouldn't go back. Part of it was the rain, it was always damp because it was close to the Puget Sound, but I went back. They say your school days are the happiest of your life and when I think of how my school days were, I say well, then Cushman days were my happiest. Now, when I'm in bed, I'm taken back there when I think about those girls and boys I knew at Cushman – I don't forget them.

Today I tell these young ones, go to school as much as you can because if you don't have an education you're nobody. People don't watch their children like they used to and that's why they get into so much mischief. When I was a kid I didn't want the willow stick, we were scared of that so we watched what we did. I don't think kids scare easily nowadays but if they want to get along they need to learn their culture and get all the education they can. It's like my uncle said, "If you don't get an education you're going to have a hard time and when you don't get along in your life, it'll be just too bad for you". He was right, you know.

Top: *Felicite McDonald (Salish/San Felipe Pueblo), one of Louise's great-great grandchildren, at Nine Pipes overlooking the Mission Mountains.*
Above: *Osprey over Flathead Lake.*

"Having fought to stay in the Bitterroot, when they finally came to this reservation Charlo and Antoine Moiese tried to stop the Allotment of Flathead land along with the Kootenai's Chief, Isaac. Charlo fought against it until he died because he knew it meant that we would lose more land . . . He was right, the Indians lost about half of this Flathead Reservation because of Allotment and today there are more white people on this reservation than Indians."

Location: *Window Rock, Navajo Nation, Arizona.*

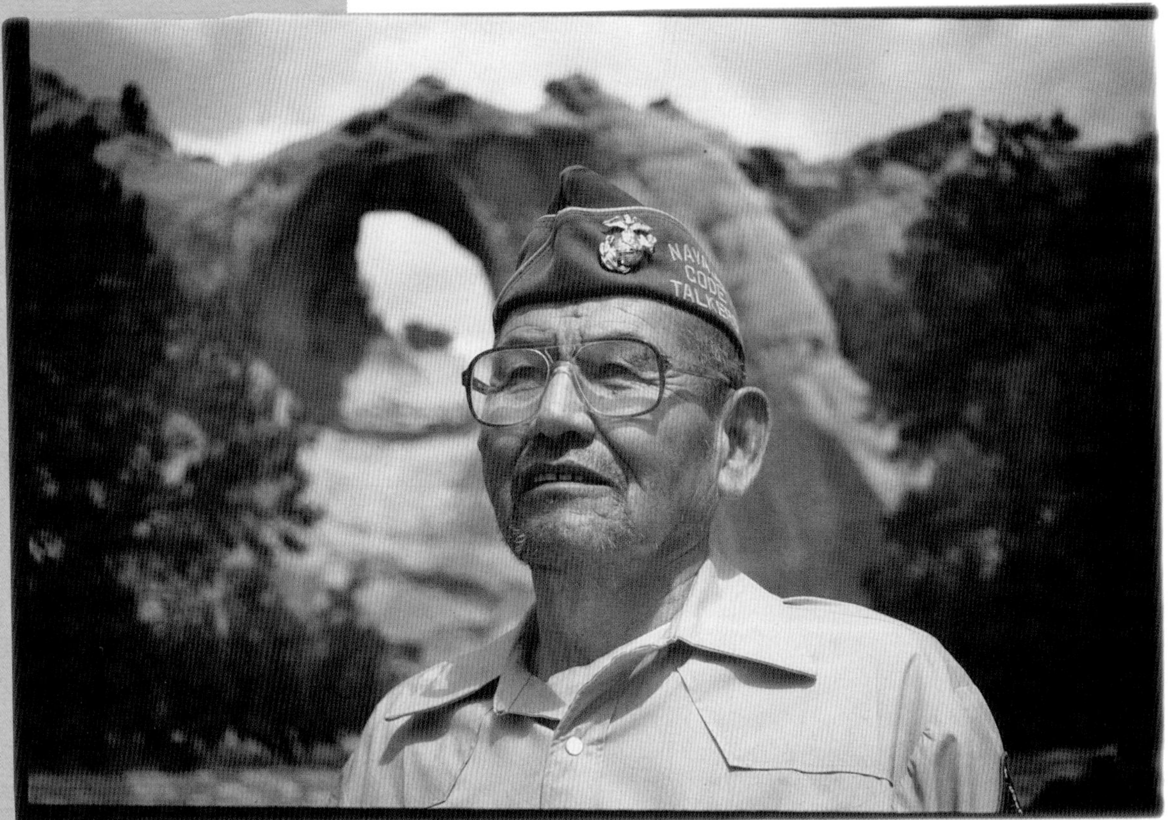

HARRY BENALLY

Harry Benally served with the US Marines as a Navajo Code Talker from January 1944 to May 1946, in the Pacific combat theatre during World War II. Harry was Ta'néészahnii (Badlands People) Clan, born for the Tódích'íi'níi (Bitter Water) Clan, his birth place being near Tosido in August 1925. As a boy he had a dream that foretold of his military service in a strange land and he fulfilled that prophetic insight, becoming a decorated veteran in a legendary outfit. Harry passed away on September 26, 2000. He was the embodiment of his Diné name, Haashkei Yitahdeeswod, 'An Experienced and Great Leader'.

Harry's story may seem like a reminiscence that can be read
at a safe distance, but it isn't.
This remembrance is courage. This memory is a situation –
a situation most never know and pray they never have to.
War.
Harry's memoir may not appear to be very long
but there are white headstones in rows
and rows of white crosses in distant fields
that each have a part of this story,
alongside those who survived and made it home
whose names and faces, like those stacked in lines upon monuments,
we may never know.
Each may not ever have understood,
but they know the sights and sounds and smells that come with war,
so others may not have to.
Here is a face to put to a name.
This is Harry's story.

"After all that schooling they gave us a test and I guess I passed it because they made me a Code Talker . . . I was shipped overseas to the Solomon Islands and then on Russell Island they assigned me out to Headquarters and Service Company, 1st Marine Regiment under the First Marine Division. We moved around Russell Island and then onto Pavuvu, Banika and Guadalcanal. Later they shipped us to Ulithi and Yap and from there we headed to Okinawa when the 2nd, 3rd, 4th and 5th Marine Divisions were fighting on Iwo Jima. We landed on the Blue Beach on April 1st, 1945 and there I helped fight in the Battle of Okinawa."

I was one of the Navajo Code Talkers involved in World War II. First I went to the San Diego Boot Camp like everybody else. I graduated from there with Arsenio Smiley and Frankie Chee Willeto, at which time we were told that they had a 'special assignment' for us. We were selected to attend communications school at Camp Pendleton, near Oceanside, California. We were trained in both sides, the English way and later the Navajo way, because they figured that was the best way for us to learn how to run radio, jeep radio, switchboards and walkie-talkie in both languages. After all that schooling they gave us a test and I guess I passed it because they made me a Code Talker.

I was shipped overseas to the Solomon Islands and then on Russell Island they assigned me out to Headquarters and Service Company, 1st Marine Regiment under the First Marine Division. We moved around Russell Island and then onto Pavuvu, Banika and Guadalcanal. Later they shipped us to Ulithi and Yap and from there we headed to Okinawa when the 2nd, 3rd, 4th and 5th Marine Divisions were fighting on Iwo Jima. We landed on the Blue Beach on April 1st, 1945 and there I helped fight in the Battle of Okinawa.

On the first day we took over the Japanese airport there. The next day we moved on and moved on and moved on, heading over the island which was about 25 miles across. We had little opposition and it wasn't too bad until on the fifth day when we were strafed by two Mitsubishi Jet Zeros. Those planes came around and went right at us and the strafe tore up our jeep and our switchboard. The sergeant got killed, a corporal got wounded and one of the Code Talkers got wounded. After it was over Colonel Kelly made the roll call. He called my name and I said, "I'm here".

He asked me, "Are you alright?" So I said, "Yes I'm alright". "Well get your combat pack ready and your rifle," he said, "I've got a job for you." He gave me a message and I put it in my front pocket. "I want you to take this message to Division Headquarters Battalion on the double! We are out of communication", he instructed me. We didn't have a radio, jeep or switchboard anymore after the attack. Then I asked him, "Which way is Division Headquarters?" And he said, "I don't know. I don't know this country. Just take off back where we came from and move back about seven miles." Then he said, "And don't ask anymore questions! Take off!" So I did. I ran at about half speed for two miles and then I was able to catch a ride in a jeep which took me to Division Headquarters.

There I found the message center personnel, who was a lieutenant. I gave him the message and he told me to wait around there. I waited for about two days and then they came up with a new jeep, new radio and new switchboards. He wanted me to drive the jeep with the new equipment back to my company but I didn't know how to drive a jeep! I never had driven a jeep so I told him, "I can't drive, I've got no license". So they got another guy to drive the jeep and another one followed us until we got back to my Service Company, 1st Marine regiment. I got back with everything and we were in communication again and we were still ahead of schedule.

". . . I shook the pole out of the ground, but when I looked down there were eyes looking up at me. I could see these eyes blinking where the base of that pole had been; I guess I had shaken the dirt off it into this guy's eyes. He was Japanese . . .

About two weeks later the army on the south side of us ran into opposition. The Tenth Army were getting wiped out and so they moved us down there to help them. We went by Naha and then south east of Naha, around Shuri Castle, where we had heavy rain for about two weeks which slowed us down. We couldn't hardly move anymore but we walked across a main wash without hitting any opposition and made it to the ridge there alright. At the ridge we were told to hold that line but all of our war equipment, our heavy machinery, was stuck in that wash. Eventually they managed to pull it out and so a few weeks later they made it across the wash with our equipment and then we were able to push on to the south. We kept pushing on, going and going and going, but we were hitting opposition. Every night the Japanese attacked us and so we'd shoot up the flare and set up the BAR [Browning Automatic Rifle] and wipe them out every night. I never knew where they were or where they were coming from, but I guess they came from underground, out of tunnels.

It was June and it was really hot. So one day William George, who was operating the radio with me, decided that we should build a shade over the radio so that it might cool off a little bit. I asked Ralph Gearing – who was a white guy from Pittsburgh, Pennsylvania – to take over the radio while we walked around and looked for sugar cane. We wanted the leaves for the top and these sugar canes were about ten feet tall and real thick. William George asked me to go ahead of him and so I did. I found a pole sticking out of the ground at about an angle of 60 degrees, so I called over to William George in Navajo. 'Do you think this pole will be alright?' Then I shook the pole out of the ground, but when I looked down there were eyes looking up at me. I could see these eyes blinking where the base of that pole had been; I guess I had shaken the dirt off it into this guy's eyes. He was Japanese. The Japanese soldiers had been coming out from down there.

At the time I didn't realize that there were likely to be Japanese hiding down in that hole! So I grabbed my rifle and put a bullet in the chamber real quick and then, in Japanese, I shouted, Get out of there! Get out of there! Or I'll shoot you. '*Tadcad Ahdikoi*.' So he laid his weapon

At the time I didn't realize that there were likely to be Japanese hiding down in that hole! So I grabbed my rifle and put a bullet in the chamber real quick and then, in Japanese, I shouted, Get out of there! Get out of there! . . ."

down and came out. And then another one came out and then another one. Japanese soldiers just kept coming up out of the ground and I kept repeating '*Tadcad Ahdikoi*' and made them line up. I didn't know it, but William George had taken off to get some help and I was there all alone with fourteen Japanese lined up and then laying on their bellies. Sooner or later this white guy came around and asked, "Did you get all of them out?" I told him I didn't know, so he asked me to cover him and he went down there to look. Pretty soon he crawled back out and said there were no more Japanese in there. Then another white guy showed up and William George came back. I covered them while they searched the Japanese and disarmed them. Once we'd cleaned them out this other white guy said, "Okay, we'll take care of them. We're safe now." So me and William George just took off and that's where we made our mistake. We didn't realize we had, but we gave our prisoners away to that guy and he claimed it all. That guy took those Japanese from me as prisoners-of-war and got the Silver Star for capturing the enemy. I lost every bit of it and never did receive any recognition. Me and William George should have just kept our prisoners, chased them over to our company and then brought them over here to Navajo country and made sheep herders out of them!

After Okinawa and the war was over they sent me to Taco, Tinshin and Peking in China. I spent another year over there and then finally they discharged me.

Adelle Cassadore Swift.

Location: *Peridot, San Carlos Apache Reservation, Arizona.*

Above: *San Carlos Apache Crown Dancer.*
Left: *Western Apache wickiups.*

Adelle Cassadore Swift

The biggest changes here on San Carlos in my lifetime happened after World War II. Before that there was a lot of discipline. When we were growing up we were trained by our people and taught our Apache ways by our parents and grandparents. They would teach us a lot of things from our early years onwards. There was no drinking or going out late. We learned how to make cradleboards, how to prepare our Apache foods, but today you don't see that. We spoke our language whereas now the children here mostly speak in English. Our Apache language here has almost faded away. Very few young people can speak it. It shows how it is when those who do want to learn end up coming back here after they have been to college or university; there was nobody left to teach or encourage them before so they have had to come to the realization themselves that they need to learn our language and our history.

There are a lot of different Apache people – the Apaches aren't just one tribe. The San Carlos Apaches are part of the Western Apaches, along with the Tonto and White Mountain

Adelle's grandfather, Chief Cassadore, was one of the leaders of the original San Carlos Apache band, the T'iis Zhaazhé Bikoh. Cassadore was a prominent personality during the tumultuous times of nineteenth-century San Carlos. Adelle absorbed her relatives' history at first-hand, along with traditional Western Apache culture, before experiencing the ensuing transitional period and pressure to live in 'two worlds'. Adelle has represented the San Carlos Apaches at educational forums in Washington, DC, and at the Smithsonian Institute. She has served on the tribe's health and housing programs, and is presently engaged with cultural preservation efforts through the San Carlos Apache Culture Center.

Apaches. Western Apache land is from here to Sedona and Camp Verde. A lot of San Carlos Apaches have what they call Pinal Apache ancestors. They settled along Pinal Creek, near where Globe and Miami are today, but the San Carlos Apaches are actually five separate bands; the Pinal, Aravaipa, Apache Peaks, Tonto and the first San Carlos people. This last band was one of the smallest and they lived around the San Carlos River in the small cottonwood canyon. My grandfather, Chief Cassadore, was one of the leaders of this original San Carlos Apache band. The other tribes got called San Carlos Apaches because in the 1870s the US Army forced them all to live by the San Carlos River, so they kind of joined my grandpa's people there and got given that name also.

It was the government who brought the white people here to work. When the Apaches were put on the reservation it was those people who taught us how to farm their way and raise cattle, that's how the San Carlos Apaches became good cowboys. A lot of other Apaches didn't want to come to this reservation here but they were forced to by the US

"So we elders are saying, 'No mines for us here on this reservation. They will kill us if we have mines. It will destroy our plants and pollute our river and streams' . . . I went to Washington, DC to

government. Different chiefs like Victorio and Naiche, ones like Geronimo, they were from different mountains; they weren't Western Apaches, they were Chiricahua Apaches with their own clans but the army didn't understand that. Things were very hard when they first started this reservation. The people were confined here and there were too many different Apache groups all being pushed together and that along with bad rations, disease and the tags with numbers they made them use instead of their names brought a lot of unrest.

It was a risk to leave the reservation though because Apache people were being massacred all around here. Even so, it was so bad that my grandpa, Cassadore, took his people away from the reservation about a year after it had been established. When the army found them they had orders to wipe them out, so Cassadore told them that his people would prefer that, to die by bullets rather than to starve to death on San Carlos. They say that their moccasins were so worn out that they left a trail of blood on the rocks. Pretty soon after that they put John Clum in charge. He was only a young guy and some liked him but many didn't. He did get the cavalry removed from San Carlos for a while though but then they forced even more Apaches to come here – Yavapais, Tontos and the Chiricahuas. About the time the Chiricahuas arrived the whites discovered silver in this area, so it was never going to work. After Clum left it got even worse. The Apache's rations never got to them because the agency workers stole them and sold them to the miners. Then, when the Chiricahuas escaped the army followed what Clum did and enlisted San Carlos Apaches as scouts to find them. Eventually things settled down and the San Carlos Apaches became famous for being Indian cowboys! Many of our people worked on Coolidge Dam which they built here between 1927 and 1930. They flooded the old San Carlos agency and that's where the lake is today. Then came those big changes I saw, after World War II.

Up until that time we were still living in wickiups and ramadas but then, a little at a time, they started to bring houses here and then we had to totally change our lifestyle. Now we have houses in every district. With these changes came drinking and violence on the reservation which never used to be here. They said that they would stop it but they never have and now it's as if we've got used to it, seeing teenagers drunk and smoking drugs. The children that they sent away to the government boarding schools in Phoenix, Nevada and California brought this back with them, this is what they learned there in the cities and it just went wild when they returned to the reservation because the other kids started to copy them.

fight for our water rights. I listened mostly but I answered their questions. After that, the tribe chose me to testify on behalf of the San Carlos Apaches . . ."

When they started mining around the boundaries of our reservation a lot of the old people didn't like it. We didn't want to lose the hills and mountains that surround us because they say that a lot of our ancestors are buried on the mountain sides. We were also afraid that we would get sick from the mines like they did in these neighboring towns, like Miami. So we elders are saying, 'No mines for us here on this reservation. They will kill us if we have mines. It will destroy our plants and pollute our river and streams.' A lot of people off the reservation are already taking our water for their orchards and farms way down the valley, going towards Phoenix. I went to Washington, DC to fight for our water rights. I listened mostly but I answered their questions. After that, the tribe chose me to testify on behalf of the San Carlos Apaches, so I travelled to Tucson with my grandpa's papers which set out who has rights to the water here and that the Apaches should be getting fair treatment – and this goes back to the old days in San Carlos. I don't want to fight for water; there should be no problem.

I would like to see our young people learning our language and culture. As it is, there are only a few of us who know it and when visitors come to the reservation from different states and different countries we are the ones who meet them at our Culture Center here. One day soon I hope there will be others to welcome them and help them understand who the San Carlos Apaches really are – that way I will know our Apache ways are strong, with the young ones carrying them on.

Location: *Lame Deer, Northern Cheyenne Reservation, Montana.*

Right: *Little Bighorn Battlefield.* **Far right:** *Elva on Rosebud Creek, near the site of the great 1876 Sun Dance.*

Elva Stands In Timber's father, John Stands In Timber, was the esteemed Northern Cheyenne tribal historian and author. *Cheyenne Memories*, his book in collaboration with Margot Liberty, endures not only as a priceless historical and cultural resource but as a significant moment in Native American literary achievement. Elva inherited her father's desire for the preservation of Cheyenne history and, like John, she sought out the elders who held the traditional knowledge to learn the Cheyenne way. Her great-grandfather, Lame White Man, fought at the Battle of the Little Bighorn and through Stands In Timber's efforts he is one of the few Lakota or Cheyenne casualties commemorated on the battlefield. An educator and advocate for the preservation of Cheyenne culture, Elva is one of the last among her people to hold some of the ancient Northern Cheyenne songs.

Elva Stands In Timber

The elders were your teachers. I hung out with my grandparents and learned everything from them. We rose before sun up because we were told that if the sun touches you and you're still asleep, it shows you're lazy. While we were getting up my grandfather would already be on his way back from the creek with fresh water. It was said that you shouldn't drink water that has been standing because when you drink water you drink the life that is in that water and the water from the creek flowed with life, so that's what we drank each morning. When I was a kid I used to ask a lot of questions, almost hounding my grandparents, but I was a listener. Some kids are always asking why? And I tell them because I was like that. My grandparents used to sing all the time and I'd sing along with them. I was a dancer too; I danced the round dance and the rabbit dance. When I look back on it, there are times when I could have asked things and I didn't and now I wished I had because there's nobody to ask anymore – they're all gone – and that's a sad part of our culture. We are not utilizing the elders like we should and I keep urging the people that are interested in bringing the language back and learning our traditions to consult with the elders everyday. Search them out because the knowledge of the elders is a precious resource.

"There's talk about the Cheyennes regarding Custer as a relative but I have never heard anybody among the Cheyenne people say that they recognize Custer as a relative! The old people would make jokes about him and tell stories about their coups there. We're Cheyennes. It's other people who make this kind of stuff up . . . I remember that my mother once told me to go and throw some of my dad's old papers away because they were filling up the little shack at the back of our house. I went back there to do it but I ended up reading in there all afternoon. He had hand written stories, about six from people who took part in the Custer battle, and that's how he started with his book."

Tsistsistas

The elders always used to stress honesty; to talk, to tell stories but not to add anything or put something in there just because you think it should be. A few of us still talk like that. Like some people try and change the story of how the So'taaeo'o and the Tsistsistas came together when this is how it was: There was a little difference in the languages but not much and they understood each other easily, so much so that one thought the other was copying from them. So one man asked the other where they came from, so he told him that he'd show him. He took him to Bear Butte and the other man told him that his people were also from Bear Butte. That's just a little bit of the story. They talked about how a long, long time ago five tribes, the So'taaeo'o, Tsistsistas, Sioux, Shoshone and Arapaho, came together in a ceremony through the Sacred Buffalo Hat and how, whatever some men might want, that it can never be changed that once, these were affiliated tribes. When the Massaum ceremony took place they would name all five tribes at the start but that ceremony has gone now. Today things are getting so crazy that you hear some people saying that the

". . . she led them that night and it was as if she could see like it was daytime. But the cavalry were chasing them and getting close, so she told the people to put their children inside their robes

So'taaeo'o can only do one thing and the Tsistsistas can only do the other, but that's not so! They came together long ago and nobody can separate them. My father was So'taaeo'o and my mother was Tsistsistas.

My grandmother was born two days after the Battle of the Little Bighorn. After the fight her folks took off in to Wyoming. She once got a write up in the newspaper saying that she could remember incidents that happened at the battle and so she would be teased about that because it was common knowledge among the tribes at that time that nobody was to tell stories about the Custer fight. Before they left the Little Bighorn they all made a vow that they would not tell the white people what happened there, so when we saw her picture in the newspaper we reminded her of that and teased her that the military police would come looking for her. When we tell that story in Cheyenne it's funny! At the Little Bighorn they were fighting for our homeland because we were being invaded. They always talked about how they knew Custer was there but that they kept saying amongst themselves that he would have to be crazy to attack them because the encampment contained most of the affiliated tribes. There should be a memorial up there by now for the Native Americans that fell in the battle. They have that big old thing for Custer but who wants to be around that? The thing about it is we killed that guy! We won that battle. I'm fiercely proud of it and I know that a lot of the other descendants of people who were there that day are. There's talk about the Cheyennes regarding Custer as a relative but I have never heard anybody among the

Cheyenne people say that they recognize Custer as a relative! The old people would make jokes about him and tell stories about their coups there. We're Cheyennes. It's other people who make this kind of stuff up.

This is what comes from the old people. It's handed down from the elders and there's no way that anybody can change it. This is the Cheyenne; it's not from anywhere else, those other parts that the white man wrote. This is what my father believed in and it is what I believe in. Some white people say that we weren't always in this land of ours but if that's true, then why would they have trekked all the way back here – home – from Oklahoma when they moved them there? The old people always claimed that this was the best country and I have always heard that this is home. According to the old people it was General Miles who, in their opinions, founded this reservation because he let them stay and hunt around here before it was decided that the Cheyennes would be sent to Oklahoma. He's the one they called Washington Big Man, and then the President made a commitment that the Cheyenne would be left with this territory. The old people always talked about how they were neither captured or conquered. How they actually came to be here was through a woman they called Sweet Woman. She *had* been captured by the soldiers and they asked her how they could approach the Cheyenne and so she taught them about tobacco and how it was used in the sacred pipe. She said the first thing that they should do is to offer the Cheyenne tobacco and then other gifts and that's what they did, they loaded a wagon up with sugar and coffee and went to Chief Little Wolf's camp. They always referred to it as, 'That's Where That Woman Made Treaties With the Cheyenne'. It was there that Chief Two Moons agreed to go and talk peace with General Miles.

and lay down. They did this and when the cavalry came upon them all they saw were buffalo sitting and laying out there. Another time it is said that they appeared as boulders . . ."

Cheyenne

When they did send the Cheyenne to Oklahoma, my father's people and my grandmother's people managed to stay behind. I have heard many stories about Chief Dull Knife and Chief Little Wolf coming back here. They were getting sick down there and people tell of how once an elderly woman so longed to be back home with the pine trees that she went out to look for some and when she found them she just fell over and died at the base of one. It was actually a woman who led the Cheyenne back up here. With that many people travelling you would have thought that it would have been impossible for them to make it, pursued as they were by all of the cavalry and bounty hunters; but one day this woman called all of the people together. This should be told in our language to understand the full meaning, so this is an interpretation; she told them that somebody came to

Cheyenne

her. At first the people weren't sure if they believed her but she led them that night and it was as if she could see like it was daytime. But the cavalry were chasing them and getting close, so she told the people to put their children inside their robes and lay down. They did this and when the cavalry came upon them all they saw were buffalo sitting and laying out there. Another time it is said that they appeared as boulders. This was before they imprisoned them at Fort Robinson, Nebraska. Recently someone came and asked me if I'd ever heard about the North Woman and I said, "Yes, that's the woman who brought the Cheyennes back from Oklahoma". Some people are surprised when they ask me questions that I haven't read any books. I haven't even gone through all of my dad's book!

Cheyenne women were never passive; we have always been independent but the role Cheyenne women had in our society has been distorted. My grandfather and my father would always tell us that the most important thing in this life is the woman. She is the life giver. She comes first. My grandfather used to say that the first thing a man must be

". . . a lot of people today claim to be 'Pipe Carriers' but I think they're crazy. In the Sun Dance, the Sun Dance priest and the dancers all carry pipes. When an individual goes through a ceremony the pipe goes along with them. That's how it is in the Cheyenne way.

is attentive to his mate because a man should only have one mate throughout his life and that woman will be the one to make a good life for him. We were told how a woman would be dressed by her husband, how he would braid her hair in the morning and of course, put paint on her face. There's a woman in every ceremony too; and the warrior societies, like the Crazy Dogs, Elks and Kit Foxes, all have four sisters in each society. They would select a young woman for her purity, often a virgin, as her purity would bring good spirits to the society. These young women were held in high esteem. When you walked into a room one of the men would bring water for you and everybody else there would then drink that water so they shared in the goodness you brought to the people. That was the way of the warrior societies but that's gone now.

Women are not supposed to view the Sacred Arrows and we are cautioned by the Hat Keeper to avoid seeing the Sacred Buffalo Hat as well; although the Sacred Buffalo Hat represents female power in balance to the male power of the Four Sacred Arrows. Sweet Medicine brought everything to the Tsistsistas, the Sacred Arrows, the military societies, our laws and government – the Council of Forty-Four Chiefs, everything. Sweet Medicine is called the Prophet and I have known people to bless themselves before they start to talk about him or tell the story of Sweet Medicine. He predicted everything that is happening today and how the Anglos would destroy our way of life to the point where we would no longer be Cheyenne. He said that we would no longer respect our traditional ways that identify us as Cheyennes and that we would even start inter-marrying with our own relatives, like an uncle or a third cousin, and even in my time this was strictly not done. Much of the sacred knowledge Sweet Medicine brought to the Cheyenne was given to him on our sacred mountain, Bear Butte, but today there are people up there who shouldn't be. It's our holy place, not a tourist attraction, and I hate to think of what might become of it in the future. I wish something could be done about it and I always say, "Maybe this is why we are going crazy, because of what they are doing to Bear Butte".

I know a lot of people today claim to be 'Pipe Carriers' but I think they're crazy. In the Sun Dance, the Sun Dance priest and the dancers all carry pipes. When an individual goes through a ceremony the pipe goes along with them. That's how it is in the Cheyenne way. There are no special 'Pipe Carriers'. I am a ceremonial person. I don't talk about that but that's who I am and it comes from my background and it comes from

There are no special 'Pipe Carriers'. I am a ceremonial person. I don't talk about that but that's who I am and it comes from my background and it comes from my people. I honor that. I don't play with it. You don't mess around with the sacred pipe."

my people. I honor that. I don't play with it. You don't mess around with the sacred pipe. A pipe ceremony is a very special occasion. My father used to try and explain that to the Cheyenne, swearing on the sacred pipe had the same importance as swearing on the Bible in other cultures. My mother once questioned my father as to how he could interpret certain things in his book because he wasn't a ceremonial man and he said, "I vowed to the sacred pipe that this comes from the old people and they gave me this gift to do this".

I remember that my mother once told me to go and throw some of my dad's old papers away because they were filling up the little shack at the back of our house. I went back there to do it but I ended up reading in there all afternoon. He had hand written stories, about six from people who took part in the Custer battle, and that's how he started with his book. I told my mom, I don't think you should throw any of it away. Then one night, when my brother was only about fifteen, he caught somebody coming out of that shack in the middle of the night. He asked them what they were doing and they said, "Oh, John told me to come and pick up these papers". Well those papers are now in somebody's collection and there are also documents that my dad showed different people he trusted that went missing.

Father became a Mennonite preacher. He used to compare the scriptures to the Old Man's word, the Cheyenne way, and he showed us where he thought they matched. For instance, he said a chief's role is much like the way Jesus lived his life. A chief isn't a king or anything, he lives to serve his people – he waits on them, he shares everything with them and a person never leaves the chief's lodge without what they need. The Anglos thought of us as the 'nothing people', that we didn't know nothing and that we were barbarians, but my mother used to say that it was the missionaries who were the savages and the barbarians. My father tried to bring the Bible together with the Old Man's word because he was afraid that one day the Cheyenne way would be gone and we'd have nothing. They always tell me that my father lived what he believed. Myself, I have seen miracles happen from within our own culture.

A person that makes a change for the people is someone that comes from the heart and that's the Cheyenne way. I don't believe that many government politicians here know much about the traditional Cheyenne way because I think right now this is a really corrupt system of tribal government. There needs to be change and that doesn't mean mining more coal. That money will soon be gone and with it will be our land, our home. I never want us to lose this reservation. Our old people fought and gave their lives so we would have this land. We have a lot of poverty and unemployment here but you can always find somebody on the reservation who will take you in and that's the way we are supposed to be. We need to start utilizing the knowledge of the elders and it has to start in Head Start for our children. I pray that the traditional knowledge will come back – if not to all, then to some who will carry it on so that it never dies. That's my hope.

"We are not utilizing the elders like we should and I keep urging the people that are interested in bringing the language back and learning our traditions to consult with the elders everyday. Search them out because the knowledge of the elders is a precious resource."

Perspectives From Native America

Marley Shebala

A Constant State of Explanation

Michael Horse
(Yaqui/Mescalero Apache/Zuni)
Actor and Artist
Twin Peaks, Roswell, North of 60, The X-Files, Lakota Woman . . .

"One time somebody asked me what it was like being an indigenous person and I said, 'It's a constant state of explanation'. It is and sometimes you get tired of it, but dealing in the movies I've learned how the system works over the years . . ."

MICHAEL HORSE

We are the invisible culture. Usually, when there are articles written about ethnic diversity, they don't mention us. They mention the black community, the Hispanic community and the Asian community but we're invisible. I have to explain to people who live in Los Angeles that the Indian community here is the second biggest urban Indian population in the United States! Then they ask, "Well where are you?" And I say, "We're all around you, but you just don't bother to look". Again it's about money; they've been selling us for years – we're the names of their cars, they make books about us, films about us, mascots, they paint our picture – and what's really interesting is that if they let us present our true stories they'd make much more money than they make now. Our true stories, who we really are, are far more interesting than anything they have ever done.

What's interesting about the movies is that we've always been portrayed as being extremely violent people, like we awoke each morning and said, "Okay, who are we going to go and beat up today". And we weren't like that. Yes, we had conflicts with other people, with ourselves, and with other nations but no more – and probably less – than in other cultures. We were and remain *human* beings. Now we're the 'noble savage', we do nothing wrong and we're continuously connected to the earth . . . But their dilemma is that once they show indigenous people as human beings who laugh, cry, love and grieve, they will have to answer for what they did to us because suddenly we will appear extremely human and not a figment of the imagination.

MICHAEL

Like I said, it's a constant state of explanation. I've talked to a lot of other actors who have attained some notoriety and who, all of a sudden, have encountered a situation where they have felt compelled to become a spokesperson for 'the entire Indian community'. But I don't think any of us want to be perceived as that! We are just individual artists, but I think that as long as we're in the hands of a system that is portraying our culture from the outside and that really doesn't bother about that, we'll end up having to speak out sooner or later. On a movie dealing with an indigenous subject, if they do any research at all the longest it will be is two weeks, which will amount to them visiting with two or three people – and that's a big study on a film dealing with native culture. How can you learn what is needed in that amount of time? You've got to come and live with the people, you got to talk with people. That's the one thing that always gets me about dealing with Native films, we're always being presented as having one overall, uniform mindset, and yet we run the spectrum of human diversity. Over the years I've seen glimpses in to my culture, but just glimpses. Nobody has got a complete picture and I don't think they're going to get the picture until they stop making 'Indian movies' and start making movies that deal with the human condition that happen to have Indians in them, or are set in a Native environment.

That's the power of the media and the medium. I am trying to establish some kind of fund for the reservations and urban Indian communities to teach young Indian kids how to become film makers. Not just to make movies and not even necessarily to make documentaries, but to be journalists. I think theirs would be both powerful and empowering to document what is happening to our indigenous people right now through our own eyes. I would love to see the facility in place so that when something happens in South Dakota, or something happens in Canada, or South America, that immediately there's an Indian film crew there to cover it because that visual impact is really strong and it's one of the best ways to teach people. In Canada they now have an Aboriginal Network which is sponsored by tribal money and by the government. It's a wonderful avenue for both non-Indian and Indian people to see what is happening in the communities; to learn about the past and have a window to the future.

People say, "Oh Jeez, what a rotten deal you Native people got but that was so long ago". Well, hey – nothing has changed! I've become involved in the struggle in South America and just like the Lakota's fight for the Black Hills and countless other nations' struggles, this is over gold and greed. The rubber tappers, gold miners, diamond dealers and their kind are poisoning entire villages. So nothing has changed. These indigenous people are once again in the path of greed. What will we lose this time? Before it was decimated, the Aztec nation was more populated than Shakespeare's London. Road systems, astronomy, great advances in medicine; all were lost in the destruction of a very sophisticated culture. Now all you hear about Aztecs is this whole myth of violence and blood sacrifice, but who knows what these people knew? Who knows if they were so attuned to that other dimension, that other side of the world, that they were capable of sending each other there. Maybe they were capable of doing that.

Being in the movies and being an artist, I've learned about greed and the system over the years. I don't know one Native person that isn't an artist. When I used to help out at the alcohol lodge down town you would get somebody off the street who, when you'd given them some coffee, would just start drawing some incredible picture on a little piece of scrap paper. It's part of what we do, it's how we relate to our surroundings. No matter what I do, I live in both parts of my world; I deal with both sides of my life everyday. But I'm always going to look at things from a Native point of view. Like culture, art is constantly changing and evolving and it allows us, as Native artists, to stay closer to our culture, because when you're dealing with our art, you're dealing with our traditions in those forms of expression. So it's a connection; every time I sit down to do my art, I have to be connected to my traditional self. Sometimes it hurts that there's so much mass production but I'm also a realist – that employs a lot of people. I do have a big problem with some of it because it's sheer exploitation and greed again, but what really gets me is when I see sacred, traditional images defiled; like Kachinas on whiskey bottles. It's a total lack of respect and sensitivity. If you make a noise about it, people say you're angry or you're an activist or both, but I say, "No. It's just that if I disrespected you and your family like your culture disrespects my culture, you'd be angry too. I mean, nobody asked if I wanted to be your mascot. You take my religious figures, you take people like Crazy Horse or Geronimo, and you tie them into alcohol and you make ridiculous movies without bothering to ask any of the people who the movie is about whether this is true. It's constant, and when you disrespect us like that it makes us angry; it would make any human being angry."

I think the positive thing is that our cultures still flourish and our religion is still alive. Even with all this pressure over the years, of trying to beat it out of us, the fact that we still exist and we still grow, and our religion is still intact is incredible. If we are that tough and have lasted through all this, we can last through eternity.

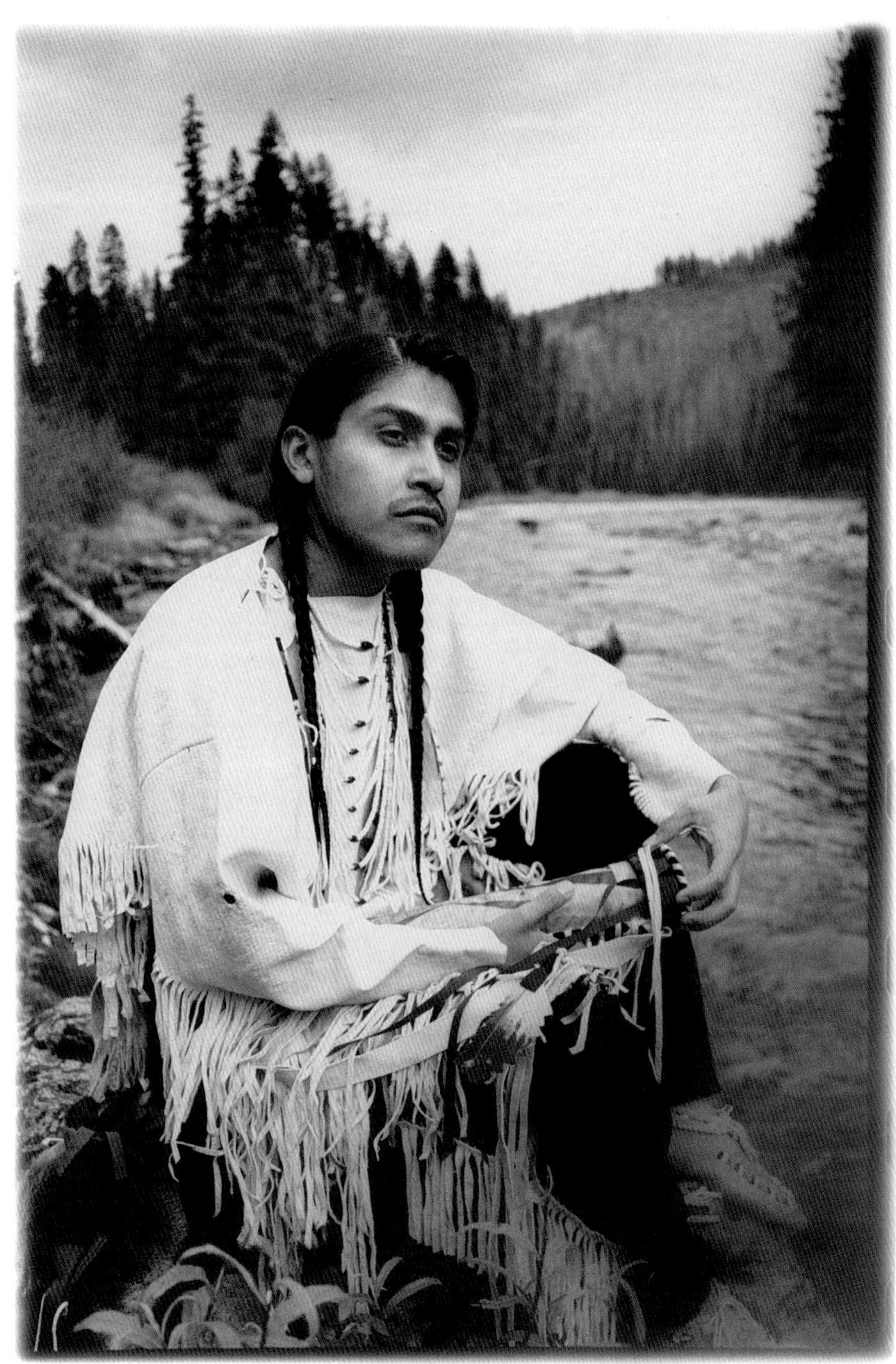

Cultural Contact

Josiah Black Eagle Pinkham
(Nez Perce)
Ethnographer/Nez Perce Tribe, Cultural Resource Department
Josiah Pinkham is a direct descendant of Tiwiiteqis, 'Old' Chief Joseph.

“Things like the Allotment Act and boarding schools were meant to completely remove all of that wisdom that we had amassed over generations. The whole idea was to make us be like the new people . . .”

JOSIAH PINKHAM

The Nez Perce people helped Lewis and Clark in many different ways; they helped them with food, with horses and canoes, as well as giving them the directions and route to reach the ocean fastest. That's what the Nez Perce had that Lewis and Clark didn't – a knowledge of the land and basic navigation skills, and without that information the Corps of Discovery would have perished. They were already in pretty poor condition when we found them so it's likely that they would never have been heard from again. It was no surprise to the Nez Perce people when Lewis and Clark were found hungry and freezing because of our old prophesies about the coming of new people. When they greeted these strangers who came out of the woods they really didn't know exactly *what* they were. My father says they were described as having eyes like fish because they were so light complected and had blue eyes.

At first the Nez Perce people were going to kill them but there was one very old lady who recounted the time that she had been kidnapped and taken from the Nez Perce people when she was very young. She talked of being taken away and sent to different parts of the country; how she was traded from here to there, bought, sold, bought and sold again, until eventually she found her way into a white man's hands and how the white man had treated her really well. After that she found her way back to the Nez Perce. So she spoke in favor of Lewis and Clark and the rest of their party. She said, “Don't hurt these new people because their kind were good to me before and without them I wouldn't be here”. Then it was discussed in council. All the old people talked about it and it was decided that we'd treat these new people well. Oral history places a lot of emphasis on the Nez Perce promise to treat these people good and that's one of the things that's been lost on the other side.

BLACK

When people come to this country they don't realize that Lewis and Clark made a promise on behalf of *all* of the new people that were to follow – that they would treat us as we had treated them. That's the way oral traditions are lost; too many people come to a new place too fast, and things get lost. I think that if people really respected the way things were conducted back then, we probably wouldn't be in as much of a mess as we are now. There would be a lot more respect paid to the people that have taken care of this land the longest. Sovereignty is one example; sovereignty is like a relationship that two good friends have who share the trust and responsibility they have towards one another, and one would never take advantage of the other – they would always heed the guidance the other person had to offer and they would listen. To me, if sovereignty really exists for us then that's the kind of relationship the US government should honor with us and share, but it doesn't.

There's a lot that's been lost but from what I imagine things were very, very different before Lewis and Clark arrived compared to what they are now. You couldn't divide up the earth by drawing lines and saying, "This is mine and this is yours". It was a lot harder to secure foods back then and food meant more because you really had to work for it; it was important for you to be at the proper place at the proper time, things couldn't be taken advantage of – there was no McDonalds! If you planned to live through the winter you had to secure enough food to make it, so you had to have a lot more forethought and that's something that we're beginning to lose. We have to regain that forethought, that respect for our future generations, and I guess that's where our relationship with the new people is very important. They bring with them a lot of ingenuity that needs guidance and that guidance can only come from one place, and that's from the people that have been here the longest. I think of the Lewis and Clark Bicentennial as a memorial to what's been lost and all of the changes that have taken place. I crunched the numbers one time and after the 1855 Treaty and the 1863 Treaty, the Allotment Act, and all of the other things that have taken place, the Nez Perce now retain less than 1 per cent of our original land; and land and culture being united, we retain less than 1 per cent of our culture, and that includes our language.

I can't really pinpoint the changes being responsible to the Lewis and Clark expedition, or the traders, or the missionaries, I think it all lends to one great big event that is still going on today. When the missionaries came it divided the people. Some wanted to learn more about the world and share another view of it, and they saw this as a great opportunity. But others said, We've been here longer than anyone can remember, perfecting this way of life. We can't change that because our future generations are counting on being here and on having resources; plants and animals, this earth to take care of them. So what great change can this new knowledge bring to this area? – And that's the debate that's still going on today, but I think the important thing is that regardless of all the changes we need to retain the idea that our future generations do have rights to all of these things, such as the trees and animals; this clean water. We're still working on perfecting that old way of life to this day.

Tiwiiteqis, or Old Joseph, was a powerful man and in many ways he welcomed the new knowledge. But then he found ways in which it conflicted with how things were always done. These new people had a different way of looking at the land; a different idea about ownership, and that was one of the things that really didn't sit right with him. He was very prominent in the treaty making process because he wanted to retain the right to be here for all, including our future generations; and that's very different from owning the land. The idea of land ownership is a different purpose and a different cause. He raised all of his kids to carry on that way of thinking about the land, and I think that is best explained through his own words. When he was talking to his son, Young Joseph, he said, "This land holds the bones of your mother and father. Never sell the bones of your mother and father." And there isn't really a way from the Nez Perce perspective that you can do that.

Young Joseph's name was *Hinmatooyalaatqit* and there's a story about that. He was born in a cave and down below there were a bunch of horses in the valley by some water, and when he was born those horses were racing across that water, making a sound like thunder. That's what *Hinmatooyalaatqit* describes, those horses going across the water and making that loud rumbling noise and how that sound carried up the mountain side to where he was born. Many refer to him as Chief Joseph and when the Nez Perce people went across this great land in 1877 they were under the leadership of many great leaders, including Joseph, but what drew attention to Joseph was that he chose to stay at Bear Paw while some other survivors went on to Canada. White Bird was one of the prominent people that went to Canada but he ended up getting killed there. But that's one of the things that has fed this misconception about Joseph being in charge of everything; that he stayed and all of the attention focused on that group and not the ones that made it to Canada. The leadership of the whole group switched from time to time, depending on where they were and who was thought to have the best knowledge of the particular area they were moving into. There's always somebody that shows forth as a leader of some certain group within the Nez Perce; not like a king with a domain, but one that the people trust to carry forth their wishes or their words, and that was the case with all of these leaders of the so called War of 1877, like Joseph, Ollokot, White Bird and Lean Elk.

I think people need to understand why that happened in 1877, and basically it was to protect the way of life that we fought so hard to retain. It was an act of trying to preserve it so we could hand it on to our children, grandchildren, and future generations. It's referred to as the War of 1877, but I think that the fighting in that summer and fall of 1877 is just a mark of something which has been going on since cultural contact – back when Lewis and Clark came – and that's still going on today. That struggle still continues, it's just a little bit different in terms of who our adversaries are. We're still trying to perpetuate our way of life; still trying to take care of our culture and look out for our future generations; still trying to care for the land. 1877 was a symbol for something that was going on and is still going on.

EAGLE

Stereotypes

Chris Eyre
(Cheyenne/Arapaho)
Film Director/Producer
Smoke Signals, Doe Boy, Skins . . .

"I can't take a screen play to a major studio with Indians living in the late twentieth or twenty-first century without the story harboring on spirituality, drunkenness or politics. If I did, they'd look at me and say, 'Well where's the story then?'"

CHRIS EYRE

There's truth in stereotypes, or else there wouldn't be stereotypes. Stereotypes get a bad rap but they only get a bad rap when people don't agree with them. When they agree with the stereotypes they can become 'humorous'. Stereotypes are stereotypes for a reason because there's a truth to them but as things change, when the stereotype doesn't change, it becomes damaging. If you get Indians looking stoic, the reason they look stoic is probably because they were stoic, because they weren't very happy with their circumstances at that time, and then they were portrayed in movies as being expressionless and consequently as culture changes that stereotype becomes damaging. People blame studios and studio executives but really what it comes down to is that there's a mold that people like to see 'their' Indians put into – in this country and probably around the world – and that's why I can't take a screen play to a major studio with Indians living in the late twentieth or twenty-first century without the story harboring on spirituality, drunkenness or politics. If I did, they'd look at me and say, "Well where's the story then?" So people are not going to buy tickets unless they can associate it in that mold, or that image, that they want to see 'their' Indians in.

A lot of times people point at studios or studio executives as being responsible for this but I think that's a bunch of bullshit because the most detrimental person is the one sitting in Iowa or wherever, the homogeneous American, who doesn't have to change because they're part of the populous. They're the one in the middle of the flock of sheep that doesn't care what's

CHRIS

trampled because they're not conscious of it. The populous dictates all those things and the populous is so detrimental that it ranks right below religion and money. It's ignorance and the worst thing about it is that they don't have to change, they don't have to see Indians differently because they're the populous! If people wanted to see alternate perspectives of Indians, I think those movies would be getting made. Hollywood's supplying a demand like any other business and people want to see their Indians in a certain form or stereotype. Indians wouldn't have been here as long as we have unless culture had changed and we had adapted.

If I had been born a hundred years ago and had my daughter like I have now, I may have been an Uncle Tom Indian that told my daughter to go to boarding school and do the best she could and become subservient, because at that point we weren't in any shape to be defiant. To fight would have meant complete annihilation, so at that time the Uncle Tom attitude was a matter of survival. But then those kids grew up and became a generation of Indians that didn't want to be Indian. The best thing about the '70s was that Indians wanted to be proud of themselves again and that is probably the earmark of what the American Indian Movement did, it fulfilled that need, AIM gave Indians generationally something to be proud of and that 'something' was themselves and the ripple effects of survival.

Indians are experts at survival but the stereotypes don't change as quickly. The stereotypes ripple on a lot longer than the changing culture, but when people ask me how I feel about the Atlanta Braves and the 'Tomahawk Chop' and all that stuff, some are appalled at my answer – which is that I really don't care. It's not something I would jump in and lobby against when I think there are more substantial and significant Indian causes like the Navajos being relocated from Big Mountain, or Yucca Mountain where nuclear waste is being deposited on Shoshone land. There's so many other things to jump on than iconic capitalist American culture. The 'Tomahawk Chop' is representative of that culture in Atlanta, whereas people in Green Bay, Wisconsin, will wear cheese on their heads at football games. They can wear cheese on their heads, they can do the 'Tomahawk Chop', and I know it's all cumulative and that it all matters, but we all have to pick our battles and to me it doesn't rank in the same realm as the BIA and the Secretary of the Interior not being able to produce documents that tell where billions of dollars that were supposed to go to Indians over the last hundred years are.

My battles are going to be fought on the screen. My battles are going to be fought in movies – hypothetically, metaphorically, and spiritually in stories. My stories are going to be funny and magical, and blasphemous to the populous, and when I talked about truth it's about scratching through these walls and finding the truth – the truth that's been lost for a long time. The truth about Indians in identifying who Indians are because I think most people in this country don't have a grasp of that at all. People have established a convention of how Indians are in movies and it's time to reinvent it.

You have to work within the system and the whole trick is to take the money from the populous and give them something they don't want with their own money. In this industry you have to get a foot in the door, and when you get a foot in the door then you walk in the room, but when you walk in the room you have to be very conscious of the fact that you can be torn apart in that room. It's a fine line and it's nothing that you can articulate. But Indians aren't alone, all people have been oppressed throughout history, most recently the Jews, Indians and Irish, so on and so forth; and I think there is a certain humanity that all people understand, or else they wouldn't have such guilt about what they've done to Indians. I think that's true of a lot of people in the film industry, which is why they have been very helpful to allow some of these issues to come on to the screen. To allow more of them to come on to the screen you don't want to bite the hand that feeds you, so you have to work within the system but also try and do a lot of shaking up within the system. That's the fine line I try to get through.

On one occasion I had a movie where I had two kids on the reservation who were playing, pretending to hunt, and they were wearing helmets and goggles. I was explaining to a distributor that this was an Indian movie and all that stuff and he said, "Well you can't tell these kids are Indians because they have helmets and goggles on". So I said, "If I put them in braids would that be better?" And he says, "Yeah! And then people would know they're Indians." And this is just the same thing Indian actors face, it's the populous that dictates how they want to see Indians, where and in what. Like *Walker, Texas Ranger.* I hate *Walker, Texas Ranger* and ironically my grandma loves it, but my grandma also loves professional wrestling and the big joke in our family is that nobody will tell her that it's not real because she enjoys it so much, but that's entertainment. But being where I am, generationally, *Walker, Texas Ranger* just doesn't satisfy any Indian sensibility for all the Indian sensibility that it uses.

That's why I mean to challenge people with movies. That's been my intention all along, to be in a place that I can help say things that haven't been said before but I know a lot of people have been thinking. The goal is to be in a position where we can tell stories in the way we want to tell them. It sounds very idealistic but it's been a dream of mine ever since I started taking pictures in high school; to mold the Indian image in the way that Indians see themselves – and that's not for me to decide, that's for the eclectic of actors and writers and other directors and so on and so forth to bring, but I know that it's long overdue.

EYRE

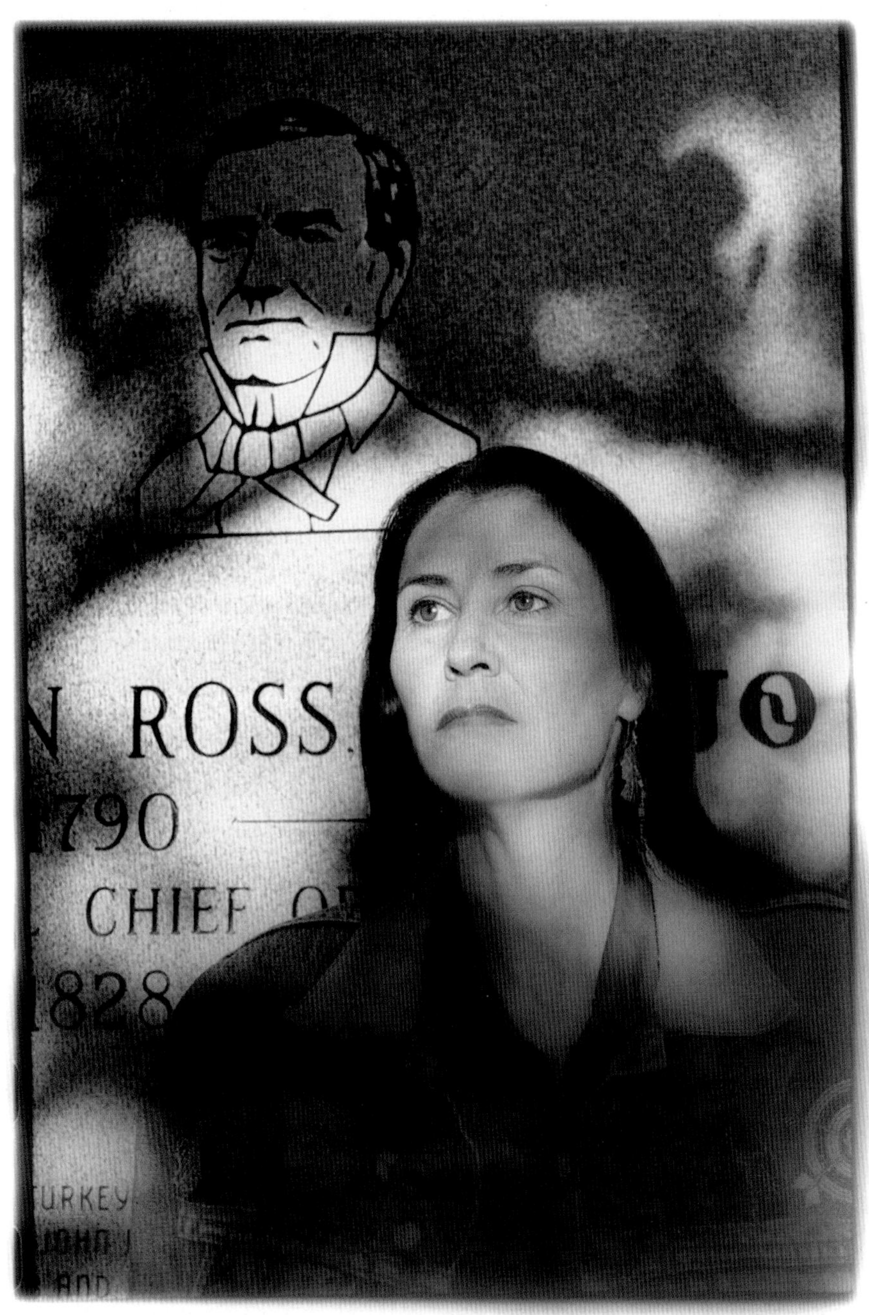

Myths and the Power of Stories

Gayle Ross
(Cherokee)
Traditional Storyteller and Author

Gayle Ross is a direct descendant of Principal Chief, John Ross.

"When did people become more concerned with fact than with truth? The story is the truth behind the facts ... Stories are living, breathing things and that creative power that is at work between the teller and the listener is very real."

GAYLE ROSS

The common association with the word myth is very disturbing because it has become synonymous with lie and that is not the true meaning of myth; myth is the way we perceive the sacred put into story, clothed with words. Therefore, myths in and of themselves are very powerful beings and so when you begin to use that word to mean a lie, you diminish the power of what the myth itself really is – a story of the sacred. Stories are in our culture, they are living spirits. The story lives on the breath of the teller and stories have a life span; we talk about stories we've lost, stories that are passed on, and new stories which are being born all the time. Stories help to define you as a people. Your myths and the power of stories are the way we explain the world around us and each other, to each other; there is a theory that stories live in a village somewhere and tell each other, to each other. So the whole business of working with story, either in telling or putting stories into books so that they travel in that way, is the business of working with some of the most sacred teachings that we have as Indian people.

The diminishment of the power of story in European culture is, historically speaking, a relatively recent phenomenon. Story is sacred to all people around the world. In all of the sacred teachings of the world there are stories at the root of how we understand who we are as human beings and what is sacred and the relationship between the two. I don't know if it was with the recognition of literature that attempts to eradicate the credibility of the story itself as a vehicle for wisdom began in European culture, but to describe something as 'just a story' now, or say they're 'just telling a story', can be almost slanderous. We Native people are just closer in time to that oral tradition. It has not been replaced with that process of writing down wisdom, we are still very close to an understanding of the power of the oral tradition. So for us it is even harder to see the exploitation or appropriation of our stories in publishing and in public performance, when someone picks up one of our stories and uses it in the manner that they are accustomed to thinking of stories; then it's a disrespect that's very, very hard to take. It's like seeing somebody pick up a beautiful hand-woven piece of cloth and use it for a dish rag because that's what they think all pieces of cloth are meant to be used for.

We all share roots in the oral tradition but certain cultures around the world are not so far removed from that power and from when it was the predominant way of teaching; of handing down information, of imparting spiritual values, of growing a whole human being; and stories teach in a way that addresses all of the different parts of a human being – mind, heart and soul. They don't speak to just one part of your intellectual understanding or of your ability to grow. Stories are living, breathing things and that creative power that is at work between the teller and the listener is the interaction that helps the story live and the power of that is very real.

When did people become more concerned with fact than with truth? The story is the truth behind the facts and what's missing when you only deal with the facts is the relationship with that reason. To say that the soil has 'X' per cent of iron oxide in it which gives it that red colour makes it a piece of information that is totally separate and apart from your life. But nothing that happens within the circle of life is separate from us and if we look at the world that way and not as an intellectual exercise, we become closer to understanding what fact and truth is. With that perception, how much more careful would we be about how we effect everything around us? Our stories are designed to teach us to see everything as a relationship that we are a part of. I don't know why industrial society evolved the way it did and I don't know where the break came in the predominantly European culture that came here and enabled the development of the dominant society to proceed in seeing itself so apart – not only from the natural world but from themselves and in that, their very existence as human beings – but I know that it plays a huge role in the way the culture that we live in today evolved and I know that it is the essential difference between the world view of Native people and the world view of the dominant society. The difference between fact and truth is like the difference between religion and spirit; religion becomes a tool for political, economic and social control and that was very much part of the dogma brought here by the Europeans, and that was entrenched in their minds when they encountered Native people for whom there is no word for religion, only for spirit.

There are a lot of different theories about what imagination really is but I believe that it is the first and most important energy in the entire act of creation. I was told many years ago that if the time comes when the earth no longer hears her creation story she will forget to re-create herself, and in our tradition the world is created new every year, and so if the time comes when no one remembers our creation and it's no longer heard, the earth will forget how to create herself and that's when this world will end. Tradition is a living, breathing, growing, changing thing – as all cultures are. I think it is important to look at not just the outer trappings of how something's done, but what the underlying meaning is that gives life and reason to the way that it came about so as to ensure *that* is what gets carried on. A friend of mine once said that tradition and ritual are the glue that bind generations together and that's really what has to happen for a people to continue in a healthy way. You can't just say preserve it, it has to be going on from one generation to the next and however that may change is what the understanding is of the power and the reasoning behind the way you do these certain things. At a lodge for example, it might be much more common nowadays to see sleeping bags, tarps and quilts piled over it; very few people say, "We do it the traditional way as we have plenty of buffalo hides lying around to cover that lodge". So superficially it's not the same but the reason people go in that lodge and how they pray there, what they learn there and what they come out of that lodge with, is still the same. That's tradition right there. It's what leads us to go in that lodge and story is the same way.

Cultural appropriation is an issue requiring a large collective voice to roar so we can't be ignored. The appropriation of spiritual teachings is probably the most visible issue, but I'm also concerned with the appropriation of our traditional stories in publishing. Publishing companies are responding to this demand from teachers and librarians for multi-cultural material not by creating opportunities for Indian writers and writers from other under represented ethnic groups, but by letting their same popular children's authors pick up anything they find and publish it. They may come across a story that was recorded at the turn of the century, then retell it and clothe it with the popular illustrations of what non-Indians think is representative of Indian culture, and then people who don't know any better say, "Oh good we'll buy this for our class in Native American Month". This is a shallow approach to something with deep meaning and there are a lot of terrible children's books on the market like that. It's just a short walk down that line into all of the ways in which stereotypes and misrepresentations of Indian people are allowed. Where do they think the Washington Redskins fan, who believes this is fine, came from? He came from that boy who saw *Peter Pan and the Wild Boys,* and one of the worst modern examples is also by Disney, *Pocahontas.* When we allow our children to accept these twisted portraits of Indian people they are literally imprinted with these diminished caricatures of who we are as human beings, so when they become adults they're unlikely to listen to our issues because throughout their lives they've had that mind set of us as caricatures of people, as opposed to *actual people*. If we degrade and devalue the work created for children, then it says that we have no respect for our values or for our entire people. They are the future.

ROSS

A Profound Impact

Joanne Shenandoah
(Oneida – Six Nations Iroquois)
Singer/Songwriter/Composer/Performer

A multiple award winner and Grammy nominee Joanne Shenandoah is the most critically acclaimed Native American vocalist of her generation.

"The Iroquois have had a profound impact on the world as we know it today. Our political system and concepts of individual liberty have heavily influenced such philosophers as Thomas Jefferson, Benjamin Franklin and Karl Marx . . ."

JOANNE SHENANDOAH

I am from the Wolf Clan of the Onyota, the People of the Standing Stone, also known as the Oneida Nation, part of the Haudenosaunee Confederacy, or Six Nations Iroquois. The Haudenosaunee are careful observers of the world around them. They realize the polarity of a life, a duality which is life taking and life giving, male and female. Accordingly, the Haudenosaunee design their culture, spiritual beliefs and political systems in compliance with the most basic of natural laws, namely that humans are entrusted with the preservation of the earth; in trust for the coming generations who have an absolute right to clean air, pure water, fertile soils and an abundance of plant and animal life.

The Iroquois have had a profound impact on the world as we know it today. Our political system and concepts of individual liberty have heavily influenced such philosophers as Thomas Jefferson, Benjamin Franklin, Karl Marx, Lewis Henry Morgan and Frederick Engles. Our food crops, such as corn, beans, squash, maple products and tobacco have affected every human on this planet. Our natural resources in our aboriginal territory have contributed untold wealth to the United States and Canada. Our forests, rivers and wildlife were and continue to be essential elements to the survival of the economy. Our Iroquois ancestors created a network of trade and information routes over water and land that later became major highways and canals in New York State. In the field of athletics, the Iroquois sport of LaCrosse has made a great impact on the world, as has hockey, our winter sport.

The Iroquois were the first to sign treaties with the United States, and treaty belts which are made of Wampum shells serve as a constant reminder of our status as sovereign nations. The Iroquois/US treaties also formed the basis by which all subsequent agreements were made with other Native nations. One of the things our ancestors have always told us about is the close friendship our people had with many of the early colonial leaders. Iroquois delegations would frequently visit with the colonial leaders to discuss trade and politics. We know that the settlers were intrigued by the Iroquois form of government and how the Haudenosaunee Confederacy managed with relatively few people to become the dominant Native political force in eastern North America. They were also interested in the great personal freedom our people enjoyed as we were governed without kings, nobility or secular classes of rulers. As a result of the interaction between the Iroquois and the colonists, the Europeans came to enjoy a higher degree of freedom than they had ever known in their home countries.

Women, as the lifegivers, are acknowledged as custodians of our Mother Earth. They assume the responsibilities of monitoring all of the resources derived from the earth and they oversee all uses of the land. Women also nominate and depose all Haudenosaunee leadership and they preside over adoption and any activity, including warfare, which places human life at risk. Family lines flow through the female, and women have the final say over marriages and divorces. Women serve as spiritual advisors, the Faithkeepers, and in the roles of political counselors and healers. They select among them the heads of their respective families, or clans. These Clanmothers then represent the interests of their kin in all social activities of the Haudenosaunee and it is believed that this method is the key to resolving human conflict since it places the lifegivers in a position to temper the aggressive nature of males.

It was the Peacemaker who established the role of Clanmother which gave Iroquois women political and social powers without parallel in the world. Many generations ago, the Iroquois: Mohawks, Oneidas, Onondagas, Cayugas and Senecas; lived in a state of perpetual war throughout their homelands in what is New York State. Many abandoned their homes and sought refuge north of Lake Ontario and among one such band of refugees was a woman and her young daughter who elected to build a small camp in the forest along the Bay of Quinte. It was this young girl who gave birth to a very special child, whom the Iroquois came to know as the Peacemaker.

When he grew to a young man, he informed his mother and grandmother that he was to undertake a great mission given to him by the Creator, he was to return to Iroquois territory with a message of hope which would end warfare among the People of the Longhouse. After an incredible journey, during which he and those whom became his disciples for peace endured the severest hardships, the People of the Longhouse were unified. A tall eastern white pine was raised next to Onondaga Lake which was called the Great Tree of Peace. The branches of the tree touched the sky for all humans to see and its four gleaming roots extended to each sacred direction of the earth. The Peacemaker instructed the Iroquois that any individual or nation seeking an end to war may follow the roots to the Great Tree where they would receive shelter. On top of the Great Tree he placed a mighty eagle who was to cry out if danger approached the people, and beneath the leaders of this confederacy of nations formed a circle by holding hands and pledging to uphold the Great Law of Peace for all time.

It was thus the world's first united nations was created by the Haudenosaunee to promote freedom, secure world peace and liberate mankind from the horrors of war. We do not use the Peacemaker's Mohawk name outside of the Longhouse as to do so is considered to be extremely inappropriate. Similarly, people should refrain from discussing any of the masks of the Ancient Ones as this also causes great distress.

Nowhere is the Haudenosaunee appreciation for women better reflected than in our music and dance. When the women dance they form a circle around the drums and rattles, and they move counter-clockwise with the earth. Their feet caress our Mother Earth as they shuffle to any one of the hundreds of verses sung in their honor. It is from this great heritage that I draw the strength to create music. My name is Tekaliwha: kwha, which means She Sings, and for over ten years I have been composing, recording and performing. I am very grateful to have been given the gift of music, which is the universal language. It is an Iroquois belief that we are all born with special talents and our original instructions tell us to use these talents with a good mind. Music is a healing force and I am proud to be just one of many Native American musicians who help to bring songs of understanding, peace, happiness and joy to the world.

SHENANDOAH

Fierce and War-like?

Michael Darrow
(Fort Sill Apache – Chiricahua/Warm Springs)
Tribal Historian

Michael Darrow is a direct descendant of Mangas Coloradas.
His mother, Ruey Haozous Darrow, is the Fort Sill Apache Tribal Chairwoman.

"... those are general characteristics of nations with a militaristic orientation and Apaches don't have any of them. In our tribe we don't have any military societies or Dog Soldiers ... We didn't have anything vaguely resembling that."

MICHAEL DARROW

When people hear the name Apache, certain connotations associated with that term automatically enter their minds and two of the most common are 'fierce' and 'war-like'. However, the Apache people have always considered themselves to be peaceful – our group does and I presume the other Apaches do – and for most non-Apaches that's a shock. An anthropologist named Morris Opler, who wrote a book about Chiricahuas in the 1940s, is the person who essentially established the term Chiricahua in reference to our tribe, which is unfortunate not simply because it's not an Apache word, but because there is a sub division of the group that uses the same name. Sometimes that's written as 'true Chiricahua' which is also unfortunate, because that implies that there are also false Chiricahua!

Without the complications of pre-established English terminology, there were the Chíhéne, Chokonene, the Bidánku and the Ndé'ndaí, and these groups were a nation. They were each independent political units and there was no name for these groups collectively but with the dictionary defining a nation as being, 'A stable, historically developed community of people with a territory, economy, and distinctive language and culture in common', those four groups together constituted a nation. It was the linguists and anthropologists who decided that there needed to be a name to refer to these groups as a single unit and so they decided it would be Chiricahua, because the name they had applied to one of the sub divisions was Chiricahua Apaches, as the Chiricahua Mountains were within their territory.

MICHAEL

Around 1998 a book was published in which the author still used the phrase 'Apache menace' to refer to the Apaches in the Southwest in a historical context. Recently I checked on the selection of terminology that's used in books, movies, documentaries and such things in reference to Apaches in particular, and Indians in general. There have been some improvements; the terms 'buck' and 'squaw' don't generally turn up much these days although you occasionally encounter them, but a term that is frequently used is 'warrior' in reference to Apaches – *such and such many Apache warriors were doing something or other.* But there's not really any standard term in our language that can be translated as 'warrior'. If you wanted to say something like that, you would have to say, "Somebody who fights a lot". There is no designation that covers the connotations that 'warrior' has in English. In English 'warrior' has a definition and connotations associated with it and yet it is never used to describe non-Indians, but it's always used for Indians, and so you need to examine why that is. If somebody was explaining some of these documented incidents and they were telling it in Apache, the term that they would use for what the historians have referred to as 'warriors', would be translated as 'men'. Not fighting people or warriors or anything like that but, '*These men did this and that*'. Not, '*These warriors . . .*'. It has a different connotation and sets up a different mind set when you use the accurate terminology, but it's very difficult to talk to historians and anthropologists when using alternative terminology because the terminology that is standard is so profoundly ingrained that they automatically use it.

As to what constitutes being a war-like or a militaristic nation; there are a lot of American Indian tribes that were like that and they had certain common traits. Militaristic nations generally have warrior societies and specific ceremonies or rituals related to them, and a certain way of dressing; ways in which you can instantly recognise people as being part of a military society. Another characteristic of militaristic nations is that people who participate in those military societies, and subsequently fighting, get special recognition and a higher social status as a result of their participation in such actions. Awards will be given for accomplishments in battle and for achieving certain levels of stature in these military societies. Those are general characteristics of nations with a militaristic orientation and Apaches don't have any any of them. In our tribe we don't have any military societies or Dog Soldiers like the Plains Indians. We didn't have anything vaguely resembling that. In our tribe you don't attain special social status by participating in something like that.

In our tribe you didn't get an eagle feather for each enemy smacked with a coup stick or killed. You didn't get awards for battle accomplishments because they generally avoided fighting as much as possible. If they had to, they would and did, but their primary concern was to avoid fighting.

Interestingly, the United States has all of the characteristics of a militaristic nation, but they keep billing themselves as peaceful and the Apaches are continually presented as being war-like, so there's a great deal of misinformation there. The United States has its military societies; the army, airforce, navy, marines, veterans' groups; people who have higher status in society and get special privileges for having participated, and in recognition they get medals for their accomplishments in battle instead of eagle feathers. But for some reason it's the Apaches that are portrayed as being war-like and that's profoundly ingrained in the psyche of any non Apaches, including a lot of other American Indians whose perceptions of Apaches are of a very fierce and war-like people, because in their tribes that is an honorable and desirable portrayal of a person. Whereas in our tribe it's not. Another effect of this misrepresentation is that even among our own tribe, the younger people are coming to view themselves by the misinformation presented in these books and movies, and not by our tribal perspective.

The Apaches, like literally everybody else, had their territory invaded and occupied by the United States. In a sense, the incidents in Kosovo provided a point of reference for the American public as to what happened to American Indians. It was ethnic cleansing, where entire populations were forced out of their homelands at gun point and they either left or died, and all of their property was confiscated and taken over by the people who were driving them out. That concept was not something that most people in the United States had ever dealt with before, but because they saw it on the news in Kosovo it was conjured into existence in their minds and now it can be explained that, that's exactly what happened to the American Indians. Several years back, President Jimmy Carter was talking about where he lived in his home state and he mentioned that there used to be Indians there but he didn't know what happened to them or where they all went. It's kind of pathetic but that's the level of information shared by most people in the United States.

In the 1850s, the population estimates for our tribe ranged from 2,000 to 5,000, but by the time they were shipped off to Florida as Prisoners of War in 1886, the population was about 500. They were actually political prisoners; they weren't prisoners because of fighting against the United States or because they committed crimes; they were prisoners because it was politically convenient that they be prisoners and they were kept until it was politically convenient to release them. However, it was still not politically convenient for them to have their own land in their home territory. The political reality of the situation is that our tribe was cut into two different parts in 1913; a bunch went to Mescalero and their destinies took a different turn to ours in Oklahoma. It is unlikely that what had been the Chiricahua Nation, that group of four peoples, will ever be reformed into a single entity again. We're still not located in our homeland. We're still in exile.

DARROW

Home

Richard B. Williams
(Oglala Lakota)
Executive Director – American Indian College Fund.

A great-great-great-grandson of the legendary Oglala, 'Old' Smoke, Rick Williams is a respected educator, advocate for American Indian youth, and historian. An editorial consultant for the TV series, How the West Was Lost, *he has appeared in numerous documentaries and is quoted in a wide body of literature.*

"We don't need an auto-parts store on Pine Ridge but economists wouldn't see that. They'd see a bunch of wrecked cars, but if you look at it like that you're denigrating the economics that exist. The economics of sharing, the economics of tribalism."

RICK WILLIAMS

If you came onto our reservation you would find people that really care about each other. People who have a spirit that is undefinable in any other context of American society, a spirit whose center is freedom. That center maybe outside the center of other people's ways, but the Oglalas have always seemed like outlaws because of that unique spirit which lifts them above the dominant society's rules. You would find a very caring, giving people. The reservation is home; it is where physically, spiritually, emotionally and psychologically you're safe – the harmful things that are there differ from those that exist outside the reservation because they're not race based or hate based. Despite all the things you might hear about reservations, for me it's a wonderful place to be – it's home and there's no place like it. There's no place else in the world that I can go to and be embraced by my relatives and where time doesn't make any difference. I could be gone ten years and go back and pick up exactly where I was ten years ago. People don't love you less or interact with you any differently based on time and that's not true of any other society, so reservations are timeless in that respect.

Although there's a tremendous amount of poverty, you won't have trouble finding something to eat or somewhere to stay on the reservation. People will take care of your basic needs. People will feed you, and it's interesting that there are no motels but you don't have to worry about a place to stay, somehow they'll find a place for you on the floor, or in the corner because there's always room for one more. You'll see things like alcoholism and winos but what you don't see with winos is a differentiation, where they are treated as less than human beings, like you see in the dominant society. If you see a wino on the street in mainstream America people walk by them like they are invisible, but the winos on the street in Pine Ridge or Whiteclay are somebody's relatives and they are treated with respect – as human beings – and that's an important thing that Indian society understands; these are not disposable beings, they're our relatives whether they are drunk or sober.

When they destroyed the buffalo they destroyed our well being and it's a well being that goes beyond economics, and that remains the major contributing factor to our problems. It has to do with the physical composition of your body and by that I mean your physical and spiritual nourishment. When the buffalo went away, part of the Indian spirit went away and that's the part that we've never really been able to recover. When you destroy a people so completely by taking away their economic means, their spiritual power, their emotional and psychological sustenance, and then put them in poverty, make them hungry and make them powerless, you nearly destroy them. When you put them in that kind of weakened state it's very difficult for them to recover and regain that strength, especially when it's tied to relationships with the earth; relationships with plants and animals and their environment. When that is no longer valued or no longer a part of the overall well being of your world, then the spirit dies. It shrinks. And that's part of the problem, the spirit of Indian people hasn't had chance to grow and flourish but just recently I think it has started coming back.

You can't destroy people like that and have them automatically recover in one generation, it doesn't work that way. I don't think the dominant society have an appreciation of that and they don't understand that to live as a human being is to live as a sacred being and that everything on this planet is sacred. The earth could live without human beings but we think that we have this value and that somehow control this whole thing, but we're nothing more than a parasite on this planet and the earth is starting to react to that. If bacteria attacks your body your temperature goes up and your body fights it. The earth is doing exactly the same thing and they call it global warming. This earth is sick and we're the bacteria that is attacking it and the temperature keeps going up. If it continues to rise and we have a five or seven degree shift this earth will no longer be inhabitable, at best there may be small pockets of the earth that are still habitable. Do Indian people understand that? Yes they do. That's part of the consciousness of planning for the recovery of Indian people and may be what it takes to bring Indians back into the situation where they are able to live in harmony with the earth again.

There's too much of a disconnect. Why do we wear shoes? We wear shoes simply because it allows us to manipulate our environment better. If we didn't wear shoes we would be confined in a smaller area and forced to live in that smaller area and develop a better relationship with that area; so something as simple as a pair of shoes can create a significant disconnect. By putting on a pair of shoes you disconnect yourself from your immediate environment to go to other environments and if you are then able to disconnect yourself from other environments, it is easy to disconnect yourself from the past – the past has no relevance to you because you've been able to disconnect yourself from that. And if you're able to disconnect yourself from your parents and your grandparents and you have no value for those connections, then why would you even think about having value and connections with historical events? Historical events where you did something wrong. It's easy for people in America to disconnect themselves from historical events and it's even easier for them to disconnect themselves from contemporary events and not realize that these have a historical basis.

Indians were made victims by the actions of people in the past. Indians continue to stay victims by the actions of people in contemporary times. Whether you're talking about the actions of a corporation or about the actions of an individual, Indian people don't like being victims but unfortunately that's the way the system is designed to work; it's designed to create opportunities for some and a lack of opportunity for others. Unfortunately Indian people have always been on that latter side. There may have been a few opportunities but they have been structured to fit in with the dominant society and have not necessarily been the best for Indian people, the best for our healing, or the best way to make ourselves whole again. To make ourselves whole again in the eyes of white society often means assimilation and giving up everything that's Indian to become white. If that's the only way to survive then maybe we would be better off extinct. But we are who we were. We have enough strength to survive. Genetically we are very similar to the people who we were a long time ago and somehow we managed to survive the worst holocaust in the history of the world, and we're still here.

One way to create an economic empowerment zone on Pine Ridge is to tear down all the fences and restore the buffalo, so you have an economy that is directly driven by the buffalo. That would help us heal and create a solid economy for us. Is it viable economically? Yes, it is. Is that something the US Government would commit to? I don't think so. But I think Pine Ridge has an existing economy that is not recognizable to economists and until people understand it and realize how to use that economy, there will continue to be economic failures and people will continue to see Pine Ridge as an economic failure when in fact it's an economic success because of the tribalistic economies and their relationships with each other, and it is so obvious that people can't see it – it's all of those junked cars that are sitting there. That's the auto parts system. They don't need an auto-part store on Pine Ridge, so what does that say about that economy? That there's a sharing.

WILLIAMS

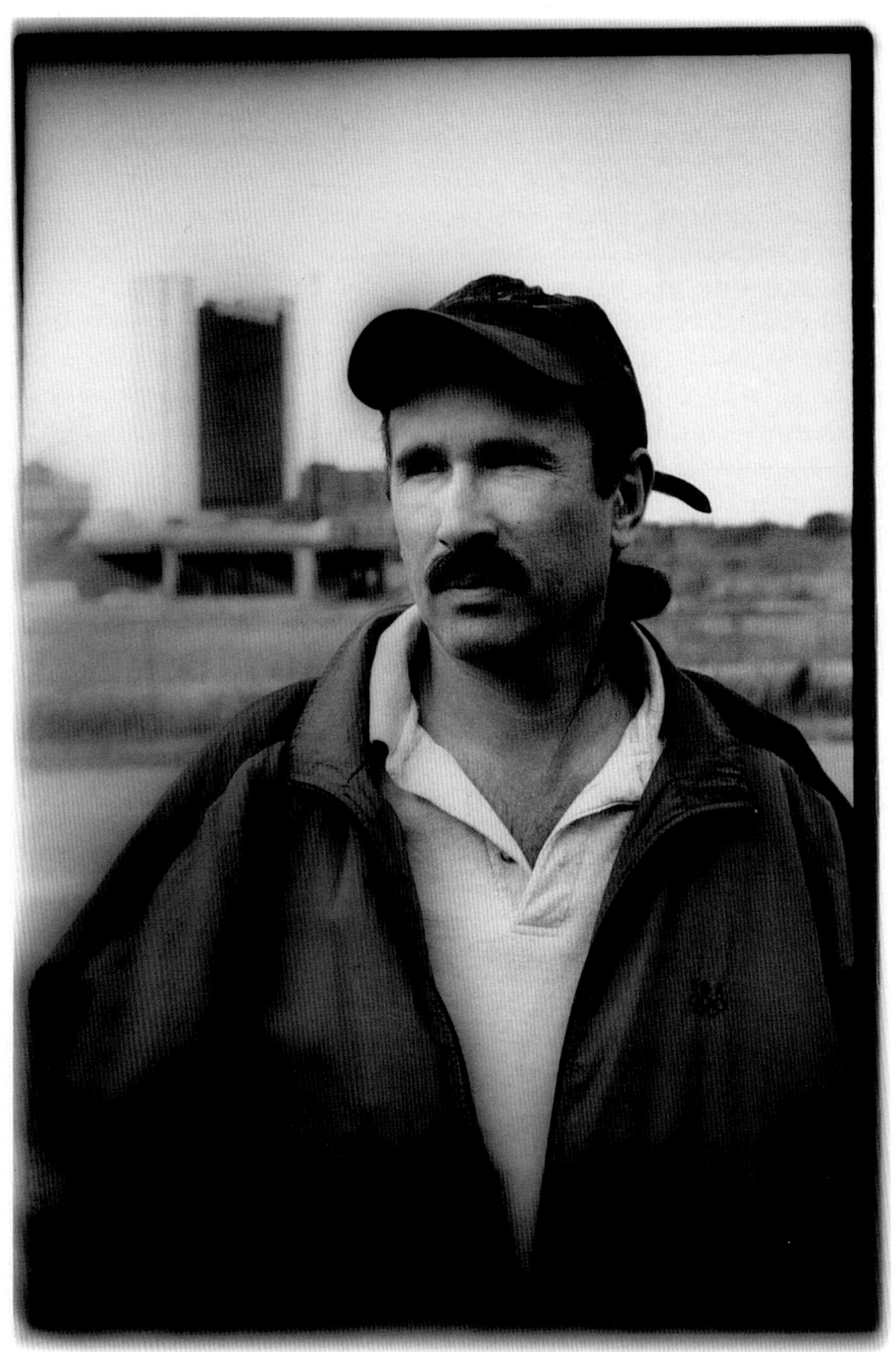

Guerrillas in the Media

Paul DeMain
(Oneida/Ojibway)
Publications Editor/Radio Presenter

Paul DeMain is CEO of Indian Country Communications, Inc. and Managing Editor of News From Indian Country. *He has served as President of both UNITY: Journalists of Color, and the Native American Journalists Association (NAJA).*

"What newspapers is George W. Bush reading, so that he actually thinks that the land claims have been dismissed in New York State and that the State has supreme power over all Indians? That goes against federal rulings, federal jurisdiction and reality."

Paul DeMain

There was a whole new level of expectation in the Native community post-World War II, brought about by our parents who had gone into the War and returned with different experiences, and from those experiences the breadth of what the world could offer outside the boundaries of the reservation gave them a different vision of how life should, or could be. It became a very important time for us in education, science and the arts, but in the mainstream press there wasn't a reflection of that day-to-day, average Native American. For example, if you look in the libraries of the *Milwaukee Journal Sentinel* or the *New York Times* what you'll find are articles using highly stereotypical ideas and ethnocentric feelings, that 'White European' society had the answers to the lingering Native problems; the first problem being taking Indian land, presenting the excuse that Native people were unable to use what they had to their best advantage because they weren't willing to do things like dig all the gold out of the Black Hills and then rebury it at Fort Knox to make someone rich in the process.

The media was portraying a mix and a match, from the poor, poverty-stricken Indian living in a tar-paper shack who retains his traditions, to the movies where non-native actors are doing things with Indian society that don't hold true in any way; the John Wayne shoots a bullet and thirteen Indians fall off their horses, kind of stuff. Part of the media portrayal was that Native traditions were keeping Indians down, and at that particular time our ceremonies had been driven underground and in the 1950s people hadn't brought them out of the deep woods for all kinds of reasons, not least the fear

PAUL

of arrest. So you went between this romantic suffering Indian syndrome to John Wayne, straight over to the militant, uppity, anti-government, in-your-face Indian of the 1960s and '70s news coverage.

The media creates figments of the imagination. With the uppity Indian thing of the '60s and '70s, in terms of Native leadership they literally created spokesmen like Russell Means, Dennis Banks and the Bellecourt brothers, because it was easy. If there was a dispute somewhere that could be linked to Indians it was easier to call one of these guys than go and report what it was actually about, because although they might not know what's going on they'd have a statement that would make it into the publication. Fundamentally that's how the media missed what was really going on in AIM and Native communities at the time, because they created these leaders they overlooked the fact that it was behind the cameras where AIM's real work took place. That's not to say that Russell, Dennis and the Bellecourt brothers don't serve a purpose, because even today if you want to get media attention you call them up. They do what I call 'guerrilla media' very, very well and a lot of people learned from it because it's been effective, but it comes out of this era of mass media and the thirty-second take for the evening news where they don't worry about the details but it looks good to have braids and feathers even if it's not representative.

Reporters and the media are not going to deal with the issues, didn't deal with the issues, haven't dealt with the issues and won't deal with the issues any better until the school systems and curriculum becomes more diversified. You will not find any revisions of the history books in the school systems of the United States pertaining to Indians until the '60s and '70s, so those reporters born and raised in the 1950s grew up in a world where all their heroes were white and all the Indians were ancient warriors of vanquished tribes, and unfortunately the legislators were educated in the same places as the reporters.

It's like when George W. Bush went to upper state New York and was asked what he thought about the land claims there and the issue of them going into federal court, and he said, "I think the State of New York and all States ought to have jurisdiction and their rulings should be the supreme law over Indians on land claims and gambling". His Press Secretary then said, "I don't know why anyone's worried about that, those land claims were dismissed a long time ago". But there's seven or eight active claims with the Onondagas, Senecas, Oneidas, Mohawks and all, on that chunk of land. Why would a US President be saying things he knows nothing about? Because he hasn't been taught. What newspapers is George W. Bush reading that he actually thinks that the land claims have been dismissed in New York State and that the State has supreme power over all Indians? That goes against federal rulings, federal jurisdiction and reality.

A person who is raised in a white community and doesn't have an opportunity to study a community that's different from their own is going to have difficulty going on to a reservation and finding the story. During the Hanta Virus scare in Navajo country reporters were running into traditional communities saying, "Tell us about Joe Whoever", and that made Grandma cover her ears and run for the hogan because you leave the person's name to rest for a year. Soon there were signs saying the press was banned from these communities and the press was astonished, "How come they're so against us?" Well think about it – you call it 'Navajo Flu' instead of the Hanta Virus, you went into communities where people were conducting funerals and resting the name but you're speaking their names, and you want information which is against the protocol of the community. That created one of the first occasions where the mainstream press utilized Native journalists instead of their regular reporters, because suddenly they were locked out of those communities

In the *Chicago Tribune* or the *New York Times* you're going to read about gaming and Donald Trump opposing Indian gaming. Or you're going to read about how Indians don't get taxed – like Paul DeMain, he's an Indian so why is he paying property taxes, federal income tax and gasoline tax? These stereotypes grow out of misconceptions. All Indians are rich because the media has visited the Pequots, 'And now there's the Sioux south of Minneapolis who have millions of dollars and they're building the Great Wall of China down there', those kinds of crazy things. All Indians are rich because people don't see Pine Ridge or wherever. Look at how the media handles news coming out of South Dakota. If a white guy is assaulted by an Indian it's called a 'hate crime' and makes it on to CNN and gets thirty column inches in the nationals, then down in a corner there's an inch about the US Civil Rights Commission going there and asking about all the Native deaths in the Dakotas! Real improvements in the media aren't going to happen for another generation because the pipeline is filled. Our challenge is putting people into the pipeline. How do you worry about getting someone into the editorial department of the *New York Times* when you've got to get them out of High School? We've got to get them into college and keep them in college.

To me one of the answers comes through Native people creating books, films and radio stations. I believe control of our own institutions is going to empower us; being able to get the story, tell our story, work and edit our stories, and then as we begin producing for ourselves and creating it for a constituency like *News From Indian Country,* we'll get to more non-Native legislatures, educators, politicians, engineers and business people. It's also access to and the power to influence the mainstream media. For the first time Native people are on the breaking edge of information technology in terms of computer systems and the internet, which means that we're going back to an old tradition, the oral visual presentation and the storyteller's credibility.

DeMain

The Sun Dance

Wilmer Mesteth
(Oglala Lakota)
Spiritual Leader

A descendant of Chief Red Shirt, Wilmer Mesteth is recognized by many as the foremost traditional spiritual leader on the Pine Ridge Reservation. He is a respected educator and Lakota historian.

"... it's shameful to see those who might once have been called Medicine Men or Chiefs catering to these people for money. Were the old chiefs alive today they would stop it but in the meantime our culture is being dismantled ..."

WILMER MESTETH

Lakota spirituality and culture are one and the same. My grandparents spoke of how things used to be and they portrayed our culture in such a way that it became something I longed to see. I have always believed that the Sun Dance and our other ceremonies should be practiced in the true Lakota way, as they were hundreds of years ago. Our people were forced into total despair when they were settled here in 1879, and by 1883 the US Government had outlawed every aspect of our traditional culture and spirituality. Ceremonial leaders were jailed and sacred items confiscated; the agent would dispatch the Indian police to conduct raids on homes or to areas where they heard drums, and many of the items they impounded like drums, rattles, pipes and gourds, were sold to museums by the agent. This regime placed a lot of fear into our people, particularly after the Wounded Knee Massacre. By this time President Grant had authorized the Episcopalians to Christianize the Lakota people but Chief Red Cloud preferred the Jesuits because of contacts he had made with them in the early explorer days, and so the Catholics entered our reservation. Initially there were three denominations of the Christian faith on Pine Ridge; the Jesuits, Episcopalians and Presbyterians, but today we have about thirty-four; by comparison, I visited Pennsylvania once and they only have three denominations there.

The influx and influence of the Christian churches severely damaged the Lakota social structure. We come from *Tiospayes*, extended family or clan groups, and these denominations pulled that apart and separated families by their allegiances to these different churches. We quickly lost two or three generations of Lakota culture and those families that hung on are the ones who preserved and passed on the culture in our oral tradition. By the 1940s our traditional culture had dwindled – the aspirations of Lakota men had been changed from the warrior society, to striving to enter the Christian priesthood. When I was a young boy I witnessed that and how they would hold these convocations of the Catholic Congress, that along with the July 4th celebrations, were attempts at replacing the social gatherings from the Sun Dance. Throughout this period, from 1883 onwards, Lakota spirituality was constantly undermined and frowned upon by these imposed authorities.

In the 1930s and '40s, the BIA Superintendent would occasionally allow a Sun Dance to take place. Until that point, the traditional families who kept the Sun Dance alive would retreat to remote areas to practice it. Piercing was still against the law then, so they used to feign piercing by placing a rope under their arms. In 1951 the tribal council wanted to bring the Sun Dance back and to turn it into a tourist attraction. They designated Chief Fools Crow to run the Sun Dance and in place of piercing, Chief Fools Crow introduced the Pipe Dance, whereby each Sun Dancer would dance with the pipe to the doorway. Piercing was not given back to the Lakota people until 1965 and even then it was strictly regulated with only top of the flesh wounds, just under the skin, permitted. My grandparents were very traditional and they would often say, "We have a true way of life that needs to go on". They were worried how these sacred traditions would survive. I had one special grandfather, George Swift Bird, my mother's uncle, who was the oldest Sun Dancer here in the 1970s. He was my mentor, my teacher, and he was well respected amongst all the traditional Lakota people for upholding our traditions.

I was already a Sun Dancer when the American Indian Movement came in 1972. When they arrived we started to take our ceremonies and traditional ways back, and for the first time we pierced the traditional way again in the Sun Dance. I liked what AIM was saying, that if we stood up for our rights we could practice our beliefs in that true way, and my grandfather adopted several AIM leaders as sons. Previously, in order to hold the Sun Dance, we had to let the Catholics come on the last day, Sunday, to perform Mass but when AIM came they pushed the Catholics aside. That was a special moment, realizing that we had the right to follow our spiritual ways again. After 1972 the Sun Dance split in four directions Part of it was due to the administration of Dick Wilson and the traditional people having to leave the Pine Ridge village area. Chief Fools Crow moved the Sun Dance to Porcupine; Selo Black Crow took it to Wanblee; we followed Pete Catches and Bill Schweigman over to Rocky Ford; and Crow Dog moved it to the Grass Mountains on the Rosebud. Traditionally there was only one main Sun Dance among the Lakota people. From it splitting into four, there are now about forty-five separate Sun Dances on Pine Ridge and I don't know how we are ever going to bring it back together. After everything we have been through as Lakota people, it may now be the New Agers who finally kill our culture. They are the main reason that the Sun Dance has splintered like this.

The New Agers who come here and steal our spirituality are consumers and there are so many Sun Dances because so called Medicine Men from among our own people have turned these sacred ways into a supply and demand business. I remember the first white man who was allowed to Sun Dance here. His name was Hogan Red Cloud and it was Edgar Red Cloud who made the special request to the tribal council on his behalf. Today he's running something called the 'White Buffalo Woman Strip Show' in Kentucky or some place. At the time my grandfather was dead set against it. He said it was wrong because these people had no Lakota lineage and they had no place in our culture; they had no idea of the meaning behind the Sun Dance; of what we suffer and why; and why we are praying and dancing.

At first the Lakota people were hospitable to these white people who came to Sun Dance because Chief Fools Crow and other leaders of that time were the ones who allowed them to do it. But look at it now. Lakota spirituality is suddenly chic and these people come here in their hundreds and pay thousands of dollars to fulfill their fantasies. It hurts to see our sacred ways dragged down like this and it's shameful to see those who might once have been called Medicine Men or Chiefs catering to these people for money, like beggars on the streets. It would have been unheard of among the old people. Were the old chiefs alive today, they would stop it but in the meantime our culture is being dismantled and sold to the point where these sacred ceremonies that were once so revered among our people, at times seem meaningless because they are continuously being degraded in this free-for-all.

In 1992 I led a protest at Bear Butte and tried to stop the bus loads of New Agers with phony Medicine Men who violate this sacred *hanbleceya,* vision quest, site. We removed all kinds of trash that they had defiled the butte with, like prayer ties made of panties. These New Agers don't see the chaos they leave behind them. They don't see families here being torn apart by what they are doing. I see a real danger of us losing our culture to this. These people bring bits of other beliefs with them and crystals, things which have no place in our traditions, and our kids are seeing this and watching as they come here with money and buy off some of our so called Medicine Men and leaders; those that won't share any of our culture with our children, but they will with these New Agers for money. Soon it will all be so diluted that there will be no culture left for our children to follow. I hold a Sun Dance and I don't allow any non-Indians to attend. We step back in time to how it used to be, how it was meant to be, with Lakota people in a true Lakota way. We practice our spirituality there in security and without any outside influences. It is our Lakota way and it's worth fighting for.

MESTETH

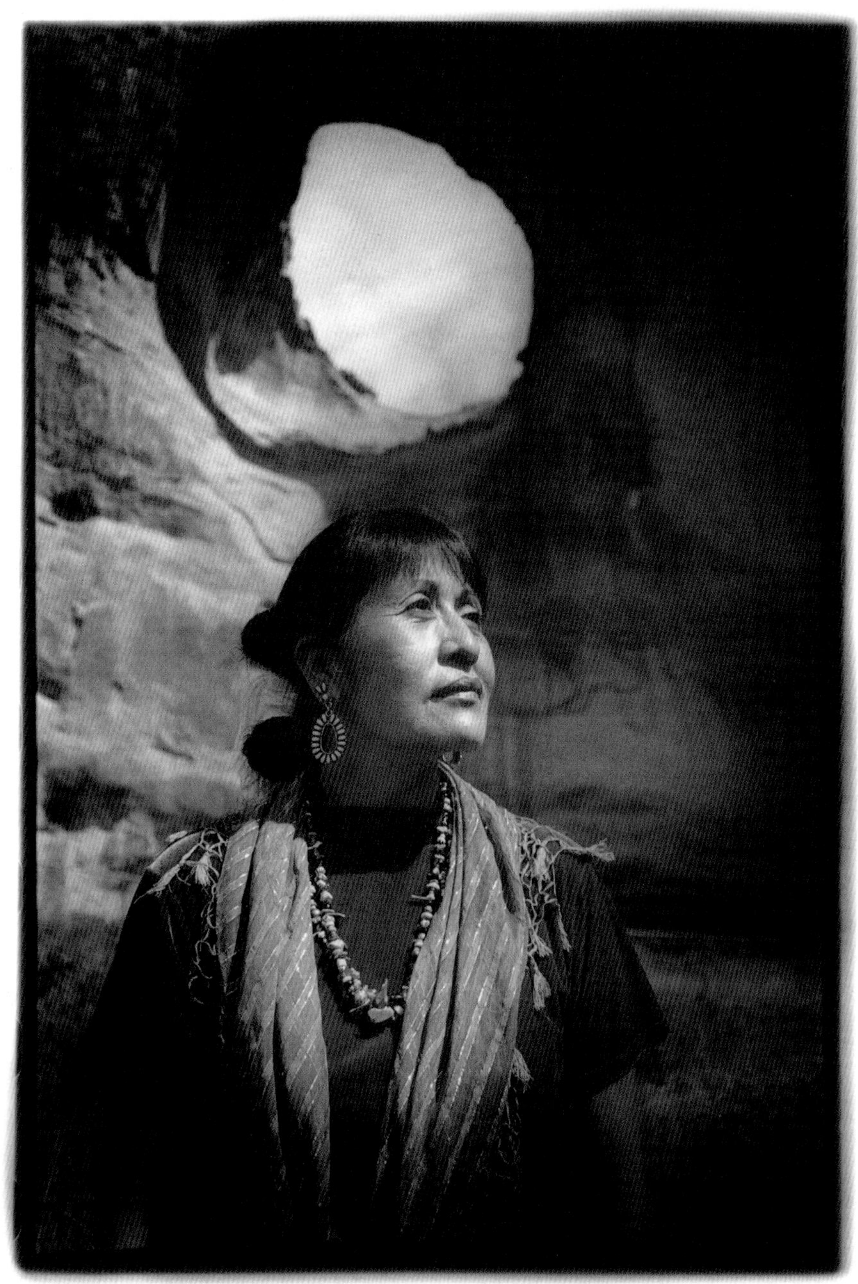

A Legacy for Commutation?

Marley Shebala
(Navajo/Zuni)
Journalist

Marley began working for the Navajo Times *in 1983 and both the newspaper and her journalism have been recognized by NAJA, the Arizona Newspaper Association and the University of Missouri. She has reported for the* Farmington Daily Times, *the* Gallup Independent, *and was KTNN radio's first news director.*

"... the MacDonald letter is part of the council's April 21, 1995, pardon and nowhere does MacDonald admit guilt, show remorse or ask for compassion from his victims."

MARLEY SHEBALA

What is a Navajo leader? Is there a difference between a Navajo leader and a Navajo politician? I was told that a Navajo leader, or Naat'aanii, became the head of the people because he knew the traditional Navajo prayers, chants and ceremonies that protected the people, the land, the animals and all life between the Four Sacred Mountains.

On July 20, 1989, two of our people lost their lives in a riot at the Navajo Nation Financial Services building. Several police officers were also wounded. I was there. I was a reporter for the Farmington, New Mexico, *Daily Times*. The Navajo Nation Council and Navajo Chairman, Peter MacDonald Sr., were embroiled in a bitter political dispute that had become physically and verbally abusive. An April 7, 1989, demonstration outside the council chamber, became violent after Navajo police failed to keep the supporters of the two factions separated.

The council, on February 14, 1989, had called for the removal of MacDonald amid allegations of federal kickbacks, fraud and racketeering and also possible violations of the Navajo Nation Ethics in Government Act involving the purchase of the Big Boquillas Ranch for $33.4 million and other business deals. But the council soon discovered that they had a power struggle on their hands. Council records show how MacDonald, over the past 12 years, eloquently convinced the council that the movement of their power to him was in the best interests of the people. MacDonald presided over the council. He hand-picked members of the various council committees, including the now defunct Advisory Committee, which held the same power as the council in emergency situations. He also selected the chairmen and vice chairmen of the committees. MacDonald decided what resolutions and individuals came before the council. MacDonald's power to make political appointments went beyond division directors and executive office staff assistants; it reached down to department and program directors. And so it was no easy task for 49 of the 88 council delegates to oppose him and call for the protection of the people's resources. I was there when the Navajo police, on MacDonald's orders, locked the '49ers' out of the council chamber and their legislative offices. They were forced to meet at the Navajo Nation Education Center, where MacDonald supporters threw rocks at them, spat on them, shoved them, pulled their hair and publicly degraded them as men.

During the April 7, 1989, demonstration, I saw the Navajo Fire Department aim high-powered water hoses at our elders. Navajo police beat men, young and old. *The Navajo Times* still has a photo of a police officer with his club held high over the head of Council Delegate Tom LaPahe. Several people, including a few council delegates, talked to me off the record about President Clinton's January 20, 2001, commutation of the remaining seven years of MacDonald's fourteen year federal sentence for the riot. LaPahe, on January 23, 2001, reminded his colleagues on the council floor that not everyone is happy about MacDonald's release. LaPahe said there are family members who will not see the return of their loved ones.

I can still remember standing on the hill that overlooked the financial services building on July 20, 1989. A lone police officer jumped out of his police car in front of the two-story building. A group of MacDonald supporters with large sticks in their hands raised them over their heads and walked towards the officer. He held his arm out and put his hand up in a motion to stop them. His other hand went to his side, where his gun was holstered. Then the crowd was upon him. A couple of other police vehicles arrived but the mob outnumbered them. A police van got stuck in the sand on the north side of the building. The driver ran down a ditch with the mob in pursuit. One of the demonstrators got in the van and exited with a police rifle.

I was running down the hill. More police officers arrived and smoke bombs began exploding. People were yelling and screaming. And then I heard gun shots. I broke through a crowd of people and saw a man laying in the dirt. He was staring straight up into the blue sky, where white clouds billowed. A soft breeze moved the smoke around him. His eyes were glazing over. I knew he was dying. I looked past him. Another individual lay on the ground. Navajo Emergency Medical Technicians arrived. The mob was acting like wild dogs. The few police officers on the scene surrounded the EMTs because people began lunging and screaming at them. I looked up at the hill and saw a larger crowd of Navajo people. They were yelling at the MacDonald supporters to go home. They were angry. A woman in her mid-thirties walked by sobbing. She said the MacDonald supporters told her it was only going to be a demonstration. She said she didn't know about the clubs and baseball bats. I saw several people, including an elderly Navajo woman and a young Navajo woman, throwing clubs and bats into the trunk of a vehicle. The two women were smiling and laughing.

I walked to the front of the financial services building. The large glass doors were smashed and the offices vandalized. I recognized Kee Ike Yazzie, MacDonald's tax director. I asked him what he and the other people were doing. Yazzie said MacDonald told them that he would meet them there. The financial services building is where all Navajo Nation checks were issued with MacDonald's signature printed on them with a signature stamp, which was kept in the building. I was reporting on a pro-MacDonald rally one night when I heard then Navajo Vice-Chairman, Johnny R. Thompson, tell the crowd that the only way for MacDonald to regain his power was to take back the 'purse strings.' Thompson pointed towards the financial services building.

The council, during the administration of Navajo President Albert Hale, voted 51–14, with 6 abstaining, on April 21, 1995, to pardon MacDonald and thirteen of his supporters, who were convicted in tribal court in 1990 on charges related to the riot. About $2.5 million of the people's money was spent on their investigation and prosecution. And of the $33.5 million that was spent on the Big Boquillas Ranch land swindle, MacDonald shared a $7.2 million profit with two of his non-Indian buddies.

During the council's deliberation of MacDonald's pardon, Chief Legislative Counsel Claudeen Bates-Arthur and Attorney General Herb Yazzie, cautioned the council about opening up old wounds. In separate written advice, they explained that in the traditional Navajo way, the victims of a crime must not be forgotten and that could only be accomplished when the offender expressed guilt, remorse and asked for compassion from the victims. MacDonald, in an April 5, 1995, letter to Hale and the council, appealed to them to pardon him of any and all convictions. MacDonald also stated, 'I wish it was possible to suffer alone but that isn't possible. When one is serving time in prison, family members, relatives, and friends serve time with you.' In his five-paragraph letter, MacDonald also talked about his age; sixty-six; physical ailments, and the traditional Navajo way. 'Ours is not a society of revenge or extended incarceration; ours is a society of khe' (clan relationship); ours is a society of harmony *(Hozhoona'has'dlii)*; ours is a society of *a'joba'* (kindness); and ours is a society of love *(Ah'yoo'o'o'na')*.' The MacDonald letter is part of the council's April 21, 1995, pardon and nowhere does MacDonald admit guilt, show remorse or ask for compassion from his victims. The day after the July 20, 1989, riot, MacDonald had held a press conference. When asked if he planned to discourage his supporters from becoming violent again, he said his supporters do what they want to do.

ACOMA SKY CITY CASINO

PEABODY WESTERN COAL COMPANY

VISIONS
FROM NATIVE AMERICA

Opposite page, clockwise from top left: *The Reverend Jesse Jackson, Sr., and Arvol Looking Horse – New Markets Tour, Oglala Lakota Nation, July 7, 1999; Cheyenne/Arapaho elder June Black, a direct descendant of Chief Black Kettle; Dr. Janine Pease Pretty On Top; Big Mountain resistor, Glenna Begay; Ga'an Crown Dancers, White Mountain Apache Reservation; Former Navajo Nation President, Peterson Zah; 500 Years of Contact – Ácoma Pueblo.*
This page, above: *Spirit World, Sego Canyon.*

The Ancients' Pathway: *Newspaper Rock.*

a landscape of indian country

BUFFY SAINTE-MARIE

"Among Indian people *on-line* as elsewhere, we continue to observe the usual gangs of unknowledgeable non-Indian and/or *'I-was-an-Indian-in-my-last-life'* opportunists and exploiters who are now upgrading their acts . . ."

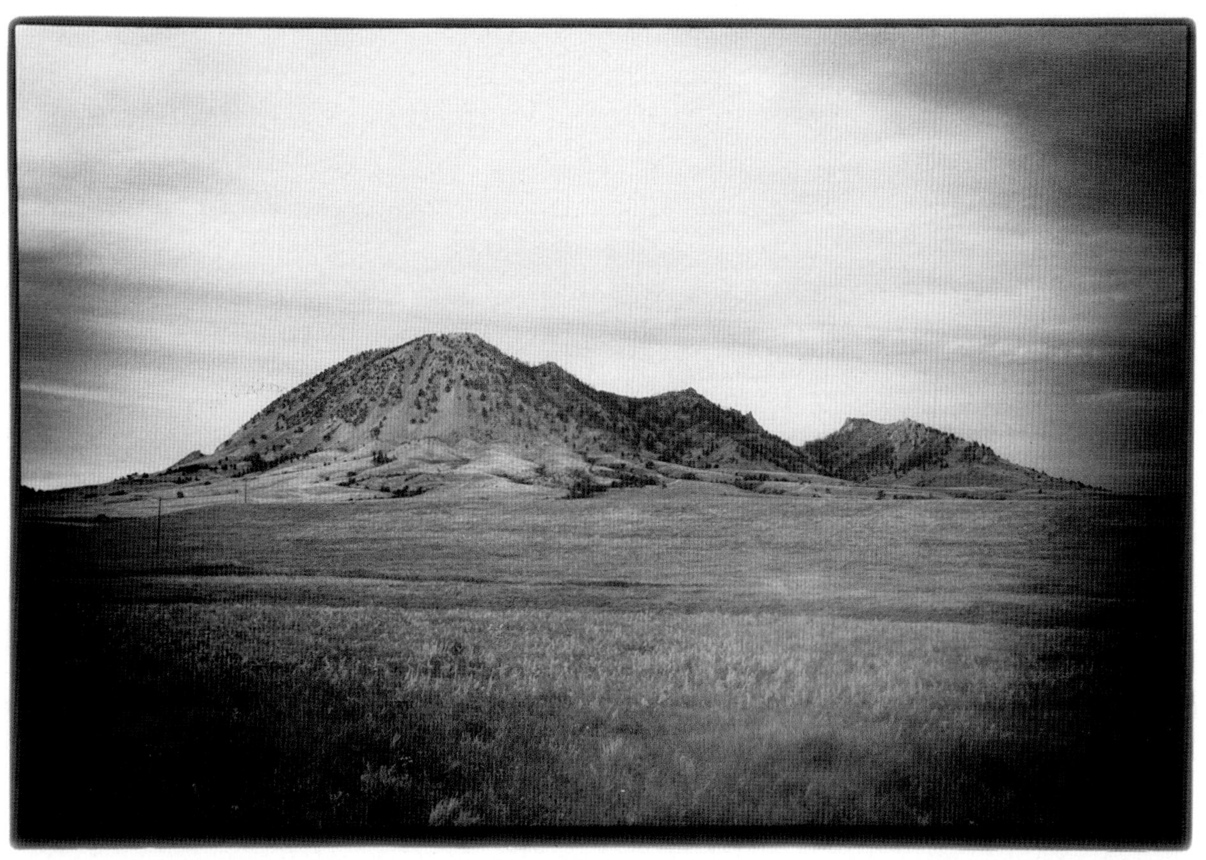

Holy Land: *Bear Butte, Black Hills.*

My digital art and my visual art comes from the 'same place' as my music. While I was creating *Priests of the Golden Bull*, I was creating the painting Pink Village. I had two computers and one swivel chair. While the painting was saving I'd work on the song. Listening to the playback, I'd work on the painting. When painting with brushes and canvas I'm usually thinking and feeling words and music. I've always been like that. I think many artists are that way but computers clarify the point because multitasking becomes so easy. When you first realize that your computer can act as an extension of your memory – record your songs, your words, your visual ideas – as well as transmit what you want to communicate to others, you can go overboard. After you've been using your computer for awhile you learn to put it into perspective. A computer is just a convenience. Computers are no more dehumanizing than a paper and pencil. They never take the place of a human thought, a puppy, a song, a community or a feeling. I use mine as a musical instrument but I still play guitar. I use it to type but I still write letters. I use it to make digital art but I still paint on canvas.

Traditional Belief: *Passage to the Kiva, Ácoma Pueblo.*

Among Indian people on-line as elsewhere, we continue to observe the usual gangs of unknowledgeable non-Indian and/or 'I-was-an-Indian-in-my-last-life' opportunists and exploiters who are now upgrading their acts, trying to take advantage of rumored tax breaks and other scams in the cyber-sector of Indian Country, but we are pretty much used to this 'vapor-speak' phenomenon, having lived with it for these past 500 years. 'Beware of White-man bearing good ideas and grant proposals' is a tacit refrain we laugh about over the phone. However, I'm glad to report that usually this observation does not interfere with honest deals among knowledgeable people of different races. Personally, I believe that we are smart enough to know who our friends are, and they come in all colors. Regarding people who are 'Indian-by-coincidence', I know a lot of people who are Native American 24 hours a day, whether it's convenient or not. I don't know much about people who were 'Indians in their past lives'. I know a lot who are Indians now. I'm so busy with real Indians I don't spend much time with 'maybe' ones. On the other hand, there are a lot of non-Indians who simply can't come to grips with the

Colonial Power: *A Reservation Story.*

horror history of their own cultures. Even in their most creative moments they can't identify with it enough to take credit as themselves, so they channel dead Indians. It's sad and I think that eventually there won't be a need for it but for the moment I try to be kind and listen to people as I find them. If I think they're full of shit, sometimes I say something if I think it will help. I know a few Indians who are full of shit too, who exploit and misrepresent far away tribes and come on like gurus to the innocent just to extend their egos and make a buck.

Sometimes I am asked, "Where did all the brain and fire of the Sixties American Indian activism go?" In my observation, in Canada we went into every field but in the United States, where things were far more dangerous, those of us who were not killed, imprisoned, put out of business or otherwise sacrificed to the uranium industry, went into education. I was talking as a teacher and only about volume level, not courage, when I was quoted in *Sing Out* as saying, "If you want somebody to hear you, you should talk softly so they'll want to hear more and turn up their ears". I do still believe that, but

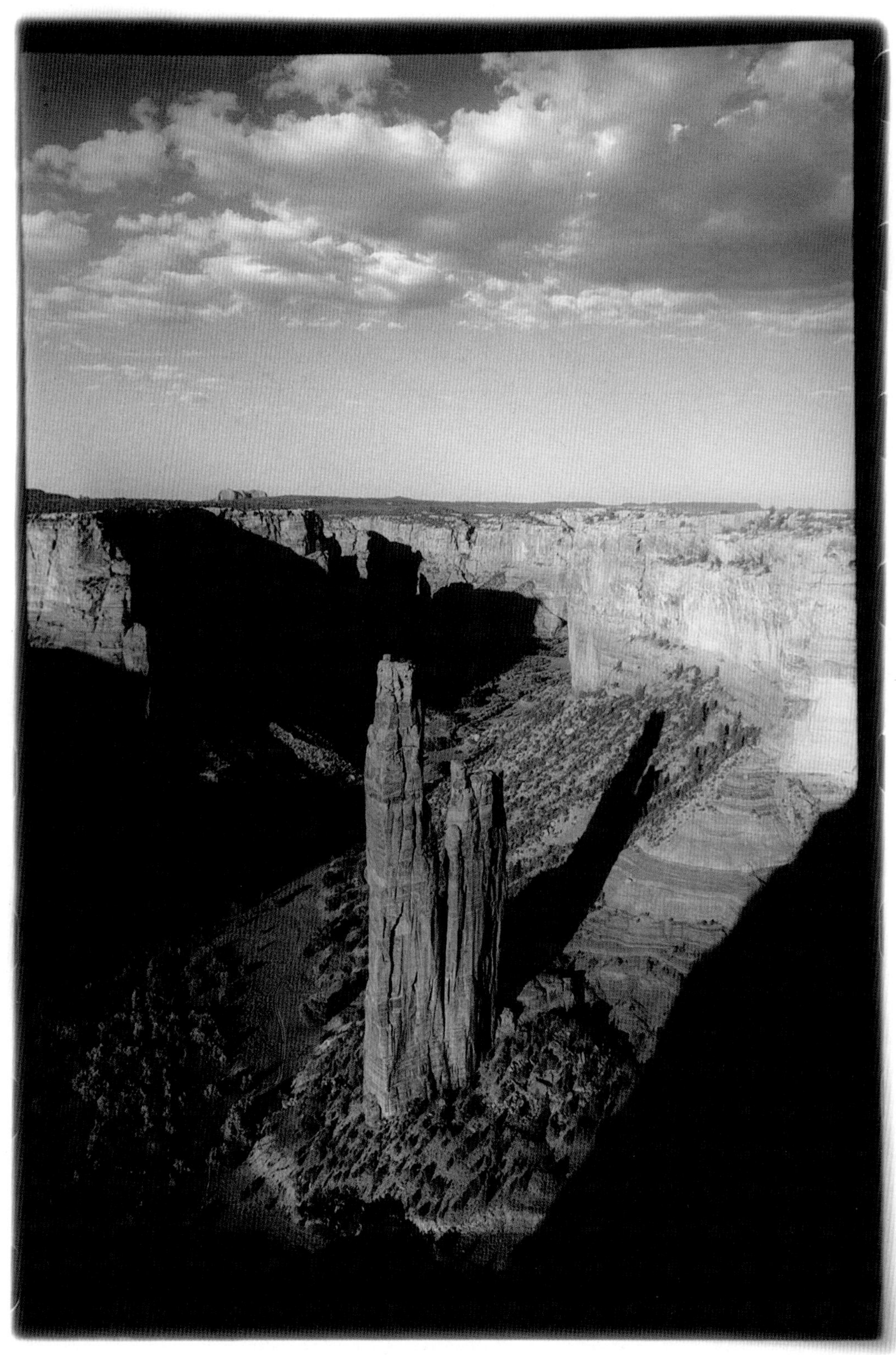

Diné History: *Spider Rock, Canyon de Chelly, Navajo Nation.*

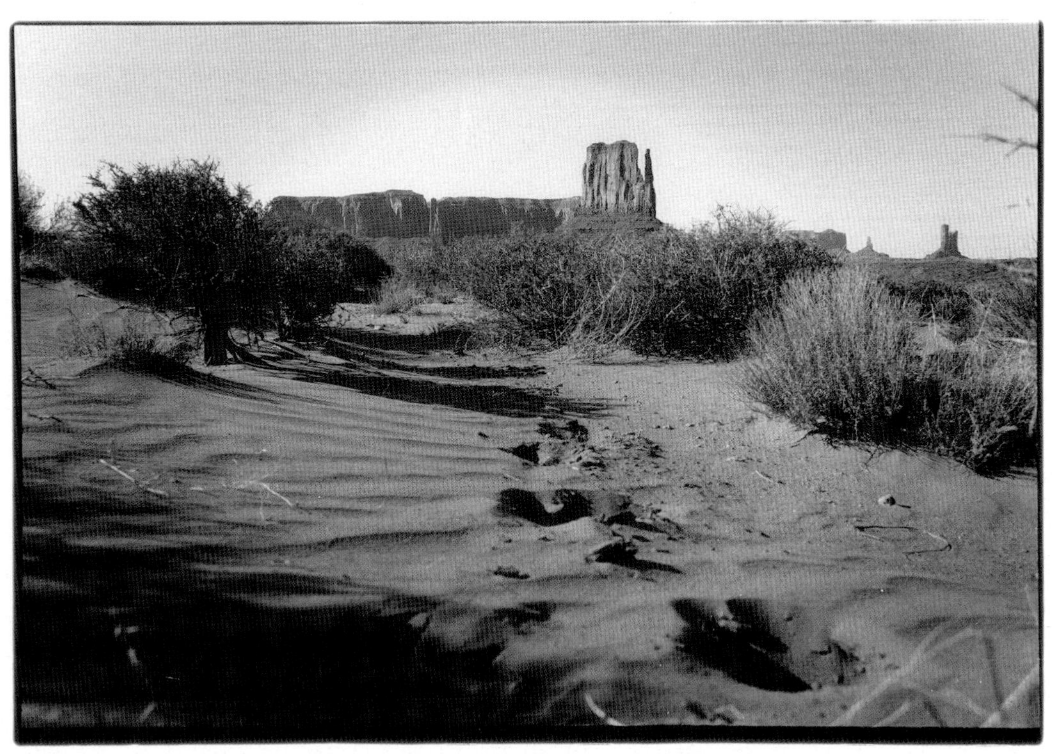

Walk in Beauty: *Monument Valley, Navajo Nation.*

"... *I learned fast* that a lot of people simply saw it as **entertainment** – 'Go *watch* the little **Indian girl cry**' – so if *I wanted* things to **change** I had better do *more* than just **write songs.**"

Tukedeka Territory: *The Shoshone's Grand Tetons.*

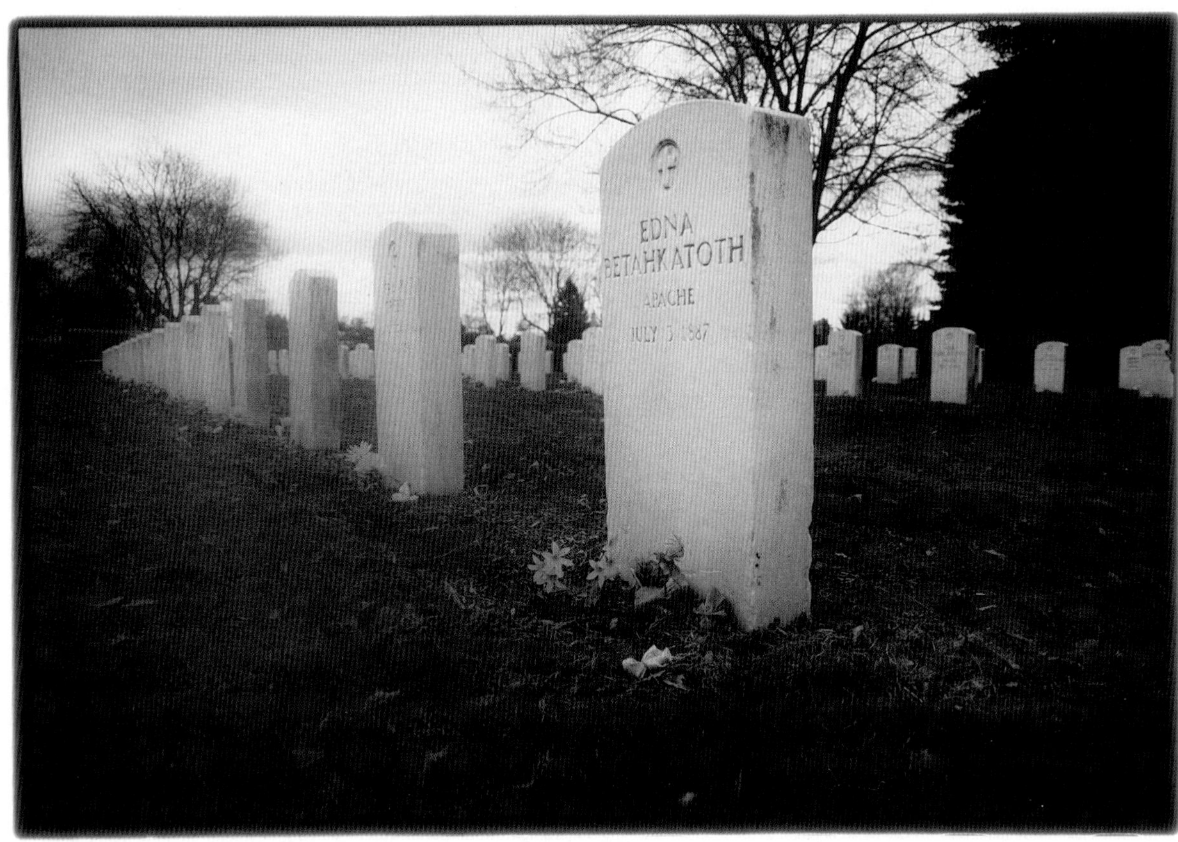

The Curriculum of Manifest Destiny: *Carlisle Indian School, Pennsylvania.*

that doesn't mean be wimpy. It would be taken out of context to apply it to Alcatraz or the occupation of Wounded Knee. I've written some real 'loud' emotional songs of protest; I just don't sing them at a high volume level. I decided to sing *Priests of the Golden Bull* like an innocent young girl who was genuinely asking, "Who brought the bomb, wrapped up in business cards and stained with steak?"

I'm a non-political activist but this only reflects my own abilities and is not meant as advice. I know precisely what I am good at and politics is not my strength. I don't agree that the system only recognizes political legislation and judicial process as a means to change. People you've never heard of make important change in all sorts of ways, they just don't get their names in the papers. I see positive change happening all the time in schools, in the grass roots and urban cities, including things that influence change to the political arena. It just doesn't have a big glow in the dark power ego like politicians carry in front. Sometimes non-political activism comes first and then politicians exploit what they see as a trend and pretend they came up with it.

On the edge of Mescalero: *White Sands*.

In the late Sixties it was hard to be blacklisted by President Johnson, after having been so welcomed by President Kennedy's administration. Johnson didn't tolerate people of color who spoke up for ourselves. He apparently wanted to be the only person to call the shots. In the early Sixties I thought that songs like the pleading *Now That the Buffalo's Gone* or the caustic *My Country Tis of Thy People Are Dying* might change things. Although they reached some people, I learned fast that a lot of people simply saw it as entertainment – 'Go watch the little Indian girl cry' – so if I wanted things to change I had better do more than just write songs. I had been involved with the national Indian Youth Council, the Native American Committee and other activist initiatives around the country. Later I met Dennis Banks, Clyde and Vernon Bellecourt, Bill, Ted and Russell Means, Eddie Benton Banai and other early AIM people, and I was real impressed with their work. When I realized that writing sad-but-true songs only did so much I put my money where my mouth was. In 1969 I founded the Nihewan Foundation through which I gave scholarships to Native American students. That helped in more ways than

Before . . . Indigenous Architecture: *Pueblo Bonito, Chaco Canyon.*

I could ever do by myself because the students went out and maximized the gift in their own communities. One recipient went on to found and preside over Sinte Gleska, which is one of the Tribal Colleges of the American Indian Higher Education Consortium.

More recently, the Cradleboard Teaching Project came about because of everything else that's happened in my life as a teacher, an artist, a bi-cultural nomad who likes people and is thrilled with the accomplishments of Native American people – past, present and future. I have seen it at powwows, in museums, in pyramids with Mayan friends, in books, in the American Indian Movement. It's Indian Country – the whole shebang from pre-Columbian inventions and the Great Law to Native Americans at NASA and AISES and AIHEC and showbiz. What I'm talking about is the entirety of what makes up Native American studies curriculum. We do two things in the Cradleboard Teaching Project and they're both real simple and together they work to solve two serious problems – that mainstream non-Indian educators can't find accurate, enriching materials about Native American people and

After . . . Rez Housing: *Blackfeet Nation.*

therefore teach *destructive, time wasting* baloney; and Native American people suffer all of our lives from this same lack of good teaching materials. The *Cradleboard Teaching Project* works to solve all that by creating cross cultural friendships through the *study* of core curriculum; history, geography, music, social studies and science, through a Native American perspective.

Sacred Hoop: *Alcohol and Drug Free Schools.*

I emphasize core curriculum because that's what the schools take seriously. Normally schools talk about Indians as a frill in the fall, with relation to Columbus, Halloween costumes and Thanksgiving. When it comes to important things like science, it all goes back to being Eurocentric. I got sick of that and decided to change it. Now we teach accurate, enriching Native American core curriculum that meets National Curriculum Standards at elementary, middle school and high school grade levels in thirteen states.

Throughout my years of travelling through Indian Country I've continually been appalled that the world knows so little about Native American anything. You can mention the tragedies, the control of the media and the involvement of energy companies – which is what *The Priests of the Golden Bull* and *Bury My Heart at Wounded Knee* are about – but I would very clearly add all the good things too. I stopped asking myself, "Why is the world oblivious to Native America?" a long time ago. Now I try to do something about it any time I can. In my opinion the dominating force in what is at times referred to as the 'international community' is not really very

Father & Son: *Leslie and Mylon Caye (Kootenai/Navajo)*

international at all. It's still the same old European and Middle Eastern suits and their friends talking only to each other instead of to their own people. Who do the newly emerging nation states listen to? Their women? Their kids? Their students, artists, elders or philosophers? No. They listen to France, England, the USA and the like. To me the entire world still suffers from what was created in one particular part of the world and reached a pinnacle in the Roman Empire. The serial killers who ran Europe during the Inquisition when the Americas were 'discovered' were following that same flawed thinking, and the same ideal is still throwing its weight around today – the basic power trip disguised as media and politics and big time money hunger. The hierarchical, top heavy pecking order rat race perfected in Rome is still the established way in North America. As individuals and as communities we should do everything we can to stay healthy and help each other in spite of that reality to compensate for the present environment. The tradition of Life in a Circle is known to lots of indigenous people but it's still not ripe in the minds of people who have only known the Judeo-Christian way.

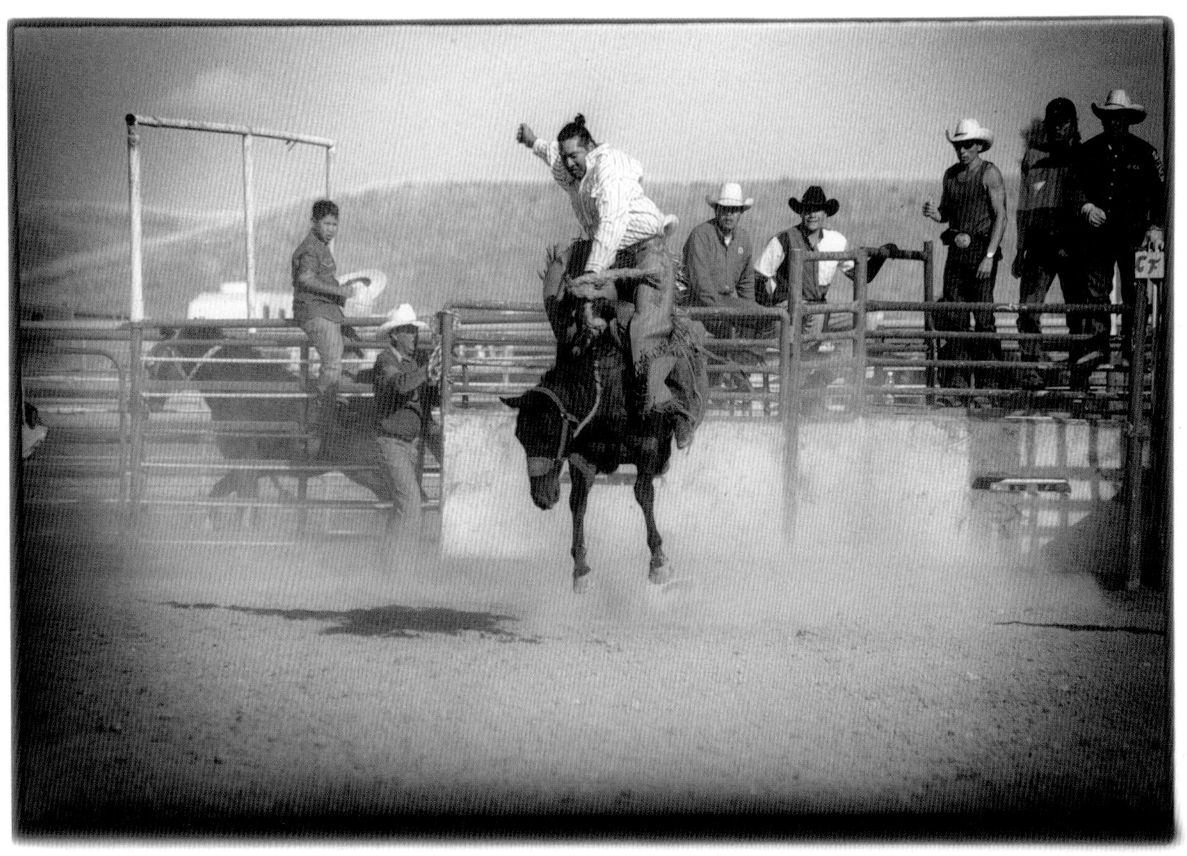

Horse Culture: *Indian Rodeo, Crow Agency.*

I believe that eventually *the pecking order* folks will discover better ways – especially if we teach them in clever and palatable ways without *burning them* or burning ourselves out in doing so – but meantime it's slow going and Mr Caesar is in charge.

Buffy Sainte-Marie
(Cree)
academy award-winning singer/songwriter, educator and tv presenter

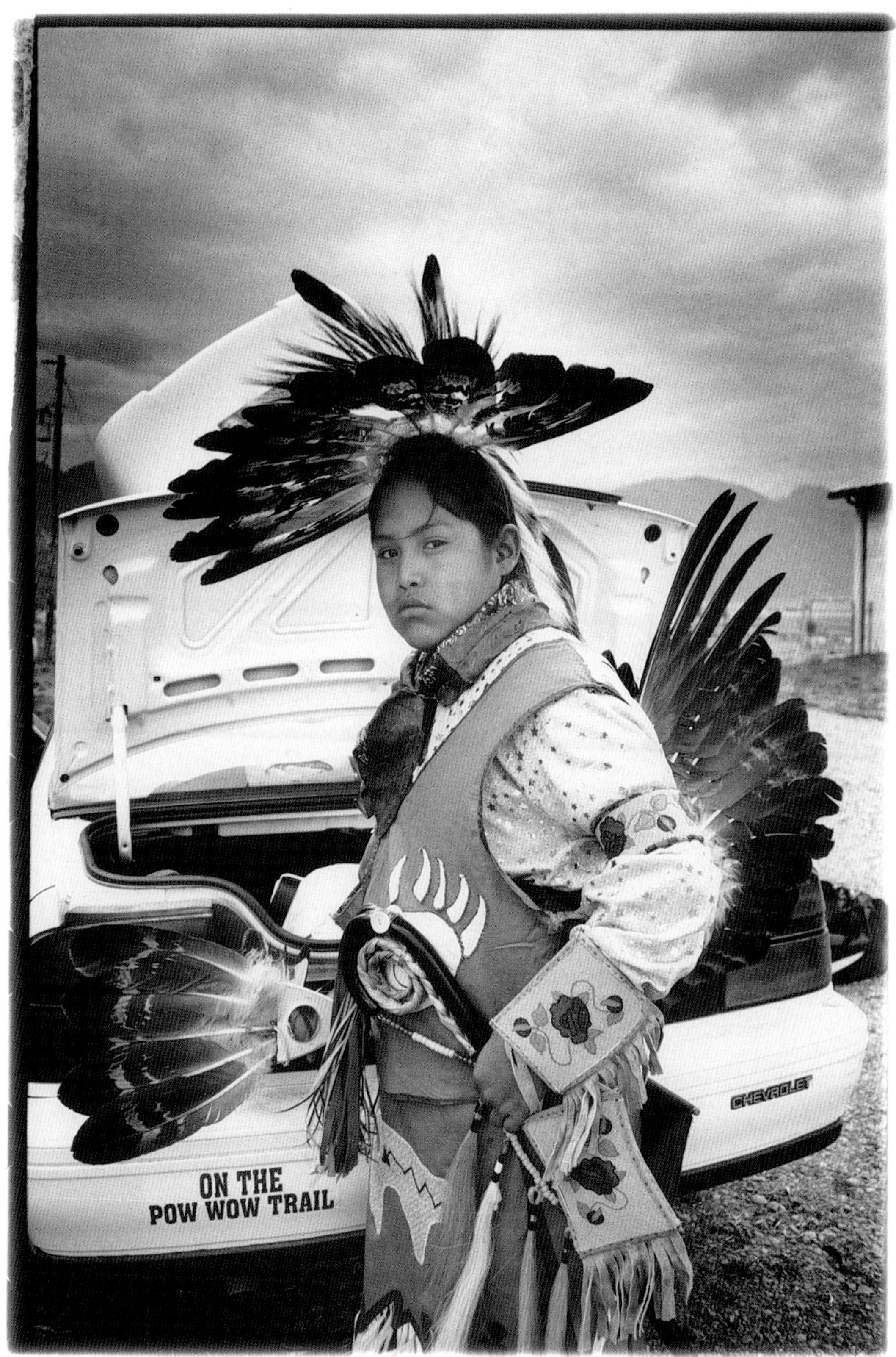

Frybread Power: *Bronson McDonald.*

bringing them home

CURLY BEAR WAGNER

"... along with other *museums and universities*, they wanted to study us to find out where we came from – *when all they had to do* damn it was ask us and *we would have* told them."

One of the main takers from the grave-robbers and looters who desecrated our ancestors' burial grounds was the Smithsonian Institution. Along with other museums and universities, they wanted to study us to find out where we came from – when all they had to do damn it was ask us and we would have told them. We took a letter to Washington, DC and presented it to the Smithsonian and said, "You can't refuse us because our ancestors were taken and we want them back off your shelves and out of any display cases". So arrangements were made for us to collect our ancestors' remains; then they had the gall to ask us, "Do you want us to ship them home parcel post?" I said, "No damn way, we're coming to get them ourselves". The Piscataway [Conoy] Indians are out that way, they're a small band from Maryland, and I'd known them for a long time. I knew they had a sweat lodge there, set right across from George Washington's house over the Potomac River, and so I went to them and presented them with tobacco and cloth and said, "We'd like to use your sweat lodge to help in the repatriation of our ancestors' remains".

We invited the Indian people who worked at the Smithsonian to sweat with us but they only lasted one round; they couldn't take the heat and they're supposed to be the ones with all this knowledge about us Indians. I always tell people that I don't mind being called an Indian. I'm just glad that when Columbus came here he wasn't looking for the Virgin Islands or Turkey! They call us Native Americans but we're not – anybody born in America could be called 'native' American. We're First Nations people, or we are known by our tribal names. Anyway, we went into the sweat lodge and proceeded. Since this happened, a number of my elders have passed on but they gave me the right for re-burying our ancestors. We brought them back home and invited the Smithsonian people to our traditional grave. At that time we still had the elders with the knowledge who showed us what to do and how to conduct a traditional burial.

Curly Bear Wagner.

Repatriation is a big issue amongst our people. I also took representatives from the Field Museum to Washington, DC for a meeting of the National Congress of American Indians, to give them an idea of how Indian people felt about the issue. The Field Museum had some of our ancestors and when they finally agreed to let them go three of us went to get them. AMTRAK gave us a free ride and gave us the biggest carriage they had for our ancestors. For two days in a row we made headlines in the *Chicago Tribune* but we were there for one thing – to bring our ancestors home. We held a sweat for them and invited the Field Museum people and they attended; then we took our ancestors and boarded the train back home. In Chicago all they had to transport them in were styro-foam boxes and so we laid tobacco in there for their journey with us and when we got back we set them at rest in a church until we could re-bury them.

We re-buried them after the first thunder, which is when our Thunder Pipe is opened in the spring of the year. With the first thunder and the opening of the pipe we could re-bury them. Those styro-foam boxes were measured so another box could be made by a carpenter into which they could be placed. We moved to our sacred burial grounds and set up our lodges there and stayed with our ancestors for four days. We held ceremonies constantly for them, preparing them for their journey home. As the moment drew closer I went up into the mountains and made my prayer and left my prayer offerings for them – praying that they would have a safe journey home. We didn't know who they were, we just knew they were Blackfeet people, and so we prepared a mass grave. One was a child, about five years old, who was mummified and still wearing bracelets and so on. When I returned, one of the tipis had burnt up. I asked if anybody had been in there but nobody had and so I said, "That's good because they obviously want to take the tipi with them on their journey". So we took the poles and everything and put it in that grave for them.

Just before we were about to bury them the elders called me over and told me that none of those styro-foam boxes would fit in those other boxes we'd had measured up and made! Clearly we weren't supposed to bury them that way and they were telling us, so we laid traditional cloth down for them and on it we placed tobacco, sweetgrass and sweet pine, along with food for their journey home. We put toys in there for the baby and some of the women placed chocolate in for the child. Then we covered them up. I remember that it was a clear day with no wind blowing but as we walked towards that grave a whirlwind came out of it and headed east. The Field Museum people saw it and I said, "I told you our ancestors are not at rest until they have a proper burial, their spirits are still wandering around". That's true and they proved it.

So we successfully brought our ancestors home and we were the first tribe in the United States to do that. I'm proud and thankful that the Blackfeet people helped get the Native American Graves and Repatriation Act to where it is today – a national law in the United States.

Curly Bear Wagner
(Blackfeet)
cultural ambassador, tribal historian and archaeologist

EDDIE BAUTISTA

eagle dance

Laguna Pueblo

The Eagle Dance is performed to honor the eagle because the eagle represents strength and endurance. Our elders believe that because the eagle flies the highest he comes face-to-face with the Creator, so we use the eagle as a messenger when we pray. When we dance the Eagle Dance we always pray first – that's the Indian way of life – and when we pray, we pray for the whole world; whether they're good or bad, everybody is included in our prayers.

FLOYD RED CROW WESTERMAN

american scream

America lives in a sense of disinformation and this causes the mass population in America to have a distorted idea of Indian people. I had hoped that by the Year 2000 we would have achieved our Nationhood; that we would have seen a move toward the removal of racist mascots in sports; and that we would have acquired a place of respect in the image of America. However, today the racism is just as high as it ever was, but our energy is also high to combat these issues.

Our struggle as a people for spiritual survival is because our traditional, cultural and spiritual survival are related to the land and these issues are our struggle for this twenty-first century. While there will be a next century, I don't believe there will be an America in the next century: I don't believe there will be an America in the next fifty years! I think it will be a different situation in this hemisphere because America is dying from within. It is morally bankrupt for leadership and it is morally corrupted – our youth are evidence of that because when youth shoot youth, you know we are at a low in society. The youth have been so corrupted that they have no direction and no respect.

The two priorities that we place in our spirituality are our children and our earth. We are fired by spiritual energy that is stronger than America. America lives off a power that is an illusionary kind of power, which it takes from our Mother Earth. The more it takes, the more negative the power becomes that they exploit from Mother Earth. We have a power from the spirit world and although it may look overwhelming our struggle is very positive.

We have a way of life to defend – America has only a society of corruption that recognizes only the dollar as a means of measuring survival; everything is for the dollar. As America struggles for profit, profit, profit, our earth is getting chewed up faster, faster, faster. So I think we have values of life to teach the country and I hope we will get to that point. I feel that we will see a great resurgence of our people and I believe our spiritual struggle will prevail.

Floyd Red Crow Westerman
(Dakota)
award-winning actor, musician and american indian movement delegate

Floyd Red Crow Westerman.

Mary Kim Titla.

MARY KIM TITLA

identity

When people ask me who I admire most, my parents are the first to come to mind. I admire them for many things but mostly for their courage and desire to break the cycle of poverty and alcoholism in their families. My father lived in a wickiup as a small child. My mother lived in a house with a dirt floor. They were poor in the eyes of those that measure wealth through material possessions but they were rich in the eyes of those who value faith, culture and a sense of family. When I speak to young people I tell them about my parents and how I grew up on the San Carlos Apache Reservation. My parents were partly raised by their grandfathers, both of whom were Apache medicine men. They grew up listening to the sacred songs of our people, including the thirty-two songs that tell of our creation. My father saw the last of the Snake Dances. I grew up listening to stories about their childhood.

"Indian youth are powerful. They *have the power* to make wise decisions, *change* their lives and achieve greatness."

In order for young people to be successful, they must draw from their past to go forward. Whether it is good or bad. They must know who they are as Indian people. They must value themselves as human beings. When I began my career as a TV news reporter, I made many mistakes and I began to wonder if I was cut out for the job. I had to remind myself that the people who seemed so talented probably started out like I did. That was twelve years ago. Now I tell young people, If I can do it, you can do it too. Everyone has the potential to do something great. Through a group called United National Indian Tribal Youth, Inc. (UNITY) I was able to realize my full potential and now I am helping others realize theirs. Indian youth are powerful. They have the power to make wise decisions, change their lives and achieve greatness. All they need is a little help so they can learn how to use that power.

Mary Kim Titla
(San Carlos Apache)
'naja' award-winning tv news reporter/presenter

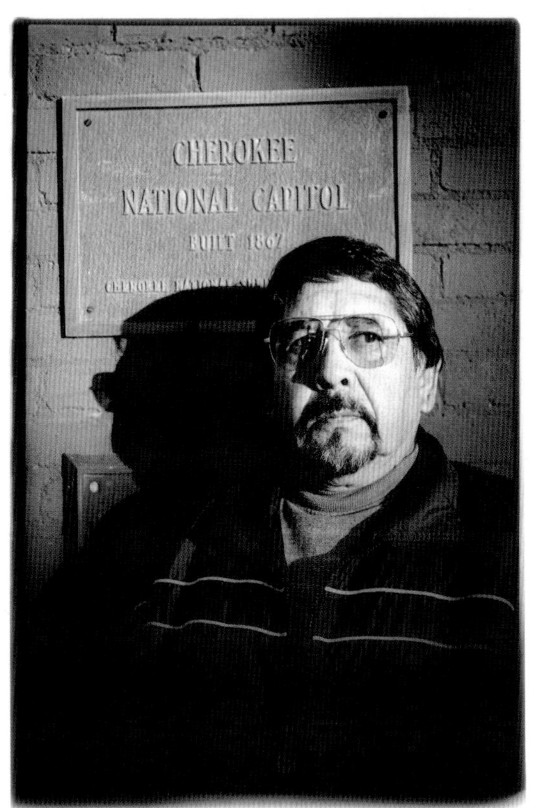

"These things happened so let's *put them in* a book. If we are going *to teach history*, let's teach it."

history
HASTINGS SHADE

When I look at history books I notice that there's a lot of truth left out to make it seem that what happened to us had to be done to create what is mainstream society today. Some of it is written as if it was done in our better interests and so now we can join this mainstream society, but do we want to? The era of relocation after the Second World War was like the second Trail of Tears for our people. I hear a lot of people say that Indians just sit back and wait and want but I always say that if we are sitting back and waiting we are just waiting for what was promised to us and has never been delivered. Through treaties, the United States promised us health, education and welfare, but any provision we have received has never been delivered in such a way to allow us self-sufficiency; it's been presented like a carrot to donkey, with pretty much the same result.

This is my home – not Oklahoma – but this land they call the United States. Turn me loose in any woods and I will survive; I'll get by because we've been taught to. My grandpa used to tell me that one of these times I might need this knowledge, these traditional ways, to get by – and I can. My ancestors still talk to me. People look at me kind of funny when I say that but if we listen as we are supposed to they still teach us. They have never left us. Their knowledge is there and their stories are there – that's our history. Many of our elders relive the Trail of Tears through stories that their grandparents told them; some are maybe a generation or a generation and a half away from the Trail of Tears.

There are many misconceptions about the Trail of Tears. You read that our people were put in stockades and taken care of, but they were put in stockades for annihilation. The Trail could have started in May or June but they began it in October so that the winter months would claim more lives. My great-great grandma was nine years old on the Trail of Tears and she said that 90 per cent of the children under seven years old died, along with most of the elders over sixty, so the first generation and the last generation were taken away from us. A lot of things she told us are not written in history books. In the stockades the women were raped in front of the men and there was nothing they could do about it. The young people were tethered to wagons to stop them running away at night. Some of the states we crossed wouldn't allow us to bury our dead because they said they didn't want the grass polluted. In other places we couldn't bury our dead because the ground was frozen. These things happened so let's put them in a book. If we are going to teach history, let's teach it.

The elders identified greed as one of the main differences between the cultures. The Creator put us here to take care of Mother Earth, not to strip and dig into her. But the dollar sign was one of the driving forces behind our Trail of Tears; gold and land ownership. The Cherokees describe gold as the yellow rock that makes you crazy. We never had any use for gold; it was too soft to make tools out of so we valued copper more. The healing is taking place but there will always be a scar. If you cut your hand and you are left with a scar, every time you see that scar you remember how you got it and that it hurt and that it bled. That's how I see the Cherokee people and the Trail of Tears.

"My *great-great grandma* was nine years old on the Trail of Tears and she said that 90 per cent of the children *under seven* years old died, along with most of the elders *over sixty*, so the first generation and the last generation were taken away from us. A lot of things she told us are *not written in history books*."

Hastings Shade
(Cherokee)
deputy principal chief of the cherokee nation

"I have a *friend* who is Sac & Fox
and he once *said* that there are
many humans *on this earth*
but there are very few *human beings* . . ."

STEVE REEVIS

being human

People might think that movies are my claim to fame but I never really thought about becoming an actor or being in movies, it's just something I fell into. Through movies, I have become recognized amongst Indian people and that little bit of recognition has enabled me to give our Indian youth a good word. I try to speak to the youth as much as I can to try and help them with the chaos they can find themselves confronting; which is often symptomatic of the social and economic conditions that prevail on many of our reservations. In the United States, when the unemployment rate hit 30 per cent it was called a depression; in some of our Nations unemployment hovers around 80 per cent, so what should we call that?

In this day and age many of us don't speak our languages or know our true tribal histories, but despite everything that's happened to our race, we all still know bits and pieces and now we are finding other pieces to go with those because the ones who know our languages and our histories are starting to bring them back to us and slowly it is returning. Our stories are returning. I don't ever want our stories to disappear because with them will go our people and identity and I never want our blood to thin to the point where we disappear into this melting pot and be wiped off the face of the earth. I want my people to live.

Life is about what you give, not what you expect or take. As Indian people, that is our true way of life. When you're giving your path will always be good and without bad feelings and traditionally that's how we conducted ourselves and to me that's true life – the path of a human being. I have a friend who is Sac & Fox and he once said that there are many humans on this earth but there are very few human beings. We need to return to that path and when we do, we will help to restore the balance of our Mother, the Earth,

Steve Reevis.

from whom all has been taken and little given. In that balance is prayer and prayer was our connection to all living things, to our environment, and to all that is above us.

We are all teachers, every one of us, from the smallest baby to the oldest person. We each have something to give and a lot to learn – the teachings of life. We may seek knowledge in profound words but in reality the teachings of life are found in the simplest things. We should never disregard anybody's words; we should always try and show respect; listen and learn. We don't have to agree but we can still learn. If you always stand in judgement you rarely learn.

Stories from 500 BC: *Barrier Canyon Pictographs*.

"*I don't ever* want our stories to **disappear** because with them **will go our people** and **identity** and I never want *our blood to thin* to the point where we *disappear* into this **melting pot . . .**"

Steve Reevis
(Blackfeet)
award-winning actor

The Truth Is: 'No kidding?' 'No.' 'Come on! That can't be true!' 'No kidding.'

SIMON J. ORTIZ

what indians?

'What Indians?' is my too-often unspoken response to people who ask 'When do the Indians dance?' Like other colonized Indigenous peoples, cultures, and communities throughout the world, Native Americans have experienced and endured identities imposed upon them by colonial powers, most of which originate in Europe. This imposition has resulted to a great extent – more than we admit and realize – in the loss of a sense of a centered human self, and the weakening and loss of Indigenous cultural identity.

Strange

April 9, 1999, 9:15 AM
Snow in soft wet knots
falling,
coming down
through gray trees.

Strange to think of Iowa and Kansas.
And Washington where I've never been in winter.
And Portland, Oregon, where I've lived
– elms and pines dripping with rain
on Umatilla Street in weather like this –

Sellwood Bridge
over the Williamette River.

Strange . . .
Nebraska, South Dakota, elsewhere . . .

Not Somewhere Else

But this is Salt Lake City, Utah.

Yeah, it could be elsewhere. In fact,

it could be Somewhere Else City,
United States of America, Planet Earth,
but this is Salt Lake City,
right smack on the western edge
of the center of the world, believe it or not.

Yeah, it's not elsewhere. It's not Somewhere Else City. It is

Salt Lake City
Salt Lake City
Salt Lake City
Salt Lake City
Salt Lake City

No where else but.
And, yeah, what a place, what a place.

Kristy Salway: *Blackfeet Tribal Police Officer.*

What a place to think of Indians.

'Where are the Indians?'
'What Indians?'
'You know, Indians.'
'I don't know what you're talking about.'

Greatest Believers Greatest Disbelievers

To believe or not to believe,
this was the question.
And THE ANSWER.

Asked and answered and believed
by the greatest believers
and disbelievers the world has ever known.

Where are the Indians?
Where are the real Indians?

There are no Indians.
There are no real Indians.

There were never any Indians.
There were never any Indians.

There were never any real Indians.

You mean . . . you mean, there were never any Indians? No real Indians? No Indians?

None.
Never.

'Indians' Wanted

Real or unreal.
Real and/or unreal.
They were made up.
It didn't matter.

They were what people in Europe believed.
They were what people in Europe wanted:

to believe.
They were what people in Europe wanted:
to believe.

Indians were what people in Europe wanted to believe. Indians were what people in Europe wanted to believe. Indians were what people in Europe wanted to believe.

'Indians' were what people in Europe wanted to believe.

'Indians' were what people in Europe wanted to believe.

'Indians' were what Europeans believed.

'Indians' were what Europeans believed.

Believe it or not.
Believe it or not.
Believe it or not.
Believe it or not!
Believe it or not!

Believing the Belief

They believed!
Oh my, yes, they believed!
Soon, very quickly, there were Indians!

If it's one thing Europeans knew how to do, it was to believe.
They still do, you wouldn't believe it even though it's true.

Oh, their belief in the power of belief is powerful!

Their power to believe was beyond belief!
It was overwhelming!
They believed, they believed!

Soon the Americans believed
since they were originally Europeans
and they yearned for 'the old country'.
Oh my, they believed!
They absolutely believed!

Rebecca Riley and Richelle Chavez: *Ácoma Pueblo Students.*

Even 'the Indians' Believed

Indians were made up?

Yeah.

They became what people in Europe believed them to be? Indians?

Indians.

Indians?

Yeah, Indians.

Soon there were Indians all over the place. But mainly in the New World, especially in America! Indians thrived in the New World. That's where they were seen the most. That's where they 'belonged'. That's where they were the most Indian!

Soon even 'the Indians' believed there were 'Indians'.
Soon even the 'Indians' believed they were Indians.

Nonetheless they were people.
They were hanoh. They were people who were themselves.
They were people who were their own people.

See Indians.
See real Indians.
See real Indians play.
See real Indians work.

But there was nothing to see.
There was nothing.
Because there was nothing there.
Nothing real
or surreal.
To see.

See real Indians.
Where?
Where?

Where.
No where.

What We Know

So where were the Indians?
What did Europeans see?
Did they see anything?
What did they see?
Did they see people?
Did they see people like themselves?
What did they see?

What did they see?
What did they see.
What did they see.

'Indians' who are our people
(The People, Human Beings, Hanoh, etc.)
knew themselves as people. Different from each other. Speaking different and distinct and separate languages. They heard each others' languages. Their peoples had different names. They wore different clothes. They ate different foods. They danced different dances. They celebrated their differences. Yes, they were different but they were all
the same:
The People, Human Beings, You, Me.

Always Just Like You Just Like Me

Meanwhile
and meantime
and always

After and before
and during
and always

always, always, always no matter what always and always and even despite the greatest believers and disbelievers in the world, they/we were people they/we were/are people we/they are people four times and without number or need for number we/they are people just like you and just like me.

Simon J. Ortiz
(Ácoma Pueblo)
multi award-winning poet, author, essayist and educator

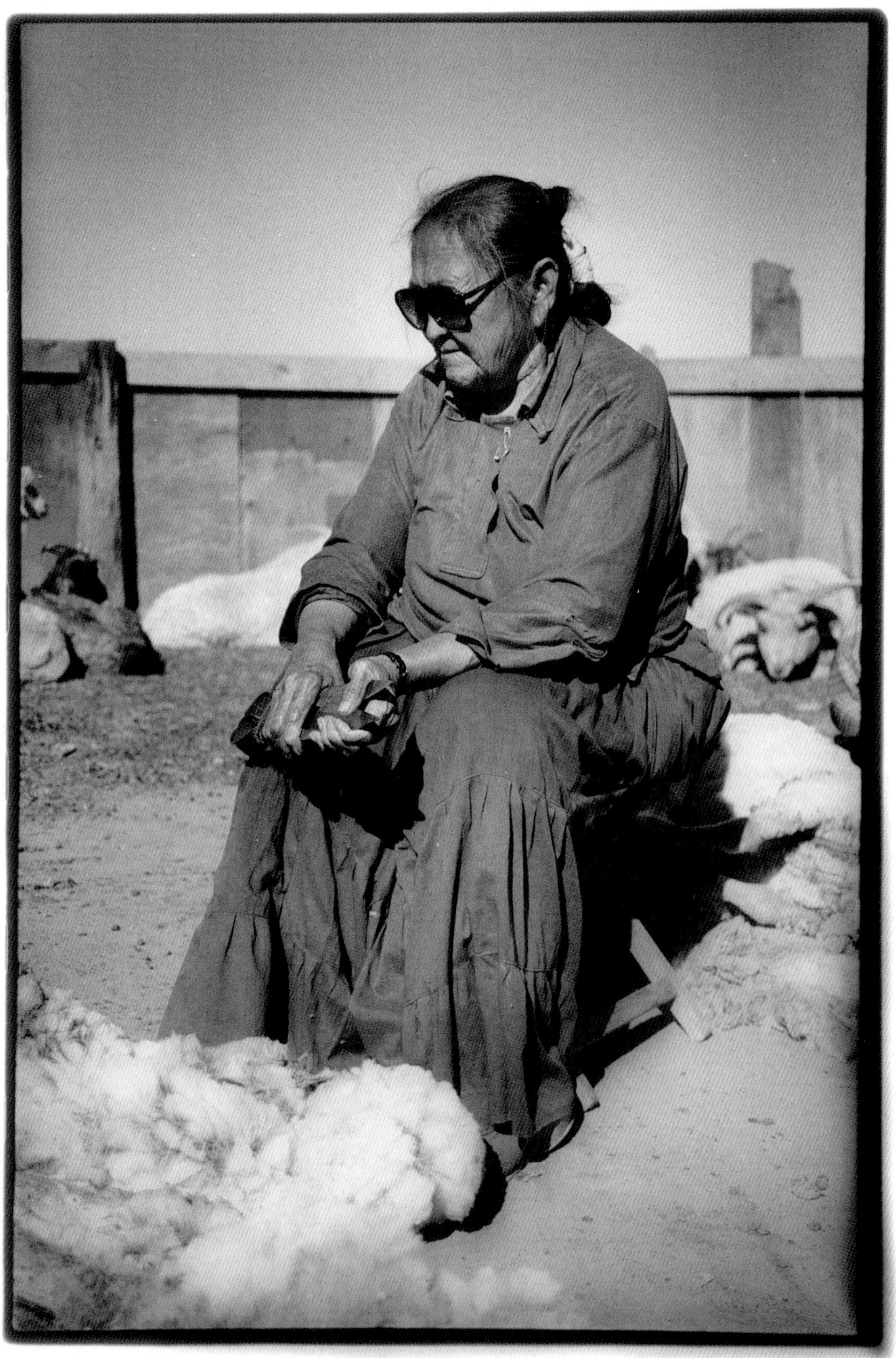

At home on Big Mountain: *Diné elder and shepherdess, Genevieve Grey-eyes.*

SEQUOIA CROSS WHITE

in century 21

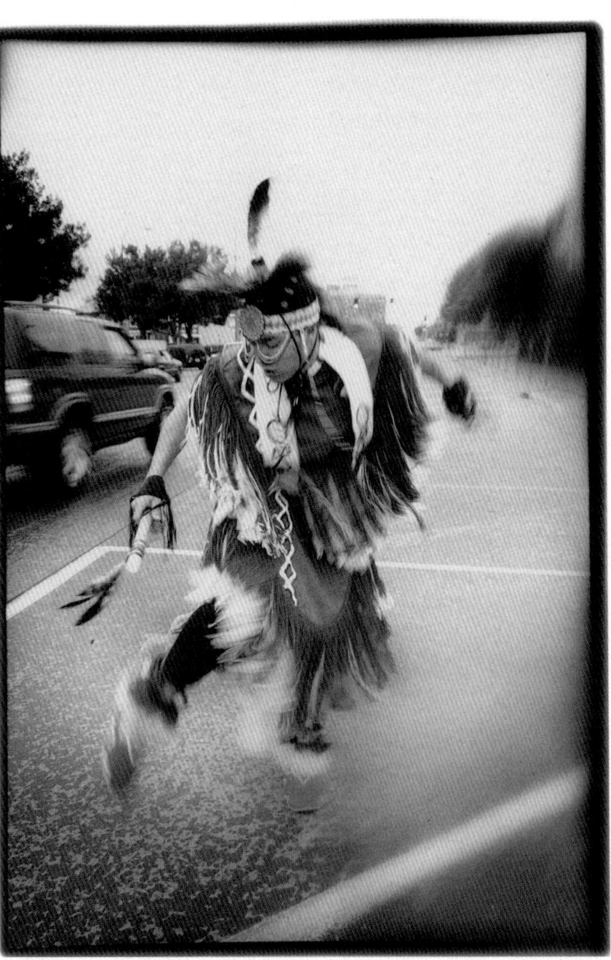

Sequoia Cross White
(Lakota)
rapper/musician

Dance for
healing
pray for the
struggle
Dance for
meaning
in this
concrete
jungle
See you may
take our lives
but our spirit
is free
Some diluted by the
lies of American injustices
You can hide the truth
but it shall shine like a light
You think you've won the battle
and we still haven't given up the fight

YASHKANDAETS'

future shock
(& the buckskin lexicon)

"*The often* used slogans that *Native* 'adult' politicians, *spiritual leaders*, elders, and activists sermonize about, *need to be* transcended to create new *strategies* for the future *by* the future; free from the neo-*colonial baggage* that seems to follow us like bad perfume."

The 21st Century has arrived: the future, according to the science fiction planetscape. And what about the future? What's the concept that is tossed around these days, borrowed from the Six Nations Confederacy? Oh yeah, 'Seven Generations'. This phrase, along with many others – sovereignty, traditional Values, etc – seem to punctuate every discussion we have as Indigenous folks, here in the futuristic days of 'tomorrow-world'. At the ripe old age of 29 trips around the golden disk, I feel as if I am about to leave the ranks of 'the youth' – to borrow another phrase from the buckskin lexicon – and yet, I still feel a greater pull towards the concerns and issues of Native Youth than I do towards the more comfortable, patient and uh, 'responsible' world of the 'Aboriginally Matured'. For quite some time now, I have felt that youth issues in our territories are not given the priority they deserve; and even worse, youth issues are approached from preachy, symbolic *cultural* approaches that use *cultural* symbols and concepts that have little or no tangible validity in the very contemporary lives of these young people. Don't get me wrong, a solid grounding in Indigenous world-views and norms is critical, but they need to be approached in a way that gives young people real tools to survive in any situation.

The matured in our communities often have a way of touting sobriety as a cure-all for our struggles, which tends to fall on many deaf ears when we see most of our 'sober', adult leadership joining the ranks of the co-opted, while at the same time going to sweats and other cultural activities. Young people see their futures being compromised away by the older members of their communities and can say nothing. Elder worship has created a situation in our communities where people hang on to every word that falls out

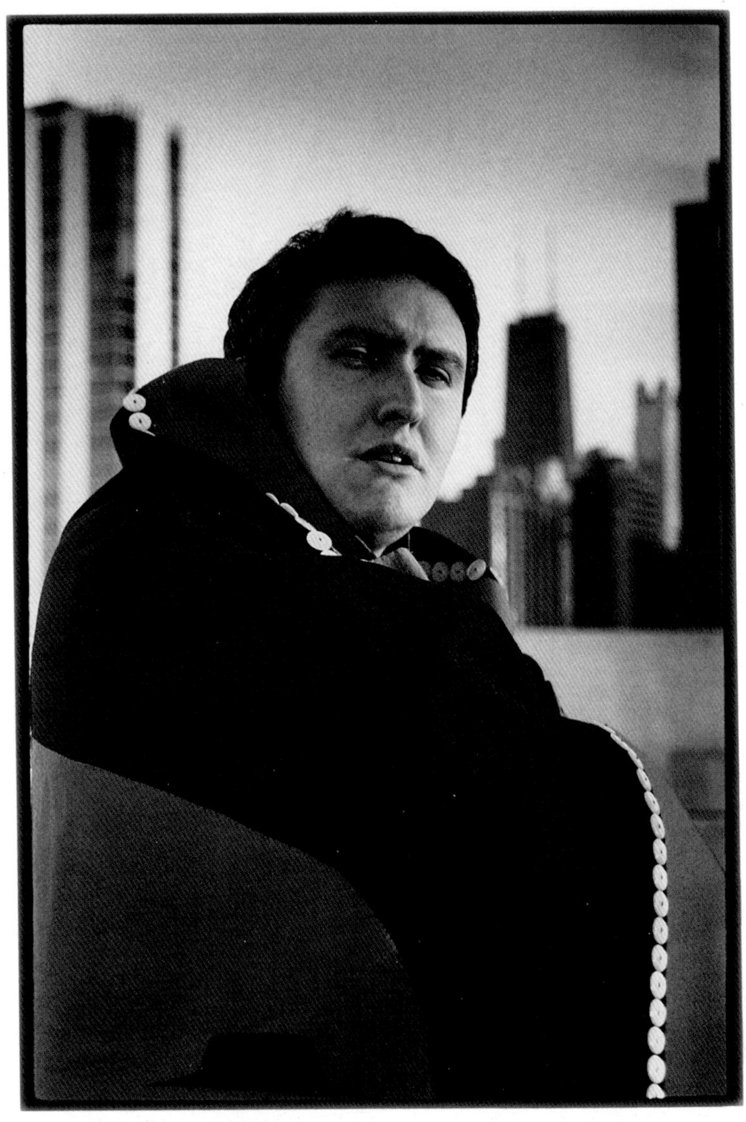

Yashkandaets' a.k.a. Sorrel Goodwin.

"Elder worship has created a *situation* in our communities where *people hang on* to every word that *falls out* of an elderly person's mouth, no matter how *ludicrous* or *flawed* their ideas may be, simply because they have *aged* of an elderly person's mouth, no matter how ludicrous or flawed their ideas may be, simply because they have aged biologically. Better, sound ideas that might be put forth by young people are hushed because, 'The elders have more experience because they have lived longer'. More experience, sure, but some 'elders' have spent their journey around the life hoop driving on empty and blindfolded, thereby creating a real hazard to the other people they share the road of life with. I have seen 'elders' who, through their colonized mindsets and re-entry into purely symbolic cultural roles, bring entire communities to their knees as quickly and as thoroughly as the *Titanic* in the Atlantic.

There has to be a distinction made between real elders and the elderly. We Tlingits have a story about a mean old mother-in-law who fakes her spirit powers when delicious foods begin to show up out of nowhere in front of her village. As the story goes, her young son-in-law, who she mistreats and looks down upon, acquires spirit powers from a sea monster and hunts for food for the hungry village. The mother-in-law is eventually found out and dies of shame – the shame of impersonating a cultural person, a healer. This story is very powerful and tells of the dangers from the abuse of age and authority disguised behind symbolic culture and pseudo-knowledge.

Native Youth, in this new paleface century, need to organize into youth communities that can network within their own 21st Century realities. The often used slogans that Native 'adult' politicians, spiritual leaders, elders, and activists sermonize about, need to be transcended to create new strategies for the future *by* the future; free from the neo-colonial baggage that seems to follow us like bad perfume. The old timers will pass away to the other world soon and the youth will be holding the bag; how can we expect leadership from these young people if we've never allowed them their own voice to speak with? Can we afford another century of adult self-righteousness thinly disguised as a cultural tradition? A window into the future? Here it is folks – Native Hip-Hop, and thoroughly modified, indigenous cultures that create new songs, new dances, new art forms, new political structures, and new nations – all done with a new indigenous savvy that is standing strong!

biologically. Better, *sound ideas* that might be put forth by young people are *hushed* because, 'The elders have more experience because they have lived longer'. There has to be a distinction made *between real elders* and the elderly."

Yashkandaets'
(Auk Tlingit)
historian/anthropologist

about carlos castaneda . . .
FIDEL MORENO
a yaqui *perspective*

'The deer represents the link to the sacred and beautiful place from which the Yoeme come . . .'

Over the years, I have heard many stories about my father's people, the Yoeme, also known as the Yaqui. The Yaqui entered popular consciousness in the late 1960s through the books of ethnologist and anthropologist Carlos Castaneda, whose *The Teachings of Don Juan: A Yaqui Way of Knowledge* set the tone for his series and the public's subsequent misconceptions. Castaneda's books made quite an impact and many people believed that they were based on actual experiences, when in reality much of the information relayed was either inaccurate or false and without any basis in terms of presenting a factual account or understanding of Yaqui people, culture, language or history. For example, the Yaqui have never used peyote in any manner related to Yaqui culture, tradition or history, but peyote is one of the core elements that the fictitious 'shaman', 'Don Juan', uses as a medium to higher consciousness. Needless to say, many of Castaneda's 'Don Juan' devotees experimented with peyote and, for various reasons, had painful experiences. The author, anthropologist and authority on Huichol culture, Jay Fikes, provided expert testimony in the award-winning film, *The Peyote,* and wrote an exposé on Carlos Castaneda entitled *The Psychedelic '60s and Carlos Castaneda,* in which he cited numerous inaccuracies within Castaneda's portrayals of the Yaqui.

As the popular frame of reference for Yaqui culture stems from such literary concoctions, for those who may have been misled I would like to offer some factual information about my father's people. My maternal grandmother's ancestral lineage and bloodline through her mother is Yaqui, but I wasn't raised in the Yaqui communities on either side of the border, so most of my understanding comes from my father's family stories and accounts.

The Yaqui people came through an intricate process of unfolding worlds, or levels of reality, to finally arrive in a beautiful world or paradise, *sea ania*, the Flower World – which accounts for our intimate bond to the world of flora and fauna. The deer represents the link to this sacred and beautiful place from which the Yoeme come, and will always belong. This relationship manifests itself in the spring, during the Catholic observance of Easter Weekend, which we refer to as the *Pasqua*, and it is a very powerful experience as it symbolizes the connection of the Yaqui to the sacred. The sacred Deer Dance is brought to the people over three nights: starting on Good Friday, it continues through Easter Sunday, when processions of *maso bwikame*, the Deer Singers, and people from the *pahko*, the Deer Dance, interact with the *maehto* and other church people; re-enacting the discovery of the Resurrection.

The Yoeme may be known as Yaqui because the Río Yaqui runs through our ancestral territory in Mexico, along which lie the historic Yaqui settlements, *Ume Wohnaiki Pweplom*, The Eight Pueblos. Tragedy accounts for why we have several communities in Tucson and Phoenix, Arizona. At the height of the Mexican Revolution, the great rebel general, Francisco Villa, lost hundreds of men in a major offensive due to using blank bullets purchased from the United States. When 'Pancho' Villa realized that the US had conspired with the Mexican government, he led his revolutionaries against Columbus, New Mexico, and sacked the town. The US government responded by dispatching several cavalry units under the command of Colonel Pershing, to pursue Villa and bring him back, 'dead or alive'. For eighteen gruelling months Pershing's men scoured the Sierras without hide nor shadow of Villa and his men until, defeated by an invisible enemy, they withdrew. Unbeknownst to Pershing, but very much appreciated and respected by General Villa, was the Yaqui's intimate knowledge of the Sierras, which he was quick to deploy both defensively and offensively in the revolutionary struggle.

These Yaqui warriors and scouts rose to prominence among the revolutionary ranks, and Yaqui units were formed and commissions were bestowed by Villa himself on the leaders of the warrior-soldier units, who often fought with their traditional bows, arrows and lances. In response to the military defeats inflicted upon them by the Yaquis, the Mexican forces began punitive expeditions against Yaqui villages, arresting any male of fighting age who would not conscribe to the Mexican army. Yaquis were massacred in their villages; survivors were shipped to the gold and copper mines in the Yucatan, where many died or committed suicide – choosing to throw themselves overboard rather than live without their families, away from their homelands. So began the Yaqui's exodus to Arizona and political asylum; all running the gauntlet of bounty hunters thirsty for any scalp that would pass as Apache. Those who survived established the Yaqui communities in Arizona, working as ranch hands, miners and railroad workers.

After generations of hardship and bloodshed, I know the Yaqui people are respected by the Mexican government. When I worked on Kevin Costner's documentary series, *500 Nations,* I met both the US Ambassador to Mexico and the Director of INI, the *Instituto Nacional de Indigena*, Mexico's equivalent of the BIA. Both commented on the strength and tenacity of the Yaqui people to survive and adapt; the US Ambassador confided that the INI director had said, "Those Yaqui's are so quiet, stubborn and hard to bring to the table to negotiate, and damned if they don't get and do what they want in the end". I just looked at him and smiled.

Fidel Moreno
(Yaqui/Huichol)
ceo and creative director: native visions arts & communications inc.

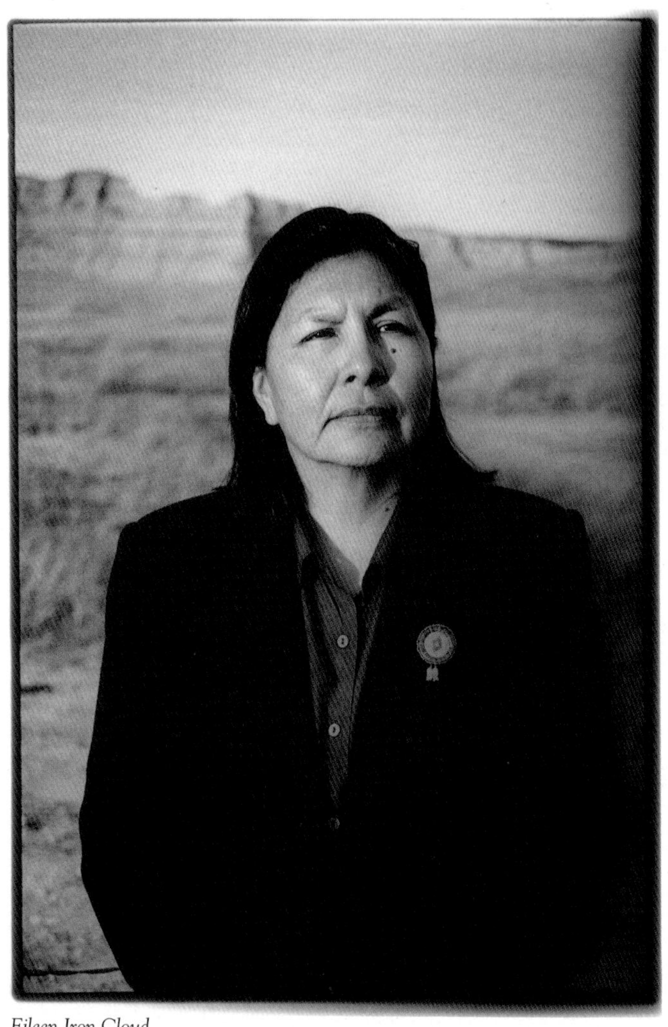

Eileen Iron Cloud.

"Look where we are today *on this reservation* – we're *tired* of being considered the poorest county in the United States and we're *tired* of what some describe as sub-standard education – we're just plain *tired* of living the way we have been for years and we *can't depend on anybody else* but ourselves to make sure things get better."

direct action

EILEEN IRON CLOUD

I have a very clear memory of standing in my grandpa Ed Iron Cloud's little two-room house that had no electricity or running water. I remember standing in his bedroom and looking at a bunch of plain white postcards that were addressed to him with all the messages written in Lakota. So I took those postcards to grandpa and asked him what they said and he explained to me in Lakota that they were meeting announcements of the Lakota Land Owners Association. So when I think about my work with the Lakota Land Owners Association, I think that's where it began.

Grandpa was very involved with Treaty work and I believe that really influenced our family. The Iron Cloud family is large, with many relatives across the Pine Ridge Indian Reservation. I have a grandpa who was a Tribal President; a cousin who was a Tribal President; and grandpas who were on the Tribal Council. I myself served on the Tribal Council and the Tribal Executive Committee. Today, I feel real commitment to the process of what some call participatory research or popular education, what others call direct action; knowledge through direct action. In this process you really value the people and their input; what they have to say and how we can be directed; sometimes self-directed; to make changes for the people.

When you take this position life can get very hard. Sometimes you have to make a stand on an issue even if it means opposing some of your own relatives. It's basically responding to the people when they call out in need. We have people appointed to official positions who are supposed to do this, to respond to the basic needs of the people, but often they don't. Often, it's only through direct action that we can really come together. We take the time to use our radio station, KILI, to bring information to the people and encourage them to talk to their council representatives or whomever can help them on specific issues. We have to be the ones to do this if we want to make some changes here for the better; we can't afford to sit back and assume that somebody is going to make good decisions on our behalf.

I'm very fortunate that my husband is employed which enables me to do some of this work, along with a couple of grants that support a newspaper we publish. It's very difficult if you don't have a car to drive across the reservation to a meeting, or if you don't have gas money even if you have a car; those are daily challenges. We're constantly working on land issues, whether they're within the Land Owners group, or are issues from the 1851 and 1868 Treaties. Many people now realize that our Treaty work is spiritual work and that it is important to ensure that the spiritual side is the foundation.

Eileen Iron Cloud
(Lakota)
stateswoman

MARY YOUNGBLOOD

trees

"My *flutes* are made from numerous woods and before I put a new flute to my lips *I always touch*, appreciate and thank the flute for its *past tree life*."

I was raised in semi-rural Washington State, in a little lake town called Kirkland. Where we lived, none of the houses had fences so we roamed from yard to yard, traipsing through to find the paths that led into the woods. There we would play for hours and hours. As rainy and wet as Washington can be, most of the time I remember it as just a light rain or mist and we kept relatively dry beneath the canopy of the trees. I was a master tree climber, as only children and tomboys like me can be. We'd make believe we were stranded on an island and had to make our homes in trees, tree forts being my speciality. The woods supplied our every need; there were huckleberries and luscious raspberries so big that you could put them on your fingers; there were blackberries, wild rhubarb and little streams to stick long grass straws into when we were thirsty.

I've always felt at home in trees. I feel safe and protected, even loved by them. In those tumultuous adolescent years I found solace in a huge Council Oak I named Brandi. I would take my drawing pencils and a pad of paper up to her highest branches and hide from the world, and she cradled me there until I was ready to face those tough teenage years again. Since that time, I have taken my own children to climb her strong, nurturing limbs.

To this day I love anything made of wood. My flutes are made from numerous woods and before I put a new flute to my lips I always touch, appreciate and thank the flute for its past tree life. I love how trees are 'rooted' to The Mother; those ancient and life giving ties to the Earth. I love their quiet wisdom and ability to bend in a storm. I love how they have always made me feel secure and nurtured, even when I felt alone in the world. I love their gentle spirit and beauty. They have given me so much in my life and it is an honor and a joy to make the 'Trees Sing' through this gift of music.

Mary Youngblood
(Aleut/Seminole)
'nammy' award-winning flautist/composer

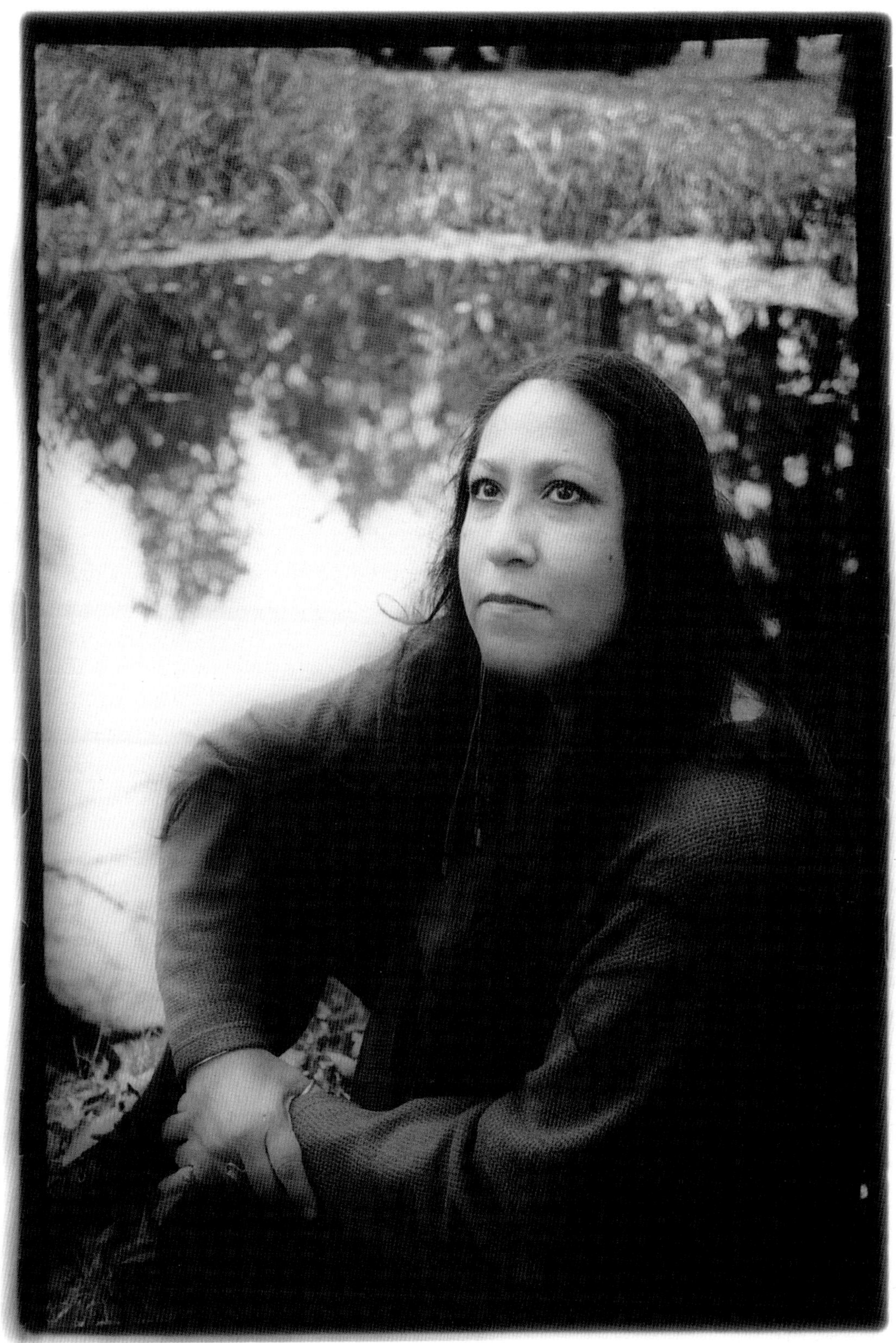

Mary Youngblood.

TOM POOR BEAR

whiteclay

My younger brother, Wally Black Elk, and my cousin, Ron Hard Heart, were found dead a few feet away from where we started Camp Justice. They were discovered in June 1999, and after we took Wally to his resting place, all the sorrow and anger that was within me left and in its place strength was given to me to do something about these brutal murders, which is when I organized the 'Walk for Justice' for Wally and Ron and all of the other victims of unsolved murders that have occurred around Sheridan County. We were about two thousand people strong when we walked into Whiteclay for the first time and it was a peaceful and spiritual march, but the headlines were made by some people who were not part of the walk – these people damaged a store in Whiteclay. That was not our intention, but you also have to look at the years and years of frustration that our Lakota people have experienced in Whiteclay where known racists have been seen physically abusing Lakota people, old and young alike.

On the second march at least fifteen-hundred people walked into Whiteclay; we had the BIA Superintendent with us, the Tribal Chairman, and also some off-duty police officers employed by our Public Safety Department. A wall of SWAT team members in full riot gear were waiting for us at Whiteclay but the BIA Superintendent told us that what we were doing was legal; it's not illegal to walk down a public highway. The law enforcement people in Whiteclay that day were there to protect the buildings but we had the right to walk and to voice our opinions. We had the right to congregate but myself and nine others were arrested; we were shackled and handcuffed to the floor of a bus and were over half-way to the Sheridan County jail when they were instructed to release us with a misdemeanor charge. Later another charge of 'obstructing a state police officer' was brought against us, but nobody was injured on any of the Walks for Justice.

Camp Justice will stand because of the injustices that our people continue to suffer because of the racial abuse they experience in areas of Sheridan County; the physical abuse as well as the verbal and mental abuse which has been going on since Raymond Yellow Thunder was murdered in 1972! Things haven't changed, our people are still being found dead in the jails, on the streets and on the land, like Wally and Ron. Camp Justice is here until justice is found and the land which Whiteclay sits on is returned to its original owners. Whiteclay has been sitting illegally on Indian land for many years and they have been selling alcohol illegally on that Indian land and it has to stop. Whiteclay is the root of it all; they get over $4 million a year just in alcohol sales – primarily from Lakotas – and Whiteclay has contributed nothing to the Lakota community, except to the alcohol problem that the Lakota people have. Whiteclay doesn't contribute to our youth; they can't even find it within them to build a swimming pool for our kids! Whiteclay could at least say, 'Thank you Mr Lakota and here, we want to build your kids a swimming pool'. Or they could build a recreation center or contribute to the programs for the elderly we try to run on our Nation. They could even contribute to help with the problem they feed

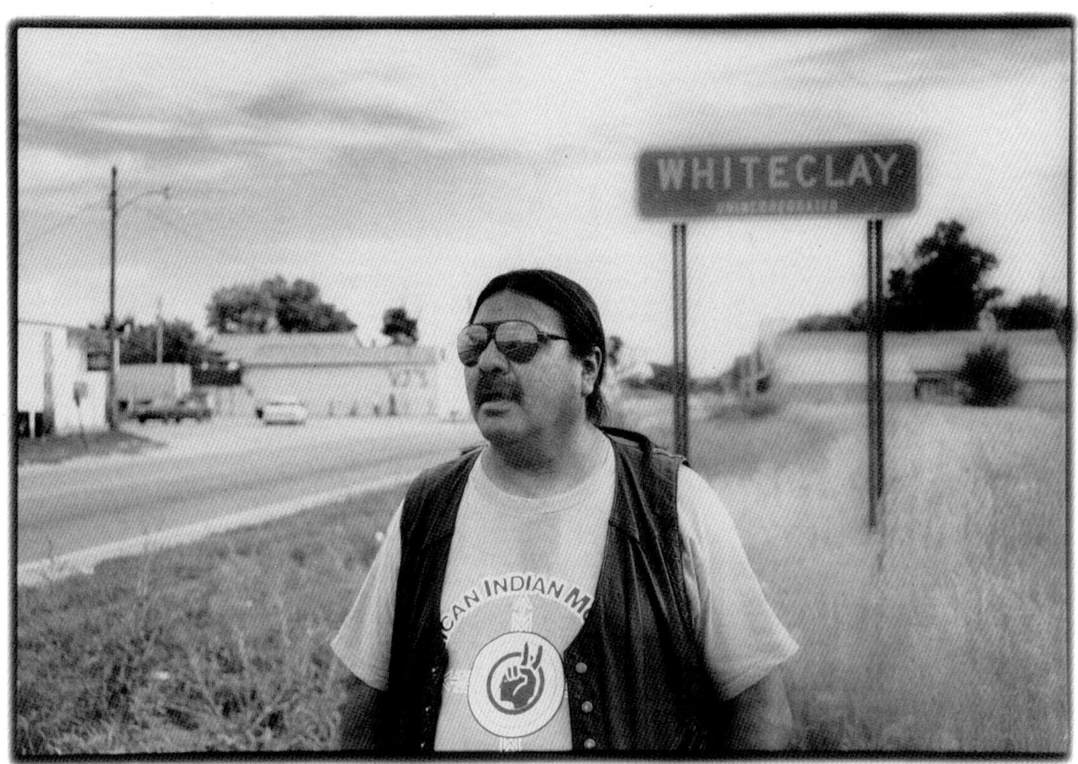

Tom Poor Bear.

on by helping us build a treatment center for alcohol abuse on the reservation; a detox center so our people don't have to sleep on the street in Whiteclay.

Lakotas spend millions of dollars in Whiteclay and there isn't even a bathroom we are allowed to use there! Whiteclay is one of the dirtiest little places in Nebraska and one of the richest and we're tired of Whiteclay laughing at us all the way to their banks with our money. It's really hard to break the habit of our people who have been going to Whiteclay for years, but Camp Justice is a symbol telling the Lakota people that it is time to stand up and say 'No More'. I remember a great man saying, 'The white man is coming and now the Indian people have to stop living and start surviving', but Camp Justice is telling the Lakota people that it's time to stop surviving and to start living as a people again with our dignity and pride. We made history when we met with Governor Johanns of Nebraska, it was the first time a governor of any state had met with a traditional form of government and he listened to our complaints and concerns and what we hoped to accomplish. Whiteclay is a town of twenty-two people and we are a Nation and we have to shut them down for the sake of our children and the sake of our people. It won't stop the alcohol problem but it will be a start. Tribes have filed law suits against tobacco companies because of people getting cancer and now they're settling out of court, and I feel we should file a law suit against Anheuser-Busch because of the liver disease and cirrhosis that is endemic among our people.

We are taking a stand at Camp Justice to say no more hate crimes, no more racial abuse and no more deaths. It has to stop.

Tom Poor Bear
(Oglala Lakota)
founder of camp justice and the walks for justice

the dance
CARMEN LONGKNIFE

During the year that I held the title 'Miss Montana State University: Northern Sweetgrass Society Senior Princess', I traveled around Indian Country representing my tribe, the Gros Ventre of Fort Belknap, Montana, and the Miss MSU title, the best that I could. I was proud to visit the Bears Paw Battlefield where Chief Joseph led the Nez Perce. Many proud and brave Indian people died there, trying to escape from the injustices of the United States government. I am a Women's Fancy Shawl Dancer, and I danced overlooking that ground for all of the people that have suffered in war and all who still endure hardships. I danced for all of our ancestors. The dance, as always, made me feel better about myself. That year was good for me but my family had to make a lot of sacrifices so that I could fulfill my obligations and represent that title.

Carmen Longknife Morales
(Gros Ventre)
miss montana state university: northern sweetgrass society senior princess

KEITH SECOLA

from kokopelli

Keith Secola
(Anishinabe)
ard-winning musician/songwriter

Everyone wants to engage the Mother Earth
Waiting for a *miraculous birth*
A frybread messiah, Quinn the Inuit,
Where's the father, son, when *you* want to quit
Up there on the high road, I blow my notes
Out there on the mesa, *sow my oats*
It's *not really* that I wanted it that way
The canyon lands are the playground *I play*

. . . This sack of seeds, I'm trying to use,
Kokopelli has *the blues* . . .

From Kokopelli Has the Blues *(Secola/Vickers)*

PAULINE ESTEVES

death valley?

Zabriskie Point, Timbisha (Death Valley).

"*This valley* is *tüpippüh*, our Homeland. The people are *nothing without* the land and the *land* is nothing *without the people*. We don't separate land from people."

We call this place 'Timbisha' and it's meaning is very spiritual. Timbisha is the red material, or ochre, found in the Black Mountains in the valley. Our ancestors, the Old Ones, believed that 'timbisha' gave them spiritual strength and it is used for spiritual healing in a lot of our ceremonies. The Creator, *Appü*, placed us here at the beginning of time and this valley is a place of life; a place of great spirituality and healing power. In our culture we refrain from talking about death, instead we refer to 'one who it has happened to', so the term Death Valley is disturbing.

Before the place became colonized by the Europeans and we were forced from our Homeland, there used to be quite a bit of interaction between the Timbisha and the other Shoshones. In those days we were not confined to any small area like we are confined here to forty acres. The Old Ones wouldn't have chosen to stay in this one area of the valley due to the sand, alkali, strong winds and heat. We were moved to this spot at Furnace Creek in 1936 and when we got here there were about twelve adobe buildings for us, all without sanitation or running water. Even at that time, some thought that these uniformed men who were pushing them around must be the cavalry and so others had to explain that they were

National Park Service officials. The Europeans first came here to prospect for gold and silver in the 19th Century but then they discovered borax and started their borax mining operations which, because of the law regarding mining claims, meant that when they staked their claims they could also claim the water rights for that area – which they did. We have always regarded ourselves as people of one nation and we took it upon ourselves to form a government under a written constitution when we petitioned for federal recognition in 1978, which we were granted in 1983. Even though we became Federally Recognized we couldn't reclaim our land but now, after struggling for many, many years, we might get some of it back and secure a land base.

The California Desert Protection Act of 1994 required the Secretary of the Interior to undertake a study and make recommendations that identified reservation lands for the Timbisha. It took a long time and a lot of discussion but with the Department of the Interior we prepared the Draft Secretarial Report to Congress outlining the agreed joint proposals for a suitable Timbisha land base. If it's approved we will reclaim 300 acres near Furnace Creek, plus 7,200 acres of Bureau of Land Management land outside the National Park that would be transferred to us in trust. It was also recommended that we purchase two parcels of former Indian allotted land, and some private land near Lida, if the present land owners would sell. I've told the Federal Government that I won't actually believe it until it happens. People with interests around here seem more concerned about us having some of our land returned than they are about having the aquifers drained by mining companies. They're more concerned about us opening a casino than the devastation that will result from cyanide heap-leach gold mining projects in the Panamint Mountains, or the high-level nuclear waste repository at Yucca Mountain about 25 miles from the park. But why would we want to open a casino? We are a people who live and work within the ecosystem, not tall buildings with flashing lights. We're on the border of Nevada where gambling is everywhere so why would we consider that to be economic development? For economic development to work it has to be done by the Timbisha people and this land would bring opportunities in several places within the Homeland, in the midst of which are our pine trees, our symbol of life.

We have explained that bleeding the natural resources in one area is not our way and why we want to follow the example of the Old Ones – it's all in the study – but when we offer federal agencies a cooperative management agreement allowing us access to our Homeland they respond with the fear that we are going to damage 'wilderness areas'! But what we would be doing is gathering according to our traditional subsistence lifestyle within the ecosystem: we wouldn't be tearing the earth up with mines or opening casinos. If we open anything it will be a cultural center. I don't think there is one Indian cultural center in Nevada that is actually run by Indian people. Up until now, they've never wanted us to be seen or for us to contribute to the visitors who come to the valley. The only information they have about us is from books and from one old man who lived here; he would tell them anything for his own amusement and they believed him.

At present we can't compare this place to a reservation: on reservations people stay, but here our people have been forced to move away because we have been confined to this 40 acres without any resources or opportunities. More than 300 Timbisha have been dispossessed here. There were about 45 of us living here but I think there's only 20 or so at the moment. As I said, people are nothing without their land, and that land is the heart of sovereignty.

Pauline Esteves
(Timbisha Shoshone)
tribal chairperson

THE OLD ONES
mitakuye oyasin

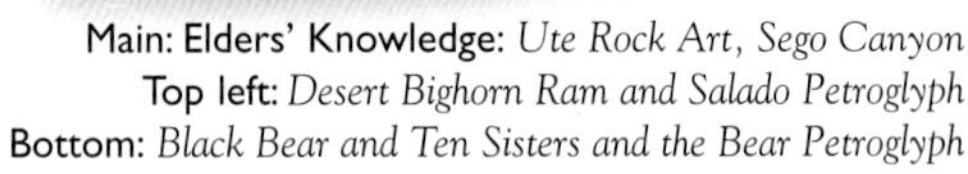

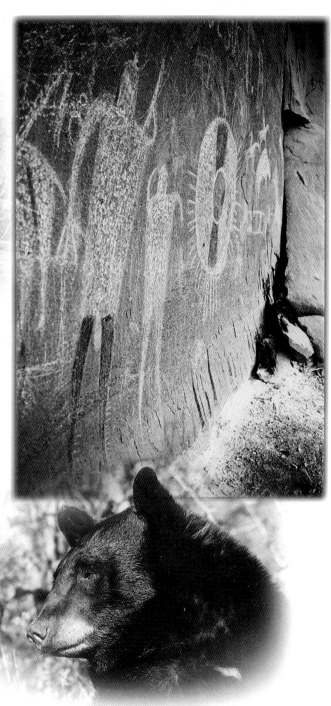

Main: Elders' Knowledge: *Ute Rock Art, Sego Canyon.*
Top left: *Desert Bighorn Ram and Salado Petroglyph.*
Bottom: *Black Bear and Ten Sisters and the Bear Petroglyph.*

HERB STEVENS

tolerance

Herb Stevens.

Every tribe in North America has always had people who are different – some good, some bad. Today it seems that it isn't seen as a good thing to be different, but back in the old days differences were considered special. Before the Europeans came here roles were very different, in our tribe men did most of the light manual work and women did most of the hard labor, but when Christianity was introduced those roles were changed arbitrarily. I have talked with elders who have told me about special people who, in the old days, were recognized as having been given a great gift – the Creator granted them the wisdom of both genders. Often they were considered very spiritual and would be artistically inclined. If given a choice, they would choose one or the other and were totally respected and never ridiculed or called names. I heard of one person like this who became a medicine man, so people visited and respected this person. Now it seems that these different people are seen as being bad but, in the end, a lot of people need to just respect others in their communities and work together like they did in the old days. So what if people are different? Everyone needs to be educated to communicate and respect one and other in this day and age.

Herb Stevens
(San Carlos Apache)
san carlos apache cultural center manager

honest abe?

FERN EASTMAN MATHIAS

Cloud Man was a Mdewakanton Dakota Chief who was born around 1780 in his father's village, about eight miles from present day Mendota, near Minneapolis. He attained status among the Santee Dakotas as a whole, and leadership of his Mdewakanton band, through his actions. He was a man who fulfilled his commitments, initially in battle in defense of his people and later in his attempts to keep the peace. His military experiences led him to instill a strict ethical code in combat that might be compared to the conventions for conduct in war that were adopted over a century later by the US and others. In war nobody from his band would harm non-combatants and in times of peace nobody would engage in combat of any kind or break that trust. Due to the geographical location of his people, Cloud Man was one of the earliest Sioux leaders of any band or nation of the Oceti Sakowin, the Seven Council Fires, to recognize the military power of the Americans and that treaties would become the means to physical survival. Some criticized his approach to the whites and willingness to accept agriculture, but at Cloud Man's village the people had been raising crops for years before the settlers invaded. Once, on a buffalo hunt, Cloud Man had nearly lost his life and those of the others in the party when they were trapped in a blizzard, and after that he believed there was a need to supplement their existing subsistence lifestyle with agriculture, so they began raising corn.

Cloud Man's youngest daughter, Stands Sacred, married Captain Seth Eastman, an officer and artist posted at Fort Snelling, and they had one daughter, Mary Nancy Eastman, who was born in 1831. Eastman was transferred a few years later and left Stands Sacred, returning around 1840 with a white wife to become Commander of Fort Snelling. Stands Sacred returned to her people and her daughter Mary became renowned in the area for her beauty. Mary had a number of admirers, and there are a few different versions of how she came to marry my great-grandfather, Many Lightnings, a Mdewakanton/Wahpeton Dakota Chief. My great-grandfather faced difficult choices in what were extremely precarious and turbulent times in the history and very existence of our people. Manifest Destiny was the order of the day, obeyed by the immigrants and armies invading our homeland. The prevailing attitude of the US government and the majority of the settlers in 1862 is represented by a famous quote from one of the government traders who operated in our territory. "If they are hungry," said Andrew Myrick, "let them eat grass or their own dung." They weren't hungry, they were starving due to government corruption, and most felt that of the two options available to them, fighting was better than starving to death.

Fern Eastman Mathias.

Little Crow was the Mdewakanton leader who, it is said by some, reluctantly accepted the responsibility to lead the campaign and my great-grandfather told him, "We will not kill women and children but we will fight the soldiers when they come". Many Lightnings was badly wounded at the Battle of Wood Lake and when the so-called 'Minnesota Sioux Uprising' ended, he was referred to as 'one of the fortunate hostiles' because he was exiled and imprisoned in Davenport, Iowa, unlike many others who were hung. Three hundred and ninety-two Dakota men were tried after this three-month fight for survival, the trials having proceeded at a rate of one prisoner every ten minutes. Three hundred and three were sentenced to death by hanging while their families starved and froze to death in a compound at Fort Snelling. Chief Mahkahto had been killed in the Battle of Wood Lake where my great-grandfather was wounded, and it was in the town that bears his name, 'Mankato', that on December 26, 1862, thirty-eight Dakotas were hung in the largest mass execution in American history. President Abraham Lincoln signed the order that condemned them in the same week that he issued the Emancipation Proclamation. People think Abraham Lincoln was a good person, but he was the one who did that and those whose sentences he commuted were imprisoned and ultimately ethnically cleansed from their homelands.

People have said and written that Many Lightnings was a willing convert to Christianity but it was, yet again, a matter of survival. After seeking sanctuary in Canada with other Dakotas, he was confined as a Prisoner of War at Fort Pembina in early 1864, and from there imprisoned in Iowa. It was during his incarceration that he converted to Christianity and became known as Jacob Eastman, adopting his late wife Mary's surname. Two other leaders who had been captured and held at Fort Pembina around the same time, Chiefs Shakopee and Medicine Bottle, didn't survive the kangaroo court and were hung. It is said that as he stood on the gallows Shakopee heard one of the first trains arriving in our country and said, "As the white man comes in, the Indian goes out". Upon his release, Many Lightnings returned to Canada to search for my grandfather, Ohiyesa. He found him and they settled with the other refugees in Santee, Nebraska, before moving closer to home, building a community in Flandreau, South Dakota. Like Many Lightnings, my grandfather survived in the white world by appearing to convert to Christianity and taking the name Charles Eastman. My grandfather became a respected physician and as the agency surgeon at Pine Ridge he was among the first on to the killing fields at Wounded Knee to try and save the survivors. He went on to become one of the first American Indians to have his work published and the books of Ohiyesa, often authored as Charles Eastman, provided the foundation upon which many Indian authors have followed.

Fern Eastman Mathias
(Sisseton/Wahpeton Dakota)
mother, grandmother and director of the american indian movement

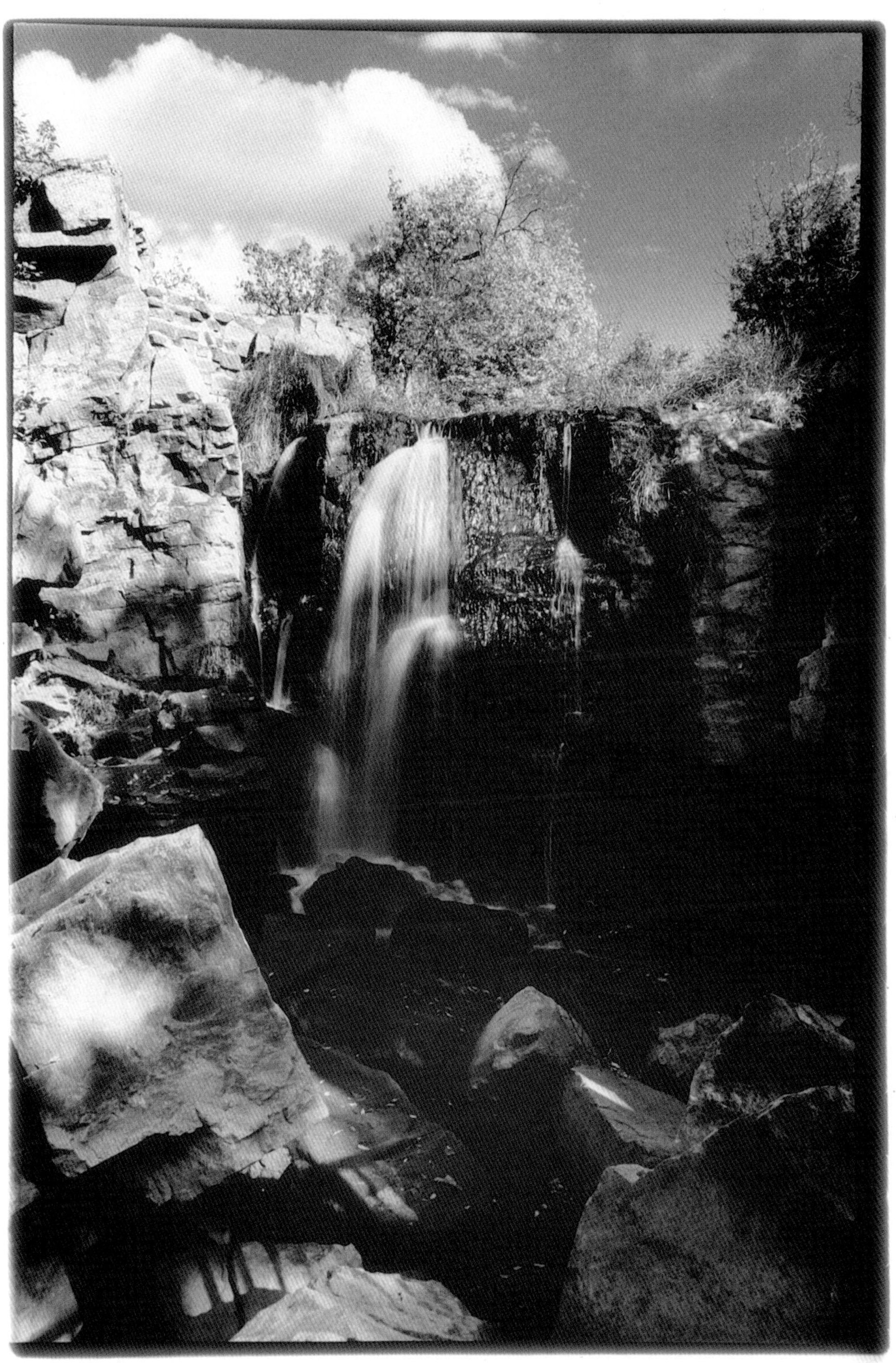

Where the Creator called for peace and water began falling from the rocks: *Winnewissa Falls, Pipestone Creek, on the sacred land now known as Pipestone National Monument, Minnesota. Fern's great-grandfather, Many Lightnings, settled near Flandreau with other Dakota survivors of the 1862 'Minnesota Sioux Uprising', approximately twenty miles west of the falls.*

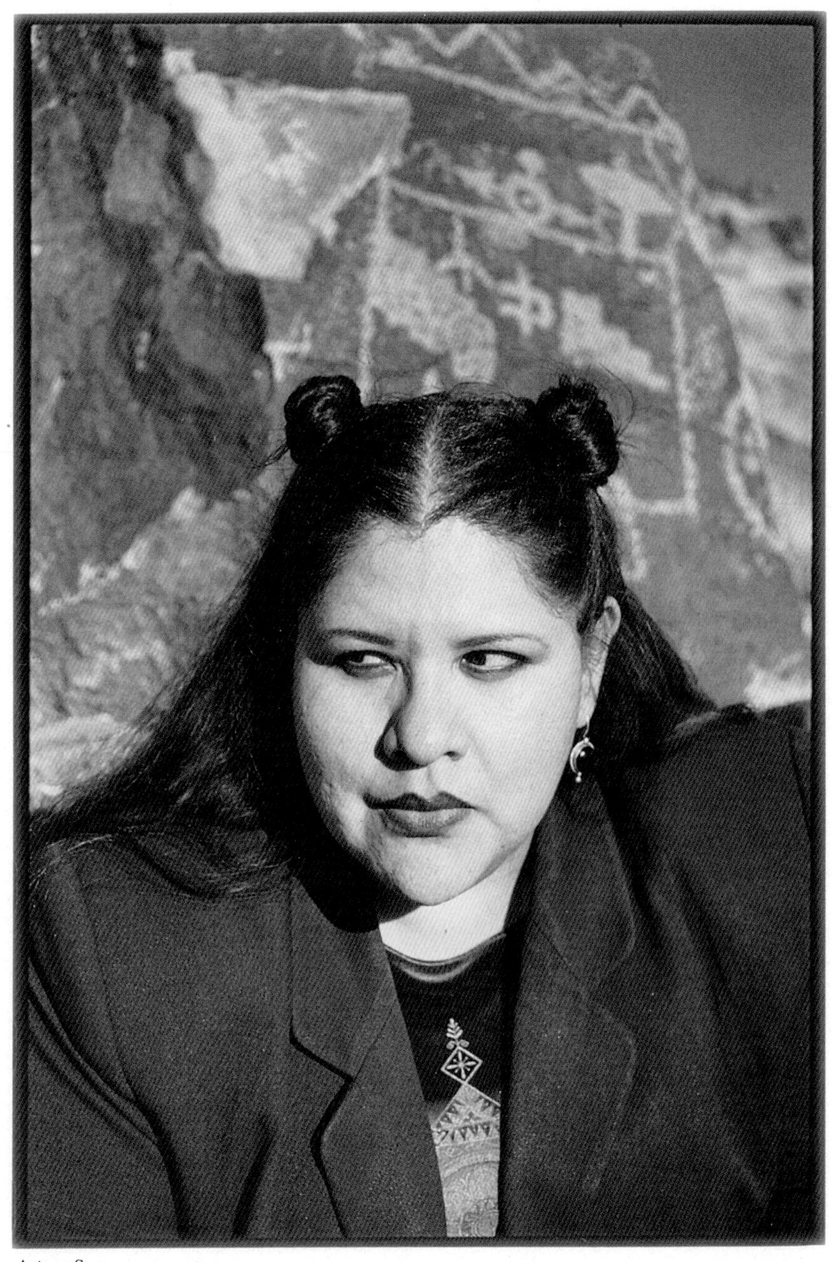

Arigon Starr.

"... *we* become activists *by* default. Suddenly, we're representing our *tribes*, the *Red Race*, in everything we do – whether we *want to* or not."

ARIGON STARR
accidental activists

It is the second cup of coffee this morning and I'm listening to the oldest Beatles CD, *Please, Please Me,* preparing to tell you about myself. For those of you expecting some mystical, shamanistic ritual, you'll probably want to turn to the fiction of Lynn Andrews or romance novelist Cassie Edwards.

I never wanted to be a 'Tribal Spokesperson' or 'Voice of a Generation', but it just seems to happen to some of us, and my Indian brothers and sisters will know exactly what I mean. I've heard this situation mentioned by several people in the community: that we become activists by default. Suddenly, we're representing our tribes, the Red Race, in everything we do – whether we want to or not. People are always asking me questions like, 'How do Indian people really feel about casinos?' 'What do Indian people think about the mascot issue?' . . . As if I'm the 'Voice of Authority' or a recognized leader of self-determination and sovereignty! Heck, I'm just an Indian girl with a rock band.

I began to write my own songs about Indian issues around ten years ago, not when I first started writing music at twelve. I had no clue what being Indian was all about when I was a kid. I saw *F Troop* and *Bonanza* and thought I couldn't be identified as an Indian unless I was in 'Plains Indian' regalia on the back of a fine Appaloosa. However, a few images crept into my consciousness which I didn't recognize until recently, so I'll blame Johnny Gage and the writing staff of *Emergency!* for turning me into an activist!

I acknowledge and respect the power of having an opinion; not being afraid to voice it and having the forum to say it. I appreciate the opportunity to be a spokesperson for the Red Race. My hope is that sometime, somewhere, an Indian girl or boy will be listening to my music in their bedroom, miming along in the mirror and playing air guitar – just like I did to music that influenced me. I also hope that they will find the courage and inspiration to forge an identity for themselves so they will not be afraid to tell their stories exactly the way they want to. There are over 500 tribes across North America. Some Indians live in cities, some live on their ancestral lands. I am one Indian who grew up urban. I will continue to incorporate my heritage into my art and my life. And listen to Beatles records.

Arigon Starr
(Kickapoo/Creek)
diva

APRYL CHATO

changing woman

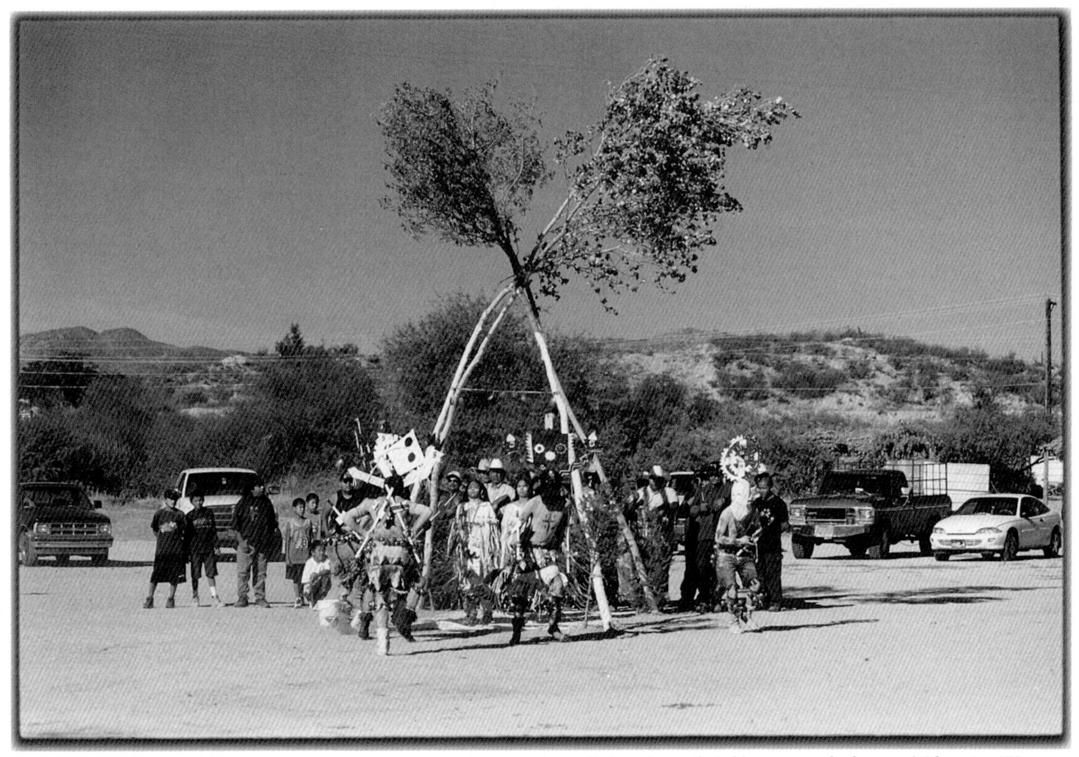

The Naiiees: *Ga'ans bring their blessings to the home of Changing Woman.*

"... *on her forehead* was placed an abalone shell pendant, the *sign* of Changing Woman, the mother of all the *Apache people*, whose spirit would *empower* Apryl during the Sunrise *Ceremony*."

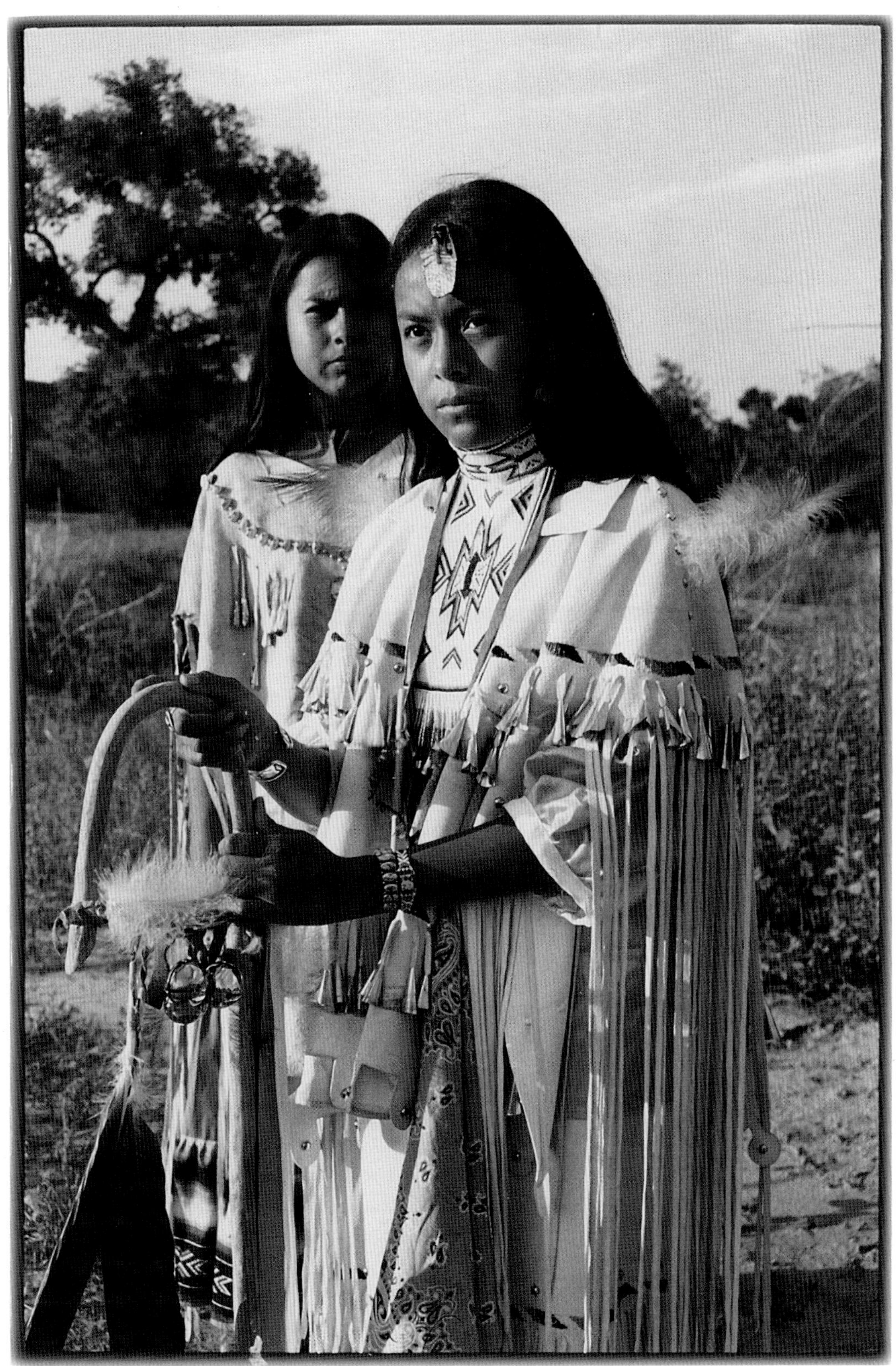

Apryl (foreground) with Jordan, her Attendant, on day two of the Sunrise Ceremony.

ba na ihl dih blessing her

Commentary by Mel Chato.

The *Naiiees,* the Sunrise Dance, is an Apache tradition that is passed down from generation to generation. The ritual, or ceremony, represents the initiation of an Apache girl from childhood into womanhood. The *Naiiees* is a four-day event that commences at dusk on the first day when the girl's Godmother dresses her; *Bi keh ihl ze,* She is dressed. We chose Andrew and Olivia Lacapa to be Apryl's godparents and as is customary, her *Naihlesn* dressed her with a buckskin cape, T-necklace, a neck string that held a cloth to wipe her face and the traditional reed drinking tube and body scratcher.

To help her live until her hair turns gray, an eagle feather was pinned in Apryl's hair and on her forehead was placed an abalone shell pendant – the sign of Changing Woman, the mother of all the Apache people, who's spirit would empower Apryl during the Sunrise Ceremony. Like all of those who have experienced the *Naiiees* before her, the sacred cane will help Apryl walk when she gets old and the feathers and ribbons that

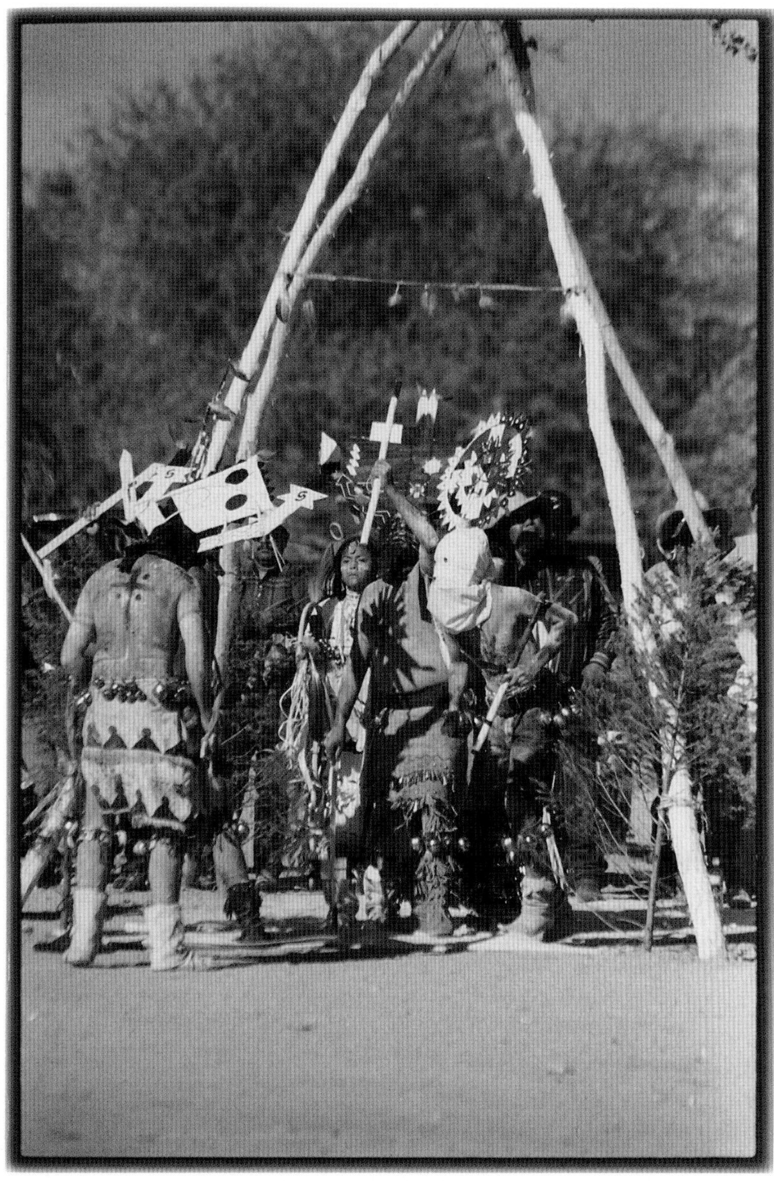

adorn it will give her a good disposition; the feathers to protect her from illness, the ribbons symbolizing the four cardinal directions, night and day, the earth and the sun.

The second day began when the men started to chant at dawn, singing the *goh jon sinh,* the Songs of Great Happiness. Kneeling on buckskin with her palms towards the rising sun, Apryl's movements signified her entry onto the path of womanhood and re-enacted the moment of Changing Woman's union with the Sun. Her Godmother then massaged her so that Changing Woman's grace would shape and influence her life. *Gish ih zha ha yinda sle dilihlye,* She runs around the cane, followed, whereupon Apryl ran around the sacred cane in four directions to ensure a long life; running to the east, south, west and north – each direction representing a stage in life, a journey others were welcome to follow. Food was then passed out so that the people will never go hungry and then, on the evening of the second day, the Crown Dancers appeared.

nja njleesh
she is painted

The Crown Dancers represent the *Ga'an,* the Mountain Spirits, the sacred emissaries of the Giver of Life, who were sent long ago to teach and protect the Apache people. During the Night before dance, *Bitil tih,* the Crown Dancers blessed the ceremonial grounds and Apryl followed in their footsteps.

As on the previous days, the third was guided by the *Di'yih,* the medicine man. Again the men welcomed the dawn with the ceremonial songs. Just as it has always been for those who undertake the Sunrise Dance, on this day Apryl received the power of Changing Woman, *bakoh di'yih,* when she was painted from head to foot by the Crown Dancers and her Godfather with a mixture of pollen, corn meal and stones ground from four colors. Inside the sacred tipi, a willow frame structure replicating the dwelling of Changing Woman, Apryl was blessed and protected from all four directions and she danced through the tipi several times so that she too would always have a home. With her Godfather and the Crown Dancers she blessed the people and they in turn blessed her and the day concluded with an exchange of food and gifts.

At dawn on the fourth day more prayers and blessings were shared until the *Naiiees* or Getting her ready – the sacred path to womanhood that recreates the story of Changing Woman and Apache creation – concluded when Apryl was undressed by her Godmother.

"... the *sacred path* to womanhood that recreates the story of *Changing Woman* and Apache *creation* ..."

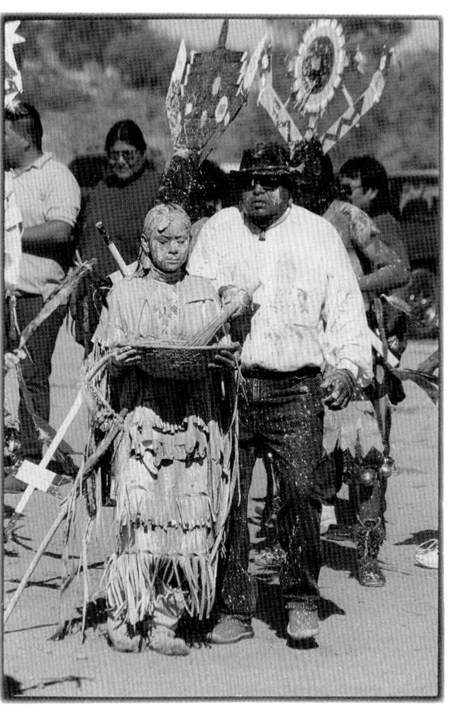

Apryl Marie Chato is Yellow Pollen Clan (Apache), and born for the Tangle People Clan (Navajo). Along with her parents, Olivia Cassadore and Mel Chato, Apryl resides on the White Mountain Apache Reservation in Whiteriver, Arizona.

ba koh di'yih

she can perform miracles

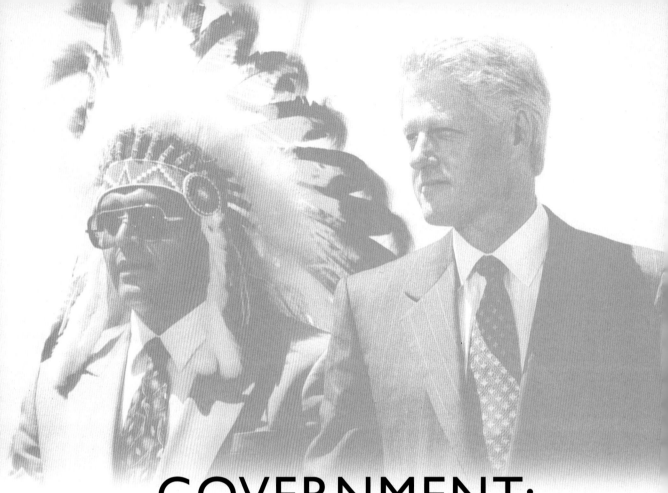

GOVERNMENT:
of, by and for the people?

Kenneth Reels, Chairman – Mashantucket Pequot Nation.
Harold Salway, President – Oglala Lakota Nation.
Chad Smith, Principal Chief – Cherokee Nation.
Raymond Stanley, Chairman – San Carlos Apache Nation.

Kenneth Reels.

Harold Salway.

Chad Smith.

Raymond Stanley.

Each of the elected leaders featured held their respective offices when the interviews for 'We, The People' were conducted.

RAYMOND STANLEY

tribal chairman – San Carlos Apache *nation*

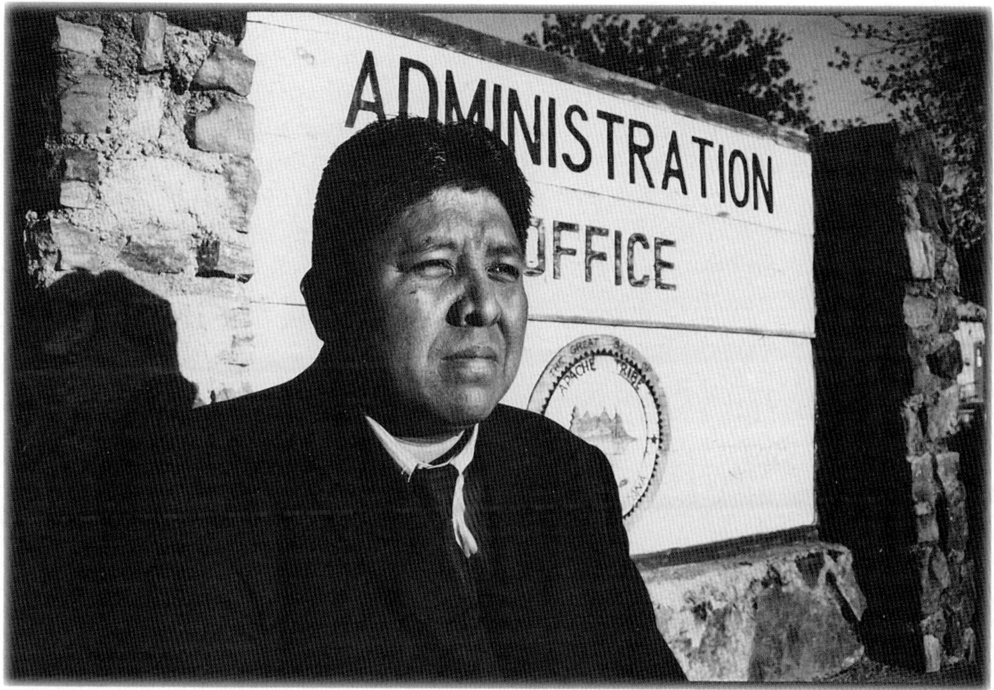

The enactment of the Indian Reorganization Act [IRA] in 1934 brought a measure of recognition for Indian Self-Determination and with it the criteria for the formation of tribal government. Most tribes started their present democratic processes by adhering to the Indian Reorganization Act. In a lot of ways the IRA sanctioned independence for tribes, but through treaty status and federal trust responsibility we're still dependent upon the US government and the US government still has those responsibilities toward us today. The IRA required the implementation of tribal constitutions and we rely upon the San Carlos Apache Tribal Constitution which embodies the statute for our elected officials, the control of our government, and the three branch system we operate – legislative, executive and judicial – which is similar to the United States Government. There are three forms of government we deal with; the federal government, state government and tribal government, and because of that I believe in a government to government relationship. I believe that we can best convey our concerns on behalf of our people through the democratic process.

I think that when the Wheeler-Howard Act was passed by Congress and mandated the Indian Reorganization Act, the San Carlos Apaches, like most tribes, came to view it as an opportunity to implement their own tribal constitution. However, the San Carlos Apache people didn't have much input into the decision to accept this form of government; it wasn't passed by vote, consensus or referendum because at that time the people were more or less wards of the Bureau of Indian Affairs [BIA] without any representation. Whether they realized it or not, it was for the better because it brought democracy and an end to BIA paternalism – the BIA being a federal government entity under the Department of the Interior.

Along the way issues of tribal jurisdiction were contested by the federal government and various state governments; that litigation subsequently ending up in the US Supreme Court, the rulings from which set precedents for our governmental functions within those contested areas as references to Federal Indian Law. Those decisions have significance to all federally recognized tribes. We lost some jurisdiction cases, including criminal jurisdiction over non-tribal members on our reservation and so, reflective of the governmental system, we have three courts to deal with – federal, state and tribal – and the resultant legal complexities. We have criminal jurisdiction over our tribal members but we have no jurisdiction criminally over non-Indians, not even civil, unless they consent. The Indian Self-Determination and Education Assistance Act of 1975 also shaped some matters of tribal administration.

"... *nine council members* represent the San Carlos Apaches as a *legislative* body, then there are the executive members of the three branch system, the *Tribal Chairman* and *Vice Chairman*. The executive branch is responsible for the tribe's *day-to-day* business ..."

We have a population of around 13,000 and the San Carlos Apache Nation is approximately 1.8 million acres of land which is divided into four districts. Each district is represented by two council members, with the exception of one district which has three council members; so in total there are nine council members who represent the San Carlos Apaches as a legislative body, or 'tribal council'. Then there are the executive members of the three branch system, the Tribal Chairman and the Vice Chairman. The executive branch is responsible for the tribe's day-to-day business and operation, but major decisions require the approval of the council through a special meeting. When it comes to the council body in entirety, myself as Chairman, and the Vice Chairman, automatically become part of the legislative body and we are considered to be part of the council and therefore have the same authority to vote on issues and resolutions. If for some reason a council meeting isn't possible, executive authority is granted whereby I can make decisions without the approval or consent of the council, as can the Vice Chairman in my absence.

When it comes to elections our Election Ordinance and our Constitution guides us. We are all elected independently. For example, I ran independently for Chairman and the Vice Chairman ran independently of me. Although a council member's term is four years, every two years somebody's term will expire; if for one district there are two council members, the tenure of their terms are staggered every two years so that they are not both elected at the same time. That's how the election is mandated. Running for office is similar to running for the State Legislature or Congress but on a different scale and without such distinct party affiliations. In our elections the eligible voters are our tribal members and I ran in 1992 as Vice Chairman and in 1994 as Chairman and in 1998 I got re-elected.

Passing resolutions requires the majority support of the council and that takes a lobbying effort as Chairman to get the council to support your issues as you have to attempt to overcome political differences for the benefit of the people you are elected to serve. We have a constitutionally mandated council meeting on the first Tuesday of every month where we meet with members of the public and then there are special meetings that can be called at any time with just cause and that's how our resolutions are introduced and voted upon. There's a big difference between the IRA system of government we have adopted and the traditional Western Apache system of governance; in the old days nobody questioned the chief. He had advisers but a lot of times he was the sole decision maker. Then, when the Apache people were confined to the San Carlos Agency, they were so restricted it would have been impossible to operate an open democracy like we have here today, and all of the decisions back then were dictated by the BIA.

Nationally tribal leaders feel that our sovereignty is not well respected; be that infringements by the state or federal government. The federal government can implement laws that affect us without consulting us and that infringes upon our sovereign status. In many ways issues like this lead us to the court room and the US Supreme Court has consistently reaffirmed tribal sovereignty so we see that as a form of security, although it remains a concern for tribal leaders that present and future US Supreme Court Justices are sensitive towards tribal issues. The only way to secure our position is to get Native Americans into the lower courts of the federal system and hope that some day we have representation within the US Supreme Court appointees.

San Carlos Apache Nation:

Location: Southeastern Arizona.
Land Mass: 1,834,781 acres.
Capital: San Carlos.
Tribal Membership: 13,000.
Tribal Enrollment Criteria: Blood quantum of 25%.
Main Employers: San Carlos Apache Tribe and the Bureau of Indian Affairs.
Unemployment Rate: Approximately 22%.
Core Business Ventures: Ranching, Apache Gold Casino, sport hunting, fishing, and mining (peridot on the reservation and copper in the surrounding area).
Government System: Organized under the Indian Reorganization Act.
Duration of Government Administration: Four years.

HAROLD SALWAY

tribal president – Oglala Lakota *nation*

The 1868 Fort Laramie Treaty was a treaty of peace, not a treaty of land cessation or otherwise. It was developed between one sovereign and another, the Sioux Nation and the United States, and it established a finite process of cooperation and responsibility that influences the affairs of both nations. However, the US federal government has continually impugned the integrity of the treaty; by Congressional Acts to supplant that relationship as sovereign, by land encroachment and the exploitation of natural resources, through to physical genocide – resultant from which is our contemporary situation. Today we live in a dual system: under the Indian Reorganization Act; and according to our traditional ways. It's a frustration we deal with on a daily basis, how to find the best approach to better the lives of our people while remaining a distinct, social political entity. This duality has created generations of Lakota people who don't know where they fit and in response I have attempted to develop methodologies to reinvigorate our traditional presence by establishing a Council of Elders to participate and advise in tribal council meetings from the traditional Lakota perspective, bringing Lakota eloquence of delivery into the legislative arena. We also have to contend with the State's attempts to undermine our sovereignty through its governance and fiscal administration towards the Pine Ridge Indian Reservation. As tribal president you run into this wall of frustration and the cumulative effect is oppression and suppression from the federal government which manifests itself as poverty and depression amongst our people.

I served the Tribal Government and Executive Committee as Fifth Member and as Vice President before being first elected at large as President in 1990. During that period, I saw how this dual system impacts upon the lives of our people, so when I first became President I travelled to Canada with numerous medicine men and headmen to participate in ceremonies with our Sioux relatives there in an effort to rekindle the Sacred Campfires and revitalize our traditional government. We placed some of our traditional foods that we use to feed the spirits on the fire and right away a blue flame shot about two feet in to the air before resting upon the wood and immediately igniting into a fire. This was a spiritual sign that the spirits blessed this initiative to redevelop our traditional form of government. Later, I was hired as Executive Director to develop this traditional government and to re-educate people as to how that socio-political structure was based around three disciplines; society's role and how it fits into the political structure; the governance of our people; and the role of our spirituality within that traditional governance. It quickly became apparent that the IRA government system suppressed any attempt to revitalize or empower traditional government but, in spite of that obstacle, today a lot of *tiospayes* are starting to articulate sustainability for maintaining autonomy.

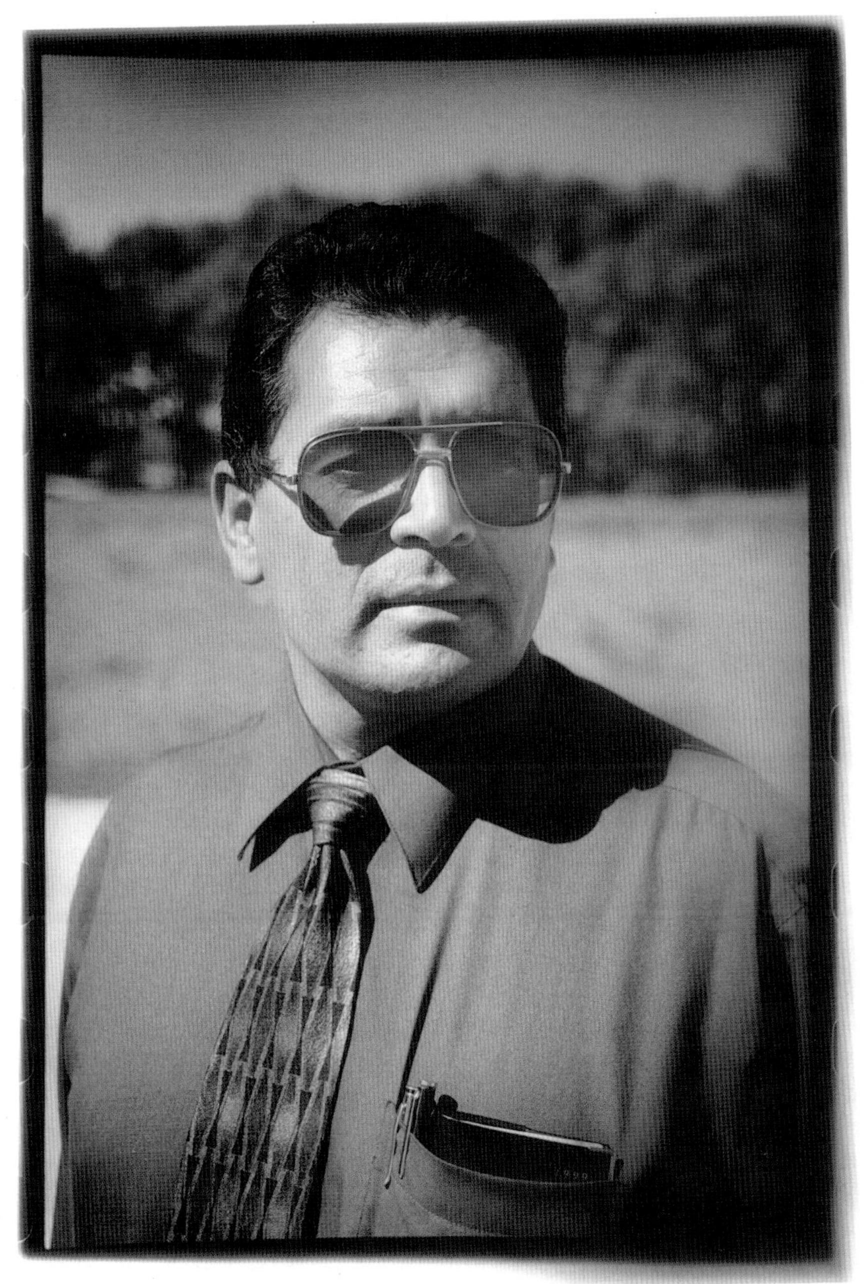

"... *I don't allow* corruption and I won't
:ondone it, but *I have seen it* and it's a daily *fight*
to maintain accountability and keep
exploitation from occurring. The IRA system *is*
antiquated and allows room for exploitation ..."

To many, the IRA system condones corruption – whereas we as Lakota people should conduct ourselves by principles that equate to representing ourselves as one with our environment. Our policy and legislative decisions should reflect that value system, based upon issues of true nationalism and sovereignty, that have good purpose for all of our people. But today we encounter people who have learned how to become politicians, not Lakota leaders, and those politicians operate in the legislative arena in accordance with the present paradigm, which is the federal government. The IRA governments were established as models of the US constitution and government, and we all know how corrupt the federal system can be. Corruption permeates throughout the institutional processes when the decision makers are corruptible and today we see that; we see tribal council members who know they can get benefits through employment and housing contracts and such for their family members or friends. I do not condone any graft or corruption but for some the temptations are overwhelming.

Some of the corruption is astonishing but it has to be appreciated that external corporations are subtle and sophisticated in their ability to exploit Native America. They go to the limit to buy people off or offer kick-backs: when one corporation wanted to develop a regional landfill depository on the northern part of our reservation I was offered money in return for my consideration, but I never accepted it and I didn't hear from them again. I conducted an inquiry into this company and found out that, around the world, they find areas of poverty and depression, then flash a few dollar bills, and most of the time decision makers accept the monetary 'contribution' and look the other way. I grew up according to Lakota beliefs and my leadership responsibility is governed by my people. In my administrations I don't allow corruption and I won't condone it, but I have seen it and it's a daily fight to maintain accountability and keep exploitation from occurring. The IRA system, in common with the Bureau of Indian Affairs and the Indian Health Service systems, is antiquated and allows room for exploitation – leaving modern, professional tribal leaders struggling to operate effectively within obsolete models of bureaucracy.

One of the primary reasons that we see such deplorable statistics and conditions here is due to a lack of funding and subsequently a lack of investment. When President Clinton visited us he brought hope with the New Markets Initiative. With the Empowerment Zone status we were granted came the possibility of over $500 million. That money could build the infrastructure of this reservation – roads, housing, manufacturing based economic stability and controlled industrial development; or whatever, with the input of the people, we could detail and develop as a model to fit within the Lakota way. Because of the political upheaval that ensued after the Empowerment Zone designation and then the change in administration, it is difficult to predict what will transpire. However, we also need to look at what natural resources we already protect as caretakers of this specific geographical area. The Pine Ridge Indian Reservation sits upon the deepest pool of the highest grade natural crude oil on the North American continent. Pine Ridge has zeolites so high in value that they are only exceeded by those found in Turkey. We have sand and gravel deposits in abundance – so we have some potential here and having such a high volume of natural resources is one of the reasons why I believe my people will not allow any type of humiliation through corporate exploitation. We have doctored people on Pine Ridge and highly qualified technical experts within our tribal membership who would return to the reservation should the New Markets Initiatives come to fruition.

Some expressed the concern that with the Empowerment Zone designation we would become little more than some form of corporate or federal serfdom but due to the aforesaid circumstances I think that is extremely unlikely. And let's be clear, I don't believe our people will allow any type of strip-mining; one only needs to revue the outcry that occurred in 1989 when strip-mining zeolite was proposed. We have a natural connection to the land and won't desecrate Mother Earth in that manner. When President Clinton came I was with him for about four hours and covered every issue I could think of, the crux of my effort being for him to recognize the 1868 Treaty and allow us to develop an economic model that is tailored specifically from our perspective. It was an attempt to get it etched into the incoming administration and supported by Congress. However, time will tell. Who can second guess the will of Congress or an incoming President's agenda?

Tribal government is still restricted by the Plenary Power of Congress, although it is limited to the IRA government and not to the people as a whole. If the people wish to come together and submit a treaty to the United Nations for a different form of government, then we are recognized as a sovereign nation. Some day soon the UN has to wake-up and hear what Native America has to offer as it has recognized other First Peoples. I see that day coming because America has become the world's melting-pot and we, the original Americans, have maintained our blood-lines, our languages and spirituality, and we are striving to retain our identities. We're durable and we're still here fighting for our land and treaty rights. For all Lakota tribal presidents and elected representatives, protecting the Black Hills Land Claim, preserving the status of dockets 74A and 74B, should be paramount. A tribal treasurer once suggested to me that we should accept the Black Hills settlement claims money to eradicate our debt. It was a very unbecoming comment as we have been fighting for years to tell the federal government that we don't want money, we want our land back. It is worrying that a tribal government official could consider that; and it is imperative to remember that along with our land comes our governance of people, which duly comes with the oversight stewardship responsibility of nationhood which maintains nationalism. Debt is endemic to most administrations because of the dysfunctional nature of the IRA tribal government, with which come the shackles of inherited debt from administration to administration.

One time I asked a Council of Elders how they defined sovereignty and they said, "It's the natural connection of nationalism and nationhood; of leading a group of people that are recognized as having the ability to govern their affairs under the context of nationalism. Therefore, you're sovereign or you're not." And we are a sovereign entity.

Oglala Lakota Nation (Pine Ridge Indian Reservation):

Location: Southwestern South Dakota.
Land Mass: Approximately 2.8 million acres (1,064,840 acres of which is non-tribally owned/allotted).
Capital: Pine Ridge.
Tribal Membership: Approximately 38,000 with 62% residency.
Tribal Enrollment Criteria: The OST requires proof of parental ancestry and the IHS requires a 25% blood quantum.
Main Employers: The Oglala Sioux Tribe (OST), the Bureau of Indian Affairs (BIA) and the Indian Health Service (IHS).
Unemployment Rate: Approximately 85%.
Core Business Ventures: Ranching, limited tourism, Prairie Wind Casino, traditional crafts and similar private sector small businesses.
Government System: Indian Reorganization Act.
Duration of Government Administration: Two years.

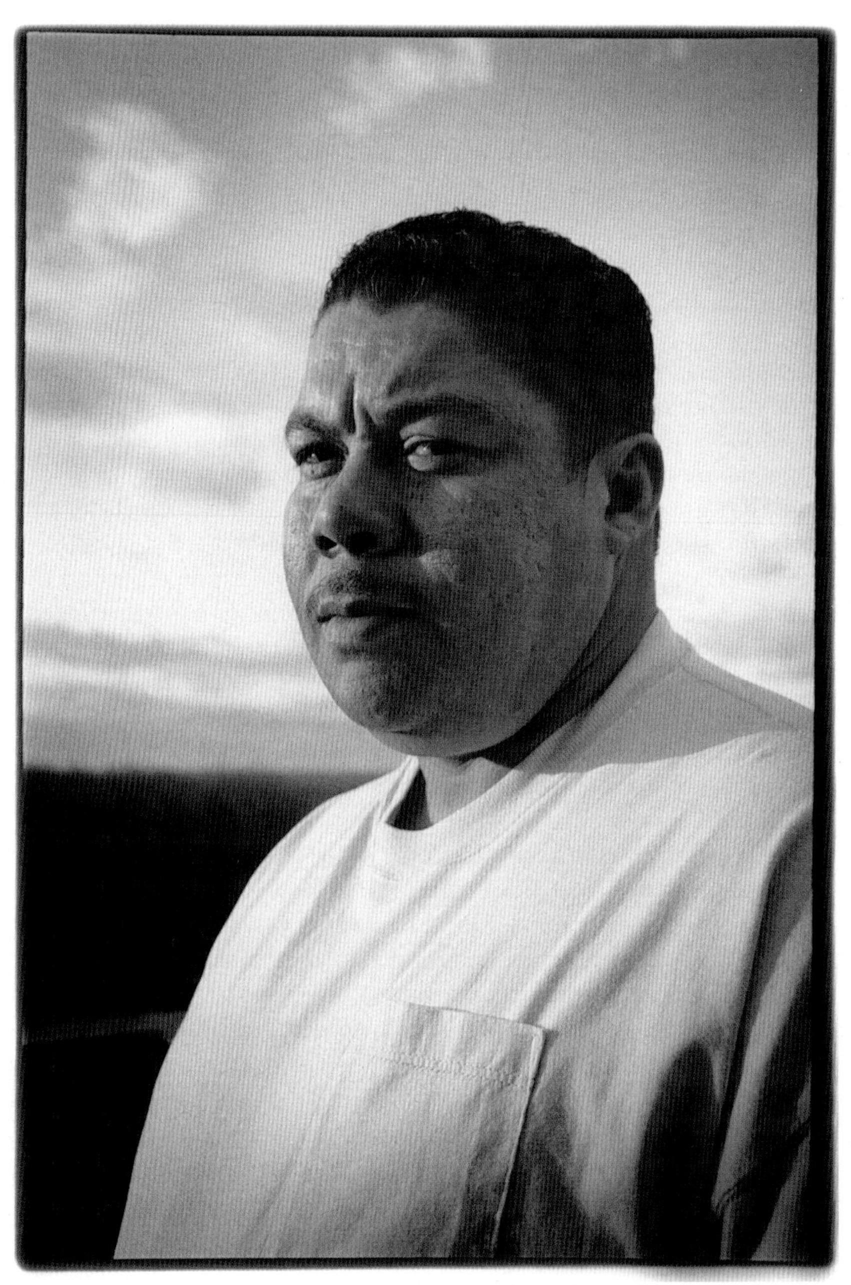

"In 1986 we started out with a *bingo hall*, which is Class 2 gaming, and nobody paid any *attention* . . . We opened *Foxwoods* Casino in February 1992 and now it is the largest gaming facility in the *Western Hemisphere* . . ."

KENNETH REELS

tribal chairman – Mashantucket Pequot *nation*

At the time of first contact, the Pequots occupied an area centered on the Thames River drainage basin. We had lived in balance with that homeland for a considerable period prior to the arrival of the Europeans, and the natural resources in that area were plentiful. Before the 1637 Pequot War, our homeland was known and respected, just as we accepted our neighbors and their respective territories. On the whole, the tribes here coexisted and many family relationships crossed tribal boundaries because of intermarriage. The descendants of the historic Pequots are now embodied in a number of modern Indian communities. The Mashantucket Pequots are one of the successors to the historic Pequots.

We originally set aside territory for the English near Mystic which, as there were only a couple of boat loads of them, appeared to be sufficient for their needs. How could our ancestors have known how many would follow? How could they have envisaged mass construction when, in our way, we lived in temporary structures; Long Houses in the winter and wigwams in the summer? After the Pequot War, we were forced into slavery and every attempt was made to destroy us and rob us of our identity and dignity. The group of survivors from which we are descended were placed under the control of the Mohegans and became known as the Mashantucket, or Western, Pequots, under the leadership of Robin Cassasinamon. The land at Mashantucket was set aside for our ancestors by the Order of the King's Commissioners in March 1665, and was granted to the Pequots during 1666. From that time onwards, I don't think that there has been a period in history when the Pequots have not had to face the threat of annihilation and the theft of our land.

At one time our territory extended from New York, to Maine, to Rhode Island, and around our boundaries were the Nipmucs, Narragansett, Passamaquoddy and Senecas. Today, the highest point on our reservation is Manton Hill and we take our young people up there so they can see what our nation once was; it's an emotional experience to see what we had and what we have left to protect. In 1983 we only had 214 acres, as of now we have 1,392 acres of land under Trust Protection. Ours is one of the oldest, continuously occupied reservations in North America.

Some claim that at one time there were only a couple of tribal members living on the Mashantucket Pequot Reservation, but that's not true – there have been a number of times throughout our history when there have only been a couple of people here! It was a matter of survival. War and slavery took its toll, after which the survivors found themselves in a position whereby they had to leave their homes to seek labor so that they could support their families, some of whom were still on the reservation. Some always stayed and different family lineages ensured that the Pequots survived. The men would be gone for two years or more, employed as whalers or farm hands, and during this period of history our women suffered a catalogue of abuse as their husbands were away. By the 1800s, families were broken apart; some joined the Brotherton Movement, a Christian-Indian group in upstate New York.

What's happening here now is the legacy of tribal elders like Elizabeth George, who protected our right to live on this reservation. Many of those who returned to Mashantucket in the 1970s were her relatives, including our present Vice Chairman, Richard A. Hayward, who was elected leader after Elizabeth George passed away. In the mid-1970s, the Mashantucket Pequot Reservation was still a rocky piece of land with no roads and only a couple of houses. In 1974 the tribe established a written Tribal Constitution. After researching the stories told by tribal elders, the tribal council became convinced of the injustices suffered by the tribe and enlisted the aid of Thomas N. Tureen who was working with the Native American Rights Fund [NARF] and who, in 1976, instituted a suit to recover lands that Connecticut had sold in 1855 in violation of the Federal Indian Non-Intercourse Act of 1790. The suit also sought to gain re-recognition of the tribe's inherent sovereignty and to establish the applicability of federal Indian land to the tribe. In 1983, Congress enacted the *Mashantucket Pequot Indian Land Claims Settlement Act*, which settled our land claim and provided federal recognition to the Mashantucket Pequot Tribe and funds for economic development, which progressed with our purchasing a pizza restaurant and initiating a successful pharmaceutical operation, the Pequot Pharmaceutical Network.

The Pequot way has always revolved around balance and storing enough to survive through the next season. Just as our ancestors stayed in balance with their environment, we use their lessons to stay in balance with the economy, our new environment. We're in the process of formulating initiatives to protect what we have. It's not what you make, it's what you save, and that's not just economics but your culture which is why we have cultural classes for tribal members and employees. We're saving to survive in the modern world and to retain control of our own destiny; we don't intend to lose control again.

It seems that people don't want the Pequots to control their own destiny, or to be part of the political infrastructure of the region. Mashantucket has had an ongoing political dialogue with the governance of Connecticut for over three-hundred years, but some politicians appear fearful of the tribe because we employ a lot of their voters. All we want is for this region to stay strong; everybody working together is to the benefit of all. Through investing in struggling businesses, the tribe have not only saved a lot of jobs for people in southeastern Connecticut but created employment opportunities and better working environments. In 1986 we started out with a bingo hall, which is Class 2 gaming, and nobody paid any attention. At the time, the Mashantucket Pequot Nation was unable to fund the construction of the bingo hall, but with loans and support from the Penobscot Indians of Maine and a local contractor, we opened it in July 1986. Then my cousin, John Holder, found a loophole in the law – the state of Connecticut promoted Class 3 gaming, slots, for a charity night once a year so, as a sovereign entity ourselves, we decided that we also had the right to operate Class 3 gaming.

It was a difficult struggle but through the vision and insight of John Holder, the council, prolonged lobbying efforts by representatives who were prepared to hear and tell our story, we eventually won our case in court. The fight with the state went to the eleventh hour as some elected officials proposed repealing the state's Las Vegas Night gaming, which would have negated the grounds for our legal challenge, but they were unsuccessful. We opened Foxwoods Casino in February 1992 and now it is the largest gaming facility in the Western Hemisphere; over 50,000 people per day come to Foxwoods. Due to this success, by January 1997 employment among all of the Mashantucket Pequot Tribe's departments, programs and enterprizes was fast approaching 13,500 employees. Across the period from 1984 to 1997, the tribe's increase in employment represented a growth rate of 379,657 per cent.

The Mashantucket Pequot Tribal Nation has a constitution which adheres to the criteria outlined under the Indian Reorganization Act. There is a division of powers between the judicial branch, represented by the Tribal Court, and the legislative and executive branches, represented by the Tribal Council. We also have an Elders' Council, which fulfils an administrative role in terms of tribal citizenship. There are seven elected Tribal Councilors, including the officers' positions of Chairman, Vice Chairman, Treasurer and Secretary, and these are at large positions elected by our enrolled tribal members over eighteen years of age. The tribe's current constitution reserves total plenary power in the hands of the general membership of the tribe. Authority over the day-to-day operations of the tribe has been allocated to the Tribal Council with some specific allocations of authority entrusted to the Elders' Council.

Like any government, our mission is to look out for the well being of our citizens. We have over 600 tribal members and as a growing nation, we strive to be economically self-sufficient so that we may preserve our culture and traditions, provide for educational and health needs, and be a contributing partner with southeastern Connecticut. As a result of our economic successes, the tribe is able to care for our elders, provide tuition for our students, offer excellent benefits and competitive wages for our employees, and donate over $1 million a year to non-profits and projects of other tribes. Over a five-year time span, the tribe has contributed over $1 billion to the state of Connecticut through our slot sharing agreement. Forty-one thousand people are directly or indirectly employed as a result of the Mashantucket Pequot Nation's economic activities, an impact which aids a cumulative contribution of $1 billion a year to Connecticut's gross domestic product.

Some people want us to give all of our money away and be poor again, so that we'll be out of the region's politics and back living in trailers on dirt roads. The Mashantucket Pequot Tribal Nation has survived only through the strength and perseverance of our elders and the generations of leaders who have preceded us.

Mashantucket Pequot Tribal Nation:

Location: Southeastern Connecticut.
Land Mass: 1,392 acres.
Capital: Mashantucket.
Tribal Membership: 600.
Tribal Enrollment Criteria: Based upon lineal descent from the 1910 Mashantucket Pequot base roll and/or approval by the Elders' Council.
Main Employer: Mashantucket Pequot Tribal Nation.
Unemployment Rate: Below or around 1%.
Core Business Ventures: Foxwoods Resort Casino, MPTN Hotel Group, Pequot Pharmaceutical Network, and Fox Navigation.
Government System: Constitution consistent with the Indian Reorganization Act.
Duration of Government Administration: Three years.

CHAD SMITH

principal chief – Cherokee *nation*

In the 1700s we were located in approximately 150 social towns up and down the waterways of North Carolina and northern Georgia. That democratic configuration continued up until around the 1770s when, due to their greater numbers, the British and American frontiersmen were in the ascendancy during the border wars against us. At that time our towns were built with stockades around them and it was easy for the British or Americans to raise a militia and burn them down, so we abandoned that kind of architecture and as we did, we also abandoned the consortium style of government. As we entered into new treaties with the British and Americans the pressure mounted for us to centralize our government. Approximately fifty towns were represented in the first 1785 treaty and each signatory was representative of a town, but by 1791 that town representation was vanishing and by the early 1800s it had evolved into somewhat of an ad hoc central government. In 1829 we enacted a three-part constitution; an executive, legislative and judicial branch. An interesting footnote to our constitution is that this concept of democracy had been captured from the Iroquois by the Founding Fathers of America because the only practicing democracy in the world in the 1770s was within the tribes of North America, as opposed to the European idea of democracy; an esoteric theory the Greeks had practiced two thousand years earlier.

After The Trail of Tears we wrote our constitution again and maintained that style of government up until Oklahoma Statehood in 1906. Although a series of Federal Acts were designed to liquidate and dissolve the Cherokee Nation, in legal theory it remained. In 1906 the Bureau of Indian Affairs adopted the posture of what one federal judge called 'bureaucratic imperialism' and it served as though the tribe ceased to exist and was basically in the function of liquidating the tribe's assets. During that the period the US President would appoint a Principal Chief – sometimes for just one day – with the sole purpose of executing documents to help complete the liquidation. That continued until 1971 when W. W. Keeler successfully petitioned Congress to affirmatively allow us to elect our Principal Chief. In 1975 we enacted a superseding constitution, which was very similar to the old form of government, and since then we have been relatively prosperous because we aggressively pursued opportunities and we had the vehicle to receive federal funding: in 1975 we received $5 million in federal funding, whereas today we have $132 million.

The Cherokee Nation is a big operation but most of the money and resources still come from the federal government; right now we are 96 per cent dependent upon federal funding. In a hundred years from now we want to have accomplished three things: to be economically self-reliant; to have a strong tribal government; and to have preserved and

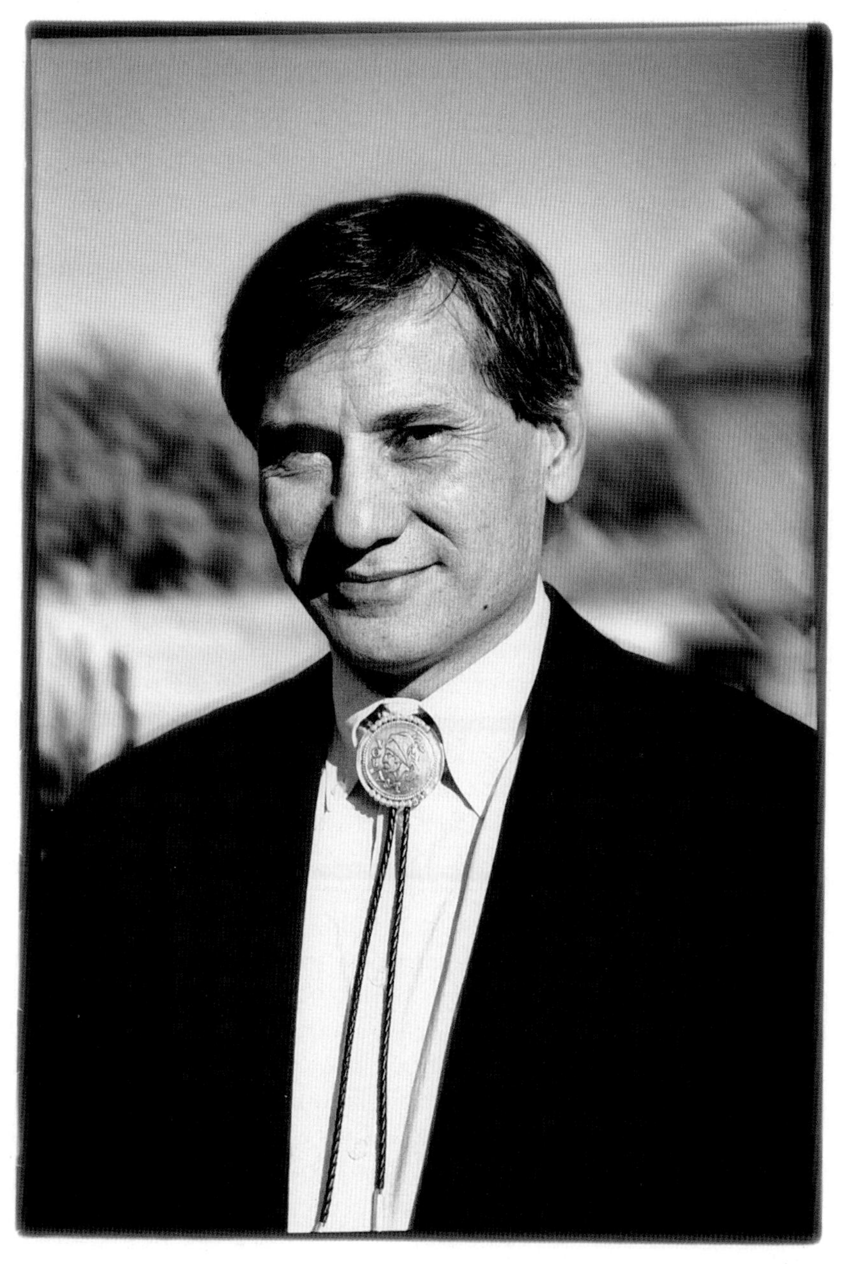

"*We need* to **reduce** our *federal* **dependency** by 1 per cent *every year* so that in one **hundred** years it *won't matter* what **Congress** says, *we will do* what **we** damn well **want to.**"

enriched our cultural identity. Everything we do now is in terms of hundred year plans to help recapture the things we had before Oklahoma Statehood. Today we have a strong, executive kind of government – we have a fifteen-person council, required to pass the laws and the budget. The Executive branch, which is the Principal Chief and the Deputy-Principal Chief, executes the laws and the courts tell us what the laws are – this is the same format the United States adopted with *Marbury v. Madison* in 1803. Within the administration we have standard administrative capacities: law, accounting, procurement, personnel and communications.

Every time we go into court it's a downward spiral in terms of losing our sovereignty, even if we win. The decline may be checked temporarily if we prevail but we never win going into court. In the global perspective, the US Congress is just a personification of public sentiment and public sentiment is driven by the media, and the media is driven by advertizing and advertizing is driven by marketing, and marketing is driven by money. Therefore, if you really want to exercise sovereignty you've got to have the muscle to do it and the muscle is money – that's economic power. What the Cherokee Nation has to do is to relieve itself of federal dependency and develop economic prowess. We need to reduce our federal dependency by 1 per cent every year so that in one hundred years it won't matter what Congress says, we will do what we damn well want to. We're never going to change public sentiment by picking on one Congressman at a time. It's a massive task and you've got to be smart enough to work your resources and smart enough to know how the marketing system works.

How can the American public understand sovereignty when the foundation for their understanding of Indians is the 1940 release of *Peter Pan, The Wild Boys Versus the Indians?* There's a poison that's been in the system since the creation of the first 'Western' Indian myth; the Budweiser commercial, the European novelettes, and then the public domain cartoons of the 1930s and 1940s. In Oklahoma, the state where there's most tribes, you see the greatest number of derogatory 'Indian' mascots for sports teams and yet find the greatest tolerance towards them among Indians. So we come back to the point about marketing and public imagery and being smart enough to control that. I think we have to grasp a more global perspective about what's in our common interests as tribes and set out a long-term plan to change the public imagery of Indians. A lot of folks say they're trite or petty, but mascot and public imagery issues have not only poisoned our people but are the main reason why when I go to court I have to tell the judge that our treaty has the same weight as the US Constitution. We all recognize that the time for Little Black Sambo passed long ago and Little Red Sambo is overdue to join him.

Our success requires strategy, thinking and looking long term. Look at your resources; inventory your resources and inventory your opportunities. If the economic and power structures start dissolving how are you going to be ready to take them over? The Mississippi Choctaws are a phenomenal model. In 1970 that area was the heart of abject racism, the social hierarchy being whites, blacks, dogs and then Choctaws. Today, because of entrepreneurial vision, the Choctaws run that county and those crackers are now working for the Choctaws and the county is dependent upon them. It was an economically desolate place but the Choctaws figured out ways to bring tourism and industry in and they leveraged federal programs and the same thing could happen elsewhere. What you have to do is get a more global view.

Superficially these 'grandmother societies' and people who claim to be Cherokee but aren't, are offensive. But I think we need to re-evaluate it and bring clarity to our understanding of their motivation; I could speculate that there's a cultural void in America and that's why these people pursue this identity but the long and the short of it is that we might be able to use this energy to the tribe's advantage because there are some good-hearted people who claim that their great-great-grandmother was a Cherokee princess! Could we educate them and get them to contribute positively by lobbying for us? We should try and make it benefit the Cherokee Nation. There is only one Cherokee Nation, period. There are two aberrations because of federal policy, the United Keetoowah Band and the Eastern Cherokees, but there is only one Cherokee Nation with a history of twenty-two treaties and a respective federal government relationship. We're a government not a social club. In regard to the United Keetoowah Band [UKB], after the federal government tried to dissolve the Cherokee Nation in 1906, during the period of general unrest that followed some groups wanted to vindicate the rights of the Cherokees. Finally, these six to ten groups convinced Congress to allow a group of Cherokees to reorganize under the Oklahoma Indian Welfare Act. I think the intent was that they would organize under a corporate rather than a constitutional provision, which they did in 1950. They plodded along until the Cherokee Nation proper was revitalized in 1970 and thereafter, in 1975, the UKB basically became a dissident group to the Cherokee Nation. People who lost Cherokee Nation elections would go over there to find a home and create discord. They then evolved into a group claiming to represent full-blood Cherokees, which is not true. Congress acknowledges them but the character of it is very limiting. That the UKB gives out 'associate memberships' speaks of how weak their organization is.

We have to chart the course for one tribe and that's the Cherokee Nation. We'll be glad to cooperate with other tribes but in terms of creating a new Tecumseh style confederation together, it's not an issue. If developing a commonwealth is so compelling why aren't more diverse nations around the world uniting to do so? The biggest challenge we face is cultural extinction and unless we do something dramatic and move immediately, in twenty-five years we won't be a tribe we'll be some brown people running a municipal government. We probably have as many full-bloods now as we did in the 1830s but we've got half as many Cherokee speakers. The revitalization of our language is crucial and the challenge is to reach everybody, the mixed-bloods and thin-bloods, so our children and grandchildren will be taught our language and history. Prior to Oklahoma Statehood we had an outstanding educational system and we want to reclaim and exceed that. Fifty years from now we want the kind of autonomy and educational prowess that will enable us to survive regardless of the government that is in power.

Cherokee Nation:

Location: Northeastern Oklahoma.
Land Mass: 3,818,085 acres (inclusive of 14 counties; 9 in totality and 5 partially).
Capital: Tahlequah.
Tribal Membership: 139,000.
Tribal Enrollment Criteria: Proof of ancestry relative to the 1907 Dawes Commission Rolls.
Main Employer: The Cherokee Nation.
Unemployment Rate: 27.5% in the area defined as the Cherokee Nation out of which approximately 11.4% is the unemployment rate amongst tribal members.
Core Business Ventures: Cherokee Nation Industries (CNI), CN Distributors, Cherokee Nation Ranch, CN Visa Card, CN Industrial Park, and mineral development lease lands.
Government System: Three branch consistent with the Indian Reorganization Act.
Duration of Government Administration: Four years.

Fern Mathias

Dennis Banks Clyde Bellecourt Vernon Bellecourt Dino Butler Bill Means Russell Means Leonard Peltier John Trudell

American Indian Movement

Principals and Moments

Leonard Peltier

John TRUDELL

Whatever all went on, it was necessary for it to happen because I think it rekindled the spirit of the people. I think that the spirit was dying and then this movement came along that took shape and form in AIM and Alcatraz, but started with the Puyallup fishing rights and the National Indian Youth Council. If you go back and look at my parents' generation and my grandparents' generation everything was lost, it was all hopeless and you had to be white or just be an outcast, and that does something to the spirit. But after the stuff that happened in the seventies, that changed. I'm not saying that it was necessary for it to happen the way that it did, but maybe it was because it *did* happen, right? But either way, the deal is that if it hadn't happened I think that we would be in much worse shape than we are now.

It was a war that was fought. It was a war and there are casualties of war. Annie Mae [Pictou-Aquash] was a casualty, Jeannette [Bissonnette] was a casualty, Joe Stuntz was a casualty, Jancita Eagle Deer was a casualty, Tina and the kids [Trudell's family] were casualties, [SA Jack] Coler and [SA Ron] Williams were casualties, Buddy LaMonte was a casualty, and a lot of people whose names we don't even know were casualties of this war. But it was a war and there is no clean way that a war gets fought.

If it had really been about law and order then it would have been different, but what we're talking about was a war for our survival – and more than our *physical* survival. I think that because all of us that were involved in this war were men, so to speak, and men are easy to like and dislike because of their failings as humans, you have to take it beyond that and ask, 'What did it accomplish?' I really think that it did accomplish a revitalization of the spirit and somewhere in the course of that, in this revitalized spirit, things are still happening. There are now more spiritual and cultural developments occurring, initiatives on a tribal governmental and political level; things are more progressive but had that not happened at Alcatraz, and then with AIM and that war that was fought, then these things would not be happening now, so I think that the net result of it was good.

Casualties OF THIS WAR

A prominent figure during the Indians of All Tribes occupation of Alcatraz, John Trudell was appointed joint National Chairman of AIM at the Movement's 1973 conference at White Oak, Oklahoma.

Russell MEANS

One of the things that brought us to South Dakota and Nebraska was a call I received from Birgil Kills Straight, who told me about the death of Raymond Yellow Thunder and that Yellow Thunder's sisters needed help because the local authorities, the BIA, and the FBI, wouldn't do anything for them and they had nowhere else to turn. I told him, "All of AIM is going to this urban convention in Omaha, Nebraska, and I'll bring it up there and see what we can do". I asked him to either come down himself or send a representative to fully explain what had happened and Severt Young Bear came to the convention with a couple of other guys. We all met in this hotel suite, AIM and others, and Severt talked about what had happened to Raymond Yellow Thunder; how he had been victimized and killed in Gordon, Nebraska, and that his killers had only been charged with manslaughter and false imprisonment and that they'd all been released on bond. We discussed this amongst ourselves before deciding that we should take a caravan to Pine Ridge. When we announced our decision to the convention we asked, "Anyone want to join this caravan?" And people from the Omaha and Winnebago reservations asked if we would pass through there on our way so that we could explain to their people what we were doing and why, which we did.

By the time we got to Pine Ridge the caravan included a bus we'd chartered and about twenty cars packed full of people, and that was a lot in those days. We held a couple of meetings in Pine Ridge with tribal officials and town officials from Gordon, and then in a gathering at the Billy Mills Hall we announced that we were going to hold a press conference on March 1 and protest in Gordon on March 6. Before we left I asked 'uncle' Joe Pourier if he knew where we could get US flags and he said the tribe had a lot, so I said, "Good, we're going to take them with us". I'd remembered a report I'd written in the ninth grade after studying the US Navy, where I'd found out that the nation's flag was flown from the top mast so that it was the first thing you would see from another vessel, which is why the

Raymond YELLOW THUNDER

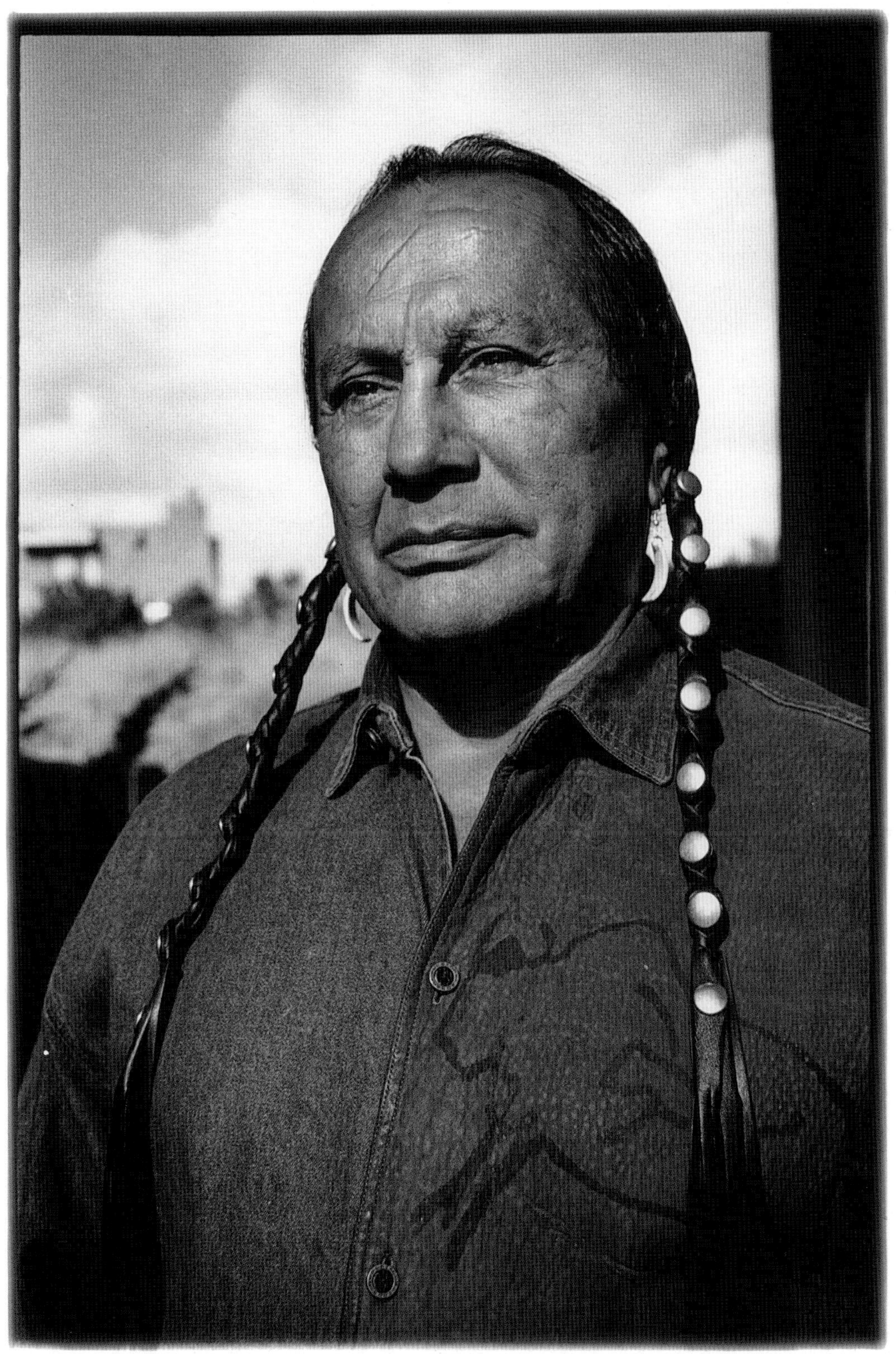

Founder of Cleveland AIM (CLAIM) and Dakota AIM, Russell Means arguably became the most outspoken and widely recognized AIM leader and the focus of the media's attention during many of the Movement's most significant engagements.

international distress signal is a ship's national ensign flown upside down. I told the group that, "We, the Indian Nations, are in distress so let's get all the US flags we can and wear them upside down". Of course, Gordon is a typical border town, about thirty miles southeast of Pine Ridge, and as we drove in there they had flags on telephone poles, light poles and some people even had flag poles in their damn yards! So there was no shortage of flags for us, even though our caravan was now one hundred cars strong.

Now this is 1972 in virgin America and they'd seen on TV how hippies had desecrated the American flag in the anti-war movement but they hadn't seen it in South Dakota or Nebraska; it was revolutionary in those days when hippies wore the US flag on the seat of their pants, and white people would beat up white kids as traitors for doing that! It still boggles my mind that human beings who have this brain can have an allegiance to a piece of cloth! They will kill for that piece of cloth, they'll cry over it like it's alive, and it's a goddamned colored piece of cloth! They don't do that with their shirts, they know when their shirts are no longer of service and they throw them away and so now they should throw their flag away as it's no longer of service. In fact, that's what the hippies of the United States were proclaiming in those days; the youth were telling their fathers and mothers and the rest of the world that this US flag is a piece of shit, it's a lie, and should be thrown away.

When we got into the center of Gordon somebody had arranged for a flatbed truck and parking in an empty lot so we used it as a stage and held a rally there, which is when we decided to march on city hall to seek justice for Raymond Yellow Thunder and for other Indian victims of uninvestigated crimes there. The mayor said, "Four of you. We want to meet four of you in the basement." I looked around and we had about one thousand Indians there. "Bullshit! You're going to meet with the Indians." We all crowded in, I mean we packed that basement, and the sheriff and the mayor were squeezed up against a table they'd set-up. Our people flooded upstairs and we took over the entire building and kept it for three days. The sheriff let me wear his hat and I did an interview on CBS national news wrapped up in a flag with the sheriff's hat on!

If you can imagine Pompeii, how after the lava was stripped away even the meals were preserved, well that's what it was like in Gordon, Nebraska. "Oh my God! The Indians are coming." White people in this country don't know anything about Indians except what John Wayne and John Ford taught them in the forties and fifties – that we were painted savages. Well, here we come! Long hair and beadwork, coming in with a drum – a bunch of 'real Indian' looking Indians. These people in Gordon actually left their homes! Some didn't even close their doors, they left breakfast on their tables and panicked and left – another glorious moment in my life. To me that was unbelievable; if we were that scary to them then that must be the reason that they hate us – because they fear us. In my experiences with the American Indian Movement, whenever the white man sees an Indian he puts a zero next to him and multiplies everything by ten, just like Custer did.

After we had taken over the town the Gordon city council gave in to our specific demands over Yellow Thunder, and then it was resolved that a biracial relations committee of local Indian people and town officials would be established to work towards racial harmony, monitoring racism in Gordon and ensuring that the local newspaper gave fair and accurate coverage to Indians after the 'it never happened' line of swill it produced about Yellow Thunder. That was Raymond Yellow Thunder in a border town in 1972, and now the same thing is happening thirty years later. Martin, South Dakota, is a white town on the Pine Ridge Indian Reservation built on land they took from us illegally, and in 1995 a white man shot an Indian in the back eleven times. The guy had to reload to keep shooting from three or four feet, and yet they were considering charging him with manslaughter! Twenty-three years after Raymond Yellow Thunder we're protesting again in the same neighborhood. It was wintertime and snow was falling and I looked over at my son who was holding his daughter and I said to myself, "Wait a minute. I protested in 1972 to stop this kind of frontier mentality so that my children – let alone my grandchildren – wouldn't have to go through this." I didn't join the American Indian Movement to win any popularity contests; in the seventies five attempts were made on my life and I went to prison so that this wouldn't happen again and so my children wouldn't have to face it, but it continues in America. Everywhere Indians live there are on-going serial killings called 'deaths by exposure'.

The protests over what happened to Yellow Thunder and our action in Gordon was what motivated Indian people on a national basis to start taking care of themselves. There's a post-Colombian prophesy that said there would be a spark in the south that would turn into a flame and engulf all of the Americas. I looked for that spark from Mexico south and all of a sudden I realized that the old-timers among my own people always called going south, traveling up; if they were going from Pine Ridge to Denver they'd say, "Let's go up to Denver". So I figured out that the white man has always looked at the world upside down and we're actually in the south. The American Indian Movement was that spark and the flame has started. Indian people in the entire hemisphere from the jungles of Brazil to above the Arctic Circle are now clamoring for self-determination and we're not finished yet, this is the beginning. It just blows me away that I got to be a part of the spark.

Vernon BELLECOURT

When Terry Booth resigned as President of Call of the Council Drums in Denver, I took over. In a meeting soon after that I said, "I think the Call of the Council Drums is philosophically aligned with the American Indian Movement and so I'm thinking of leaving and starting a chapter of AIM". Everybody said that instead of breaking up we should just change our name, so we did and that's how the American Indian Movement got started in Denver. In the meantime I had heard of Alice Black Horse, an elder who had walked into Washington, DC with Dr. Martin Luther King. So I went to look for her at a powwow organized by the White Buffalo Council, a group run by Chuck Trimble who was on the Mayor of Denver's Council for Human Rights. When I got there I recognized a guy called Willis Little Wolf and I said, "I'm trying to find Alice Black Horse, is she here?" He pointed her out and so I walked over to her. "Mrs Black Horse, my name is Vernon Bellecourt. I'm the brother of Clyde Bellecourt and I'm wondering if you've ever heard of the American Indian Movement?" She was looking down, doing quill work. "Yeah, I heard about the AIMs. I heard about that. That's good," she said. "Well I'm thinking of starting an AIM chapter out here", I said. "I'll help you", she replied, and that's all she said.

By September 1972 we were preparing for a meeting at the Albany Hotel in Denver. We were bringing in the Indian leadership from across the country and out of that meeting came The Trail of Broken Treaties. Alice Black Horse, Rod Skenandore and I were sitting there talking about The Trail of Broken Treaties and the campaign to follow. We wanted something to put on a bumper-sticker and Rod Skenandore, who was an artist, said, "I'll do a nice eagle feather but let's do something different here". As slogans we already had 'AIM for Unity', and 'AIM for Freedom', so I said, "Why don't we say 'AIM for Sovereignty'?" So we decided to order 1,000 'AIM for Sovereignty' bumper stickers and held a meeting to show them to our board of directors. Vivian Locust looked at us and said, "Where did you get this communist phrase?" "Well," I said, "you've got to look in the dictionary." But that's how confused our people were then, they thought 'sovereignty' was communist rhetoric. The three of us that day, Alice Black Horse, Rod Skenandore and I, started the contemporary sovereignty movement.

Trail OF BROKEN TREATIES

Vernon Bellecourt co-founded Denver AIM in 1972 and went on to become the American Indian Movement's National Representative and head of the Movement's internal security and intelligence.

The Trail of Broken Treaties to Washington, DC, was billed as one last effort to bring about peaceful, corrective change. Our people started to arrive in Washington on November 1, and I think we got there the next day. Despite what had been planned in advance, what awaited us was the rat infested basement of St. Stephen's Church, and we declared that we weren't going to stay there and perpetuate the poverty syndrome endured by a lot of our people in their everyday lives, and so we decided to go to the Bureau of Indian Affairs as the 'Great White Father' was supposed to take care of his wards! We went there to challenge them and Louis Bruce, who was Oneida, and the Commissioner of Indian Affairs, welcomed us into their auditorium and before the day was out we decided that we were going to stay. Then, while we were securing the doors, some of the federal guards started beating some of our people and that's when we barricaded the building and started that whole take-over. We were under siege for seven days in the BIA headquarters, surrounded by Federal Marshals, the FBI, CIA, and Lord knows who else.

Frustration, coupled with the fact that we already had agent-provocateurs infiltrating the Movement, resulted in a tremendous amount of destruction to the BIA building and their records. Carter Camp led an effort to try and burn the building down without any regard for what would happen to the people in the building or whence they left the building. I was woken-up after not sleeping for three or four days by people running in shouting, "Oh my God! They're trying to burn down the building!" And I personally went and put two or three fires out. Then a few months later in Custer, those same people tried to burn that community down. So we saw that pattern and the roles of agent provocateurs develop on the Trail of Broken Treaties.

By the time our negotiating team met with the White House staff to resolve the siege, Nixon was already ranting and raving because the Presidential election was upon them and they were already trying to cover-up Watergate. Nixon directed John Wesley Dean to contact the FBI, the Justice Department and other agencies, to develop dossiers on those of us they thought were leaders of AIM, and our names are listed in the FBI's response to him. This became a program in which they admitted to recruiting 'extremist informants' to infiltrate the Movement, individuals capable of extreme actions who they characterized that way because they didn't want to say that they were FBI agents.

The Trail of Broken Treaties negotiating team was led by Robert Free and eventually they came back with an old used black brief case stuffed with $66,650, mostly in $100 bills. But here's what I wanted to do when they brought it back; I said to the leadership that we should take those $100 bills, crumple each one of them up, and take them out onto the sidewalk and burn them in front of the world – burn that $66,650 and tell the US government that there's no deal and restate our objectives, the implementation of the Twenty Points document we had presented. That didn't happen but because of the Trail of Broken Treaties we saw the American Indian Policy and Review Commission established, which was a four-year study that led to the abolishment of the BIA as we had known it.

Dennis BANKS

My feelings on that first day when we went into Wounded Knee were, *aaah*! I was having heart palpitations because of the adrenalin that was just racing through my body and it was almost like I was developing small beads of sweat on my brow due to the excitement. It was so strong that I couldn't focus my attention for too long because it was *so* exciting. People would ask me something and I would say, "Let me talk to you later". I didn't want to talk to anybody because I was seeing a great event unfolding. Some years earlier, when I was in prison, I had said that I wanted to become part of a movement that was going to create change and at Wounded Knee not only was I a part of a movement, I was in a leadership role creating change – I was the primary mover and the principal founder of the American Indian Movement.

That isn't to take anything away from all of the founders of AIM who came together on July 28, 1968. It doesn't say anything less of George Mitchell or Harold Good Sky or Clyde Bellecourt or Mary Jane Wilson or Peggy Bellecourt or my cousins, Ches Brown and the Brown family, they were all there. But at that moment in Wounded Knee, I could see this great event unfolding and it was like my dream come true: I wanted to be part of a movement, I wanted to create change, and here I was on the eve of a most significant event in Native American history and I was at the center. My name, Nowa Cumig, means in the center, and there I was. I didn't want to talk to anybody, I just wanted to absorb it and embrace it. I wanted to just bask in that sun and I wanted it to give me power. I wanted to think about what I was going to do and what my role needed to be. "What should I do?" And then I realized that the Creator had given me this opportunity, the very wish that I'd had in prison, and said, "Here it is. Now take it. We want you to be strong. We want you to be strong in your delivery. We want you to be strong in your words. We want you to lead this moment." And that's what I felt. It made me feel so good and I have never experienced that feeling ever again. Maybe I will in another set of circumstances where I must step into another role as an elder or as a spokesperson and deliver it again.

WOUNDED KNEE *Liberation*

I didn't want it to end! I didn't want Wounded Knee to end. It was sad because Buddy LaMonte and Frank Clearwater were killed. I felt sad and I questioned myself, Was it my fault? Could I have said to everybody at Wounded Knee, "Okay, let's lay down our weapons today and let's go in". Could I have said that? Yes, I could have said that, and Buddy LaMonte and Frank Clearwater would be alive today. I think of things like that but I also know that we needed to stay there to tell the government that we had every right to be there and that we would fight. I personally felt stronger, and I felt stronger as a leader on the last day. I was barking orders, telling people what to do, giving directions and providing answers. "This must happen, that must happen. We are all going to be having high bail so this person must get bailed out first, then try and get this person bail money second, and we need this person in the field." I felt strong but I also felt sad that it was coming to an end, and I felt sad that Buddy and Clearwater had been killed.

One of the worst moments of my time in the American Indian Movement was inside Wounded Knee when Buddy LaMonte was killed. That was the first death that I felt that I was responsible for, the second was Pedro Bissonnette, and the third of course was Annie Mae's death. Buddy was at war, he was killed in action at Wounded Knee, and as a principal leader of the American Indian Movement I felt responsible for his death. I felt questioned by it. Pedro Bissonnette was a warrior and a personal friend of mine. After Wounded Knee the government wanted to separate Pedro's trial from ours and they wanted him to inform against the American Indian Movement but he said, "No. I will defend the Movement." He said no to the government's plan. Annie Mae Aquash did battle against a very powerful enemy, she did battle against the government of the United States. She was at Wounded Knee not as a cook or a waitress, she was there as a combatant; she was there as a fierce soldier and she was there as a sensitive mother, aware that her life would be snuffed out and that her children would never see her again.

AIM understands the language of murder, we understand the language of prisons and we understand the language of pain, deep pain, but we never dwell on it, we move forward. Sixty-four people of the American Indian Movement were killed – gunned down – through 1973, 1974 and 1975; we stop to remember them, offer prayers, and we move on. We still keep with us the memories of those who were killed, of Buddy LaMonte, Frank Clearwater, Annie Mae Aquash; we remember them all the time, and now we are adding to that list of people those were killed in the 1990s in Rapid City, in Mobridge and elsewhere. Nothing has changed apart from the names of the victims. We were in Rapid City thirty years ago trying to get them to change the curriculum and history, but nothing changed. We offer our prayers and songs and then we move on. We can't dwell on why they were killed.

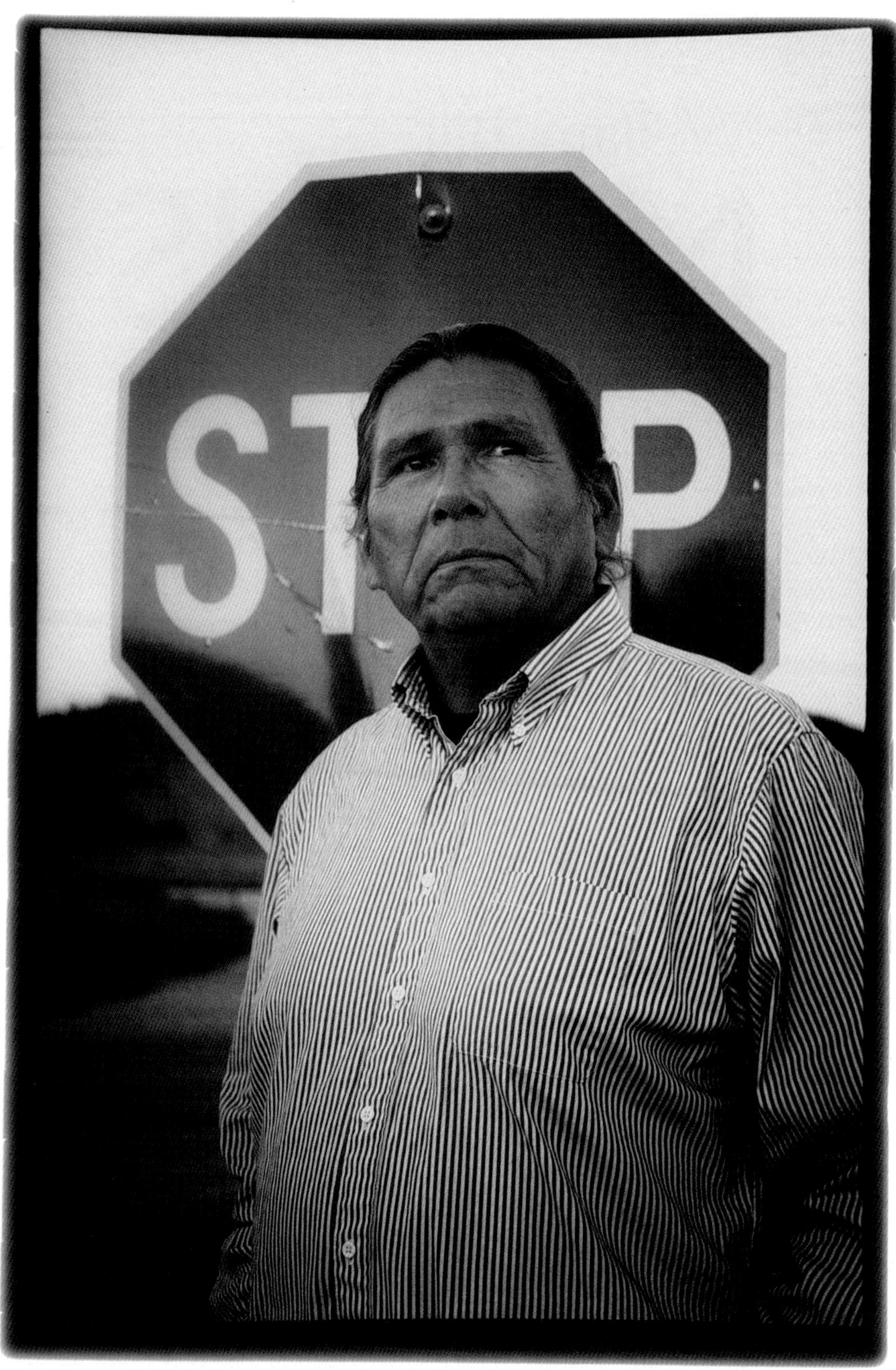

Co-Founder and National Field Director of the American Indian Movement, Dennis Banks first established AIM in Minneapolis/St. Paul alongside Clyde Bellecourt and with the support of attorney Douglas Hall and Twin Cities Black Panther's advocate, Matt Eubanks, all of whom had served with the anti-poverty program, Citizen's Community Centers (CCC).

William 'Bill' MEANS

The International Indian Treaty Council (IITC) was founded in 1974 at a historic time in the evolution of the American Indian Movement, when over five-hundred people were on trial for various incidents that came out of the Wounded Knee liberation in 1973. The so-called 'leadership trial' in St. Paul, Minnesota, in which the two defendants were Russell Means and Dennis Banks, was until recently one of the longest trials in the history of the United States. It was a very public trial in terms of local, national and international media coverage and it really brought Indian people to the forefront, not only nationally but internationally. As a result we undertook a lot of speaking engagements and organizational meetings in and around AIM because people were constantly coming into town as either witnesses, or organizers for political and financial support, not only for the trials in St. Paul, but those that were taking place in Sioux Falls, South Dakota, and Lincoln, Nebraska. We helped to organize the Wounded Knee Legal Defense/Offense Committee (WKLDOC), a team of volunteer attorneys who represented all of these defendants, and all of this took a tremendous amount of coordination, most of it being directed from St. Paul.

When the trials started we decided that we would try and put together a conference in June, 1974, that would be an international conference where we would invite Indian people from throughout the Western Hemisphere as, for the first time in the 20th Century, we felt that Indians had the attention of the international media. We were beginning to show that Indians had not all been killed by John Wayne and our message was, 'We're still alive. We still have our culture, our way of life, our land and our resources.' We saw that other liberation movements were operating in the international community and we thought that it was time for us to enter. During and before the Wounded Knee trials we had met, or were in touch with, members of the African National Congress in South Africa, the Palestine Liberation Organization, plus various other movements in Central and South America who we were in solidarity with as we had identified an international common interest: through its foreign policy the US government was heavily involved in

Trials, Treaty Council & Faction

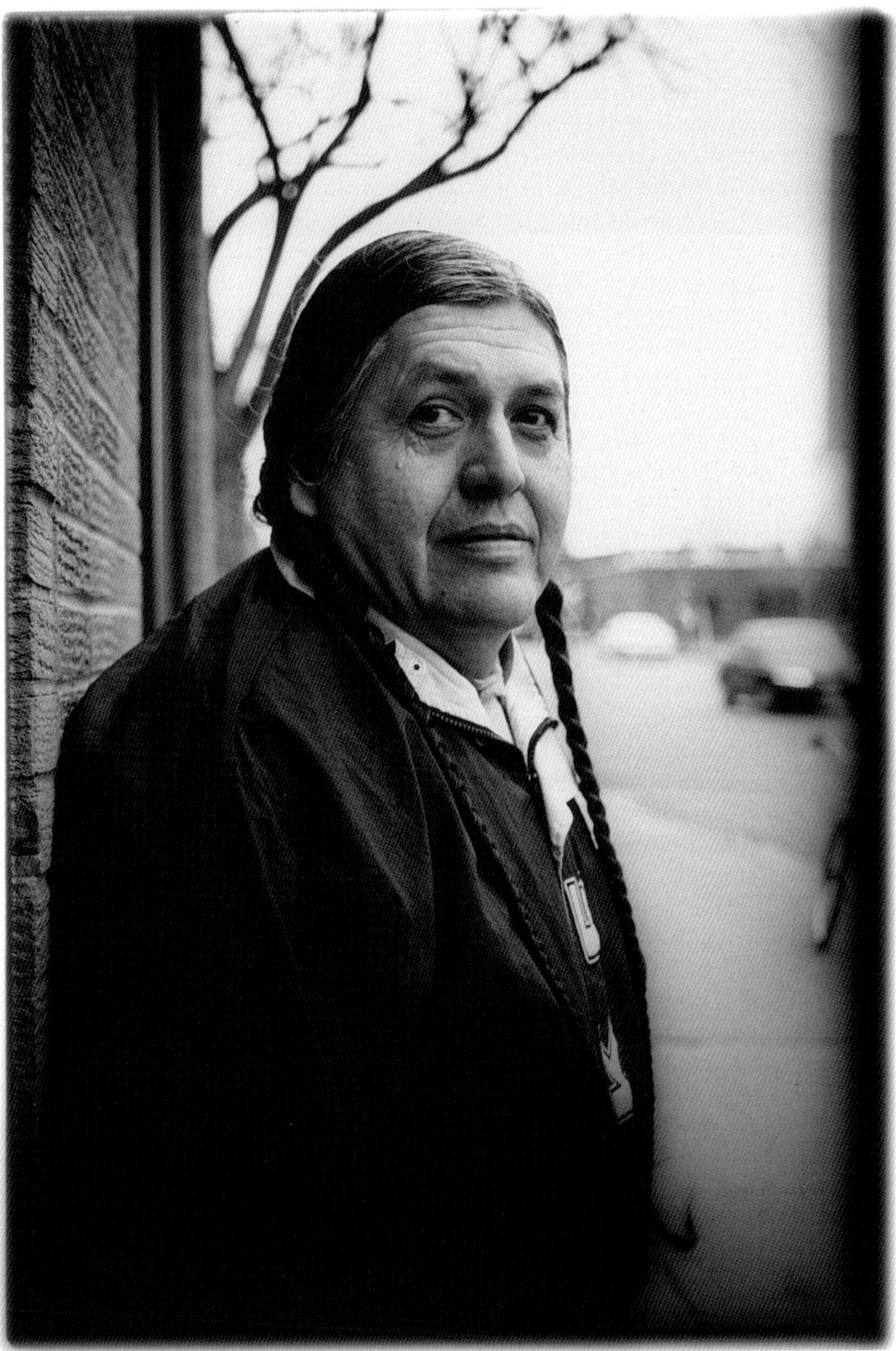

Bill Means, President of the International Indian Treaty Council (IITC), AIM's sister organization representing Indigenous Peoples of North, Central and South America, and the Pacific. Recognized as a Non-Governmental Organization by the United Nations, IITC participates in the UN Commission on Human Rights, the Working Group on Indigenous Populations, and the International Union for the Conservation of Nature.

what was happening to indigenous people all over the world. And from those meetings surrounding the Wounded Knee trials, myself and probably three or four others, were given the responsibility of organizing this international conference to bring these people together and focus on the Western Hemisphere. We decided that the Standing Rock Reservation should be the location for the conference as it was one of the few places at that time that had a very progressive tribal administration; most of the time in the history of AIM we had a very adversarial relationship with tribal governments. When the time came, in June 1974, over five thousand people gathered there in Standing Rock Sioux Country for the '1st International Indian Treaty Council'.

There were always certain factions within AIM but one consequence of the Wounded Knee trials was that some people moved further apart; either they were tied up in court, or members of the leadership were, and unity suffered. I always tried to steer clear of the factionalism and I was able to do that because of the fact that I lived in Rosebud; most of my brothers lived at Pine Ridge, the Bellecourts lived around Minneapolis, Carter Camp and his group were in Oklahoma, and Dennis Banks was all over. So in terms of people who may have been considered AIM leaders, Crow Dog and myself were pretty much isolated being down in Rosebud and so I was able to keep from getting a label. Of course, my name is Means so everybody naturally assumed that Russell and me were together, but I was good friends with Clyde and Vernon [Bellecourt], I remember Peltier kind of had a group, and basically I was able to move amongst all of the factions. Like the day the incident happened with Peltier at Oglala: I was at Banks's trial in Custer and the governor of South Dakota had the highway patrol ask me and Dennis if we would fly in the governor's plane to Pierre to meet him. We agreed and so they took a recess from Dennis's trial and brought the plane in and flew us to meet the governor. The first thing we were asked was, "Did AIM just declare war on the State of South Dakota?" And we said, "What's going on?" Then we heard about the incident at Oglala. So that's the level it came to, people thought that AIM was starting a war against white people and South Dakota.

I remember one time before that, towards the end of Wounded Knee, when a group primarily from Oklahoma talked about making an offensive against the forces that surrounded us. They had some good, tough Vietnam Vets in their group and others who were well known for their ability to defend themselves and so this wasn't just a threat, it was actually discussed as an alternative. Militarily, had we taken the offensive, the US forces at Wounded Knee would have been no match for us because they had been trained as domestic law enforcement and we had not only been trained militarily, we had combat experience. But the voices of the chiefs, headsmen and women at Wounded Knee always said, "These people are only here as law enforcement, they are not our enemy. We're not here to kill people, we're here to defend the treaties and our land." And that was our position.

Leonard PELTIER

Whoever killed Anna Mae Aquash, whoever did the dirty work for the FBI, I think they were duped. Those guys were tricked into doing this and I don't believe that they had any personal dislike for her or just wanted to hurt her, I think these people were just mislead. There was such hysteria about people being FBI agents and we knew that the FBIs put out shit about Anna Mae. You know, you can tell an informer. I knew with Doug Durham, I just knew there was something wrong with him. I'm not going to say it's a gift or whatever but I've been able to sense it, my instincts have been real good. One time when I confronted Doug Durham I saw the look on his face and Leroy Six Toes was standing next to me as my witness. When we walked away and we looked at each other I said, "That guy's a rat", and Leroy said, "Yeah, I seen it too. He's a rat." I've been able to sense it about these people and that's why I had gone in to question Durham, but at that time he was so close to Dennis I couldn't say anything about it. Of course I told Dennis, "Hey, there's something wrong with this guy. How well do you know him?" And Dennis got kind of irritated and looked upset. Doug Durham wanted me out of there and he'd say to Dennis, "Why don't you give them some money and they can go back to South Dakota", stuff like that.

I think it was around that December when I heard that Anna Mae was dead. I was in that jail over there in Canada right around whenever they exposed who she really was and what she died from, but I believe I didn't hear about it until December. When people say that she tried to contact me, that's a lie. If she'd have tried to contact me then she would have been with me, and there's no doubt in my mind because the Indian people knew where I was; certain people knew where I was at. She would not; I mean, I know she didn't try to contact me. This is something that has to get out, out there: some of these people are just outright lying. I know it because how in the hell, all of a sudden, are they involved in this twenty-five years later? 'Oh, I know this. I know that.' Well, they didn't know shit before and all of a sudden twenty-five years later they know something? All of this information that these people are going around this country with is the same information that we had through our investigation back in the seventies. Right after it was revealed that the body they buried as 'Jane Doe' was Anna Mae Aquash we immediately began organizing and trying to get an investigation going, and all of that evidence that we uncovered from that time is what these people are going around the country using.

Everybody has their own agendas now. As the years go by with these so called brothers of mine, these Sun Dance brothers, I imagine that there's some jealousy about the symbol that I've become, but one of the things I want them to know is, 'Hey, I'll trade you places. You can have this place.' I never wanted it from the beginning and I don't want it now, but we don't turn against our people. We don't turn against our own. This is an oath we made in the Sun Dance, this is an oath we made on the *canupa*, the sacred pipe – we do not turn against our own. And some of you guys out there are doing that, you're turning against your own like a bunch of goddamned hyenas. Because they have personal vendettas against each other and they dislike one and other, they are going around and making all of these accusations in the media to not only gain attention for themselves but to try and cause harm to a fellow American Indian Movement brother and in any place in the world that is not only an informant, in prison you would be considered a goddamned rat. And that's what they are, they are rats.

I had a guy on my visiting list who told me that he could get me out; he specifically said, "I talked to these people and they said if you can help us in any way to get a conviction over Anna Mae that they will immediately move you from this prison. The minute you say yes, they will immediately move you from this prison, give you some protection, and then it will just be a matter of time before you're released." He didn't say them by name but he had talked to the prosecuting attorneys in Denver, Colorado. I said, "Well, I don't know anything". Then he said, "You could still help us". So I sat back and I looked at him and said, "You're asking me to be a Myrtle Poor Bear then? Do you want me to make something up? What makes you think that's going to help?" And he said, "Well, with your influence, more Indians will come forward and then we could be sure that we'll put these bastards in prison". Or that's what he thought. I said, "I'm not going to do that! Your full of shit. Don't ask me that shit." I took him off my visiting list after that and if I was outside I'd kick his ass. So that's what they're doing right now and the end result is that these people will suffer like Myrtle Poor Bear did. Myrtle Poor Bear has been ostracized by her own people. Every place she goes they are continuously brutalizing her – they're not killing her, not like this here – but they'll beat her up. She has been going through her own mental torture for the last twenty-five years from her own people.

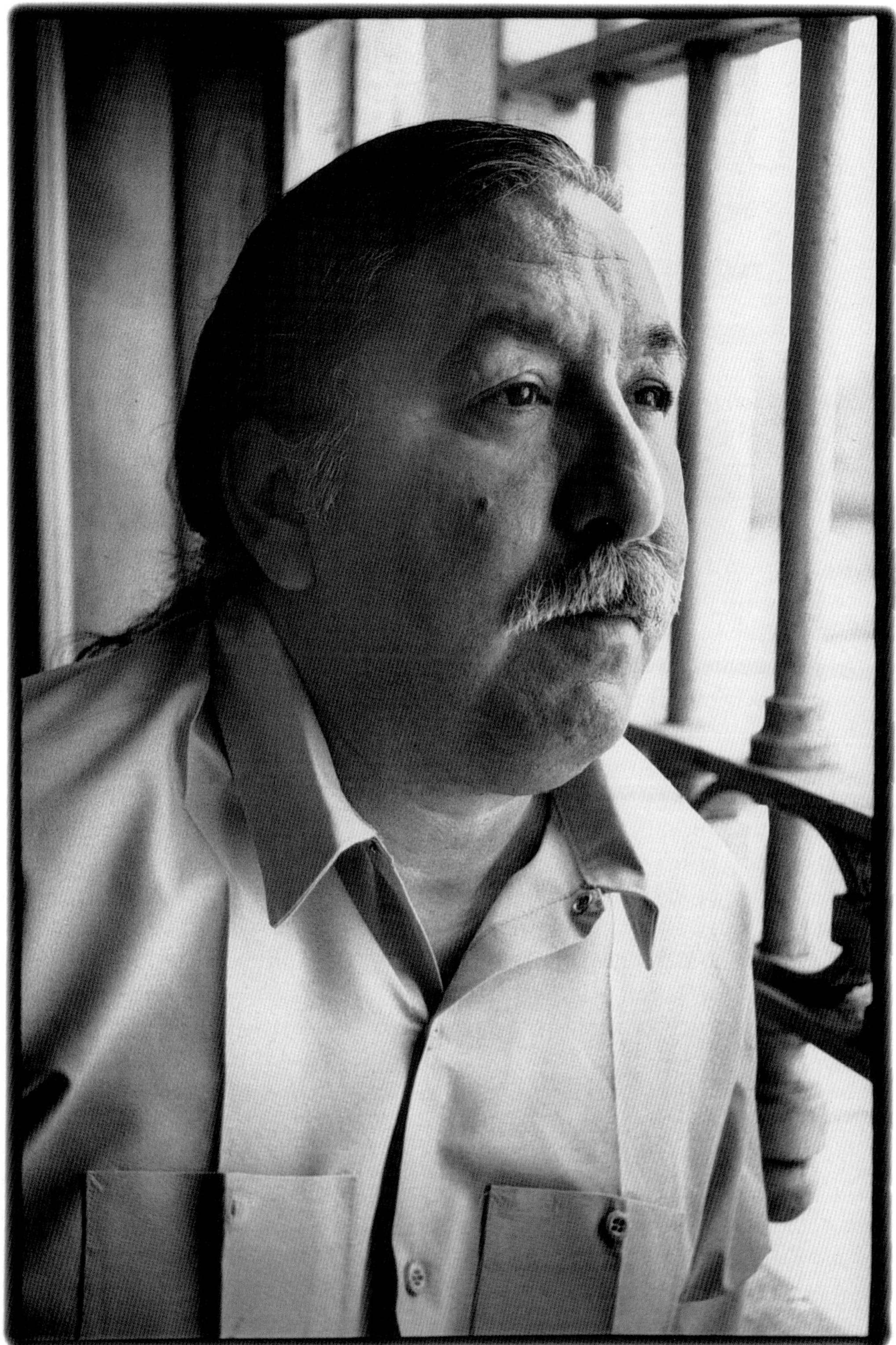

Introduced to AIM by Vernon Bellecourt, Leonard Peltier was appointed bodyguard to Dennis Banks at AIM's 1972 Leech Lake conference. He acted as security for the The Trail of Broken Treaties negotiating team and later became an influential voice at AIM's encampment on the Jumping Bull property in Oglala. In Fargo, North Dakota, on June 1, 1977, he was sentenced to serve two consecutive life terms, having been found guilty on two counts of murder in the first degree for the deaths of FBI agents Jack Coler and Ron Williams at Oglala on June 26, 1975. The incident, investigation, trial, verdict, sentence and subsequent appeals continue to arouse controversy and are steadfastly contested by Peltier's supporters.

Darelle 'Dino' BUTLER

Peter Matthiessen's book was put on hold for a long time but he eventually won that law suit and then he came out with the second edition [of *In the Spirit of Crazy Horse*]. In that edition the change in the story was that a Mr X had killed the agents [at Jumping Bull, Oglala, June 26, 1975] and it's bullshit. When David Hill moved out to Oregon that summer he started chumming around with Bob [Robideau] and although I didn't really trust him, I acted civil towards him. Then Bob told me about this story of Mr X; that David told him 'maybe we could help get Leonard [Peltier] out with this story about Mr X'. Bob wanted to know what the rest of us thought about it so I mentioned it to John [Trudell] and Nilak [Butler] and a couple of other people and we felt that there should be a meeting about it, so we called for a meeting to be held at Max Gail's place. Max Gail had a sweat there at his house, so we had a big sweat and after that we all went down in to his yard. Bob was there and we talked about this Mr X story, about all the pros and cons and everything. The meeting lasted at least an hour, maybe even two hours, and when it came down to me I just told everybody that my feeling was that it wasn't the truth and that we'd always based our struggle on the truth, and if we started creating lies to fight the liars then we're no better than them and we'd lose in the end. I said, "I can't support this because it is a lie". So after that we had a vote on it and everybody agreed that we wouldn't use that story.

We all went on our way and it was supposed to be settled; it was unanimous, we had agreed that the story wouldn't be used. I went to the Sun Dance at Green Grass that year and when I came back I went over to Bob's house in Portland and he told me that he wanted to talk to me. He said, "How about if you come back later this evening and we'll send everybody to the movies because I want to talk to you Dino, in private?" I wasn't suspecting anything so I went back that night and Bob sat me down and said, "I called up Oliver's writer and I told him that I had information that nobody else has, but that I wasn't at liberty to say it over the phone and if he wanted this information then he should get on a plane and fly up here and I would

About Mr X . . .

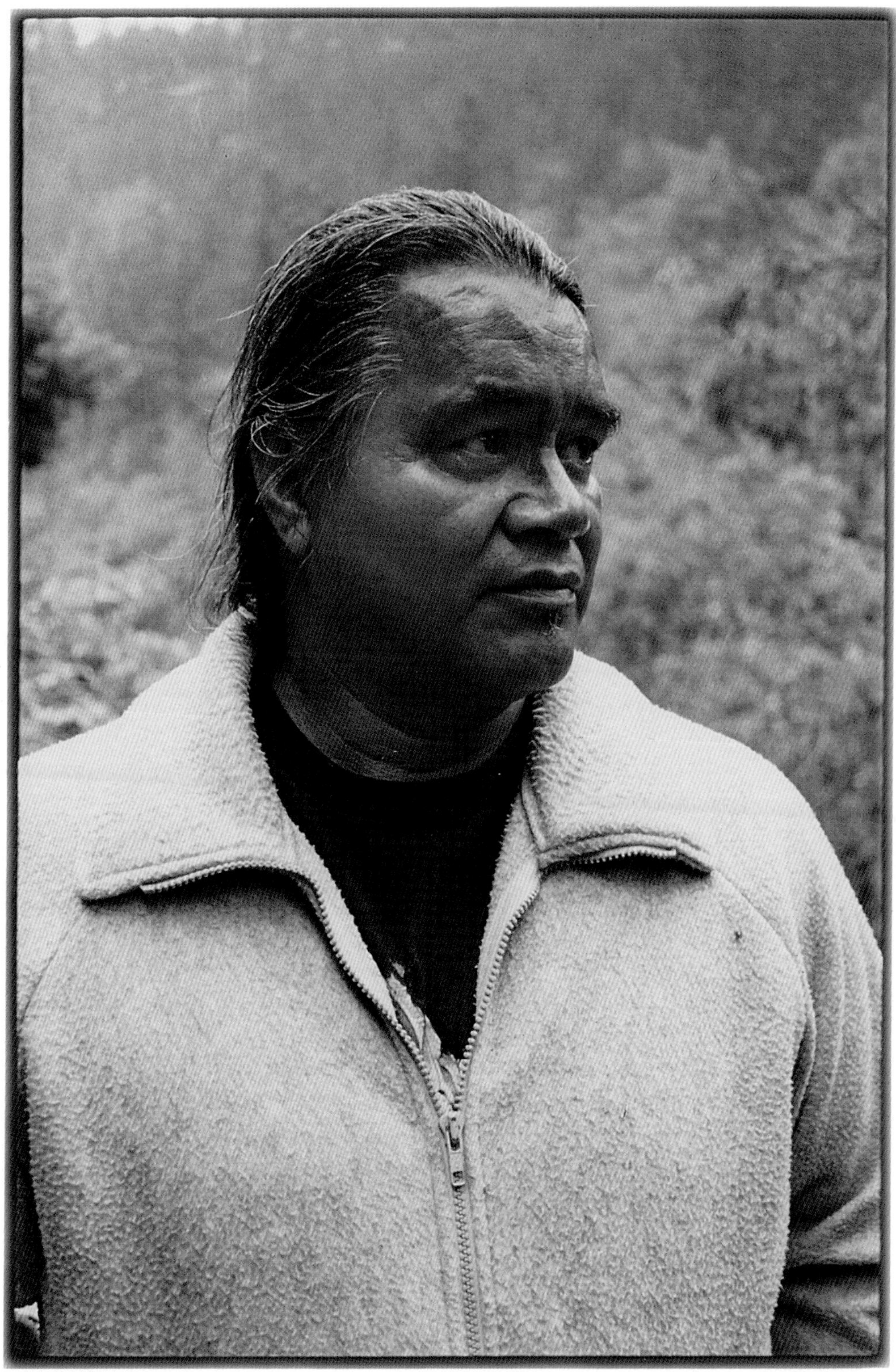

Having first worked for AIM's national office in St. Paul during the Wounded Knee trials, Dino Butler was among the coordinators of AIM's LA-based West Coast communications center before participating in the AIM/Menominee Warrior Society takeover of the Alexian Brothers Novitiate in Wisconsin and the AIM/Navajo Warrior Society occupation of the Fairchild Plant in Shiprock, New Mexico. An organizer at the Jumping Bull encampment in Oglala, on July 16, 1976, in Cedar Rapids, Iowa, he was acquitted of all charges stemming from the June 26, 1975, firefight at Oglala in which AIM member Joe Stuntz and FBI SAs Jack Coler and Ron Williams were killed.

pick him up'. At that time Oliver Stone was making a movie about Leonard. So this scriptwriter went for it, he took the bait, and Bob brought him to his house. They were there for a couple of minutes and then the phone rang and Bob said that Dave Hill was on the other end of the line and that he talked to this writer for a couple of hours on the phone and gave him this whole story about claiming to be Mr X and that he had shot the agents and everything.

The reason Bob now wanted this private meeting with me was because he wanted me to verify this Mr X story that he and Dave had given to this writer. Bob said that after the writer got off the phone with Dave, he sat down with him and he verified his part of the story; he told Oliver's writer that he and Joe [Stuntz] and me were down by the agents' cars and that this pick-up came in and that someone had gotten out of this pick-up and shot the agents and jumped back in and driven off. Since Joe was already dead he couldn't verify it and so he wanted me to verify the story because they had placed me down there with them. "Bob," I said, "that's not true, man. And why, after we all agreed that we wouldn't use this story?" And he said, "Well, it's a way to help Leonard to get out and you're either going to support this story or you're not and if you don't support it then you're not helping Leonard and that's the way it's going to be taken – that you're unwilling to help Leonard". Then I got really upset at Bob and said, "I'm not going to verify this story. I'm not going to do that. It's going against everybody else and I'm not willing to do that." And he said, "Then as far as we're concerned you're unwilling to help Leonard". So I said, "Okay then, if that's the way it is", and I left his house.

Eventually I ended up back in California. I stayed up in the mountains there for about five years and during that time, I think within a year, I sat down and I wrote a letter to Bob. I told him that because he and Dave had done that against everybody else's advice that I could no longer trust him and as far as I was concerned the Bob Robideau that I knew was dead, and I haven't talked to him since. He just kind of turned against everybody from then on and that's the way that Mr X story came up and I believe that it was just concocted to keep Leonard in jail longer. At that time Leonard's appeal was going before the Eighth Circuit Court and that's when the government changed their story, saying that they knew that they couldn't prove that Leonard was the trigger-man but that he had information about who did kill the agents so that justifies keeping him in jail – and that's exactly what happened. At that time Leonard's lawyers had gotten the FOIA [Freedom of Information Act] paper about the FBI ballistics tests to link Leonard's gun to killing the agents and how they couldn't prove anything about that gun, which cast a lot of doubt upon their whole case. The way I see it today, that is why the Mr X story was brought up; they had to change their story and that's how they did it.

Dave Hill is the one that brought that Mr X story up and so maybe he's got a hidden agenda somewhere. I think Robideau sold that story twice for $10,000 each time; first to Oliver's writer and then to [Robert] Redford's scriptwriter. In that letter I wrote to Bob I told him that I would not interfere with the Oliver Stone movie by saying that it wasn't true but I said, "I'm not going to promise that about the other movie and if anybody asks me then I'll tell the truth to them about that". But he went ahead and sold that Mr X story to Redford's scriptwriter anyway. John [Trudell] was in touch with Redford's scriptwriter and he called me up and asked me to come down there and we went and talked to him; we sat him down and told him what that story was all about so they never did use it.

When I made a public statement denying that there ever was a Mr X, Leonard called me up and asked me why I did that and I told him, "Well Leonard, it's a lie, that's why". I said, "Imagine Leonard if I'm the President of the United States and there's this piece of paper on my desk to release this Indian man who was convicted of killing two FBI agents but now he's gotten so much support that people want me to release him; but this Indian man is sitting in prison and he's saying, 'Yeah I know who killed those agents but I'm not saying because it's the warrior way and I don't snitch on my own people'." And I said, "Me, as the President, I'm not going to release you. Nobody is going to release you. You came out after that Mr X story and that's what you said, 'Yeah, I know who Mr X is but I'm not going to snitch on my brother, that's not our way'. So who do you expect to release you Leonard? Don't you see why this story was created?" But he fed right into it and no matter what he says now, he said that and that's always going to come back on him.

Peter Matthiessen also called me and he was pissed-off and asked me, "Why did you say that? Don't you know that just attacks my credibility?" And I said, "Peter, you put my life in jeopardy and you put the lives of my family in jeopardy by putting that bullshit out in your books. Why didn't you call me and ask me if that was true? Everything you said in that first book, you would call me; you would call Nilak; you would call John; you would call all of us that were involved and ask us 'Is this true?' and we would tell you but you didn't do this in the second edition. You went out and you put this Mr X in there when it was all lies." And he said, "Well, I didn't believe Bob would lie to me". I told him that I thought he could repair his reputation if he tried to prove that this was all part of a counter-intelligence program to discredit everything, and that's how he'd get his reputation back, not by calling me and accusing me. I said, "If you really care about your reputation and if you really care about Leonard and our people then that's what you will do".

Clyde BELLECOURT

The Longest Walk was conceived during the period that Dennis Banks was confined to the state of California. Dennis had been convicted on charges arising from the Custer protest in 1973, and was fighting extradition to South Dakota when the Longest Walk was planned. People who Dennis worked with at D-Q University were involved with it and I think Dennis and Lee Brightman began the walk at Alcatraz but by the time they were approaching Kansas, Dennis had lost control of it because he couldn't leave California. Dennis called me and asked me to go out and take over it for him because by that time not only had they been pretty heavily infiltrated by FBI informers, there were more mistakes than logistical coordination! For instance, they never lobbied once on the way from California to Kansas, so they had no governmental support, they had no labor union support, and no student bodies and societies backing them. Up to Kansas, they were running through all of these towns without even holding press conferences. At the time that he called me, the Longest Walk was about 95 per cent non-Indian, they had all the hippies and those kinds on the walk, so Dennis asked me to take over and coordinate it.

Ernie Peters was supposed to be heading the Longest Walk and he was supposedly carrying Leonard Peltier's pipe and somewhere along the line he was calling himself the 'chief of all chiefs' or the 'chief of ninety-eight tribes', which he wasn't – there happened to be ninety-eight tribes represented on the walk, but the issue wasn't appointing yourself 'chief', it was communicating what the Longest Walk was about and they weren't doing that. They weren't getting the word out and they weren't exposing the twenty-four anti-Indian bills that were then before Congress. They weren't speaking about American Indian Religious Freedom, the thousands of Indian women who were being sterilized in a covert government program, the desecration and robbing of graves, enforced relocation and removal at Big Mountain; none of these major issues were being addressed and highlighting those issues was the purpose of the Longest Walk. That was a sign that they were pretty heavily infiltrated

Prophesy & THE LONGEST WALK

Co-Founder and National Director of the American Indian Movement, Clyde Bellecourt first became involved in Indian advocacy groups through the influence of Eddie Benton Banai while both were inmates at Stillwater State Prison. Along with other AIM co-founders, Dennis Banks, George Mitchell and Benton Banai, he initiated one of AIM's first major projects, the 'AIM Patrol', to monitor police conduct in the Twin Cities Indian communities, emphasize civil liberty, and provide social and welfare support through the Movement's office on East Franklin Avenue.

and they weren't doing their jobs. They were sending flyers out to all of the tribes along the way but for one reason or another, that information never got to the tribes and so nobody knew what the hell was going on, or whether or not they should support the walk. They didn't even have the National Congress of American Indians or any of those groups behind them

I received Dennis's call here in Minneapolis and against the wishes of all the local people here who didn't want me to touch it, I agreed and started by organizing a 600-mile run from the Heart of the Earth Survival School, moving from Fort Snelling, Minnesota, all the way down to Kansas. When I got down there I went out to the walk's encampment and found that it really was a rag-tag operation. I started questioning people to find out when the information went out and what had been going on, and I found that information had been destroyed and there was a lot of fighting going on. I asked why they weren't stopping in any of these towns, why they weren't doing any lobbying; and why right when they were on Highway 40 there was no media exposure? Crow Dog gave Ernie Peters the name 'Long Walker' and for whatever reason Ernie refused to relinquish control of the walk; he said that he was carrying Leonard Peltier's pipe, and I said, "You can carry any pipe you want to. We have a pipe here, and this is what we're going to do." So I called a big meeting there and just took complete control of it.

At that first meeting I told the people that I knew that we had been heavily infiltrated and that if I caught anybody I thought was an FBI agent or informer I wasn't going to kick them off the walk, I was going to keep them on the walk, but that they wouldn't get to eat from there all the way to Washington, DC, and so when we got there I would just dump their bones on the steps of the J. Edgar Hoover Building. That night, about two hundred of them left the walk. I set-up an advance group and crew which went ahead of the walk to meet with all of the government officials on our route, and also to prepare the parks where we would camp, organize catering facilities and appeal for donations. From there on in, we held press conferences everywhere we went and got the word out to all of the tribes and the non-Indian support groups, and the unions. We addressed every local government, every mayor, every city council, and every state government; we went into the state legislatures and had complete support all the way to DC which is why we defeated every one of those twenty-four bills. But to me, prior to that, the walk was strictly an FBI operation after Dennis lost control.

We tried to make it a very spiritual walk; I had the advance crews setting up sweat lodges so we had ceremony and prayer with us, and spiritual leaders from other faiths joined us like the leaders of Japan's Buddhists and the church leaders who had supported us throughout the Movement. To build momentum I contacted people like Dick Gregory, Mohammed Ali, and

Marlon Brando who supported us and walked with us, along with prominent political figures. Senator Jim Abourezk was head of the Senate Indian Affairs Committee and I went into DC with an advanced crew to meet with him and he gave us a lot of logistical support. I was in his office when he was talking to different agencies and telling them what we wanted, and if they said they couldn't do it he'd say, "What do you mean you can't do it? I've got your budget right here on my desk." When we got into Washington, DC there was a big bus strike and he arranged out of a federal fund that buses from Baltimore would be brought in to bus our people back and forth, and he got the National Guard to come in and put showers up for us, supply meals and medical attention. When the National Guard first showed up some of our people didn't want them around but I said, "If anybody had told me at Wounded Knee when we were surrounded by APCs and military hardware that five years later the US Army would be feeding us I would have said they were crazy! So now we're going to accept their help."

Initially they had planned to march down Embassy Row and I said, "To hell with Embassy Row! What the hell would we march down Embassy Row for? I want to march through the Nation of Islam territory. I want solidarity with the black community who are struggling and going through a lot of suffering and pain like we are, that's where we'll have our rally." I just changed the whole scope of it and everybody went along with it. When the Longest Walk reached Washington, DC it was the largest gathering of Indians in the Twentieth Century and the biggest march since the Poor People's March. Laws were established in DC after the Poor People's March whereby nobody was allowed to erect any kind of camp there, but kids at the Heart of the Earth Survival School had put together a tipi, painted it, and then sent it to me. I'd put it up all along the way and we held meetings and lobbied in it so, when I went into DC about a week and a half before the walk arrived, I decided to put it up. In the middle of the night we put that tipi next to the Washington Monument. At that time of year up to twenty thousand people a day went through there, so that's where we wanted to lobby.

On the first morning I spotted President Carter and his family at the White House and we waved back and forth to each other with binoculars and then I waved them over. They came over and I asked him if he was going to be there when the Longest Walk arrived. He apologized and said he couldn't be there because he was going to the Berlin Wall to condemn the Soviets for human rights violations. I kind of chuckled at that because our human rights are violated every day, every treaty had been broken, and here were these twenty-four bills pending before Congress to strip us of everything we had left and yet he was going over there to condemn the Communist countries for supposedly doing what the US was doing to us!

Nee-Gon-Nway-Wee-Dung/Clyde Bellecourt, Co-Founder of the American Indian Movement.

The American Indian Movement is a fulfillment of prophecy. During the Longest Walk I looked down from a hill on North Pennsylvania and through the mist I could see hundreds of fires all around me, the fires our people were building. The prophesy said that in the fifth generation we'd be the ones to bring the drum back and the songs back, and that when we did the fires would burn again and bring the people home. When I looked across our camp that day, that's what I saw. We built the fires of prophesy, the fires Thomas Banyacya and other spiritual leaders told us about. AIM is a spiritual Movement, regardless of what people say about us, or against us. Those same people who criticize us wouldn't be where they're at today had it not been for the American Indian Movement.

The passages featured in this section are brief segments of extensive interviews taken from BLOOD SWEAT AND TEARS: INSIDE THE AMERICAN INDIAN MOVEMENT *by Serle Chapman © 2001 (ISBN 0-9528607-6-7). With previously undisclosed insights and accounts of the 'incident' at Oglala, and the persecution and murder of Anna Mae Pictou-Aquash, the book includes the thoughts, recollections and perspectives of over seventy interviewees including other members of AIM leadership, grassroots AIM members and supporters, WKLD/OC attorneys and aides, federal and state prosecutors, FBI agents, BIA officials, federal and state politicians, and local residents with contrasting experiences and opinions of the events that shaped the Movement. (In connection to The Trail of Broken Treaties, 'Mr X' and the Longest Walk, those identified within this section of* We, The People *offer their own interpretations of these episodes in* BLOOD SWEAT AND TEARS.)

Voices
From Native America

Wes Studi

N. Scott

MOMADAY

"I think the sacred is something that is purchased with sacrifice. Actually, I believe that the words sacred and sacrifice are probably related in some important way. To me that which is sacred is earned. The obvious example would be a battlefield, land that is purchased at the cost of blood, which makes it sacred. But there are other ways in which it can be sacred. Somebody has said that where words touch the earth there is the sacred, so I think it is possible to endow the earth with a sacred aspect by means of language, by means of story, by means of words."

Described as 'The dean of Americar Indian writers' by *The New York Time Book Review*, Kiowa author and artis N. Scott Momaday has created a celebrated body of work since firs rising to prominence in the late 1960s. In 1969, he was awarded the Pulitzer Prize for his debut novel, *The House Made of Dawn*, since when his honors have included a Guggenheim Fellowship, recognition from the National Institute of Arts and Letters the Golden Plate Award from the American Academy of Achievement and the Premio Letterario Internationale 'Mondello', Italy's foremost literary accolade A graduate of the University of New Mexico and Stanford University, Scott Momaday was Professor of English and Comparative Literature at the University of California at Berkeley before moving to Stanford, then the University of Arizona, and fulfilling commitments as a visiting professo at Columbia and Princeton. While lecturing in Moscow, Professor Momaday's second volume of poetry *The Gourd Dancer*, evolved, succeeding *Angle of Geese and Other Poems*. Scott Momaday's other books include *The Names*, *The Ancient Child*, *In the Presence of the Sun: Stories and Poems The Man Made of Words* and *In the Bear's House*. Of his own works *The Way to Rainy Mountain* remains his favorite

I think that in the Indian world story is one of the principal creative elements in language. People address each other in terms of story, they tell stories – that's part of the conversational mode – and they explain the world in terms of stories. Everyone does to an extent, the story of Creation in the Bible is a story, but most people in general society don't employ story or use story in that sense. For them, story is something you read in a book or you tell to your children at bedtime. They don't think of story as a pervasive element in language, which I think it is, and the Indian understands that because it's part of the oral tradition. The trick is bridging the gap between that perception and the other. I have a story which is predominantly a dialogue between God and the Bear, and the element of belief is one of the things that I mention as principal unifying information in the story. You have to believe, that's part of the contract between the storyteller and the listener. In effect the storyteller says, 'I'll tell you a story and what I ask of you is that you believe it'. You have to invest belief in it because that's part of the vitality of the story. If you don't play that game there's no point in going on, but if you do, if you will believe, then we can realize wonderful things.

I think the sacred is something that is purchased with sacrifice. Actually, I believe that the words sacred and sacrifice are probably related in some important way. To me that which is sacred is earned. The obvious example would be a battlefield, land that is purchased at the cost of blood, which makes it sacred. But there are other ways in which it can be sacred. Somebody has said that where words touch the earth there is the sacred, so I think it is possible to endow the earth with a sacred aspect by means of language, by means of story, by means of words. I think the sacred is endless. In a sense I am more willing to share my perceptions of the sacred than other people might be because I'm so concerned to convince people that it is important and so I talk about it because this is a way of enlisting the attention of other people, and the belief or investment of other people in it. But there are a lot of things that I keep to myself as well. Perhaps it's impossible to draw the line.

It does occur to me that I might be misunderstood by people who have a New Age perspective but it doesn't particularly bother me because I know that's going to happen and that it can't be avoided. The alternative is that you can't reach people, and I find that when I talk about certain things that are sacred, I get a lot of sympathy and discover a lot of agreement amongst people; their perception of what I'm saying seems to grow as I tell them what this is and that's gratifying. That's worth all the rest. That's worth the risk of being misunderstood. In a way it's taking a chance but it's a chance worth taking and I find, more often than not, that I think I can be meaningful and convincing too, on that subject. The spiritual is much more general than religion. I think it probable that most people think of religion as a system of some kind with rules and boundaries and so on, whereas the spiritual is more general and may be deeper. When you use the word religion, what comes to one's mind is a structure, whereas with spirituality that's not necessarily so.

N. Scott Momaday

I believe that the sacred goes on and, as with ceremonies, stories or songs, just because they aren't practiced or heard anymore does not mean that they aren't still there. In *The Way to Rainy Mountain* I wrote of how my grandmother was present when the last Kiowa Sun Dance was held. I think that there is some kind of spiritual information in the Sun Dance which goes on. It is so in oral tradition. I know there are mysteries involved in the retention of things; you tell a story and it may appear to die away but in my experience some of these things, many of them, have come back – even across generations – which is something that I don't understand. It's as if it goes into the blood somehow and it crops up down the way, and I think that can be said of such things as the Sun Dance. I think that information exists and that it's not beyond recovering, but I don't know that it will be recovered. The Kiowa's sacred Sun Dance symbol, *Tai-me*, is still extant and it is in the family – I think from the last official *Tai-me* Keeper who died back in the 1930s. It still exists but as far as I know, no one has the right to open it. It was exposed once a year during the Sun Dance and then when the Sun Dance died away there was no reason for the Kiowas to expose *Tai-me*; so it became a kind of closed bundle. The bundle still exists, nobody opens it, but what happened to it I do not know.

The beginning of the Kiowa's journey south, toward the dawn, from the mountains of western Montana, was a great story in itself. It must have been very difficult for the Kiowas to become a Plains people; this requires an adjustment that must be very great and maybe impossible to imagine. And then following the sun southward through that gray sea of grasses and always encountering new people and new landscapes, that's a wonderful odyssey in a way; and then to come among the golden age, to end the migration in the Southern Plains and then to be the lords of the land for a hundred years. That's a very exciting story and there are many things along the way that interest me. The Kiowas have several calendars that contain the landmarks of that journey, and in a way the calendars are the landmarks, so there are stories and events along the way and it's a wonderful epic. The whole thing fascinates me, and from the time that I made that pilgrimage there are probably a good many things that will always stay with me. I have stood on the Southern Plains and imagined that I was in the place of Satanta or Satank. That's a very satisfying and profound spiritual sense and one way to express that is to say that it moves me to prayer. I go to my grandparent's graves at Rainy Mountain and I go to the arbor where I was given my Indian name – it's still there – and I go to the place where my father was born in a tepee where that arbor stands, and I go to the place where the old man *Koi-khan-hodle*, 'Dragonfly', prayed the sun out of the ground and I stand where he stood. And that, to me, is as if there is some kind of continuum in the blood that I'm celebrating. Being there and having the knowledge, or having the blood memory of it, is a great fulfillment and this happens to me many times, especially in terms of the Kiowa's journey.

I think that in a sense nomadic is an accurate description of a facet of the Kiowa's lifestyle; you know, in the heyday of the Plains culture everything was portable and there was movement all the time, people never stayed in one place very long. They were always ranging and that was a part of their lifestyle, and I think that also still exists in the blood. I think that I am moved to rove; something in me is compelled to do that, which I think comes from that tradition. I don't think of nomadic as wandering without aim; there was some purpose in the Kiowa's movement. It was an expression of their spirit. That is what we do, pack up our camps and go to the next place.

I don't know that we can tell who, years from now, will be spoken about as Satanta is from his time frame, but I think that people in the Indian world are emerging as individuals of accomplishment. They will be talking about people we don't even know about as yet, who will have written great things or been great Statesmen or whatever. I don't think we'll run out of people to talk about, and I think there will always be people who come to the fore and make themselves very visible. We don't know who they are, but I think there's a lot of movement in that way. Heroes will emerge, and such things are always fictionalized too, they become mythic. Crazy Horse is to me a great mystery; we don't know much about him but we are willing to believe that he was a wonderful, God-like man, and that's important. We probably did the same thing with Christ, and that's the oral tradition, that's how it works. As in *The Way to Rainy Mountain*, we go from the mythic to the historical to the personal reminiscence to the myth; it is all a wheel and it renews itself all the time and gains force. Time in the Indian world is as static. In the general society we talk about time passing, time drawing near and time receding but it doesn't, it's the other way round – we go through time. Once I took a trip through the Grand Canyon on a raft and I was very keenly aware of that there, where you move through geologic time and look at the walls around you and you understand that they are there and they're going to be there and there's not much you can do about that; there they are and you pass through them and you emerge on the other side. In the Bear/God dialogues I have a dialogue on Time, which explains it from my point of view.

In my own life I have not been an angry person but I find myself becoming angrier as I grow older when I think about some of the injustices that have been perpetrated on the Indian people. I don't act upon anger, I don't reveal it particularly, but there is an anger and I hope it's creative; I think it can be creative if it's controlled. I'm not outraged, though I can be reminded of a lot of outrageous things. In part I agree with the idea that while there's nothing you can do about the past and what has happened, nor can you forget it as that would be another kind of injustice. So you appropriate it to your experience, you live with it, you try to make something positive out of it and that's all you can do. I don't know if I have found words from anger. I suspect that I've found some but they issue from a reasonable kind of anger, and not rage. I don't think you can find words from rage. Rage does not sponsor creative language, at its best it can sponsor just wild, irresponsible language, per se – explosions! But I think a little of it can inspire language.

I don't know the answer to what my creative process is. I can sit for hours and not write a sentence. I know that there have been times when writing has been completely frustrating to me, but I think it's been a matter of waiting it out. If you sit there and endure the frustration eventually something will come. I was once listening to the radio when somebody was interviewing a writer and they asked the obligatory inane question, Is it difficult to write? And the writer said, 'No. No, there's nothing to it. All you do is sit there looking at the blank page until beads of blood appear on your forehead.' And I thought, yeah, that's pretty much it! With my painting I would say it's different. Both things are creative and they both express parts of my experience, but they're not the same thing. I find writing much more concentrated and it requires concentration. Painting is a relief from writing; I can listen to music and paint but when I'm really writing I can't listen to anything else, I just have to be so concentrated on the writing itself. I think that's what makes it so difficult and why I find you can't stay with it too long. If I can write for three hours a day, that's a lot for me. I shoot for something like a page; that takes time and that's a good day's work, and when I've reached that limit there is a kind of exhaustion. I can turn to painting then, or to something else, but I can't go on writing. I think that there is a kind of ceremony to writing, and it does irritate when people say they just 'dash it off'. Somebody might come to me at a book signing and say, 'I wrote a poem today', and I will say, 'Like hell you did!' It's not possible!

I can relate my paintings to pictographs and petroglyphs. I think about images all the time when I'm painting, and frequently I think of cave paintings because they are so important to me. I've seen petroglyphs and pictographs, and I've seen the rock paintings in Altamira, and those things are maybe the best art I've ever seen. So when I'm working those things come into my mind and I hope inform my work in ways that I don't know. I don't know if we will ever truly understand those images and what is being communicated in pictographs and petroglyphs. It will be difficult I think because we have a long way to go in terms of understanding those things. I hope that happens, but I'm not willing to say that it will. If it does I think it will take a tremendous effort and a long time. I would say that those who think that there isn't great meaning in these images, and a connection to ancient tribal stories and explanations, are wrong. There's a whole network of relationships and these things are related in ways we don't know yet and we may never know, but clearly they are connected. Some of these stories are not only ancient, they cross continents; some are world-wide.

As to how those ancient people came to be on this continent, I don't think I have anything definitive that will end the controversy one way or the other.

All I have ever said about that is that I don't believe, with regard to the Bering Strait, that we're talking about a theory; I think we know for a fact that people were crossing the Bering Land Bridge twenty thousand years ago and maybe much before that. Whether that was the only entry way into the continent I doubt, I think there were probably other avenues of entry. I don't know what they were, but we seem to be finding more and more evidence that people were coming in boats to parts of the Americas, so I think it's an open book. I know there are a number of people who say, 'No, people were not coming from Asia. That's not right, we were always here,' and I respect that, but I don't believe that is true for all of the First People in North America – but it could be true of some, why not? We say that man was born in Africa and we have a lot of evidence to support that, but we may well turn up evidence that man was also born in North America. I wouldn't be surprised. I think it's pointless to try to figure out where the first man emerged from the soil. I think there are a lot of possibilities and I don't want to exclude any of them.

The Kiowa language is hard to understand. As a child, I used to hear my grandmother pray in Kiowa. I do not speak Kiowa, so I never understood the words of her prayers, but the Storm Spirit understands the Kiowa language. Where language touches the earth, there is the holy, there is the sacred. I heard the Navajo language when I was young, living in Shiprock, Tuba City and Chinle. I was so young that when I first heard it, it evoked nothing in particular because it was quite natural; it was like hearing any language or my own language. Navajo was something that was in the world and I was exposed to it, and I took it for granted. Now, however, when I go back to the Navajo Reservation and I hear Navajo spoken it evokes a lot of memories of those times in my life when I lived there. I have an ear for Navajo simply because I heard it at the right age and I can mimic most of the sounds of Navajo, which are sometimes very difficult, but it's in my head somehow. I can deal with the pronunciation but I don't begin to know the language. I know something about it, having heard it and I studied it for a time one summer, so it's wonderful for me to hear it. The memories it evokes are very good ones. And I loved the time that I spent in Canyon de Chelly and Monument Valley; all over the Navajo Reservation there are some great places, very strong, spiritual places, and when I'm there I feel good, and good about people. No Navajo has ever expressed to me that they objected to my usage of 'House Made of Dawn', although on reflection I think it might well be true that some Navajos might object to it. *House Made of Dawn* is not from a secret prayer. It is sacred, but language is sacred. All words are sacred in a way.

I completely disapprove of what has been happening with coal mining upon Big Mountain, and the consequences of that. It's been going on for a long time and I don't know why; well, maybe I do understand why it's permitted to go on but it's a very bad thing, it seems to me. It's so blatant, so obvious, that's what I don't understand. How can that happen? I know that it is happening, but how do you justify it? I think any alliance of government and corporate interests to dispossess people is shameful. I think it's an obscenity. I think it's completely indefensible. If I had stronger language I could probably apply it! I don't even know that we can conceive of that kind of thing. It's like ethnic cleansing, it's beyond the imagination.

I sometimes think that we create states of being and conditions that enable us to live the life we want to live. So we'll make war for example, because there's something within us that depends upon war, it fulfills a desire. Maybe poverty is like that; is poverty necessary, in one way or the other, to the functioning of general society? It is wrong, but if the question is if poverty is created to satisfy some need, whether imagined or not on the part of the general society, I would say that's entirely possible. I think poverty is largely imposed in the case of the Indian and comes about because the white man has beaten the Indian down to such an extent. The Indian is controlled, has to withstand persecution, and has been diminished in certain areas, so that Indian people existing under these conditions are simply targets; they are victims. I would say these things, like alcohol and drug dependency, are brought about by exploitation and persecution; that they are imposed upon indefensible people. When we are talking about children as addicts, they are completely indefensible, completely vulnerable.

Clearly it suits the general society and the powers that be for these problems to exist among the Indian. I do not think it would be so if it weren't alright with the society at large. It may not be a conscious and malicious thing but it's certainly criminal. I think a lot of it is indifference and misunderstanding and carelessness, but it's nonetheless wrong. Some of it is intentionally wrong. There is malice. There is hatred, but much of what exists is not because people act upon hatred, but just because they simply don't care or don't understand. It's convenient to overlook these things because it enables us to maintain the status quo and as long as we're comfortable with that, you know, the hell with everything else.

Sovereignty, I suppose, means in the long run the ability to take responsibility for oneself and to control one's destiny, and that ought to be the right of tribes as well as the right of individuals; to define themselves. That's my idea of sovereignty, but I'm not sure that it's the right idea or the best definition of the word. I'm involved with Buffalo Trust and the idea behind that is to return the elements of heritage to Native Americans. I think that is where you can begin to make a critical difference, you can enable children to define themselves. That's wonderful and that's the first step; you can prevent children being defined by other people who will rob them of their heritage and their identity, sometimes consciously, sometimes not. My advice to young people is talk to your elders; understand as much as you can about your heritage and think of yourself as an individual. Define yourself, don't let other people tell you who you are, but tell other people who you are in terms of your heritage. Easier said than done, but I think it has to be said. ”

JOHN

John Trudell

Trudell

"Everybody is indigenous to the planet. We're indigenous to different land bases and to me, our DNA physically comes from those land bases. But we've got to know who we are – to know our identity – if we're going to make it. A tiger knows it's a tiger and it does tiger things; a wolf knows it's a wolf and it does wolf things; and we're human beings but we're not doing human being things. We may be doing human things, but we're not doing human being things because the 'being' – that's the balance. And I think that's the most crucial thing, to know who we are. If we know who we are and we seek to find that, then we will understand the gifts that we have and our abilities."

With his 'Radio Free Alcatraz' broadcasts, John Trudell became the voice of the Indians of All Tribes Occupation of Alcatraz Island. Some seven months before the occupation closed, Trudell painted Plymouth Rock red during a national day of Indian mourning on Thanksgiving, 1970, and from the rocks of Alcatraz and Plymouth to the present day, the juxtaposition of art and activism for which he is recognized continues to resonate throughout the Indigenous Rights Movement. As National Chairman of the American Indian Movement John Trudell brought an eloquence and intellectual dexterity to AIM's leadership platform, a quality that did not escape the FBI which, in the 17,000-page file it compiled bearing his name, reported 'Trudell is an intelligent individual and is an eloquent speaker who has the ability to stimulate people into action'. On February 11, 1979, he burnt the Stars and Stripes outside the J. Edgar Hoover building in Washington, DC, during a protest against the US Government and the FBI's modus operandi in Native America; some twelve hours later, John Trudell's wife Tina, their three children and Tina's mother, were killed in a fire 'of suspicious origin' that destroyed the family's home. Amidst the loss and devastation, Trudell began to write. 'About six months after the fire the lines came. The lines were my bombs, my explosions and my tears. They were my everything.' Those lines became a series of books and albums, the former beginning with *Living in Reality*, the latter including the 1999 Jackson Browne produced *Blue Indians*. In the interim, Bob Dylan described his *AKA Grafitti Man* as 'the best album of 1986'; he gave an award-winning performance in the role of Jimmy Looks Twice in the movie *Thunderheart*; and many came to regard him as one of the finest poets in America. "John Trudell," says Kris Kristofferson, "is a crazy lone wolf, poet, prophet, preacher, warrior full of pain and fun and laughter and love ... He is a reality check."

"Rolling hills, water, trees, hot summers and cold winters. When I think of Nebraska that's what comes into my mind. That's home. I think home is a place. Sometimes it's a physical place and sometimes it's a place of memories because it's not physically that way anymore, but even if the place is only in our consciousness, home is still a place, otherwise there would be no word. That's where I'm from, the Santee Reservation in Nebraska. Being Santee is important to me because it's a part of who I am and all the parts of who I am are important to me. I think my 'Native me' is an integral part of my reality, so to be from my tribe is very important because I still have the identity of my past, ancestrally speaking. The Santee Dakotas were prisoners of war when they were put on this reservation in 1862 after what the government called the 'Minnesota Uprising'. That uprising ended only to be replaced by others. It's not 1862 and we're not in the same physical world environment. In one sense, when they hung the thirty-eight Dakotas at Mankato that rebellion ended, but it ended only to be replaced by the uprisings of the descendants.

Maybe in some theoretical sense it's the same struggle today but in other practical ways it isn't the same; we're surrounded by computers and high-tech surveillance and napalm and Grand Jury indictments and shit; whereas then, they just took them and had that kangaroo court and hung them. But we've changed and that's why it's not the same struggle. The perceptional reality of the Santees in 1862 was shaped entirely by their life experience at that time, ancestrally, environmentally and physically. But since that time we, the descendants, have had other experiences and so our perceptional reality has been altered from what their perception of reality was. That's why I would call it a new uprising. I've never imagined myself as being one of them or being in their place at Mankato when they stepped up to the gallows, but I do know the pain of the past and what happened to the people of the past. I have been one with the past. I have been one with the survivors of the murders. I have been one with the murdered. In my own way I have felt the experience of 1862 in Mankato, and I've felt the experience of Wounded Knee in 1890, and I've felt the experience of Sand Creek and the Trail of Tears.

The most significant event that's happened to me in my life is leaving the womb. I have the DNA of two continents, which I think may be to my advantage in some ways, and in this hemisphere I have DNA from the north to the south. I have that DNA within me and it brings different points of view and perceptions but it does not necessarily have to bring conflict. I understand that there are different perceptions and different points of view and I know there may be an abundance of those things internally within me because I'm part white. It may bring conflict in the European perception of reality, because in that there has to be conflict if there's a different point of view, but I don't think that's part of a Native

John Trudell

reality, there doesn't have to be conflict in Native reality just because there might be a different point of view. So I look at the way my personal DNA is split up as more of an advantage, and no matter where the DNA comes from it's out of the earth.

Growing up, I lived between those two worlds, the Native and the non-Native, and in this day and age, where we are at now, I think they are both part illusion and part reality. Crazy Horse said we live in the shadow of the real world and I have my own understanding of the truth of that. I think reality is real and the world is real but it's our perceptions that become altered and become more unreal. When I moved between the reservation and off the reservation when I was growing up, some things were more real to me in my Native world than they were in the non-Native world; things of the human essence; but in the non-Native world, for want of a better term, some of the cruelties that I saw were real to me. I mean they were *unreal* but they were real! It gets confusing but I figured out that it's got to do with our overall perception. The real problem is that we now live in a time when it's harder to know who we are, and when it's harder to know who we are, then it's harder to understand our purpose, and when it's harder to understand our purpose then it's harder to deal with anything. We are part of an evolutionary reality but part of the purpose of this technological civilization is to erase our memories and erase our identities. And I think that the real problem is the erasure of the identity; genocide erases identities, right? All technological reality does. If we know who we are and if we take the time to remember who we are – *we're human beings* – if we take the time to understand that and to know that, then I don't think it's so hard to shift from one reality to the next – from the Native to the non-Native.

I can't romanticize the past. Before this technological reality appeared for us, in the past life was still hard. It was good and we were free but it was hard. To live with nature with nothing but the natural resources of nature around you, rather than converting it or mutating it with technology; life was hard. Being able to feed oneself year round and being dependent upon what your climate and your environment was to live; life was hard. But we knew who we were and we knew what our purpose was and in that, that's what made us free. So to me it's back to us re-identifying who we are, and it's very difficult. Let's look at the Sun Dance: to do the Sun Dance is a very difficult thing to do and thinking about moving from that Rapid City world, that technological reality, to the Sun Dance, is not that easy for most people. The Sun Dance is not an easy thing to do anyway, it's a serious challenge, and in a way that challenge is to remind us. It's not to save us and make everything go away and change everything instantaneously, because that reality does not exist. This prayer, this ceremony, is to remind us about what sacrifice really means so when we go back into that technological reality we should go into

John Trudell

it strengthened because we've just come from this time of prayer. Sacrifice means many, many things and to give up food and water is just a way of telling us that sacrifice means many, many things. So we sacrifice some of our pettiness and some of our weaknesses, we conscientiously work at giving those things up and getting rid of those things. And that's what ceremonies should be, strengthening that part of our reality and making it easier for us to do that. But if we don't understand that, then it can make it even more difficult because when we go dance and pray to the sun something's going to happen and it's in our best interests to understand what's happening. If we don't understand what's happening, it's going to happen anyway; we've made that communication to spirit, to the Creator. And in a way it's got to do with us knowing who we are.

Once you become engaged in that spiritual energy system it kind of goes both ways but if you don't understand what you're doing, you're seriously going to mess yourself up. Like these people who are going around selling ceremonies don't really know what they're doing in my view. Personally I don't agree with it but I'm not going to quarrel with them and I'm not going to start any wars over it. I'm not going to have a fight with these people over it because I don't agree; because I don't agree I won't do it that way, I'll do it the way I think is more appropriate to do it. What I do know is this: I know that when you have ceremony and you make that prayer, that prayer will be heard and there will be an answer. All the people that run to those who sell ceremonies don't know what they're doing, so that means they're not really going to learn anything anyway. As long as they're not physically dangerous to us I would rather see them in that confusion than to see them thinking that they're fucking Neo-Nazis! I wouldn't do it but I think of what Chief Joseph said, 'We do not want churches. They will teach us to quarrel about God, as the Catholics and Protestants do on the Nez Perce reservation and at other places. We do not want to learn that. We may quarrel with men sometimes about things on this earth, but we never quarrel about God. We do not want to learn that'. So I'm going to remember that and I'm not going to engage in this fight because in a way it is a variation of how to fight about God. Again, everything comes back to us knowing who we are and these people who we say misuse the ceremonies are a bunch of Europeans looking for an identity, they want to know who they are. Their behavior isn't malicious or aggressively deceitful in a malicious way, it's more the behavior of the confused. And the people who sell the ceremonies to them, well I don't know what their confusions are. When someone comes out with a brand new made-up Indian name and they're out here peddling it, I have a problem with that as well, but I'm not going to engage in a war with them either because I'm not giving them anything. If I engage them in a war I give them energy and I figure that if I don't agree with it, then I don't give them anything.

If you're going to fight a war against cultural appropriation then really that war has to be waged against the colonizer himself. We're held in economic bondage. Religion has imposed it's bondage but it's all part of the economic bondage and if anything is going to take us out, this is what's going to take us out, not some Indian man or some wannabe out selling ceremonies somewhere. That's not what's destroying us, it's the economic manipulation and the whole lack of recognition of our sovereign natural rights that's imposing the greatest pain and the longest term danger. This is the thing that's trying to alter our identity and alter who we are, this is the most dangerous thing. I understand that to some degree this selling of ceremonies is connected to it, but it's connected at the peripheral edges. The danger is the religions that are imposed upon our reservations and the economic hold that they have upon our reservations, and the economic hold that the government has on our reservations through the programs and all that stuff. These are the dangers and this is what's going to wipe out our identity. The other thing is not going to wipe out our identity. I know it's a big thing but it's like this fight about who is more Indian, and what the fuck is this? Who is more Indian? It's a useless fight. It's a useless argument. We're not Indians and we never were Indians. Only in our oppressor's terminology and language were we Indians. We're the People. We're the Human Beings. That's who we've always been but for 500 and some years we've been 'Indians'.

This whole thing about people selling ceremonies is a very emotional issue too, but quite frankly I think anybody that engages in the fight over who is spiritually right or spiritually wrong loses. This whole idea of spiritual warriors? No, I don't think so. Wage a spiritual war? Whoever is going to wage that war? Well, however they're going to justify it and rationalize it they're wrong. If they want to use spirituality then pray, but this turns into just another crusade and watch out for that crusade stuff! If anything, the creation of this war and the prosecution of this war will, in the end, serve the effect of replacing our whole spiritual reality with a religious reality. Who is to say what is between you and this Great Spirit? Who is to tell you that this is the only way you can talk to this Great Spirit? Who can tell me or you or anybody? Who has that right? If these people are wrong then it will play out and those who are misusing it will answer to the responsibility of that, but if we get engaged out of emotional reactionism then it becomes our crusade and then we're in the middle of it and we're upsetting our own balance.

Things have changed on reservations since I was growing up. There's more technology on reservations now. And it used to be alcohol on reservations and now it's drugs and alcohol. But it depends upon which reservation you're looking at because some of these gambling governments have got more money than they possibly need and their reservations are wealthy, so things have changed there, but if you go to Pine Ridge, Pine Ridge is still suffering the consequences of Wounded Knee and the Oglala incident. The US government is still being very repressive towards Pine Ridge and so you go in there and they have nothing, absolutely nothing – there might be no more than a half a dozen dreams left – it's a hard situation there. I think in every situation it has changed for the young people, it's a faster world than it was when I was young. On some reservations maybe they're speaking the languages more because they are being taught to the young now, whereas in some places it remains the same.

I'm going to say that the biggest change on reservations has been an economic change, because economics change the politics. To me Clinton's trip to Pine Ridge was theatre and it did not represent anything of substance that has to do with real change and any type of positive outlook for the people of Pine Ridge. I don't actually know what Clinton wanted, and it may be that what he intended wasn't what the people he worked for wanted, because it isn't about what the President wants; when we're talking about policy and shaping the industrial economic future the President does what that industrial ruling class wants him to do. No matter what the Americans say, that's how it is for Presidents in America. Whatever Clinton did there and whatever his motives, for him it was PR, but for that industrial ruling class there was a little bit of that serfdom pitch which might have had nothing to do with what Clinton really wanted. One of the things I do notice on reservations that have access to this Public Health, which used to be Indian Health, is that the Indians that don't go to it unless they absolutely have to are usually better off than the Indians that run to it every time something's wrong with them. Then they have to keep going back and I think there's a lot of experimental crap that goes on, on the reservations because nobody pays any attention. So in a way there is a form of biological warfare going on, on reservations. I think a lot of this goes way beyond the sterilizations too. It's the New World Order.

The Federal government and its agencies are paranoid, armed and dangerous, and never forget it. What they're paranoid of is people who think differently. The Inquisitions of AD 1100/1200 in Europe had to do with how people think; when the Church waged a war of Inquisition against the people to get them to stop thinking the way they thought and to think the way the Church wanted them to think. And that seems to be the nature of the State now as manifested through its law enforcement agencies and its National Security apparatus and all of that – they are paranoid of how we think. I don't know if it's so much that they are paranoid about how we think at this point, more that they are paranoid that we *might start* thinking. I think that civilization has evolved to the point now where we probably spend 90 per cent of our time with reactive thought rather than initiated thought; reactive thought meaning we react to the emotional

John Trudell

intensities and data we've been programmed with all our lives so we just react to any circumstance. I think their paranoia is that they know that we carry within us the ability to have initiated thought and at any time that initiated thought can spark in our consciousness, and if it sparks in one consciousness and they can get it to another one, then it might spark for real and people will start to see things differently. I think that's what makes them paranoid. Or the more evil the empire, the more paranoid the society!

I see sparks all over the place and maybe the main spark I see is that most people that I encounter really do want to see differently. They want to *think* but it's just that everybody is so confused and befuddled by everything that's going on that it's hard to see clearly or even take the time to understand to see clearly. In a way part of this reactive thing is that we've been programmed to seek answers but I sense amongst more and more people that they want more than answers, they want understanding, and that's a spark. Answers aren't enough. We've been conditioned to seek answers and not understanding, and we're programed to believe. We're programed to believe rather than to know or to understand. But this goes back to our identity again – we have to know who we are – I think that's very crucial. We're human beings, that's who we really are. We are shapes of the earth; our physical reality, our form, is made up of the earth's metals, minerals and liquids; we're this form of the earth and we have 'being'. I think we really have to understand that and what that means because that's our relationship to the reality of power. As human beings we're part of an ancestral lineage, our DNA comes through the millennia, so our relationship to power is in the earth because that's where we physically come from and our relationship to power is in that DNA ancestral lineage because that's where the 'being' part of us has been riding all this time. And our relationship to reality is in that – that's our identity of who we are – and I think that all the programing that has taken place, has taken place to remove our identity.

If you look at European Americans, when they look at their ancestral lineage they know they've got great-grandparents – maybe. They might know their names and might even have met them – maybe. But beyond that they don't think in terms of ancestral anything. So once that's been erased it's almost like they've been severed from their spiritual power, their relationship to the past, and I think that this is one of the first things that comes in to make people feel powerless, because the power's being diverted over into something else. I think all the programing has got to do with affecting our perception of ourselves and who we are. And how do we get past it? There's no easy way through this. But the way we get past it is to look at ourselves to see who we are. I think that's the first step. I can't tell people how to do it but I think we've got to, in some kind of a way, be real to ourselves. Let's go back to our form – human beings – and let's call it the

John Trudell

'being'. And all the things of the earth are made up of the same DNA, so all of the things of the earth have 'being', and we live in a reality where we understand that they can take uranium out of the earth and put it through a mining process and convert the 'being' part of that uranium, that DNA, into a form – a mutation of power – that is energy; electrical energy that can be controlled by man. A mutation of power can be controlled by man. We know that they can do that and we know that as a result of that mining process it leaves a toxic waste in poisons and pollution. We know they do it with fossil fuels; they take the fossils out, the dinosaurs out of the ground, put them through a mining process and convert it into gasoline which is then converted into another electrical energy system and it leaves behind its pollution. And what I'm saying is that they're doing this to us – they are mining the 'being' part of human through our intelligence. They are mining the 'being' part of human and converting that power of the 'being' part of human into a form of mutated power called energy and they use that energy to run their authoritarian, material, technological systems; we're the gasoline that runs it just like the dinosaur runs that internal combustion engine. But as a part of that, we know that from those external systems that mining process leaves pollution – and the pollution that is left from them mining the 'being' part of human is every doubt, fear and insecurity that we have – that's the pollution that's left over and it keeps us from seeing clearly. If we can't see clearly in every sense of the word then we cannot be clear, and so now here comes that reactive thought. Everything now becomes a reaction to this haze. That's how that mining process works and how we get past it is to understand the reality that this may be a very real process that's taking place, and looking at ourselves in relationship to that.

Everybody is indigenous to the planet. We're indigenous to different land bases and to me, our DNA physically comes from those land bases. But we've got to know who we are – to know our identity – if we're going to make it. A tiger knows it's a tiger and it does tiger things; a wolf knows it's a wolf and it does wolf things; and we're human beings but we're not doing human being things. We may be doing human things, but we're not doing human *being* things because the *being* – that's the balance. And I think that's the most crucial thing, to know who we are. If we know who we are and we seek to find that, then we will understand the gifts that we have and our abilities. I think that if we understand who we are as human beings then we will better understand what the reality of our intelligence is, we'll understand that we have purpose and our intelligence is there to help us serve our purpose. If we understand and really know we're human beings we'll know that we're physical entities in a spiritual reality and our purpose is to perpetuate and maintain that spiritual reality.

The spiritual reality of life is about responsibility and that's what I was saying about those quarrels that come up over selling ceremonies. Everybody is responsible for what they do so if somebody's doing something that I disagree with and I then behave irresponsibly, they didn't make me, the deal is that I did what I did through my own thought process – either a reactive thought process or an initiated thought process. The gift we've been given to protect us as humans is our intelligence. Our intelligence is our medicine. We were not put here defenseless to be eaten up by this mining process. Where does this mining process take place? It takes place through our intelligence. It goes after our intelligence, so if we understand the value and power of our intelligence then we could influence through our consciousness how our evolution is going to go. And we can't help but influence that, it's an inevitable reality that we will influence our evolution. If we use our minds for mindless things and don't respect ourselves and understand our intelligence and all the things that we have going for us then that's how we will influence it, but if we understand the power of it and use it as clearly and coherently as we can, as often as we can, then that's how we will effect the evolution. The reality of it is that we are a part of an evolutionary reality. Revolutionary reality is like putting a Band-aid on the cut, but the evolutionary reality heals the cut. I think we really need to have an understanding of that as human beings, no matter where we're at.

Our cultural identity is getting stronger and I think that is the biggest accomplishment that came out of that period of political activism. It rekindled the spirit of the Native people at large. It re-lit that fire. One of the things that made that all fall into place for me personally was that whole summer of '69. I was going to school in San Bernardino but by then I had basically dropped out because I had a disagreement with them, but I just hung on to enough classes to keep my checks coming in; the GI Bill deal. I had just started to do some film work and Buffy Sainte-Marie was sponsoring a Cree artist, Alan Sapp, in LA and so I came down to film him. Then these two students, Ray Spain and Chuck Nacho, came over from UCLA and told me what was going to happen up at Alcatraz but I couldn't go because I was making this film. Then the Alcatraz occupation happened and I hitch-hiked over there from San Bernardino the following weekend. I just knew I was going to go. I used to have these conversations with a friend back then and I'd say, 'I don't know what it is but whatever I'm supposed to do is coming and I just got to wait'. I remember having that conversation with him many times. And I didn't get it that, that's what it was when these guys first told me about Alcatraz but I knew I was interested in it and when I got there I knew that's where I was supposed to be, I was just waiting. The Anti-War Movement was going on, the Black Student Unions, the Civil Rights, and the Women's movements, everything was going on except us! And I remember waiting for it in that summer of '69 and when I showed up at Alcatraz, that's what it was. When I got to the island I talked to Richard Oakes and some other people there and decided, this is where I want to be.

JOHN TRUDELL

My lasting memory of Alcatraz is that when we went there we wanted the title to the island. We wanted that island and we wanted to build our cultural center there and we went through that whole occupation and through various negotiations. At the last meeting we had with the US government they offered us money. They offered us a quarter of a million dollars and a lease, and we were to receive the money in $50,000 increments from five different federal agencies and all we had to do was put the proposals together and we told them, 'No! We don't want your money, we want the island.' And that's my lasting impression. We built a community there and I have many, many pleasant memories about Alcatraz and many wonderful things happened to me there, my son was born there; but it was this, that after 18 months we didn't want their money. 'We'll do it ourselves.' And I never had that experience again. *I never had that experience again.*

Before Alcatraz I had been in the military but I just erased that from my mind. That was something I went through and got through it and I didn't compare any of the stuff we were involved in to anything I had to do with the military. To me that whole Alcatraz and AIM time was about idealism. In my mind hope never had anything to do with it. Never. It was our idealism and our youth and our mobility; we could be mobile because there was no place in America for us anyway, be it in the workforce or any of that stuff. It was a very energizing time and out of that our cultural identity became stronger and more visible. Whatever the hard times were and remain, there's still this other element that is there and I see it. Our identity is coming back to us in much stronger ways and it was slipping away from us before that all happened. There was excitement during that whole time and there was purpose. We had a purpose. I had a purpose. There was something we had to do. It was a revitalization and there were many good times as well as the hard times. After that time was gone, and I look back at it, for me personally it was a very valuable time because I learned so much. When it's time to look back, I learned so much.

There are some things about it I don't think you can express. There are some things, like what happened with the goons, the death squads, and all you can say are words, but this is about a feeling. With certain things all that you can communicate are words and if you want the feeling for some of these things you have to have the experience. I can tell you about someone putting a gun to your head, or to my head, and all I'm doing is telling you, but when that gun's at your head then you know what I'm saying. Then you truly know what I'm saying. When you know the motherfucker on the other end of that gun is crazy enough to pull the trigger, just mean enough and hateful enough, and that they may be wearing badges or representing the authority. But you have to be there for that, you seriously do. And fear? I'm sure there were times when we felt fear, but we weren't afraid. I think fear is a natural instinct but I think that the reality we live

John Trudell

in, where it's an obsessive neurotic fear, that's something else. But fear itself, I am thankful for my fear because if nothing else it stimulates the old adrenaline and makes you perk up there and look around! It might have you trembling and shaking but my fear tells me that I'm alive.

The neurotic fear that manifests in this society tells the society that it's dying; it's the distortion of the 'being' from that mining. Fear as we know it now in society is very dominant, everybody's afraid of everything! Afraid to be who they are, afraid of what other people might think or not think, afraid to stand up for themselves – even love is now entwined with fear. This has to do with love, fear and possession, and the descendants of the tribes of Europe. By about AD 1000 those descendants didn't know that they had come from tribes because they didn't have that tribal memory anymore – 1,500 years passed in which they had been turned into serfs and landlords and royalty had been created, and they were now the property of these creations. They had no tribal memory in the sense of their tribes but they still had a part of their spiritual memory, so they still prayed to spirits and they prayed in their old ways, and so that 'being' part was still active to some degree. Then in about AD 1100 when the Church decided that it was the authority of God on earth, basically God's government, it launched its war for the possession of the souls of the 'heathens' and if you thought differently to how the Church wanted you to think then you were guilty of heresy and you had to be tortured and executed, then the Church would take your property. This was a religious ritual, accusation, torture, execution and seizure of property, and it ran for five hundred years in Europe. So this war was waged against the descendants of the tribes of Europe, now the peasants, serfs and fiefs, to get them to perceive reality differently – which was they had to now love what they feared – and what they feared was now possessing them, so love and fear and possession became one then and the Western perception of reality has not been able to unweave that thread. They're so intertwined now, that in this perception of reality, love is not really about caring, love is about possessing, so love and fear became neurotic then. It was no longer whole, it became neurotic with possession. Fear in the natural sense that we are born with is there to warn us and to give us a sign that we are alive, but his exaggerated fear, this fear of everything, means that the human being is possessed by fear. Due to the way the mining process has taken place and the way we've been manipulated and our perception of reality has been manipulated and exploited, that fear is now almost like a companion to most people.

We have another perception because we still have our relationship to our ancestral past. The Natives have it in ways nobody else on this land base does. We know we came from here. It doesn't get erased. We know this is where we are from. We know that wherever we go, our ancestors have roamed here, they lived here, they went through every experience here and they are buried here. And we know that yet. Throughout the treaty process we have maintained that position, of wanting to be who we are. Treaties were legal agreements so America has a legal obligation to us, it may be called a treaty obligation but really they have a legal obligation because treaties are laws. Our approach to America has always been, 'We want to be different. We want to be who we are and we just want you to fulfill the law and the legal agreements you made with us.' Our struggle didn't start with wanting the right to vote in their system because we know that their system is corrupt. When we were the majority here they wouldn't let us vote, but now that we're the smallest numerical minority they want us to vote. For the blacks, their whole recognition had to do with civil rights within the American system whereas our whole relationship had to do with the treaty rights outside of the American system. I think that is the main difference in what happened to the two of us; when the blacks were brought here as slaves they were ripped away from their roots so they have to go through many, many millennia to establish new roots here. The Europeans severed their own, but our roots were always here.

They needed to keep the blacks alive to be slaves for them. Other than in the minds of some good people who spoke out about slavery being evil, the Civil War had nothing to do with freeing the slaves, it was about the Industrial Revolution. The economic reality was that if the US was to be a world empire the use of slaves was going to hold it back in its destiny because the machine had arrived and that was going to be more effective than slave labor. It was the North telling the South that they were going to take this technology and industry and do everything that the North said because this Industrial Revolution was happening all over the God damned world and those in the South weren't going to hold them back. At this point those good people who viewed slavery as wrong got to have a voice and then this war was fought over it. If it had really been about slavery being wrong, after the Civil War had been fought and the blacks allegedly emancipated then their economic reality and living conditions would have changed but that didn't happen; the mantle of slavery was lifted only for them to be kept as sharecroppers. This was a property they had and they needed to have the blacks there. It was like a livestock deal but for us, they needed to kill us, so the legacy of that behavior is that there are a couple of million of us compared to twenty or thirty million blacks. They tried to make us invisible. Part of this thing about the Constitution is that America has always claimed citizenship over the blacks, even if it was through ownership, and when the blacks got separated from their cultural roots they could only hang on to what the memories would allow them to hang onto. Basically they had to start over in many ways and consequently they may now have many of the same goals that this overall society claims it has because that's what they've been taught. But we know we came from the earth and I think that's got a lot to do with the differences between our experiences and theirs.

Let's look at the human part of us again: the human part of us, the bone, flesh and blood – our DNA – is literally made up of the metals, minerals and liquids of the earth, so we're shapes of the earth. Everything of the earth has the same DNA, it's just the form that is different. As humans we recognize that we have 'being' – spirit – and all of the things of the earth are made up of the same DNA so it means our DNA has 'being'. So the physical is the *visible* visible, and the 'being' is the *invisible* visible; we know it's there. I think that when the human dies the 'being' does not die. If the 'being' was to die inside the human then it might be the sorting out process, the impurities, like the salmon that don't make it up the stream because they can't cut it to carry it on. Maybe what we're going through here is this whole technological reality where if the human eats up the 'being' while the human is alive then that's it, they don't get to participate in anything anymore because these are the imperfections that would prevent the Nirvana, the place of balance, or the heaven or whatever people want to call it. It's possible that may happen, but generally speaking I think the human dies but the being doesn't. When someone we love dies and we bury them, in a way what really changes is how we communicate with them. If we say in our mind that they're dead, then they're dead because that's how we choose to communicate with them because we can't see them and touch them. But if we understand that the 'being' part of living still continues to live, that their spirit is still there, then I think our communication changes but it's still communicable.

What lives in the heart and the mind – *that's what lives.*

We haven't lost. This society at large may want us to think that we've lost but we haven't. We're oppressed but that doesn't mean we lost and it doesn't mean we're conquered, it just means we're oppressed. Let's examine our own intelligence and check out how to use it. ”

JOHN TRUDELL

TANTOO

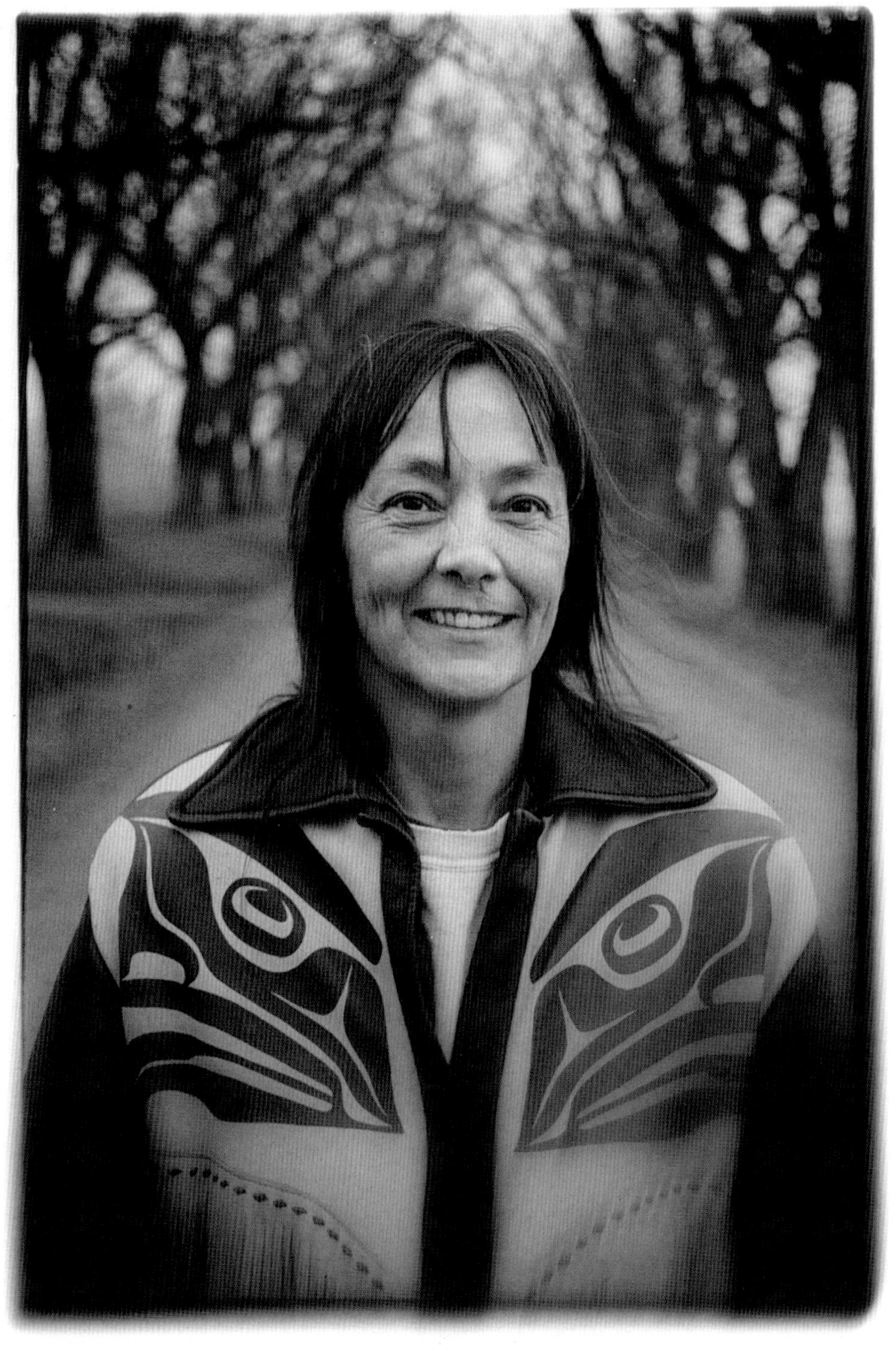

CARDINAL

"I'd done a number of films before I knew I was an actor and that this was going to be my life . . . It was in about 1982 that I finally realized, 'Well, this is your career. This is something.' It's not easy and it's never been easy at any time along the way. As an actor there are barriers that come from being brown and from being a woman but you're born into that struggle and you have to push harder. For an Indian actor to win an Oscar would be amazing, for an Indian actress to win it first would be miraculous."

Tantoo Cardinal made her cinematic debut in 1975, since when her performances in a prodigious body of movie and television work have gained her recognition as one of Canada's leading actresses. Arguably the most successful and recognizable First Nation's actress, her forty-plus screen roles include her award-winning portrayals in *Legends of the Fall*, *Dances With Wolves*, *The Education of Little Tree*, *Where the Rivers Flow North,* and *Smoke Signals*. Tantoo Cardinal received both a Gemini award, and Toronto Women in Film and Television's Outstanding Achievement award, for her role as 'Betty Moses' in the critically acclaimed TV series, *North of 60*, in addition to which she has starred in the TV productions *Doctor Quinn, Medicine Woman*, *Lonesome Dove: The Outlaw Years*, *Grand Avenue*, *Lakota Woman: Siege at Wounded Knee* and *Tecumseh: The Last Warrior*. In 1999 Tantoo directed *Stories from the Seventh Fire*, and she continues to play multi-dimensional characters in theatre productions. Tantoo Cardinal is the recipient of the National Aboriginal Achievement Award for arts and culture.

"First Nations is the term that I think best describes who we are and what our position is in North America. First Nation's people in Canada have endured essentially the same experiences as those in the United States. The Americans did it mostly with guns and the Canadians did it with paper, but after a certain point the Canadians got into guns and nooses as well. The border doesn't make any difference to the indicators of sickness in our societies; alcoholism and substance dependence, abusive domestic situations, the high suicide rates and depressing statistics are on both sides of the border after generations of brainwashing and assimilation. We have to get rid of that brainwashing in order to reclaim healthier communities and at least in Canada First Nation's people have a higher profile than in the States. I think that the way the emancipation has been dealt with, and the way that leadership has proceeded, has made a difference in Canada. We are really behind in the US so far as receiving any kind of recognition as a people but in Canada there's something in the newspapers relating to First Nation's issues nearly everyday. Those contributions that are natural for us to make to society and civilization, that we haven't been allowed to make for generations because of colonization, are closer to the surface in Canada but in the US I think that African-Americans have the strongest civil rights profile.

I try to stay out of political structures now, to me they are too man-made and it's a twenty-legged race in order to accomplish anything. You can't get away from the twenty-legged race though because when you're filming that's what it is, but it's more comfortable for me to work through those barriers in the arts rather than politics. There were different events and situations that brought me to this arena. When I was a child there was nothing to say, You gotta be an actor! There was no such thing. We never even had a television or radio and we didn't get electricity until much later. We hauled our own water and chopped our own wood, so in a sense I grew up 'a long time ago'. I come from a part of the world where the Church and the government had done their thing and had brainwashed a number of generations, telling the people that Indian ways were of the devil and not only were they unlawful, Indian beliefs were shameful, sinful and evil. My grandmother raised me and it was very much alive that you had to be ashamed and should hide 'Indianness', so even though I came from that culture and that community where people visited one another and shared experiences and told stories, the structure was gone and the ceremonies were gone – it was all Catholic. So it was rage that got me into acting and of course that is what also got me into politics.

I understood that the lies the Church and the government were spreading were outrageous and were hurting a lot of people, so I decided that I was going to play a part in exposing them – tell the truth, find the truth. I had to go through that process and unburden myself of the lies that had found their way inside of me. We had been fed that Indians were stupid and simple, savage and pagan – whatever that was – and all that bad press. I became involved with the Native Youth Organization

Tantoo Cardinal

and one of the things we did in finding the truth was to look at the statements made by our Native leaders at the time that the treaties were signed and then look at the difference in thinking. In the late 1960s all this stuff started emerging about Indian ways and what those philosophies really are, and then what the army and the government had hidden, and what the Church had hidden: how they had twisted it all and presented it back to Native people so that when brainwashed and emasculated the people themselves became a part in the oppression. Why? Because we stood in the way of their money and political gain. We belong to the land, but they had to rip it up and turn it into coin and there was no time for sharing or respect because they believed they had a superior position in Creation.

The damage that the Residential Schools did is very deep. The unnatural separation of children from their parents and brothers from sisters, the severing of those bonds and the regulations that left those kids in the clutches of those perverts from the Church who had no respect for Indians anyway, was an abomination. The arrogance of those who did it, perpetuated it and established laws to sanction it is absolutely disgusting. After all the emotional abuse, sexual abuse, physical abuse and psychological abuse suffered by those Native kids they weren't even given a proper education – they were trained to be domestic help or hired hands. When they went back to their communities they were strangers. They had been punished at these schools if they ever spoke the languages of their mothers and fathers and they hadn't been allowed to pray in their God-given natural way or allowed to sing those songs, so they could no longer communicate with their parents or people. They had been taught that their parents and relatives were unintelligent and that Indian people were inferior. And now, in this day and age, people are talking about and crave the wisdom of Native people! How come all of a sudden Native people have got wisdom white people want? I didn't go to a residential school but everywhere you turned that devastation was there because it wasn't only happening in the school system it permeated through the government and Church to the mines and to the people in the towns.

Basically we've got the same challenges that we've always had, mainly to break through this big, thick barrier called the European mind-set. It's the same challenge but I think that we're getting closer and closer together as human beings now because the environment is going to shit and we all share the fall-out from polluted waters and air and acid rain, and we are coming to the realization that our children are inheriting the same earth. The gifts that we have as First Nation's people are in the blueprints of our culture and in those blueprints is the wisdom that is going to be needed for this civilization to survive. We're just starting to understand a lot of the things that have kept us in the darkness of oppression and as we as First Nation's communities struggle to break free and to breathe, the same thing is happening in other communities. So much of the journey that I have traveled has been about breaking through this oppressive machine that has made us lesser human beings in the minds of its operators and in their children's minds and in their legislation and procedures. Now our children and their children are sharing common experiences and there are incredible changes going on, not just among First Nation's people but everyone, particularly amongst women.

Women's rightful place is to be overseers of this movement in the community, society and civilization because women were given the incredible gift of creation and the honor that goes with it, the responsibility of carrying new life. Men weren't given that role, men are helpers, but where we are now in our evolvement as physical beings means that we have to get the guys off the pedestals they've made for themselves because they are damaging much of what we need for our children's futures in the pursuit of control, manipulation and power. Dealing with that oppression is something that we, in First Nation's communities, have had to do for generations – ever since that first boat hit the shores – but people are now starting to deal with issues of control and oppression on personal levels too. If we were in Atlantis, the First Nation's people would be the Believers in One, with the philosophy that all of this energy and power is for the betterment of the whole and not just for ourselves. We are all a part of Creation and the circle is the foundation of who we are.

A lot of people who don't know what their Indian heritage is say that they are Métis and quite a few who have no Indian heritage but would like to are starting to call themselves Métis. I was born into my mother's family and my grandmother who raised me was Cree, Chipewyan and Sioux. She didn't belong to a reserve or have a treaty number because her father was considered a renegade by virtue of the fact that when the treaty was signed, he split. That made him a 'Wanted Indian' and the cops found him when he was living with the Sarcee, just outside of Calgary. He was Cree and Sioux and he married a Chipewyan woman, which is where my granny came from, and then my granny married a guy who was half French and Cree. I was raised by her as my mother left when I was very young and my father left even sooner. My step-grandfather, the man I grew-up calling dad, was from Cornwall, England via Garry, Indiana, and his name was Winston Plews. When I was 15 years old I left Anzac, which was just a few houses in the bush, to go to school in Edmonton. There were certain places where people would look at me and then take a second look at this brown girl and I used to get the feeling that they didn't think it was appropriate for an Indian to be there; they were uncomfortable by my being there. But to me, the fact that the guy I called dad was English, meant to me that I could go anywhere I wanted to; and then I came to feel that we allow ourselves to be imprisoned by prejudice, whether we're conscious of that energy or not. I said to myself, 'Whether they like it or not, I'm here and I'm going to go where I feel compelled to go'. Not everybody was like that. I'm thankful that I've also met strong kindness along this path.

I'd done a number of films before I knew I was an actor and that this was going to be my life. In those days I still had the brainwashing tape playing in my head, telling me that I was stupid and ugly and no good and that I couldn't contribute anything to society. Then, one day I remembered that everybody has been given a gift from the Creator and I decided, I'm going to find out what my gift is. So I just did anything and everything that I could in my life, whatever inspired me, and that's how I eventually found it – acting. It was in about 1982 that I finally realized, 'Well, this is your career. This is something.' It's not easy and it's never been easy at any time along the way. As an actor there are barriers that come from being brown and from being a woman but you're born into that struggle and you have to push harder. For an Indian actor to win an Oscar would be amazing, for an Indian actress to win it first would be miraculous. Occasionally you feel that burden, that additional responsibility to your community, but without this vision of work that has to be done I wouldn't be here – things have to change, the truth has to be told, the misrepresentations have to be eliminated – so we have a responsibility to act because it is what we can do that might make a difference. Today I don't feel like it's a responsibility, it's just a place to be. It's my life and it's a gift to have that purpose.

I've met some incredibly strong-hearted people when the odds against us have been pretty thick; beautiful, generous, kind, dedicated people with vision and passion – to know they're out there is an exciting part of all of this. You throw whatever it is that you've got in the pot and they put what they've got in the same pot and then this new idea comes out! Of how we can all work together, no matter what culture we come from. There can be conflicts when you're working on a story or a scene but I'm really hopeful because I have seen a good progression. Years ago there were so many people in a crew or on a set that were ignorant and just followed the misrepresentations they had been fed. Situations of racism and sexism were rampant but it's exciting that in the recent past the crews and the groups that I've found myself working with haven't been like that, they've been people who understand the circle and that place of putting energies together and working together. Maybe that speaks of how many independent films I've done! It's a broad generalization but money has a funny way of affecting people and making them separate from the humanity part of themselves.

There are many factors that come into deciding what roles to take. It has to have something in the script and this is how I support my children so I have to get paid! Money is a factor but sometimes the right script has no money but you still have to do it, even though it might cost you more than what you make from the film; you have to do it because of its passion or the writer's vision, the creative energy. I think of every movie I've done as being part of a process. Each one of them has been a victory for me in the struggle of trying to get things closer to the truth.

TANTOO CARDINAL

There's been something that had to be addressed on every single production I've gone on – whether it was characterization, wardrobe, or a prop – and even where you wind up in the shot all the time, the 'Indian woman' is always back there, even if she's supplying the lead, like she's the mother of the lead. This industry is so male-gestated and so sometimes I have an incredible struggle: where do women fit in this whole scheme? So there's the process of trying to make it habitable for that circular way of operating and being. As an actor your power is limited because by the time you get to work most of the decisions have been made: the development has been done, the characterizations, the dialogue – even the shots have been decided before you get on board.

Black Robe was a film I turned down twice and then finally I recognized that it wasn't up to me. The force that guides let me know, 'Just shut-up and go to work'. That's what the grandmothers were saying. I literally felt like I was being pushed out of the door to work on it and I didn't want to do it because I was tired of being in situations where you talk over the script with the people who are in charge and try to work on changes, and there was so much in that script. I didn't want to deal with it but when I got there all of these other actors who wanted to get at these issues that were not right in the script were all sat around the table! That's a scary thing to a lot of actors because they don't want to create conflict with the directors and producers because it can jeopardize your livelihood but friction is one of the essences of creation. The film was really from Church records and Bruce Beresford, the director, did the job that he was asked to do by making it from the colonial perspective. We did as much as we could to try and bring in some truth and we made the changes that were available to us but there was only so far that we could go because it actually was about the colonial perspective. I think it accomplished its purpose in that it made people react; maybe some non-Native people who saw it wondered, 'How could they do that? What were they thinking?'

There were some things that happened during the filming of *Black Robe* that told me that there are certain things that we as human beings have to do and that there's a force that goes beyond that. That's where the power and strength is, being guided by that rather than people, politics and words – those are all a part of it but they have to be guided by that essential spirit. There was a scene where a baby was still-born and in the script my daughter was braiding this white guy's hair while I was taking down down tipis and everybody else is just walking back and forth like, 'So what, she's putting her dead baby out', as this woman was putting her baby out to the trees. It made us look like we had no heart or feelings attached to that incident. I'd used up all my bargaining chips in terms of getting changes and I was depressed about it going into work that morning, thinking it was wrong – firstly my daughter wouldn't have been braiding some guy's hair while I was working, and on and on. Then, when I got to the set, there had been a problem in continuity so my daughter couldn't have been braiding the guy's hair so they had her taking down the tipis which left another woman and I available to come out of the tipi with this woman and her baby because in an earlier scene we'd refused to be sleeping while she was giving birth, so we could be with her. At that we were asked to say something to her as she came out carrying her still-born baby, a 'There, there. Never mind' kind of thing. So we found something to say but it was too quiet as the point of the scene was for the Jesuit to see us, so it had to be louder – so I thought about a song. They would never have allowed us to bring a song in there so I decided not to tell them and that I would just do it and by the time they called 'action' again, the song had come. I started singing and all these guys who were supposed to be just walking back and forth, oblivious, stopped and paid respect to this woman – and it just happened – I could never have negotiated that but it happened in that moment and it was a big moment for me.

I think both *Black Robe* and *Dances With Wolves* had something to contribute to the overall feeling of what's in people's hearts and minds. I think the power of *Dances With Wolves* is that it brought some positive images forward that we were really, really needing and that was extremely important. For some it touched a place of spirit and belief and it made people feel good. *Black Robe* was darker but the darkness didn't make it more truthful as some people tend to think. That's one of the problems we have in this industry, that we can't get at the truth. *Smoke Signals* did that, but overall it's so hard to handle with a sense of humor when all this horrible human calamity is going on – especially when it's being written from a place of guilt because it's not written from within the community where it can be more personal.

The magic of art is that people can look at the same thing and get something completely different out of it. As long as it inspires thought and it inspires discussion and some kind of dialogue! As an artist you work from that place of soul and energy and when we work we try to touch those places in other people. If we do, we somehow become a part of them, just like people whose work I admire has touched my heart and soul. That's our job as artists."

VINE

Deloria, Jr.

"There are hundreds of conferences on sovereignty where people just get up and talk and talk and talk and talk, but very few will do the hard work to go out and exercise the sovereignty that already exists. They spend all of their time trying to define sovereignty more clearly and that's absurd if sovereignty means that any political entity can negotiate on an equal basis with any other. Period . . . So sit down and work out a deal! It's very difficult to get tribes to see that. A lot of them are so enthralled with this sovereignty idea, 'Oh we can't talk to anybody, it would infringe upon our sovereignty.' Well, if you have sovereignty and you refuse to exercise it you don't really have anything, you're just stuck. That's one of the big problems that I see out there today."

Variously and frequently described as the pre-eminent American Indian author, scholar, lawyer and philosopher, Professor Vine Deloria, Jr., is quite simply one of the most influential and respected voices in that which constitutes the 'Indian World'. Without his crucial literary contributions, including the acclaimed *Custer Died for Your Sins*, *God Is Red*, *Behind the Trail of Broken Treaties* and *Red Earth, White Lies*, life would have been lonely for those with a genuine thirst for knowledge and understanding of the complexities and myriad issues encountered by tribes and their members. Among his latter works is *Singing for a Spirit: A Portrait of the Dakota Sioux*, a chronicle of the Yankton Dakota interwoven with the story of the Deloria family, many of the perspectives and experiences having been shared by Professor Deloria's grandfather, Chief Tipi Sapa, and his great-grandfather, Saswe. Vine Deloria, Jr., founded the Institute for the Development of Indian Law in Washington, and was a founder of the National Indian Youth Council. He served as Executive Director of the National Congress of American Indians, as a board member of the Oglala Sioux Legal Rights Foundation, and was Chairman of the Repatriation Committee of the National Museum of the American Indian. Following the OSCRO/AIM reclamation of Wounded Knee in 1973 and the ensuing siege, he acted among the defense counsel during the 'Wounded Knee Trials'. Professor Deloria is the recipient of three honorary doctorates and numerous awards, his recently published anthology *Spirit & Reason* is defined as '. . . a collection of the works of one of the most important thinkers of the Twentieth Century

"To understand tribal government today you really have to go back and see what it had been. Shortly after the reservations were established, various agents started organizing governments along Western styles, but by 1860 the Osage and others had already adopted constitutions, so it wasn't just the the Cherokees, Choctaws, Creeks, Chickasaws and Seminoles, the member groups of the Five Civilized Tribes, who had organized themselves along similar lines with tribal constitutions that were adaptations of their old ways, and were so named because of their adaptability in developing institutions comparable to the European models. However, on a lot of reservations in Montana and South Dakota the old councils of chiefs and leading men were trying to govern their reservations, while the Indian agents and federal police were wanting to enforce a whole new set of laws, out of which the Court of Indian Offenses developed and proceeded from the mid-1880s to the First World War.

In this transition from the traditional tribal government which basically performed a quasi-judicial function, to the modern tribal council which performs predominantly executive and legislative functions, around 1914 legislation was introduced to provide Indians with the right to vote for their agents, which was a significant effort to establish the Western style of government on the reservations. The legislation authorized the formation of a business committee to hold an election to approve or disapprove the agent, and then once the election had been held those people who served on the election board would somehow become the tribal government. But this was all just ad hoc and didn't provide any means to operate effectively on the reservations. In addition, by 1916, the effects of the government boarding schools were becoming apparent; you had an 'educated' class of Indians there as well as the traditional people, and you started to get tribal inter-marriages to a much greater degree, particularly at Haskell and Carlisle and all those places.

The idea became that the federal government should have a tribal government that looks like itself to negotiate with. Some Indian historians claim that there was never any recognition of tribal sovereignty or political status by the federal government, but there had to be because they were busy trying to transform the whole council into a new governing body, and you don't need to institute a governing body and such procedures unless sovereignty already exists and you have a political entity there.

In the late 1920s, the Klamath came in with a plan to turn their reservation into a corporation. The Klamath had a great big reservation near Crater Lake, Oregon, and the BIA stole a lot of their timber; so under this plan they proposed to kick the BIA out and have a federal district judge supervise the operation of their sawmill business, so creating a corporate form of business corporation. This caught all the reformers short because they didn't understand how an Indian tribe could think that far ahead, so there was a lot of controversy and people like John Collier struggled to keep up with where the Klamath wanted to go. But unfortunately, there were three tribes on that reservation, the Klamath, Modocs and Shoshones, and every time the plan looked like it was going to be approved these groups started fighting with each other for who was going to have the major influence. So in 1932, Senator Lynn J. Frazier from North Dakota, introduced what's called the Indian Tribal Councils Bill, which was strictly a self-governing political proposal to govern the reservations, setting up tribal enrollment, the rules for elections and so forth. Frazier's bill was supported by the reformers and the three or four white men who ran around Washington, DC making Indian policy – John Collier, Nathan Margold and people from the Indian Rights Association in Philadelphia; Oliver La Farge and the like. When Congress closed in 1932 they didn't get the bill through because it was an election year.

Now, this group who worked together on Indian policy were originally interested in conservation – they knew each other and similarly were known – so when Franklin Delano Roosevelt was elected and was trying to fill his cabinet with the best people, he more or less put it to these people, Harold Ickes, Nathan Margold and John Collier, that they could have whatever positions they wanted so long as one of them became Secretary of the Interior and one of them became Commissioner of Indian Affairs. And that's the way Roosevelt worked: pick about five guys and hand the whole thing over to them. It could have gone in any direction, but it ended up with Ickes as Secretary of the Interior, Collier was Commissioner of Indian Affairs, and Margold became Solicitor of the Interior. Margold then brought in Felix S. Cohen, who was a working lawyer from New York City who was into all kinds of reform things, and Collier put a bill together which was going to restructure all of the relationships between Indians and the US government. Collier's bill provided for self-government, it provided for vastly expanded educational programs, it provided for land consolidation, and then it provided for a Court of Indian Affairs that would handle all litigation involved with Indians, and be a regular federal court. It was a brilliant idea. The guy's a hundred years ahead of his time, but he goes out in the field and preaches that Indians must go back to their original culture which means pooling all the allotments and going back to a sovereign state reservation, which was also a good idea.

The problem was that after being allotted, the pressure was put on educated Indians to sell their land. This immediately checker-boarded all the reservations with ignorant white settlers who moved in and usurped the educated Indians who were pushed off their own land. So Collier's bill was sabotaged in Congress and they passed this crazy bill that's currently federal law – the Indian Reorganization Act – which is basically a rehash of Frazier's bill of 1932 without Collier's reforms. Nobody knew what the situation was and the

IRA was rushed through before Congress adjourned in 1934; on the day Roosevelt signed it he must have signed some fifty bills. They didn't know what to do and they had to find a way to rescue Collier's original proposal so in the fall Felix Cohen issued a Solicitor's Opinion known as *The Powers of an Indian Tribe*, which defined all the political powers that already existed in Indian tribes, with the interpretation that the Indian Reorganization Act had only added three powers to this other reservoir of powers that tribes already had. This opinion saved tribes and prepared us for the modern time because all of those powers were regarded as inherent sovereign powers; that meant the political entity had those from the moment it became a political entity and it's not possible for anyone else to take them away. So the three powers that Congress added then become delegated sovereign powers, which means Congress either seeds part of it's power to the tribe, or it gives the tribe permission to exercise those three powers which it believes, rightly or wrongly, did not exist before this. Those three powers are the right to hire a lawyer, the ability to issue charters of incorporation for business purposes, and entitlement to receive loans for tribally chartered corporations for economic development purposes

They then go out and try and to organize all these tribes; organizing reservations politically. Then comes the question, 'Who handles land consolidation?' because Collier is big on getting the reservations back into their original form. So they write another Solicitor's Opinion which says that these governments that they are setting up for IRA are in reality federally chartered corporations for the purpose of economic development, and in doing so they mixed what should have been public and private forever. Therefore, from the beginning of IRA, nobody has known whether they were supposed to be a political organization looking out for appropriations, having law and order, taking care of child custody, zoning, and all the things they're doing today – or alternatively – if they were just a little corporation set up to represent the economic desires of the people and designed primarily to go out and initiate economic development; it's a total mix and it's just about impossible to pull it out, separate it, and see what's going on. So in fact, you don't have true governments, you have governments burdened with a special responsibility to take charge of the economic welfare of the people. They always have to make a decision between the spiritual welfare of the people or the physical welfare of the people, and a lot of people don't make that distinction which explains why, when the Bureau of Indian Affairs push economic development, they look at the reservation as a resource but the people living on it look at it as a residence, resulting in clashes every time someone proposes to do anything.

Jumping ahead to the 1950s, the federal government think they're terminating tribes but in point of fact when the movement switches and they have to go back and re-federalize all those tribes they terminated, their excuse is, 'Even though they're not federal Indians, they're still a tribe with all this authority and all we did was sever the financial relationship between the tribe and the federal government', which just adds to the confusion. What happened in the Twentieth Century was that they did things they didn't understand, by following the moods of the country and of the Indians. They had to think of new ideologies to explain why they did the wrong thing in the first place, and it's been wrong from the beginning. The situation now is that there are very complex tribal governments with millions of dollars in budget every year, and yet they have less *actual* say in what happens on the reservation than the 'uneducated Indians in from the wild' did in the 1870s and 1880s. They made decisions regarding land and annuities and so on, and through the Nineteenth Century nobody ever had to approve tribal actions, then in the Twentieth Century the Secretary had to approve everything. It has been down hill all the way.

Now, in modern times, we have to sort all of these things out. The fact that Congress didn't understand what it was doing in the IRA and said, 'In addition to the existing powers the tribes should have three additional powers', is federal recognition of the inherent sovereign powers of those tribes. If you have a sovereign power you can use it anytime you want, but now you have residual sovereign powers – powers that you have but don't exercise – dealing with almost anything any other political entity can deal with today. That is the way modern political entities have to exist. Industrialism just pushes things together that should not be together, so then you have to use law and governments to try to resolve those questions. Some of the progress that some of the tribes have made is absolutely astounding in such a short a time: in the northwest they have fishing councils, they have authorities on the river and on the Puget Sound, and they have court systems everywhere; and that raises another question – since those are all foreign institutions, how do you take those institutions and turn them towards the service of the people who live on the reservations rather than the efficiency reports of the BIA?

You're going to have constant turmoil all the time dealing with these things and the tribes that will succeed are the tribes who fight back against the BIA and say, 'No, this is the way we're going to do it'. To solve things for the future, you take either your economic function or your political function and reform them. What you could do politically is elect people, stagger the terms, expand the council and elect people for a longer duration and have them represent definite constituencies. Those little villages and little settlements out on the reservations should have some status within the tribal government; just as the state of South Dakota has charters for Sioux Falls, Aberdeen, Rapid City and wherever, so those little settlements should have charters. Each one of them should be a little village with police powers, with court powers, and so on. They could organize informally and without having everyone on salary, but they could then take charge of that and also take responsibility for the commodities and distribution. The tribe could then deal politically with the state, tribal and federal governments. You could then take your education and economic development arms and set them up as long-term operations that are subject to severe scrutiny by the tribal council to make sure they're working. However, what you have on reservations now is that every time you have an election all the jobs change place and everything is in chaos. If you're electing your chairman every two years you can forget it because you're never going to achieve anything. Pine Ridge is evidence of that, it never, ever, ever makes any progress because you have to satisfy all kinds of new people every time.

What you want to do is politically develop your relationship with the United States and call the United States to account for all of these disasters visited upon the reservation under federal policy. When they had the Claims Commission Act they reviewed transactions to see if the true value of the land was received. If they found it wasn't and money was owed they would award it and in theory that brought everything up to date. But you have to then ask, 'What was the effect of the Allotment Act on these tribes economically?' Examine what they were doing: the head of the household received 160 acres, 80 acres went to his wife, and 40 acres to their kids. It was obvious that in ten years those twelve year olds would be twenty-two year olds and they'd be wanting to start a family, but how could they start a family on 40 acres in that environment? So what you can highlight is that there was a deliberate design to put Indians in poverty to make them sell their land, and this would be a violation of the trust the United States has. Based upon that, it should be possible to put together all the facts and figures and negotiate in Congress for rehabilitation for what the government has done; you could take other parts of federal policy in to demonstrate very easily what the cost has been in human lives and suffering, etc. If you got an award, then that award would go to the tribal council and not to the economic development arm. In doing that, you could educate Congress, you could educate your own people and you could educate citizens around you as to why there is poverty and why there are broken homes and so on. I think by making what happened in the past very clear, you can find the first step to move things along. Look at the Puyallup settlement and how the tribe documented what the real damage was to the Puyallup people and how they got a $100 million-plus settlement. Both Indian and white people get a little tired of hearing, 'Well you broke the treaties'. That's obvious, so be specific – how did they break the treaties? And then go into the facts, that there was never a chance to escape poverty because of the way the Allotment Act was administered.

I think that would be a first major step in a reform movement. Then you could go in on land consolidation and propose that instead of all this litigation and constant fighting back and forth, it would be simpler to have Congress set up a bill resulting in repatriation and consolidation being turned over to the tribes. You could then have viable rural industries. I've been a very strong supporter of the buffalo movement because that animal gives you everything and the earth is as good after the buffalo has moved on as it was before, because they're a sustaining animal. I keep hoping for a big snowstorm in South Dakota to totally do away with all those cattle and let people see how great the buffalo are. I think that in order to look at a lot of reform issues properly you really have to find out how things got the way they are. The BIA doesn't have any memory at all, their idea is simply to control what Indians are going to do. It's the tribes themselves that have got to research these things and present them in a very responsible, irrefutable way and then propose some solution to them and eventually that would lead to very innovative ideas. If you're going to have computers and bank accounts and participate in society the way it is then you'd better gear up and prepare yourself for going through a long struggle. A number of tribes really need a research arm; they need to put money into research, they need to put money into public relations, and they need to tell their story. Tribes need to always be factually ahead of the government and they have to develop their own scholars who can crank things out and answer all these problems.

On a lot of reservations in the West, the original residents were often the fugitives from Indian Wars. A reasonable distribution are the Sioux people up and down the Missouri River and over toward the Black Hills. With all the military oppression that culminated in Wounded Knee, the feeling among the Sioux people was that Red Cloud had the most influence with the government so people would naturally flee to Pine Ridge to hear Red Cloud speak up, which results in all kinds of others residing there at Pine Ridge *in addition* to the Oglalas. Now, you can't possibly keep jamming 15,000 people into a place that has a declining land base, so what you really ought to do is begin to train people to run a sustainable community there with the buffalo or some other resource, and then propose to the government that they allow a certain number of people to set up a new reservation on land the government provides. The federal government has a lot of land sitting there and it ought to relieve population pressure on some of these reservations because when they constructed the poverty housing they didn't build houses way out in the respective areas for people to live in, instead they clustered them all together in certain areas which created urban slums in rural areas. There's no reason why some part of southwestern South Dakota or Montana or Wyoming can't be utilized and a new reservation established there and prior to it, design how to develop the economics there and then get families – not individuals – get whole families to move in and occupy that reservation, then have an election and set up a new tribe. If all of these ranchers are going bust, I don't see why the government couldn't also come in and buy some of that land to use for an initiative like this, which is what they did in California in 1934; they had all these homeless Indians in California so they started buying ranches and said, 'Anyone who wants to live on a reservation can come here and set up housekeeping'. They got a former ranch in Rancheria, California, called XL Ranch.

If you're going to live in a rural area you need to be partly self-sustaining. Ranchers are going broke now, but what do they do? Often, if they live thirty miles from town, misses gets up and drives into Eagle Butte or wherever and buys milk, eggs, bread, etc – all of which they could be producing – then drives back; so they're living an urban lifestyle in a rural area. Fifty years ago, when I was a kid, they didn't have fancy houses or television, but they were all well fed because they grew stuff on the land. And in the old days, you never had a camp of more than two hundred people because you couldn't feed them, and that's exactly the situation you have today – you can't feed all of these people. If you look at the federal records, in the 1870s when all of the buffalo hunting tribes were placed on reservations, you find that there are numerous bands that don't appear in your average 'anthro' books. They used to get together for religious ceremonies but the rest of the time they were in smaller units so they could sustain themselves; they didn't have to kill five hundred buffalo to feed two hundred people, five buffalo could keep them for a week, and economic development could be viewed in similar terms.

It's possible to solve these problems. Another example is the Hopi-Navajo situation. I suggested that if the Hopi and Navajo in that area wanted to live together and it was just the tribal councils that were fighting, another line in the sand should be drawn that contained all of the people who wanted to live together, then an election should be held and the new Hopi/Navajo reservation declared: have three tribes there instead of two. Nobody would have to move and the government can then pay off both tribes, 'This is for your loss of land, and this is what you're contributing to create a new reservation to solve this problem'. All of these things are possible but people have to think beyond the confines of where their minds are at the present time and they're not doing that. There are hundreds of conferences on sovereignty where people just get up and talk and talk and talk and talk, but very few will do the hard work to go out and exercise the sovereignty that already exists. They spend all of their time trying to define sovereignty more clearly and that's absurd if sovereignty means that any political entity can negotiate on an equal basis with any other. Period . . . So sit down and work out a deal! It's very difficult to get tribes to see that. A lot of them are so enthralled with this sovereignty idea, 'Oh we can't talk to anybody, it would infringe upon our sovereignty. We can't have an independent school on the reservation, it would infringe upon our sovereignty.' Well, if you have sovereignty and you refuse to exercise it you don't really have anything, you're just stuck. That's one of the big problems that I see out there today. If for example the state sits down with you, they'll lose sovereignty too because that agreement is going to bind both parties. It's very simple, and the good thing about setting up negotiations and finding an agreement and working together is that if it doesn't work, you can always go back and negotiate for another agreement, there's nothing hard and fast. If you go to court there is a winner and a loser, and if you're the loser you don't have it anymore, and that will stand until you're able to go back in and try to get it reversed. Litigation is a real hazard, it's like throwing the dice. About the only thing Americans can do politically is figure out a compromise where everybody gets a little bit of the pie and solves the problem for two or three years, and then you go back and try it again. That's why there are so many treaties with some tribes in the United States; that was the process – keep negotiating back and forth.

Too many people are trained to just think in the little arena and as long as you're in that box, you're never going to go anywhere. If you can step out of it, then look at it and say, 'What the hell is this?', then you realize that if you can make an officer a gentleman you can do any damn thing you want! For instance, plenary power only exists where the court says it does, it's not something standing there and staring you in the face. They don't teach you that in law school, but if you read enough litigation on Indians and don't read it as a lawyer but as someone trying to figure out what they're doing, then you see that the court wants to solve problems; they think up the easiest, most acceptable way to phrase their decisions and in very few cases do they actually say, 'Plenary power allows them to do this'. Generally, they fudge and go round it. Even in *Lone Wolf v. Hitchcock*, which has the great definition of plenary power, they continue their opinion and say, 'Well really this is a business transaction and we're transforming the investment, we're not breaking the treaty'. So even that court didn't understand what it was doing. When they make problems with Indians they take the white man's education too literally and they think that it's real when it really isn't – it's just a hodgepodge of emotions put in English. Once you can get through that barrier and see it, you say, 'I don't have to worry about this stuff, I can figure out a way to deal with it'. A lot of very good young lawyers we've produced in the last twenty years are trapped in the idea that federal law is finite and therefore you have to stay within the confines of it.

I would favour creating a new entity called the Sioux Nation to which all the Sioux tribes contribute. This would start at 1851 and put out a massive 'renegotiation of treaties program', systematically renegotiate all of these things like the Mitigation Act that keep arising. That way there would be one entity that everybody would support and this entity would post good information and make top-level responsible moves with relation to the government, as opposed to the way it is now where everybody runs around and then ends up fighting with each other over everything. I'd also favor trying to go back to the old *Tiospaye* band structure of settlement and begin to get people to look at who is really responsible for the tribal government and all of these things, and try to adopt some of those traditional ways in terms of accountability and operation. Try and pull families together first, because if you can get two or three elders who represent two-hundred people, then they can be a political force almost anywhere. You need identifiable human interests on the reservation but right now the reservation governments treat their membership as the US treats it's citizens: a conglomerate of individuals, each of who's opinion is as good as anyone else's. And that's absurd. There are very smart people and very experienced people, and there are very stupid people, and if you're going to set up a government where stupid people can out-vote the wiser and more intelligent people, then you get what we have today.

Tribes already have the right philosophy in their traditions. At conferences everybody screams, 'Elders, elders, elders, elders!' And yet they really don't pay any attention to those elders and they should! They don't set up structures where the elders' wisdom can come to the fore. When you go to an Indian meeting on the reservation a loud-mouthed drunk has as much say as the smartest medicine man on the reservation because of the way they run it, and that's nonsensical. I've been to the Sioux summits where you get all the Sioux from different reservations, but we don't even sit in a circle where we'd all be equal, we have a stage and a panel, and then we have everybody in the audience; so they're running around talking to each other and it's total chaos. You're not going to stop anybody from doing anything if you're not organized. You have to get your people emotionally organized around their responsibilities to their relatives, and then that can become a voting block of political influence; then they're the ones who can say, 'No, no, no, you can't do this'. The way it is now, you just cut out any intelligent discussion by having an open meeting and that's why all the white cities are so badly governed – there's no one representing the spirit of the town and the developers can just run wild creating more slums. Society is going totally mad, speeding at 90 miles per hour toward a granite mountain and nobody is even aware of it.

I think the traditional form of government was very efficient, because what you had with chiefs and headmen and warriors was a way of pinpointing responsibility. If you go into social contract theory – the reasoning of John Locke and Charles de Montesquieu – it basically says, 'We can't trace the descent of Adam, but if we knew who Adam's direct descendent was we'd make him king of all the world, but because we can't we'll have to start out with the idea that all people are created equal and they all have a right to vote for a government. They then give up the right to kill each other and the government does it for them and then you have a society.' But that didn't account for the cultural, social and family profile of that individual who wanted to vote. In America there were the middle class merchants who didn't want to pay any taxes to England and they weren't the smartest guys in the colony by any means; they were disgruntled rip-off artists who were having closing sales everyday and never closed their businesses, like the car dealers of that era, and these were the guys in the American Revolution. So an institution is created which says you have rights against your neighbor and you have rights against the state and that's an adversarial social contract that never defines what your responsibilities are to your neighbor and what your responsibilities are to the state. Now if you move to the Indian way, within the kinship system and the clans you have responsibilities to every person you know and they have responsibilities to you. So you're contrasting two different forms of government: the Indian one is a government of responsibilities and duties, while the white one is a government of rights. You can't have anything but turmoil in a government of rights because every individual has the right to assert his rights against everyone else, making it the dream universe for lawyers; the only way you can solve anything is to fight according to the rules society establishes. When you go to the Indian way you find all of these responsibilities and if you violate your responsibilities you then have all these people saying, 'You failed, this brings shame on our family, the other families look at us and say we can't control our relatives. This is a disaster, our name's besmirched, we're no longer one of the leading families.' And that's a terrific punishment there, and if you're totally out of control, they say get out of the tribe – and the tribe is all you have! With the social contract thing if you screw up, they're going to put you in jail. In both instances you're leaving society, but the fact that you convict someone for armed robbery and put him in jail doesn't have any effect in teaching the rest of society to behave themselves. There really is no educational feature in the criminal law system, it's just retribution – you steal a car and we'll put you away for three years. So this person goes to jail and learns how to steal even bigger things and comes back out and starts stealing again; they didn't learn, society didn't learn, and building prisons is the fastest growing industry in the United States.

The fishing rights struggles in the northwest that started in the 1960s provided a model for traditional values with the Franks family. Old man Franks was in his 90s during the fishing rights struggle, and it was basically that one family and their in-laws who fought that whole thing out. Those were family groups who took responsibility and tried to live in the traditional way and forced the federal government to change everything it was doing. So it's entirely possible and probably the only way that you're ever going to do it. Now, I think the recent Makah situation in the northwest is a little different. There are a lot of things behind that reaction and one of them is that the US is a totally urban society and the majority of American people truly believe that milk comes from the supermarket, along with meat, eggs, and so on, and that there's nothing else involved! Then the Makahs go out and kill a whale and people go absolutely crazy, 'They're killing Willy the Whale!' And nobody asks the question, 'Well haven't the commercial whalers been doing this all along?' Well yes, and it's okay for them but it's not alright for the Indians. It comes down to a small group of people and one whale. At the time one guy wrote, 'How could they kill a sentient being?' Well what about all the dolphins that are killed? And there's nothing more sentient than wolves and coyotes but they've eliminated most of those. So you think, Wait a minute, what planet is this guy living on? He doesn't understand that when he buys bacon that some pig somewhere died, or what? But there was a lot of anti-Indian hatred up there for a long time among the average rednecks. Washington State is an amazing place, you had enough intelligent white political leaders who sat down with the tribes and worked a lot of things out, but you're always going to get very weird people. We lived in Bellingham and they believed that the Russians had divisions in Canada who were ready to invade the United States and that they were going to head for Bellingham because we had the largest toilet paper factory on the west coast, and if the Russians wiped that out then by the time they got to LA all the Americans would be sitting on their stools in their houses and would be easy to capture. Now these are not just nuts, the rank and file of Bellingham deeply believed that!

All we're really seeing in American history is the working out of the failures of the protestant reformation. These people thought they could live in a feudal society by proclaiming their conscience – Calvin, Luther, etc – but they ended up being abused in Europe and hating Europe, so they came over to the New World and paid a terrible price to settle on the East Coast; casualties in some of those colonies were 80 per cent over a twenty-year period. Almost a third of the people went back to Europe, but those that stayed were afraid of the Indians, afraid of the land, or afraid of each other – the American people have needed someone to fear and someone to hate from the very beginning. The Berlin Wall goes down and you get all these nuts bombing federal buildings; people hate their own government. We desperately need aliens from outer space so we can all hate them and pull the US together again. So that's what you're looking at when you look at American history, just hate and fear alternating with never a chance of setting up a decent society. There are all these European ideas and institutions in this society that can't ever become indigenous here and the prevalent attitude is a foreign attitude. Now ecological historians are attacking Indians right down the line, 'Indians did away with the buffalo, Indians did away with the hard woods, Indians did away with . . .' and why is that? They're trying to become indigenous and they think that if they smear Indians then they'll become the true ecologists, but it doesn't work and they're just getting more and more frantic. Everybody here is a fugitive with a fugitive mentality. You look at Kennewick Man and the doctrine is that we were the only ones here, and now they're trying to change the doctrines so they can play with it. They desperately want an Anglo to have been the first one over here and they don't care how they do it, but what you end up saying is that nobody has any roots here and no one can ever feel really native here. America is the most dangerous country on earth and the only way you can establish American identity is through violence.

If you look at who's going to be the last person standing in North America when the whole thing goes, the Indians have got such a lead that you can forget about it! The whites are all clustered in the cities so they'd better stop fooling around with these little countries because if they decide they're really going to go after the US, the way the cities are, with germ warfare you could start one hell of an epidemic. With the environment, look at global warming, it's becoming catastrophic. That Ice Cap up there is melting and so you're going to see a total ecological breakdown in Alaska very shortly and everything there will change radically. I don't know what's going to happen then because that oil pipeline is built on the premise that you have permafrost underneath and nothing is ever going to give way, but Alaska is just a big deposit of muck from a tidal wave of a planetary catastrophe. You drill down in that muck and all you have is trees, broken bones, and mud; that stuff has been frozen for God knows how many years and now it is going to come loose. It's going to be a hell of a mess and they are finally going to have to admit that there were gigantic catastrophes on this planet. But the Indians are going to win in the end because there's undoubtedly going to be a Cree or Blackfoot up on some mountain in Canada that won't get the word when everything collapses and everybody kills each other, and they're going to come down out of those mountains saying, 'What the hell happened?' ”

VINE DELORIA, JR.

JOY

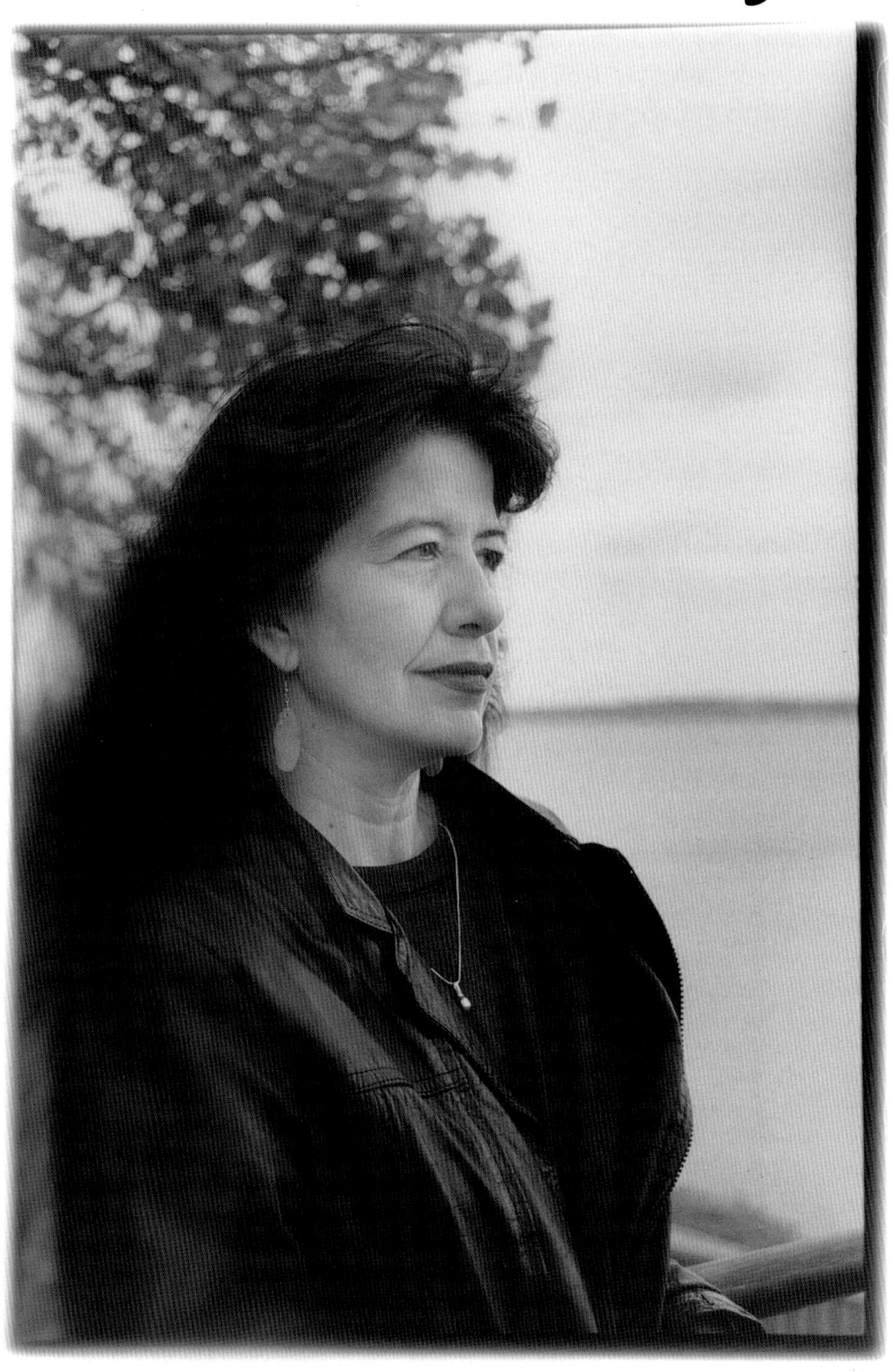

Voices from Native Amer-ica

HARJO

"The world is dense with layers of meaning, layers of being. This is true for everyone, not just for Muscogee peoples, or Diné or others. It's a human reality. Some cultures haven't separated the spiritual from science, as has the Western world. Some chose to develop this perception instead of building skyscrapers. When you travel outside the Western time chain you understand that everything exists within this moment; there is no separation from your actions and the affects of your actions, and there is no separation from the heart and the mind."

Joy Harjo has received the Lifetime Achievement Award from the Native Writer's Circle of the Americas and her critically-acclaimed and best-selling collections of poetry include *A Map to the Next World, The Woman Who Fell from the Sky, In Mad Love and War, She Had Some Horses*, and *What Moon Drove Me to This?* In recognition of her outstanding literary accomplishments, the American Indian Distinguished Achievement in the Arts Award, the William Carlos Williams Award from the Poetry Society of America, the Josephine Miles Poetry Award and the American Book Award, are among the multitude of honors bestowed upon her. In 1992, Joy Harjo was the recipient of an Honorary Doctorate from Benedictine College, and in the same year she held her second National Endowment for the Arts Creative Writing Fellowship, one of several individual fellowships granted to her. A member of numerous panels and advisory boards, her professoriate chairs have included tenures at the University of New Mexico, the University of Arizona and the University of Colorado, having previously served as a lecturer and instructor at ASU and the Institute of American Indian Arts. The saxophonist and vocalist with her band, *Joy Harjo and Poetic Justice*, their album *Letters from the End of the Twentieth Century* won the First Americans in the Arts 'Album of the Year' Award. A descendant of the Muscogee patriot Monahwee, in 1998 Joy Harjo received a Lila Wallace/Reader's Digest Fund Writer's Award to develop the non-profit body, Atlatl, to provide literary resources to the Native American community.

"I don't know that you explain, The Earth is our Mother, you just live it. The earth gives us many gifts and expects so little from us. The one philosophy that appears to connect the over 550 tribes in the US is that the earth is alive – the planets, stars, all of us, all creatures and life forms are alive and deserve respect. That's the basis. A common misconception of non-Indians, and even many Native peoples, is that we are 'Native American' or even 'American Indian'. Many recognize 'Indian-ness' from images cooked up from a pseudo-Plains culture, first described by the Wild West shows. This is not a true culture, but many cling ferociously to it. I've been to Germany many times to perform both solo and with my band. Once, a man came to interview me before a show and he was disappointed when he saw me. I don't look the part, and he was even more disappointed when I refused to give him back the rhetoric that he wanted to hear. If I had been male with long flowing hair, wearing a ribbon shirt and giving him a high five we would have gotten along. Instead he turned and walked out. He would have been disappointed with anyone other than those who look like the image Hollywood has promoted, which is again, Indian men with long flowing hair who often tend to find themselves on the backs of horses wearing mid-1800's drag. We are human beings who are all related, but belong to very distinct cultural groups. And it is no longer the mid-1800s.

Most Americans have an adolescent sense of time and space. The perception of time varies according to culture and relative human age. An infant enters this world carrying a sense of eternity. For a child a day is nearly forever. For an adolescent there is no future nor past, everything is now, in the moment – and most Americans have not grown past this age. They have no sense of history, place or family and their relationship to it, which I attribute to severe dislocation that came about with colonization. Colonization is destructive to both the colonized *and* the colonizer. In order to conduct acts of genocide and attempt to destroy cultures, the colonizer goes into a state of denial of the pain and destruction he is causing. Or he rationalizes it. Hence, there are 'Indians' who exist in the imagination, not in real life. And there is no history; or history is rewritten to exclude these acts. But what is denied actually does exist and eventually comes to the surface, just as any truth will eventually surface despite acts to hide it. To confront the truth of the matter would open the wound and it would heal, but instead of doing that everyone steps around it, wondering why their children are picking up guns and shooting at them.

I think it's very important that those who have been colonized abandon the victim mode. Yes, the Battle of Horseshoe Bend happened. I've walked those grounds. I have seen the war and the aftermath. I am descended from one of the leaders of that attempt to stand up for what is right, to stand up against destruction —Monahwee. We have the stories and the songs and they live within us and will continue to be part of the story. I prefer to think of the destruction as ways that we have been tested – and we have been tested terribly. Maybe we were tested so hard because we were beloved. Maybe I am being a fool. It all still hurts. But we as Native peoples keep being told by images – by others' versions of us – that we have been defeated and that we are not acceptable as ourselves. It can be difficult to step out of the paradigm of defeat, but it is possible.

If I communicate anything during my tenure here in this particular life it would be that Native peoples are human beings! That we human beings are all related in complex yet simple ways, and that this whole existence is sacred and divine . . . and then riff in words and music some of the wildness and sweetness of this existence. That's rather basic, and maybe even shocking, yet, as I travel around the US and the globe, I find that people have a hard time seeing us and knowing us beyond cheap Hollywood images. Any living culture is an open system; that means that it is in flux. Its soul has a particular imprint, and maybe even a promise to grow, to change. And it has to change for vitality. Colonization was like a rock falling on a flower. That kind of change is drastic and it's difficult to recover. But it's possible. I always admire flowers that erupt from concrete.

Where do words come from? It is the same source of creation that gives birth to songs, or to any other kind of creative expression. I honor it, I hammer myself against it, I am in awe of it, I respect it. Words, or rather stories and songs, are what humans do. We go out during the day and return with stories and songs that intrigue us, that we share. It's an ongoing process. All literary traditions are oral in basis, the written word came much later. The written word made us lazy because then we no longer had to remember. Yet, I find the written word intriguing because it combines elements of our oral traditions with the images of the letters, the words themselves. There is energy in what is spoken, in what is thought and the manner in which we perform our thoughts and words. I think of a poem as an energy field, related directly to songs.

I believe in a society in which everyone is valued for what they bring to the mix. It disturbs me to see anyone disrespected because of race, sex, culture, economic status or sexual preference. I believe there's room for all kinds of permutations of being. I have found those societies that are called 'traditional' to be the most accepting; they understand this. Often those societies influenced heavily by Christianity are the most rigid, as are the 'born-again' traditionalists. There is one central law that you will see repeated all over the world and that law is the golden rule – treat others the way you would like to be treated – kindly, and with respect. It's very simple, but I believe that it comes down to that. The opposite of love isn't hate, it's fear. The misogynists, the white supremacists, the fundamentalists of any kind, all might be full of hate but fear is the predominate source of their passion. Ultimately they are afraid of themselves.

I see myself as a human-being who is also Muscogee and female. To be female in this world isn't easy, especially in a male-dominated culture, as is what I call the 'overculture'. I've disregarded many of the cues of so-called femininity and keep in mind that the soul is ultimately neither male nor female, or both. At least that's how I see it. On the stomp grounds women are treated respectfully, both sexes hold value. In the Euro-American culture, I think the feminists are on the right track; feminism is about equality and respect and I think the movement has made inroads. It does have relevance to Native women because we deal in worlds in which women are seen as having less value. Again, much of this is due to particular interpretations of religious sects and to males who are afraid of female power and again, ultimately, themselves. Of course, at the root of many of our tribal cultures women are central, but others aren't quite so evolved. I always like the story I heard of a Maori woman who stood up to speak during an assembly. One of the young men had gone away to school and had learned the ways of the Europeans, so when he returned he took offense that a woman was assuming authority to speak. He asked her to sit down. She then turned to him and asked, 'Where do you think you come from?' And then lifted her dress to her knees. 'Every human comes through the door of a woman. Don't forget it.'

When I think of great woman warriors I always think of Anna Mae Pictou Aquash. I wrote a poem for her and Susan Williams, her brother John and I, made a song. Most warriors will never be seen in our text books, their names will not be known to the wide public. They are the ones who get up early in the morning to cook, dress the kids and send them off to school then head to work, then come home, cook dinner and do everything needed to ensure beautiful humans in the world. I think of my daughter, Rainy, too. She has three children she has given birth to, and three daughters acquired through her partner, Tim. She is a fine mother to all of them; patient, strong, inspirational, and funny. I've never heard her complain, though she has had many tests in this life. She's also a fine writer, a better poet than I was at her age. She's only twenty-six.

My music and poetry are inspired by the acts of such warriors, both male and female. What deeply moves me is to see people overcome terrible acts and turn them into something beautiful. I pull from many sources in the poetry and the music. We call the music of Poetic Justice a 'tribal-jazz-reggae-poetic-rock', when in essence the influences are even more than that. As a Muscogee living at the beginning of the 21st Century I am, as we all are, exposed to a diversity of music and sounds we never heard in the 1950s in Tulsa. We heard rock and country on the radio, sometimes live music, stomp dance and country. I remember country guitarists at our house, and once I heard my mother sing a ballad with a country band. I grew up to all of those sounds and then after I went to high school in Santa Fe, I experienced powwow, Navajo and Pueblo. They are all a part of me, a part of the influence. So, lyrics to Anna Mae over a jazz infused reggae is a natural expression of the poem, and what the song means. Musically what caught my soul was John Coltrane's horn. And then Jim Pepper, a Muscogee horn player who was incredible. He was encouraging, and became a friend. Another unbroken, inspirational musical experience comes from being involved with my ceremonial grounds. Those songs wind through my blood.

The definitive moment for me in terms of poetry was hearing Simon Ortiz read poetry – his own poetry. It was the first time ever that I realized that you didn't have to be white from Europe or New England to be a poet, to write poetry. It was then that I understood that poetry could be written from my experiences as a young Muscogee woman, a teenage single parent trying to get through school. That was a major revelation.

The world is dense with layers of meaning, layers of being. This is true for everyone, not just for Muscogee peoples, or Diné or others. It's a human reality. Some cultures haven't separated the spiritual from science, as has the Western world. Some chose to develop this perception instead of building skyscrapers. When you travel outside the Western time chain you understand that everything exists within this moment; there is no separation from your actions and the affects of your actions, and there is no separation from the heart and the mind. I have a great faith in humans and in human nature, despite the rampant destruction of spirit we see occurring at this shift in time. I think we will keep on, though the worlds might turn and we start all over again. It's important to keep creating and to keep thinking for ourselves: think good thoughts and keep singing. ”

JOY HARJO

WES

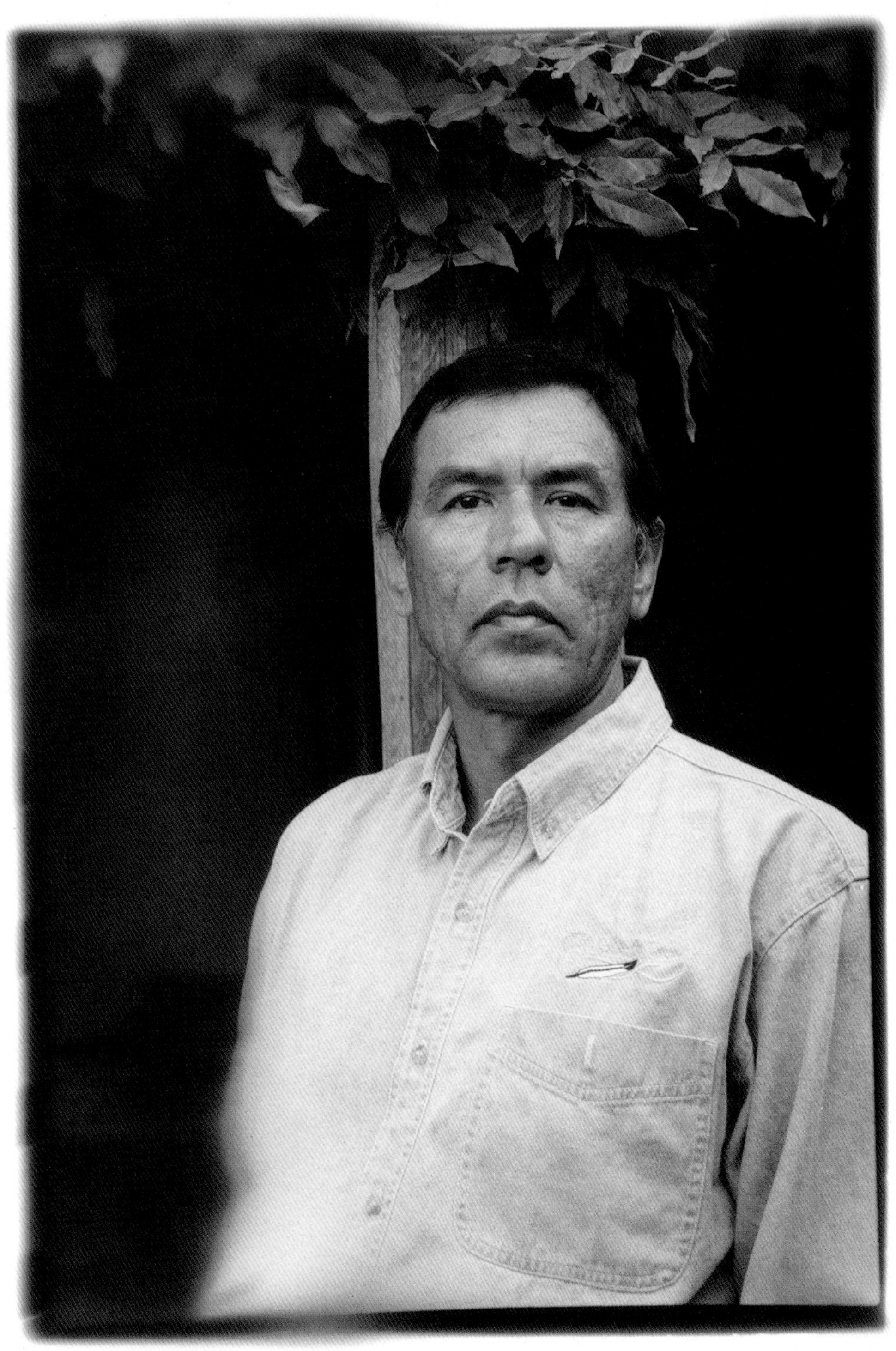

Voices from Native America

STUDI

"I can relate every part that I've ever played to something in my life. The Indian parts I've had have been easier in that respect because those roles have called for a look into the past, which has meant looking into what still angers me about the relationship we have with the government of the United States and other colonial powers. So from that perspective those are fairly easy to connect with in terms of people like Magua, Geronimo, or Red Cloud, but the difficulty is that men are much more complicated than history would have them. With the ethnically non-specific parts I can also connect something from within my own life that has relevance to what's going on in that character's life at that time. . . I don't think I've played my favorite role yet but out of those that I've done I would lean towards Magua and Geronimo, although I also see myself as that guy in Heat *too."*

Wes Studi

Although possibly best known for his portrayals of Magua and Geronimo in *The Last of the Mohicans* and *Geronimo: An American Legend* respectively, Wes Studi has achieved that which has eluded many of his contemporaries: he has torn through Hollywood's buckskin curtain to be recognized as an actor, period without the platitude 'for Native American roles'. Parts in *Heat* opposite Al Pacino and Robert DeNiro, and in *Deep Rising*, helped change the emphasis and since the mid-1990s his portfolio has alternated between 'Indian' and 'ethnically non-specific' roles, as evidenced by the aforementioned plus the likes of *Street Fighter*, *Mystery Men*, the TV movie *Crazy Horse*, and *The Streets of Laredo*. Internationally he came to prominence as the 'Toughest Pawnee' in *Dances With Wolves*, since when he has received numerous awards; many believe his performance as Magua merited an Academy Award. In addition to his screen work, he performs in theatre productions, wrote and performed a one man stage show, and directed *Bonnie Looksaway's Iron Art Wagon*. He is the author of two children's books and he plays bass in the band *Fireca[t] of Discord*. Prior to his career in the arts, he served in Vietnam and upon his return became active in the American Indian Movement. He later wrote for, and helped found, the forerunner to the *Cherokee Advocate* newspaper. In 1999, Wes Studi was honored by the Cherokee National Historical Society.

"I think that we as Cherokees have always had divisions amongst ourselves and I doubt that you will find many groups of Native people here, in what is now the United States, that have always acted as one, in unison, throughout their history. The Cherokees are a large number of people who were confederated into one nation by virtue of language but before removal, back in the east, we inhabited a large portion of the present day southern states. That was our territory before contact with the Europeans, when first the Spanish came from the south, then the English from the east and the French from the north. We had contact with all of those Europeans as well as other tribes from the north and south, and I think at times divisions amongst us were created by the separate alliances that were made with those different peoples. In terms of The Trail of Tears, that happened a long time after initial contact and by then we were dealing with 'the Americans'. It would probably have behoved us at the time to have embraced a more nationalistic flair and attitude about ourselves and had we done so I think that we may have been more successful in retaining our homelands, but because of that divergence of opinion within the Nation it was easier for President Andrew Jackson and the state of Georgia to execute their policy of removal, resulting in The Trail of Tears.

In the east the Cherokee Nation had established a democratic form of government with a recognised council and leaders, so we began early in terms of organizing a democratic forum to meet the demands of dealing with the US government. We had begun to forge ahead as a Nation, but geographically within the United States itself we were virtually locked between the northern states and the southern states and the ideologies of the North and South had a lot to do with forming ideologies, and as a result overall plans, by different factions within the Nation about which way the Cherokee Nation itself should move. That's really what happened in terms of The Trail of Tears. The Ross party was mainly Republican in ideology but the Ridge party was more or less aligned with the Confederates and the slave holding states and, at the time, the Federal government was equivocal and that's how it came to make the agreement with the Ridge party against Chief John Ross and the Cherokee Nation government.

The Cherokee Nation government was fighting hard to oppose removal and sought remedy through the courts. In March 1831, the *Cherokee Nation v. Georgia* was rejected by the US Supreme Court on jurisdictional grounds but in February 1832, without the question of jurisdiction, the Cherokee Nation won in the matter of *Worcester v. Georgia*, the Supreme Court ruling that neither the state of Georgia or anyone else had the right to seize our lands or force us west of the Mississippi. However, President Andrew Jackson defied the Supreme Court and said that if they were able to enforce that decision, then they could go ahead and enforce it. Jackson advised the state of Georgia to continue its actions against the Cherokees, and he was part of the group that made the agreement with the Ridge party of John Ridge,

Wes Studi

Elias Boudinot and Stand Watie, that made it all possible. By 1834 the unity of the Cherokee Nation began breaking apart; Ridge and Boudinot had celebrated the 1832 Supreme Court ruling just as John Ross had, but by 1835 they had made their agreement with the US government, and Cherokee was going against Cherokee on the question of removal and survival.

Interestingly, by that time a lot of Cherokees had already begun to move simply out of distaste for the living conditions that had come upon them in the east; things were changing too quickly and they wanted to keep the lifestyle that they had so they began moving west of the Mississippi. They moved into areas of Missouri and Arkansas and were known as the Western Cherokee for a good twenty years before removal happened. They had to go out and fight Osage, Pawnee and Sac and Fox people who already lived there, but they carved out a pretty good homeland until removal when, more or less without being consulted, they were also dragged into the area that was to be demarcated as the Cherokee Nation in the west. In the main I think that the divisions that may still exist follow along those same historical lines, with the addition of those who readily and enthusiastically joined up with missionaries of different kinds, primarily the Baptists.

With hindsight it's easy to think of Stand Watie as a man who only had the worst in mind, but given the context of the times in which he lived I think that you have to give him some credit. I personally don't think a whole lot of his actions, but on the other hand I wasn't there or part of the political situation as it existed around and during the Civil War, and the South might have won. I think that possibility may have weighed heavily on his mind and should that have happened, the Cherokees who followed him may have been able to mark out their own territory and secede from the States. My understanding is that Stand Watie and the Cherokees who entered the Civil War as Confederates lived a lifestyle compatible to that which the Confederacy sought to preserve; some of the Cherokees to the south of where the Nation is now situated were slave-holders with plantations, and I think that a large proportion of the Cherokee Nation's mixed-blood population followed in that direction.

Up to a certain point I think that Watie did what he thought was right but why he continued until he was the last Confederate general to surrender, and why he employed tactics similar to Sherman's 'scorched earth' strategy, I don't know. The people who suffered most from that, when they went in and burnt down and destroyed everything with the idea that it could be rebuilt later, were those who wouldn't join-up with either the North or South and tried to remain neutral, and the majority of full-blood and traditional Cherokee people fell into that category. In the main everyone suffered for what Stand Watie and his people did because their active support for the Confederacy provided the Union forces and the Federal government with the rationale to forget that we also had people fighting for the Union, and they more or less punished the whole Cherokee Nation by taking away huge tracts of land. But when considering Stand Watie you always have to remember that the South could have pulled it off and had they been able to, who knows where the Cherokee Nation could have been. As it was, the Nation was devastated by the Civil War and the growth and prosperity that people had achieved in that short thirty-years since The Trail of Tears was shattered.

Cherokee was my first language. I always hesitate to say that my family were traditional; we were survivalists, I think. We attended all the things that other Cherokees attended and as a child I didn't even know that there were other people who looked that much different from us. I don't remember seeing an 'American' or 'Oklahoman' or whomever until I started going to school at about five years old, because our whole life was made up of Cherokees. Our family was part of the community, we did what everybody else did in the area which actually wasn't that much because our religious practices were banned at the time. I remember one of our sisters getting involved with the Church when she went off to school and her coming home and trying to tell the family about it and my grandpa's reaction was, 'I don't want that in my house'. Not that he offered that much either in terms of religion or any kind of belief system except that we would go to the Stomp Dance now and then, but we didn't really know what the deal was with that, other than it was a big gathering and a big feed and it was good to get out there and learn those songs. And it was always on the sneak because our dances and ceremonies were against the law; a lot of times I hear Cherokees say that we only do our dances at night and I think that's a holdover from those times when we had no choice but to only do them at night because they were totally outlawed.

I think preserving cultural traditions is just a matter of being able to practice them. If they are a viable part of a family's survival, be that subsistence or whatever, and therefore are a part of a community's economy, the traditions allow families to define themselves spiritually and economically, and I think that's the basis upon which it works. One of the reasons why I think the Stomp Ground in the southern part of the Cherokee Nation has survived is because it plays a part in everyday life there. People interact with one and other there; they're able to trade goods, trade jobs, and do favours, and what brings them together is the Stomp Ground. The dances and traditional teachings that happen once a year keep them together, and all of these people also interact in economic terms; they're all in one area and all share the same beliefs. Those of us who don't live in that immediate area can also share in the beliefs that are taught there on a yearly basis, although we're not part of everyday economic life there or the day-to-day function of that traditional unit.

A lot of people like the idea of being Cherokee because it gives them some sense of being part of something that's bigger than themselves. I used to be really disturbed by people who do that, who claim to be Cherokee and aren't, but after thinking about it somewhat they must have a really high opinion of who we are as a people if they want to say that's what they are! Hopefully that's what it is that drives them. What made me think that these people shouldn't be doing it is because they haven't lived the life that, as a Cherokee, I've lived, or had ancestors who went through what ours did because of the fact that they were Cherokee. If these people look at being Cherokee as joining some kind of social club I don't respect that at all because it belittles the efforts made by our ancestors to keep our people together as a unit, as a tribe, and as a Nation.

I've heard of people 'buying' memberships to groups who claim to be Cherokee, but there is a defined method of being able to get a card that says you are Cherokee which is based upon your Cherokee blood quantum, and therefore your ability to establish ties with someone who was at one time recognized as a Cherokee. People who try to fake this are like those who con people by trying to sell ceremonies, they belittle the belief system or the tradition or ritual they are claiming to offer. They also take advantage of some people who are honestly looking for something to help them with their lives, they prey on what they perceive to be that weakness. Thankfully they're almost always found out because they can only live that lie for so long. They're hustlers and when selling ceremony doesn't pay off anymore they'll go on to something else or get drunk and die! I think they find their just desserts as time goes by. I don't know that I give these people that much attention now because I don't intend to give them that power, if you will.

If I only played Cherokee roles I wouldn't have work. Well, maybe I would on *Walker, Texas Ranger* but unless you're 'Walker' I don't think you'll make much of a living at it! This is a business that is entirely dependent upon image, and by that I mean the definition of image you find in the dictionary, by which I'm an American Indian and that gives me a broader spectrum in which to play as an actor, rather than being identified solely as Cherokee. Acting is what I do, it's my work, and when I'm in that mode of thought I accept myself as being whatever my image is in that context. That is also when I have to accept myself somewhat on other people's terms by accepting that this business is what it is and I am capable of working in it by virtue of what I look like first and then by what I am capable of delivering as an actor. When I'm in the acting mode then that's what I am, an actor. I'm fortunate that in my career I have been able to cross-over from those parts that are entirely ethnically specific, like the one in *Deep Rising* which didn't call for anyone to be ethnically specific.

This business works on demographics and we as American Indians make up a very small part of the entire population of the United States and a minute part of the world's population, so if I was to show up in braids for a part that was ethnically non-specific it wouldn't help me that much because I would be identifiably American Indian. If, however, I was willing to take those braids off and look less identifiably Native, then I think I'd probably stand a better chance of scoring that job. On the other hand films have to be ethnically-specific in certain cases, particularly when it comes to telling a story about Native Americans, as I think those who play those parts will bring a certain credibility by virtue of their appearance, mind-set and even accents. Similarly, if you were going to cast *Boyz N the Hood*, you're telling a story about a black neighborhood and so you're definitely going to have black people in it, right? But then when you get into stories that are ethnically non-specific, it comes down to image and the ability to get into the story as an actor. I've shaved my head a number of times for roles, once to look more like a Pawnee, once to look more like a Huron from a specific period, and also to play ethnically non-specific characters a couple of times. I personally believe that my appearance is definitely Native American and definitely Cherokee – that's who I am – so I feel that whatever I do with my appearance, I'm still who I am. If I was so attached to a certain aspect of my appearance, like if I was so attached to those braids that I couldn't take them off to do a part, then I would say that I was in the wrong business.

I can relate every part that I've ever played to something in my life. The Indian parts I've had have been easier in that respect because those roles have called for a look into the past, which has meant looking into what still angers me about the relationship we have with the government of the United States and other colonial powers. So from that perspective those are fairly easy to connect with in terms of people like Magua, Geronimo, or Red Cloud, but the difficulty is that men are much more complicated than history would have them. With the ethnically non-specific parts I can also connect something from within my own life that has relevance to what's going on in that character's life at that time and so there's always something in there that looks like Wes Studi. I don't think I've played my favorite role yet but out of those that I've done I would lean towards Magua and Geronimo, although I also see myself as that guy in *Heat* too. I've turned down a part or two because the role wasn't very effective in the story that's being told and/or I personally felt that it was somewhat demeaning to us as American Indians. I don't hesitate to do that but it hasn't happened to me too many times. I think to some extent every 'Indian' stereotype you might be presented with in a role is still alive but I think that people are beginning to shy away from dealing with the world through stereotypes and I think that's a good first step

A film that I would like to put together would be one that speaks to the concept of arrested development in terms of a large group of people. Something that explores what kind of personality develops from a mind set that has perhaps dwelled too long on the idea of arrested development and has asked too many times, 'What would it have been like had we continued to develop as we were?' And I'm relating that to European contact. If everyone had stayed where they were supposed to stay, where in the world would we be now and what kind of people would we be? That's the kind of story I would like to work on.

With regard to the consequences of European contact, including our issues today, I don't know that a lot of media coverage would make any difference because the majority of the American public view our issues as things that should be taken

Wes Studi

care of by their government. They're not really affected by them until you reach a point like the Oneidas getting a bunch of land back which might dispossess some people; that's when it affects them and causes a ripple in the public's perception. Mostly I think that the American public's view of our issues is something they only deal with after a film like *Dances With Wolves* which was hugely popular, or something dramatic like Wounded Knee in 1973. Then public persuasions are pushed in one direction or the other, sometimes in our favor and sometimes not, and they begin to read about this and that and offer an opinion. But I don't think the American public's perception of us is that much of a force because they are fairly powerless, and most decisions that affect us have to do with either governmental or corporate decisions that are made at either state level, federal level or county level. The most damaging threat to us remains the move to terminate and abrogate the special relationship we have with the Federal government. If I could, I would introduce legislation that would put tribal governments on a par, by law, with state governments.

Being an Indian certainly doesn't hold you back and to our younger generations I would say be who you are and grow to be better. You're as good as anybody else, so now become the best 'you' that you can be in whatever it is you choose to pursue. If something is holding you back it's not that you're an Indian, and if it's a hurdle then you might be dealing with the wrong people. I used to envy people who decided early in life what they wanted to do for the rest of their lives but it's not a decision that anybody needs to rush in to. I've seen people who started out wanting to be this or that as a profession early in life and with the passage of time have become disillusioned with it, feeling like they're stuck doing this one thing for the rest of their lives. I think that we should remain open; a person doesn't just have to be one thing throughout life. If you decide to do something I think you should do the best possible job that you can within that particular activity, you should take it all the way there and then if it no longer pleases you, look for something else. You have a fairly long life span and a person can do many things in life. I think that's one of the things that keeps a person interested in life; being able to do different things and undertake new endeavors and challenges; continuing to learn. For instance, it takes a while to master shooting a bow but once you achieve a certain finesse in that you also have to learn something else – I think that's pretty much what life is – discovery and finding different things to learn. By the time you die you should be practiced in many different things and you should have done all of the things that have ever entered your mind to do. ”

Henrietta

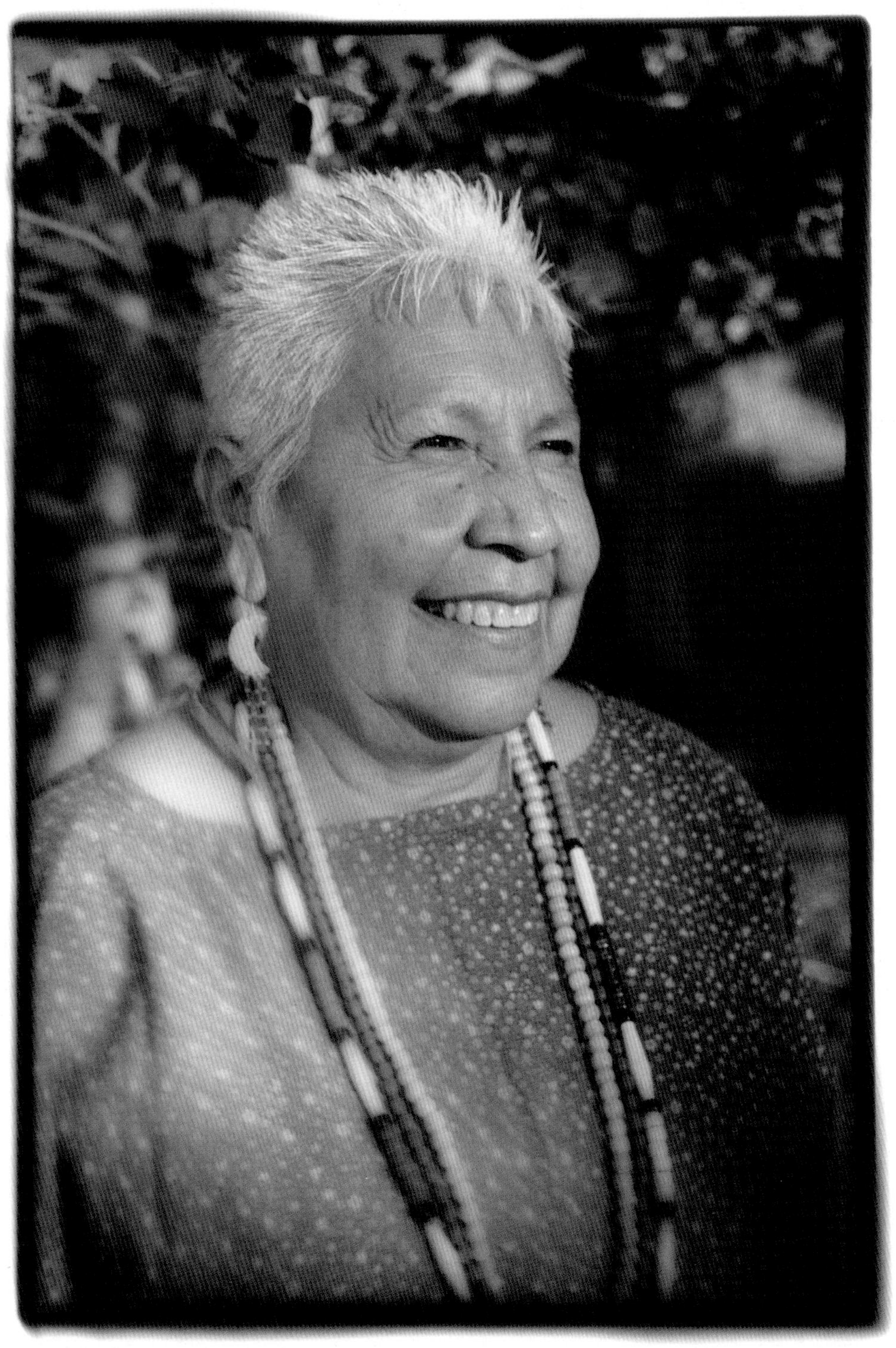

MANN

"I can forgive but there are certain aspects of my history, whether it's solely as a Cheyenne or as an Indian person, that I cannot forget because Native Americans never want to go back and relive that horror. We told everybody that Freedom of Religion is not guaranteed in this country and that what happens to us could happen to you. In 1953, Felix S. Cohen, who is considered to be the father of American Indian law, wrote in the Yale Law Review *that American Indians were America's miner's canary in terms of the treatment we have endured. Today, we are still this country's miner's canary when it comes to the erosion and lack of protection of First Amendment rights."*

In 1991 *Rolling Stone* magazine heralded Dr. Henrietta Mann as one of the ten foremost professors in the United States, and her distinguished career in higher education has included tenures at the University of California at Berkeley, Harvard University, Haskell Indian Nations University and the University of Montana. The National Women's History Project named her among the elite 'five *20th Century Women Educators*'. Dr. Mann was the highest ranking American Indian woman in the administration of US President Ronald Reagan serving as Deputy to the Assistant Secretary of Indian Affairs/Director of the Office of Indian Education Programs, and she later completed a two-year term as a Commissioner for the National Commission on Head Start Fellowships of the Head Start Bureau, an office of the US Dept. of Health and Human Services. Dr. Mann was the National Coordinator of the American Indian Religious Freedom Coalition, and the numerous boards upon which she has sat or continues to hold membership on include Native Action, the Council of Elders (AISES), the Native Lands Institute, and the Board of Trustees for the National Museum of the American Indian Smithsonian Institution. The TV and film documentaries *How the West Was Lost*, *In the White Man's Image*, *Paha Sapa*, and the Ken Burns/Stephen Ives produced *The West* all feature Dr. Mann's work in the capacity of interviewee, consultant or technical advisor. Dr. Mann was the Cheyenne language consultant for the movie *Last of the Dogmen*, and she is the author of *Cheyenne-Arapaho Education, 1871-1982*. Henrietta Mann has been honored as Cheyenne Indian of the Year, and National American Indian Woman of the Year.

"*When I came* to walk on this earth it was in 1934, so I guess that makes me a 'Depression' baby. I didn't have any sense of what the Depression was, but most American Indians have always lived with the state of depression, we just didn't know there was an era for it! I was born in Clinton, Oklahoma, the first child of a Cheyenne man and a Cheyenne woman who had met at a BIA Boarding school and married young. Both my mother and father had become Christianized, my father was a Baptist and my mother was a Mennonite. I spent my formative years in Hammon, Oklahoma, which is just a small, small town, but at least there were Indians about; Cheyennes all around – we had surrounded Hammon! I grew up in our extended family, not knowing about the depression or the economic situation; I didn't know about poverty – it just was. Four generations of us lived in a three-room home on my grandfather's Allotment and my great-grandmother was the matriarch. She passed on to that final camp, as we Cheyennes call it, when I was two years old, but I know that she taught me so much in those two years.

My great-grandmother had already raised my father whose mother had passed away when he was an infant, and she taught him and then he passed on those teachings to me and so I have a very intimate knowledge of her and what it is to be a good Cheyenne woman. It takes a lifetime to achieve good-heartedness and to be consistent about it and I was blessed with a good Cheyenne heart, which means that there are standards and values I am expected to maintain in terms of who I am and what I am as a person; what I'm expected to do and not do. My aunt reared me as most Cheyenne aunts do and I think that environment and upbringing really gave me a strong sense of identity as to who I am. My mother and father made a very special vow, one which Cheyenne people could make, vowing not to have another child for ten years so that I could be taught all the things that would make me a good-hearted person and a person blessed with a Cheyenne heart. Had they not fulfilled that vow, it would have resulted in my death, so I did not have any siblings until I was twelve years old.

In the meantime there was this world of relatives who contributed to a very rich education, at least from the Cheyenne cultural perspective. As my grandfather's oldest grandchild there is a special relationship between he and I that transcends life, he was my best teacher – all my joy – and he was *very* Cheyenne. My grandfather had instilled in me a love of knowledge and so I wanted to go to school to learn, and at five years of age I did. I convinced my grandfather that as my cousins went off to school and came back and taught me English that school must be a wonderful place as they seemed to have a lot of fun, and whether they did or not, that was my conception of it. I was very wilful then and finally my mother said, 'Okay, you can go to school but you've got to get permission first'. This was the time of Indian agents, so we went to ask the Education Agent if I could go to school and he looked me over almost like you would a horse, he did everything except check my teeth, but I stood there trying to look as intelligent as I could with my

Shirley Temple look and he agreed to let me go to school. He said, 'She'll get tired real easy and then you can take her back out', and of course I heard that. Finally, I think in the fourth grade, I marched home from school after some racial tensions and I guess a good dose of prejudice, and informed my parents that they could take me out of school now. That was when I learned that education was a life-long process. I ran over to my grandfather and he said, 'When you start something you carry it through. A good Cheyenne doesn't quit.' And so I graduated at sixteen.

Even though I went to school, my father got one of his cousins to come and live with us so that when I got home I'd also have my Cheyenne lessons. My aunt taught me language, culture and so forth in my own private one-on-one Cheyenne school with her and I loved that. So having grown up as that special child, because of the vow my parents took, I guess in a way I was really given to the people and I would never change what it is to be a woman of the people. When my mother first brought me home from the hospital my great-grandmother was there to greet us. She was a midwife and she was a medicine woman, and traditionally babies were introduced so she took my small body in her hands – I am told she held me like men handle the pipe – and she offered me to the Grandfathers that sit at those four sacred directions of the universe and then offered me above and then below, microcosmically tracing my journey. I'm sure that was a wonderful prayer and I think it's a prayer that has guided my life. There are some of us, certain individuals within a tribe, who are looked upon as bridges and they have to function us bridges between, and interpreters of, culture. I think that was the way my grandfather and my great-grandmother saw me and it is the view that I have of myself today, which is why I teach at a mainstream institution.

I work very hard to educate myself in a non-Indian context, following those first students who went off to places like Carlisle, Pennsylvania, or St. Augustine and Fort Marion, Florida. I have taught at the higher education level now for thirty years and it's all been about American Indian studies because I saw that gap in the higher education curriculum; it's as if we, as Indians, are not supposed to exist, much less have any place in the world of academia – their place of knowledge. But we are very much a part of American society and so for the past thirty years I have attempted to teach, or to provide some kind of information about the beauty and the reality and the harshness of what it is to be an American Indian in today's society. Contrary to the perceptions of some individuals, I have not disappeared into the world of academe; I function there but I am always on the periphery. I'm not really accepted as a part of their world but there's nothing they can do to get me out because I work very hard to have the same kind of credentials that they do. At the age of forty-five I went back to work on my doctorate degree and finally got a Doctor of Philosophy degree at age forty-eight.

I won't go back to another Anglo institution but I still have a lot to learn about what it is to be that good-hearted Cheyenne. I am one of the many ceremonial people and I never thought that once I'd fulfilled my vow, that I would return to that Sun Dance Arbor; there are others now, and my children have. I didn't think that I would instruct anybody and pass on the teachings of my teachers and their teachers but a young woman came to my sister's house with her offerings, with her tobacco, and asked me to instruct her – she wanted to go through the Sun Dance. Those ways that we have of maintaining and sustaining ourselves are exceptionally important and after she asked I sat there and I prayed about it. Then I thought, I go all over the United States and I have gone to foreign countries, always to instruct the children of my white brothers and sisters – and that was a big dilemma for me, that I teach everyone else's children but my own. So I thought, you start with your own, and so I consented to instruct her in our ceremonial ways and it feels good. I'm very happy about being back on that sacred ground – in that Arbor – that center of place, to help in my own small way to recreate and renew a world that is in great need of renewal. We as the adults of this world have not modelled the kind of behavior that is going to promote and encourage among our children the very respectful and inter-personal kinds of relationships between humans and everything else in the environment; our relatives that are rooted in the ground, the four-legged ones, those that fly and those that crawl. We have to set the example and to learn not only how to get along with one and other but how to be respectful and to live in inter-dependence with all life and it worries me that the adults of the world can still engage in one conflict after another and perpetuate inhumanity.

I don't know about individuals who can forget about the horror of places like Wounded Knee, and more specifically for Cheyennes – Sand Creek and the Washita. Can we forget about being literally herded onto reservations and having to live in the kind of poverty that we have been locked into for centuries? Or the loss of an entire continent that is constantly being desecrated and violated? I come from the school that says, 'Yes I can forgive but there are certain aspects of history that you can never forget'. This is part of history and the whole evolution of this country called America that, unfortunately, has a history of religious suppression, and persecution, of American Indians. You can't look at it as if it suddenly ended in 1934 when John Collier supposedly reversed the policy of banning the Sweat Lodge. You can't forget that the Sun Dance was classified as an 'Indian Religious Offense' along with all of the other similar ceremonies. I think forgetting in that regard would further prolong this society's existing state of denial and enable individuals to ignore their own history and a situation that could be likened to the holocaust. I can forgive but there are certain aspects of my history, whether it's solely as a Cheyenne or as an Indian person, that I cannot forget because Native Americans never want to go back and relive that horror. We told everybody that Freedom of Religion is not guaranteed in this country and that what happens to us could happen to you. In 1953, Felix S. Cohen, who is considered to be the father of American Indian Law, wrote in the *Yale Law Review* that American Indians were

America's miner's canary in terms of the treatment we have endured. Today, we are still this country's miner's canary when it comes to the erosion and lack of protection of First Amendment rights. We cannot forget this earth that was the first to nurture us and needs to be renewed. So we go back into our ceremonies, because if you forget one aspect of your history that could lead you to forget a lot of other things, and we have these sacred mandates and these sacred missions in life to ensure that our ceremonies continue, because as long as our ceremonies continue then we're alive. We seek life through our ceremonies and so long as we perform our ceremonies, the world will continue to exist.

In one respect I think that the schools and the Federal Government succeed to a certain extent: in their obsessive need to destroy us as a people – not just with the diseases that they carried with them but by devastating our ways as people, our languages, the things that sustain us spiritually and physically; the ceremonies that provide us with the means and belief in transformation. People can always change for the better and even in the midst of the horrors of cultural assimilation we clung to that hope of a better tomorrow and that there could be better people, people that would really love and respect each other. We still hold that hope. I hold a certain hope for the young people. Among young Indian people, schools have created very negative self-images and if I had to live in this time I do not know whether or not I would take the path of least resistance like many do and engage in substance abuse or suicide or teenage pregnancy, or any of those social crises that young people face today. The way I grew up provided me with a very strong sense of identity and provided me with a foundation of right and wrong, but unfortunately there have been breaks in our culture. Several generations who were sent to residential and boarding schools did not readily experience what it is to be a good parent in terms of being modelled, or the modelling of healthy domestic environments where you can demonstrate love and respect for one another. I think that's generational, so now I believe it's up to every one of us individually and culturally – as tribal nations and groups – no one else is going to save us, so we'd better save ourselves.

When there isn't a very strong sense of identity and the languages are no longer being spoken, our communities seem to be in disarray. You don't see that strong sense of family, but you do see tribal government officials not getting along and the spoils system at play. Alcohol is one way to numb the spirit from all of the insidious cultural erosion and when you've got the kind of poverty that exists on many reservations people turn to what's most readily available and often that's alcohol. Children in Lame Deer and on nearly all the reservations can get high for what, two dollars a day? A dollar a day? Or whatever it costs to manufacture that poison, be it crank or whatever it is that's available. Some have lost that sense of hope. I work with a project there, on the Northern Cheyenne reservation, called the Seven Cheyenne Stars and Hope and those eight little girls who make up that group are the light of my life. It's a combination of a cultural leadership and development program and they're in my finishing school. I just want them to be all that they can possibly be and know who they are as Cheyenne girls. So you take that core and you work with them and hope that those kinds of successful programs or projects can be replicated. We as family members, we as members of our respective tribes or nations, really have to take the time to teach our young ones. We took them to Bear Butte and I sat and told them about our relationship to that particular piece of land, how it holds our souls, it holds our spirits, and it's our origin as a people. If I never do anything else, at least I know there are eight little girls who know what it is to be culturally grounded. The program has a language component to it and languages are critical to the lifeblood of a people's culture, and ceremonies have to be conducted in those languages.

You've got the churches declaring their war on drugs and the Federal government declaring their war on drugs and yet on reservations most people know who the drug lords are, but the Federal government seems to be powerless to do anything about them. These drug dealers become an institution unto themselves as they prey upon the most vulnerable in our communities, our young people. I assume some of them are getting very wealthy and it's their livelihood, so either you've got rogue federal or tribal officials and court personnel that may themselves be involved at some level and do not want to stop the drug traffic, or with all of this manpower and alleged infusion of funding they really are powerless to stop it. I think we as tribal members, community members, parents and grandparents are going to have to get angry enough to say this has to stop and maybe then we can use those that pay lip service to remedy these social ills that they have created. We didn't create them, the government created them by this five-hundred-year history of oppression and if they don't have anyone else that they can arrogantly consider inferior, then they are going to want to keep us there and I for one am not content to let us stay there.

Many Indian people are physically sick today because of what they have to live on; the high fat, high starch and high sugar content of commodity foods simply feeds diabetes and heart disease and so on, so by modern day tactics the Federal 'Commodity Program' to Indian reservations could be classified as genocide – it's the same end result without the cavalry. The genocide of our people, whether it's physical, spiritual or cultural is still there but we're still very much a part of this land. We're still very much alive and we have not been driven to extinction or vanished. I think it troubles society that we are still very identifiably Indian and it has certainly astounded and confounded those policy makers that we didn't disappear. They came with their concepts and doctrines of Manifest Destiny and Imperialism. They wanted the land – but we are still very much a part of that land – and they still want it. I guess it's still Manifest Destiny: subdue the earth, take what you want, and never mind its impact upon those children yet unborn. Satisfy the 'I' generation, the 'me' generation, of today and don't think down the road

about those that may not have any natural resources or may not even have a land to live upon.This is a very voracious society that is taking the natural resources from the ground that most of us look upon as our Mother, and those resources represent the internal organs of our Mother the Earth. A lot of disruption is caused by this lack of vision on the part of those that are doing it and the policy makers allowing it who have no respect for culturally different points of view. We sit here living within this great circle of life in an inter-dependent relationship with caretaking and stewardship responsibilities for the land and all that is on it, above it and below it. We live by that understanding, that mutuality and reciprocity; if you're going to take something then you give, but with all of this coal, oil and gas extraction – the plundering of the earth's natural resources – what are *they* giving back?

When we were given our way of life as a people and our prophet, Sweet Medicine, was talking at Bear Butte, he spoke of the day when those that would come to live with us, who we call *Ve'ho'e*, the Spider White People, would tear up the earth with their hands. He said that when we Cheyennes started to do it with them we would become lost as a people. I haven't seen it done yet but the Northern Cheyenne people have had to deal with the matter of coal since the Bureau of Indian Affairs approved leases for coal development on the reservation in the 1960s. They were eventually declared null and void in the 1970s but the spectre is still there with the contemplated Tongue River Railroad that may cut through the eastern boundary of the Northern Cheyenne Reservation to transport coal. We may see coal trains rolling over land which is considered to be the most sacred part of the reservation, where people go to gather their medicinal plants, where they go to fast and to pray, where they go to make their offerings and where they go to bury the afterbirth of their children. I think granting permission for coal extraction and coal development on the Northern Cheyenne Reservation is certainly a sovereign right of the tribal government but I would hope that they would think very far into the past and very far into the future before they gave that permission. They should think about coal development in the context of the prophesy of Sweet Medicine and what the impact would be on us culturally and spiritually.

It is very important not to cross the gender lines that exist when discussing certain aspects of our culture and to be respectful of this, but I will say that when Sweet Medicine bought us our way of life as a people, he also instituted our government. Along with the traditional form of government which we refer to as the Council of Forty Four Peace Chiefs, he also instituted the Warrior Societies and he gave us our law-ways as a people and told us how we were to live – that we were never to murder another Cheyenne. The spiritual and medicine people of the tribe were vested with the highest authority and the four major laws he gave us prohibited lying, cheating, marrying relatives and intra-tribal murder. Sweet Medicine also devised our value system, consisting of love, respect, cooperation, generosity, understanding, humility, and maintenance of the Cheyenne way of life.

He lived with us for 446 years and gave us a wonderful way of life and through those values he brought to us the laws and the way we governed ourselves and protected ourselves. We still have the traditional council but it has no decision making authority in terms of policy that can affect the economic and social well-being of the people, although there is still a ceremonial responsibility. In 1934 the United States Federal government enacted the Indian Reorganization Act and set in place its form of government which supplanted the traditional forms of government for those tribes that elected to organize and adopt constitutions and by-laws pursuant to the provisions of the Indian Reorganization Act. The Northern Cheyennes organized under the IRA form of government, as did the Southern Cheyennes in Oklahoma, so essentially two different governmental bodies then existed, one traditional and one a Federal government/Bureau of Indian Affairs imposed structure intended to take the governmental power from the traditional form of government. This created tension that we have never really overcome as one group is often played against the other, so the Federal government placed us in a cultural dilemma by extending their form of government and the reorganization efforts that completely supplanted the traditional form of government organized and established by Sweet Medicine as it was sent to us from Grandfather Creator, The Great One Mysterious. Maybe the Federal government likes to play God or thinks it's God! Because of this, the policy of divide and conquer is still very much alive and well in places where they have been able to create puppet governments in their own image so we might just do ourselves in.

I think many American Indians today have a love/hate relationship with the Bureau of Indian Affairs, but as long as it's there I know that the Federal government is carrying out its treaty commitments to us as a people. From that standpoint I look upon the BIA as being more or less symbolic, but even with all its ineptitude and paternalism as long as it's there I'm one of those that say, 'Okay, the government hasn't forgotten its promises to us'. On the other hand, having at one time served as the highest ranking Indian woman in the administration of US President, Ronald Reagan, working for Indian education in 1986, I experienced government at a high level and I would say the most powerful entity is the Office of Management and Budget where things can be decided very expediently and expeditiously based simply on dollar amounts without any regard for the human toll and impact, and I remain very critical in that regard – we don't need that kind of government at all. I think the Bureau of Indian Affairs would like to get out of the Indian business and maybe it should, but I would probably be out there leading a protest to keep it because of those solemn and binding agreements that many of our Indian Nations entered into with the United States, of which it is symbolic. But it needs to change; it needs to be more sensitive and more humane as the agency charged with the responsibility of carrying out the Trust Agreement of the United States of America with the First Peoples of this country.

In more traditional times women's roles and men's roles within tribal society were very well defined and the first ones to come along and blur those gender lines were the fur-traders and trappers. They tended to have a subservient view of women, born out of the role to which Eve was relegated after the fall of Adam and their expulsion from the Garden of Eden. That was their point of reference and their version of Creation. The Cheyenne Creation account, at least as it was put together by the Northern Cheyennes, falls into the Earth Diver category. Most historians place us in the Earth Diver type of Creation account where you have this great body of water and an animal of some kind dives down to the bottom of this great salty water and brings up some sort of soil from which this earth is made and consequently all life. For us Cheyennes, our Creation as a people is preserved in our ceremonies; the male ceremony relating to the sacred objects that Sweet Medicine brought to us from Bear Butte that I cannot mention; and the Sacred Buffalo Hat that the other prophet, Erect Horns, brought from a mountain that from a distance looked as if it were black, believed to be in the Timberline Mountains of Minnesota.

Our Creation is preserved in those ceremonies that accompany those two sacred objects that came from different mountains and every year when those ceremonies are performed we are taken back in time, to Creation, the time when life was most sacred and most holy. In those ceremonies we are re-centered spiritually and renewed to walk that good road again in a good way. Our Creation account talks about human beings being created from elements in our environment, from earth mixed with water, and how the Creator called the winds from the four directions to come and give us the breath of life. So in the way I understand our ceremonies and our Creation account, you don't see that subservient role of woman propagated by Genesis. We did have role definitions and the women knew that the children were their responsibility, as was the most secure of all places on earth – the home. Without a woman, the Sun Dance cannot take place for the Cheyenne people. But over time we have seen the erosion of egalitarianism by external society and some of our people have embraced Christianity and its attitudes.

It's easy to identify the grave socio-economic conditions on reservations and look at the high incidence of alcohol and drugs, but we've never had the benefit of anything like the Marshall Plan being instituted after we were invaded – and we were never in the business of striving for world domination like Hitler's Germany! All of these present, fragmented services provided by the various branches of the Federal government ought to be brought together in a way that's going to result in very positive changes in Indian Country and somewhere along the way we as Indian people have to take some responsibility. We have to say, 'I'm not going to live this way any more. I'm not going to allow my children to destroy their minds and their bodies with alcohol, drugs and so forth.' We have to participate in that process of building healthy communities and rearing healthy children, but we also need an infusion of all of the services and available funds to help us make ourselves well. ”

HENRI MANN

Kevin

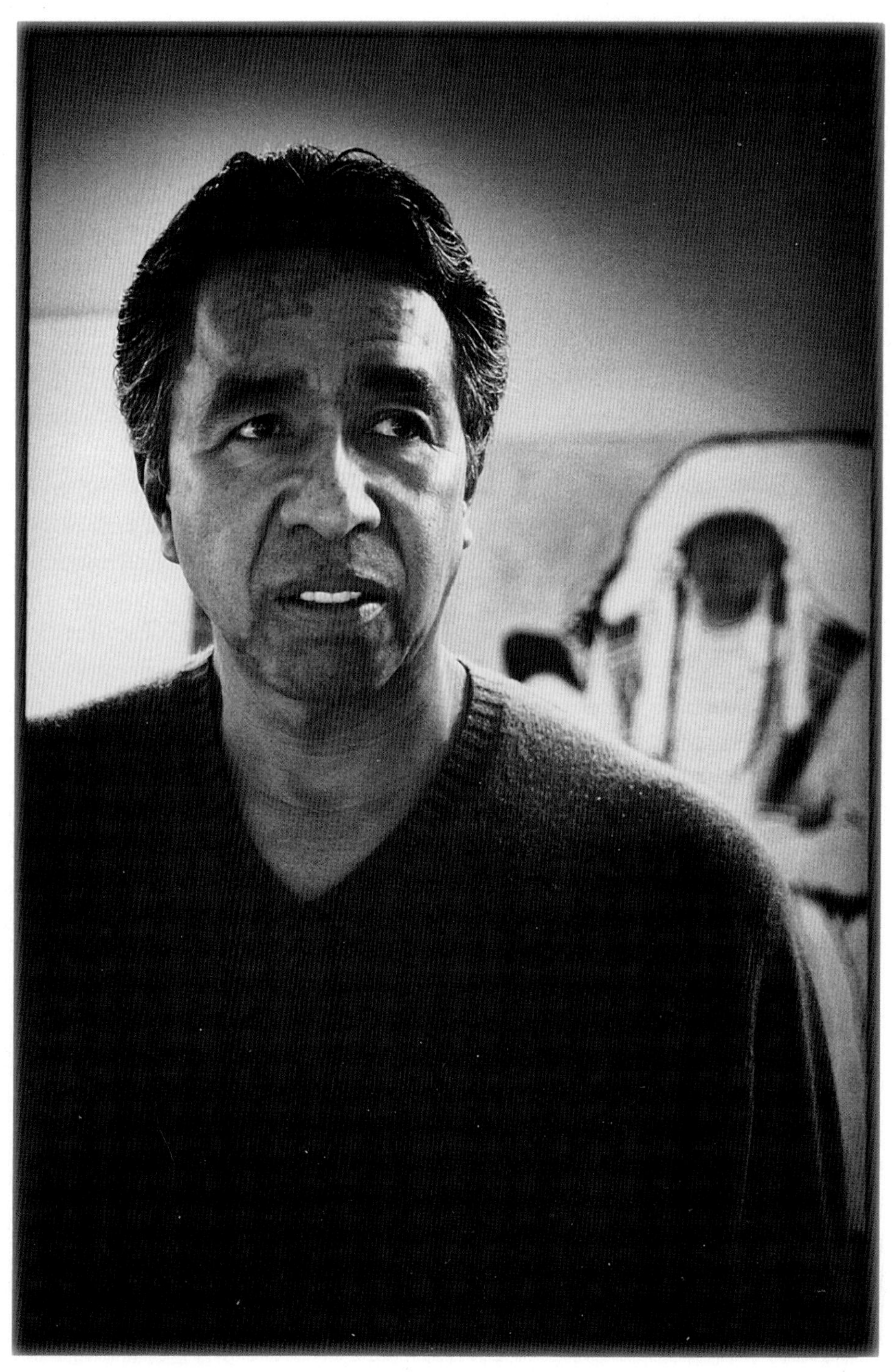

Red Star

"I never pondered if my work was going to sell or not because I never cared, I just produced. Some young, up and coming artists ask, 'What if people decide not to buy your art at some point?' To which my reply is, 'I don't even consider that. I'll still produce. I'll still paint for my self-satisfaction whether that happens or not.' I think when a person just creates without confines they move energy around, like an energy is created in the universe that comes back to you. I feel that because I believe in the Creator and I see myself as being part of a chain that receives the inspiration that originates from the Creator . . ."

'He is among the Masters and will, during his life, enjoy his status as such,' declared an art collector, an opinion of Kevin Red Star shared by critics, connoisseurs and fellow artists alike. Red Star has been in the vanguard of the arts for over thirty years, first within the circle of American Indian artists, and then the international sphere of the art world in all its incarnations. In 1962 he was among the initial 150 students selected to attend a fledgling Institute of American Indian Art (IAIA) in Santa Fe, since when the academy has become a fixture – with Red Star's work hanging within it. The IAIA's museum is one of many around the globe to hold Kevin Red Star originals in a permanent collection, the others include the National Museum of the American Indian-Smithsonian Institution, the Heard Museum, the Whitney Museum of Western Art, Denver Art Museum, the CM Russell Museum, Eiteljorg Museum, and the Buffalo Bill Historical Center. In addition to the Pierre Cardin Collection in Paris, and China's Shenyang National Art Museum, Red Star's work is held by museums in Germany, Belgium and Japan, and was featured in the US State Department's 'Art in the Embassies' touring program. He returned to IAIA as one of the first Artists-in-Residence, and completed similar tenures at Roanoke College, and the Russian Academy of Art in Moscow. 'Painted with light' on canvas, Kevin Red Star's impressionistic odyssey through Crow and Plains Indian culture adorns galleries, museums and imaginations around the world. He is the recipient of an honorary Doctor of Fine Arts degree from Rocky Mountain College.

"Where I'm at with my art is pretty much an easy flow at this point in my life. Over the years I've done a lot of research, when I was younger I visited all the museums I could when I traveled to the big cities and today when I have a show in Los Angeles, or Denver, New York or Chicago, I allow myself that extra time in those cities or wherever, so that I can continue to research. Now, as back then, I go to museums or libraries where I've heard there are great Plains Indians collections so that I can study and absorb the artifacts, the visuals and paintings, and over the years I have stored those images away in my memories. Sometimes I will pick up postcards or have slides of these items, but often it's just the memory and inspiration and I work from those as they become ideas. Those ideas can also serve to illustrate in my mind the Crow legends I heard from my father and uncles when I was a young boy. I create and recreate those situations, and ideas are created from them; I will create a setting from the stories that I've heard. I'm a romanticist. I read all the Crow legends and stories and then I put them together and create a setting for an image, be that a camp scene at night or however I translate it in my own way. I try to make these settings as authentic as I can and, because I never lived in that era, that's where these items from that research come in for me; the Crow designs, maybe the design on a Crow warrior's shield, or how a Crow warrior marked his horse compared to how a Shoshone, Arapaho, or Blackfeet might.

I was born in Lodge Grass on the Crow Indian Reservation and raised in a household where there was creativity. My mother was a bead worker and so art was always there with items on the walls, Crow designs and fringe-making material, her moccasins, vests, hair barettes and appliqués, so I grew up surrounded by Crow art forms. My father was employed as a police officer and chief game warden, but he was a musician and he and his buddies formed a band called the Reservation Hot Shots when they came back from the war. They'd come over and have jam sessions, playing all those old Hank Williams Honky-Tonk/Country songs, and I remember those and being impressed that everyone read music. My dad played steel guitar and I just remember them having a great time, and that was the household I grew up in; I was a young guy surrounded by music and art and that combination is still with me when I work. Musically I'm from the sixties and when I'm initially preparing, mixing paints and stretching my canvas, I like to listen to music from that era. I go to The Beatles and some jazz as I go through the preliminaries and when I'm doing background and fill-ins, but when I'm into my next half of the painting I like more subtlety, maybe some classical. I like music in the background of my life. I think my parents instilled creativity in me and it was nurtured through them. When I decided that I wanted to go to art school they didn't hesitate, they wanted me to do something with my life.

When I graduated from the Institute of American Indian Art (IAIA) in Santa Fe, I then went to the San Francisco Art Institute, and then to Montana State University in Bozeman. I went back to Santa Fe in the mid-1970s as an Artist-in-

Residence at IAIA and set-up a studio space in the area. I stayed around there for about seventeen years and that really gave me a chance to explore the art world and experience a great camaraderie that existed amongst some artists there during that time. That camaraderie makes a lot of difference to you when you're young, or it did to me; I had sculptor friends and printer friends and we would always be sharing ideas. There were American Indian artists too, like Allan Houser and Dan Namingha who were also IAIA alumni, and some Kiowa friends of mine; guys like TC Cannon, Earl Biss, and Doug Hyde all went back to live around Santa Fe. It was a very exciting time, we were all young and had either graduated from college or come back from Vietnam; some were teachers and decided they didn't like that so they became working artists like myself. I don't know if that happens nowadays, but we shared a lot; I was already an established artist there so if one of my collectors came and wanted to see my studio I'd also invite them to visit my sculptor friend or my other painter friends and later, in turn, they would do the same. I grew up in an age when we shared a lot.

When I was starting out I never really had any role models from the art world until I went to school. I was impressionable in the sixties, and I liked what was happening on the east coast with Warhol, Robert Indiana, Jasper Johns, Rauschenberg and that abstract, expressionist movement. It was exciting to see and art was suddenly in the news and so we started exploring those forms as young artists. At the time I was studying the Crow culture and was encouraged in that by one of my instructors, James McGrath. I had heard the Crow legends and was looking for those artifacts, shield forms and symbols, and myself and others used that east coast style in collages we created with our own tribal imagery, symbols of horses and buffalo. That fusion and excitement was there, how those artists on the east coast were interpreting those articles from their experiences and we were using the ideas that the Plains Indians were noted for, and we needed that. I needed that, to play with something exciting. But we weren't copying them, we were relating the idea to our ancestral memories and environments. We were exposed to the spectrum; from the Renaissance to post-modernism, the European art of Michael Angelo and Rubens to mixed media; and so the whole meeting of image and influence was inspiring, but in general I would say that there are many ideas but not one sole artist who has influenced or inspired me – so many people bring so much. Maybe being healthy creates the greatest inspiration.

My work has evolved and it's still changing. There are times when you're young that you explore and try different things, I went through a more abstract stage in my life and I really liked it but then again I didn't want to divorce myself from what I'm known for. Now I remember that I had formal training in the traditional techniques of an oil painter, and remember that when you have that you're able to explore and break it apart, just tear it up and create a whole composition with an image that you conceive without having a realistic or impressionistic boundary; on occasion I've gone beyond that, I've torn it up, and I've created something real exciting for my own satisfaction. I went through a similar stage when I was doing a lot of collage work using leathers, using feathers and pieces of wood and other materials in the late 1970s and then I thought, 'Maybe I shouldn't explore so much because my collectors might not like it!' And that was just my insecurity at that age. People are sometimes reluctant to change or explore because they don't want to leave an area that's sellable and while that may be understandable if you're a working artist, I've seen artists follow such a formula and never lose clients but they don't grow; I see a lot of that all over the arts, not just in the Indian art world. If you're a musician and you've had some hits in a certain style then some repetition might be necessary but you still have to have some new stuff or the hits and creative expression stop pretty quickly. The collectors, the people that have followed my painting for over thirty years now, like a little movement and even now I do a few things that I did in my early training; some very impressionist, almost abstract pieces, and I feel comfortable with that and so do my collectors because 'they want something from Kevin Red Star', so I have that freedom. Early on I was vulnerable like most artists, but I got over that quickly and I just said, 'I'm going to produce no matter what! Whatever comes to me, I'm going to produce and not really worry about anything.' And I don't really have any regrets in my art.

Everything I do is an experimental state but I'm positive it is going to formulate into a good state. I try to give it this nice balance, whatever the struggles around me, and maybe if I can put a solid over here, or maybe with another color here, I will find that balance and that's my enjoyment; can I make it work with a little swash of red over here? And that might give the whole balance. And that's me, that's my personal satisfaction in the studio. It's a personal expression. Interestingly, I also feel that describes abstractionists. 'Abstract' is a freedom of expression but once again it's from an idea, maybe an idea others wouldn't recognize because it is such a personal expression and involvement between the painter and what appears on that canvas. I've gone through that with collage work and I just got into values and tones and just how far you can come off the canvas, and that's an expressive style of work.

I think that there is a point of conception with a piece and today that is pretty much the same for me as it was when I first started. When I started to paint I also had some practical considerations, I wanted to produce art as best as I could with whatever materials I had, so I set goals to buy better brushes and quality paints, but when you're young and you're starting out you often can't afford them. Fresh out of college and with some good art and ideas I still couldn't afford them so I did that bit by bit. My studio was always my apartment; I never called them apartments, they were always studios because they became my primary work space, my living room and my dining room were my studio! And even though my circumstances have changed I still feel that way. I'm more confident in creating after all these years and my art has given me a sense of fulfillment, but my selling or not selling has never been an issue with me. I never pondered if my work was going to sell or not because I never cared, I just produced. Some young, up and coming artists ask, 'What if people decide not to buy your art at some point?' To which my reply is, 'I don't even consider that. I'll still produce. I'll still paint for my self-satisfaction whether that happens or not.' I think when a person just creates without confines they move energy around, like an energy is created in the universe that comes back to you. I feel that because I believe in the Creator and I see myself as being part of a chain that receives the inspiration that originates from the Creator, almost like that channels through me and manifests as the art I produce.

I take Sweats and I try to take care of my body, even taking a walk in the foothills or in the mountains makes a lot of difference to my well being. For me this is an aspect of spirituality, I believe in the Creator and He's definitely there when I'm producing. When I decided to be a full time painter and not a teacher, some people felt that I should have something to fall back on but I never thought about that. I didn't have a net to fall on, I just went forwards with that guidance and belief and I think that made me a stronger person in the arts.

About twenty-five years ago I got this thing called Lupus. I didn't know what it was and nobody in Billings, Montana knew. One of the doctors came to me and said, 'You're going to have to let us know Red Star or we can't help you. What are you taking?' And I didn't know what he was talking about. Then after he left I worked out that he thought I was taking some kind of drugs! That really upset me, I was diminishing, I was dying, and that's all he could say! So I said to my mother, 'I'm not going to die here'. Then a visiting physician from east India diagnozed Lupus. After that I respected everything, I really respected my art direction. It made me consider if art was what I really wanted to do, and after that I got back into my art. I've always been an artist but at that point in my life I really saw everything clearly and I realized just how much I really love what I am doing.

In my own style, I now kind of see myself as a recorder of the Crow arts; contemporary arts. I would like to think that in fifty or a hundred years from now a young Crow student might consider my work when they are conducting their research and find this body of work from the 1960s onwards that can be very abstract and loose but always with an element of the Crow; perhaps a design, a symbol or a message. If I can leave a message for them saying that Crow art and creativity has never died, or maybe one of them might want to come up with something like Kevin Red Star did, then I will have achieved what I wanted to. I think of my art as being a part of that great circle of Crow art from the last century, the century before and even before our migrations. I see it in the context of those shields and designs in museum collections, and I have to remember that I'm in some of those same museums now!

KEVIN RED STAR

I think the research that Native American artists do concerning American Indian art is at an honorable level, artists show that dedication and commitment to their art and their tribes more often than not and I feel that's needed for the young people to grow so they can ask, 'Okay, where was Kevin Red Star at this stage?' Or maybe one of the Pueblo potters, or one of the many fine artists from the southwest, in New York or on the northwest coast. If we can better ourselves now, our younger generations will see that American Indians were, are and can be in the mainstream of the arts. For myself, I don't just look for galleries that carry good Native American collections, I go to galleries that are different and being in those galleries makes a statement not only for me but for the Indian world. I'm not playing it too safe as far as that's concerned, I want to be pretty universal and want our other artists to have that opportunity. Being accepted by a museum is also an honor and I'm thankful that I am and that it may give the upcoming Native American artist, potter, or sculptor some incentive to look and see a fellow Indian in there, letting them know that they could get there too.

It's tough getting your work into museums, so by making inroads now for the future generations is a good feeling. When people refer to me I don't mind if they use 'artist', or 'American Indian artist'. I am American Indian and I'm considered in the art world in general. I am a representative of my particular tribal group, the Crow or Apsáalooké, but I'm also representing American Indians as a whole, native Hawaiians, and even Indians in Central America. When I had a show in Paris, France, I said that's how I felt and I do. That's how I present myself because I feel that if one of us does well in any field, it's a reflection for all Indian people. I'm not expecting people to say, 'Oh, we're proud of you'. I'm just saying, 'Hey we're doing this and we should be noted'. So that's how I try to represent the indigenous nations of this continent, so others learn that we are still here and so that we can take pride in all of those who help us to take pride in ourselves as Indian people. It's not about me but us.

When I begin a piece at this point in time I already have it in my head, I can already picture it so as I'm doing it I have the other ideas I'm planning to incorporate. It used to intimidate me when I saw a big canvas, I used to wonder how I was going to cover it! But not now. They're pretty deliberate now but if I start out on a piece and it's just not going to a direction or to an area that I really feel good about or where I thought it would go, I just set it aside and go back to it later and in the meantime move over to another canvas I might be working on. I have so many things I want to do and there are so many ideas I want to portray on canvas. Even when I was younger in New Mexico, I was quite prolific; I'd paint on anything that was available, drawing paper, print paper, anything that was there; I just enjoyed the art so much I wanted to produce. I don't know how many of my paintings are out there. It's really tough putting price tags on art but it has to be done, so I give that job to my daughter who manages my gallery! I change my prices probably every four to five years and I never got out of hand with the pricing of my work, whereas some of the young artists put a price way up there without any

recognition or any substance to their painting career and then they get discouraged because their work doesn't sell. An unknown artist might want to think about his price if he's asking $7,000 for a piece! I was just slow and steady.

The first piece I sold was years ago and it was to an art instructor, he was a jeweler, and this piece was an oil painting on canvas. I didn't know what to say because I'd never really sold anything at the time and I think I ended up selling it for something like $275, and to me that was a lot of money back then. It was a large piece – a Plains Indian dress, very pastel, with very thick paint. It was a Crow woman's dress with fringes and the elk teeth were created from squeezing paint from the tube, and it had a dark background. I thought it was pretty impressive and I had a hard time over it but my painting instructor told me, 'If you're going to be in art you'd better start selling'. I guess that painting is somewhere in Arizona, in Hopi land! I'd like to see it again one day and I know that if I found it tomorrow I'd be happy to put it up alongside my other work. I have labored over every piece I have ever done, they were all challenges to me.

I really enjoy the idea of creativity and finding out that it was legal made me feel so good! But I didn't know what an artist was, then going to school in New Mexico really opened up my eyes. I didn't even consider myself an artist then because I didn't know what their philosophies were, what they did or didn't do, or what they were all about. So through my training and going to galleries and museums I broadened my horizons. Before you know it you're immersed in the art world and once you start producing you're an artist. I guess I came back from IAIA to the Crow Reservation an artist, or at least my friends called me an artist! But living the arts, living in this existence and loving the form, makes art an existence for me and art encompasses a lot; theatre, films, architecture, landscaping, visual arts, literary arts – that's all art alongside enjoying and respecting this existence we human beings lead. Everything I do revolves around this thing called art and I just respect this existence called art. It surrounds me, I breathe art and I wouldn't put in any gauge that says something is 'high art' or 'low art'. If you live the art, you are portraying a feeling, communicating an emotion; it's a human connection, or rather a connection between human beings. ”

POSTSCRIPT

BY

Maka Citomini Omani Win

LORI LEA POURIER

"For those who have already searched the many faces and read the many stories told here, I have one more for all who will allow a moment. It is the story of a dear friend and the gifts she left . . ."

Warrior Women

A VOICE BRIDGING GENERATIONS: A TRIBUTE TO

INGRID WASHINAWATOK

Within the covers of this book lie lives and moments of people – indigenous people – many of whom I know, men and women whose lives and accomplishments deserve recognition, and more importantly, pause. For those who have already searched the many faces and read the many stories told here – which in itself is a victory in our fast-moving media landscape – I have one more for all who will allow a moment. It is the story of a dear friend and the gifts she left. Her name is Ingrid Washinawatok, a daughter, mother, wife, sister and self-proclaimed, 'ordinary girl from the rez'. She is here in spirit, for all those who will pause with me.

On March 4th, 1999, Ingrid Washinawatok's extraordinary life came to a shocking and brutal end while working for Indigenous rights in the U'wa territory of Colombia. At the age of 41, this 'ordinary girl from the rez' was executed by the FARC (Revolutionary Armed Forces of Columbia), a leftist guerrilla movement. All the evidence points to the fact that after a week of captivity, she was marched by her kidnappers a short distance across the Venezuelan border, blindfolded, bound and murdered along with two of her traveling companions, Lahe'ena'e Gay and Terence Freitas.

"On March 4th, 1999, Ingrid Washinawatok's extraordinary life came to a shocking and brutal end while working for Indigenous rights in the U'wa territory of Colombia . . ."

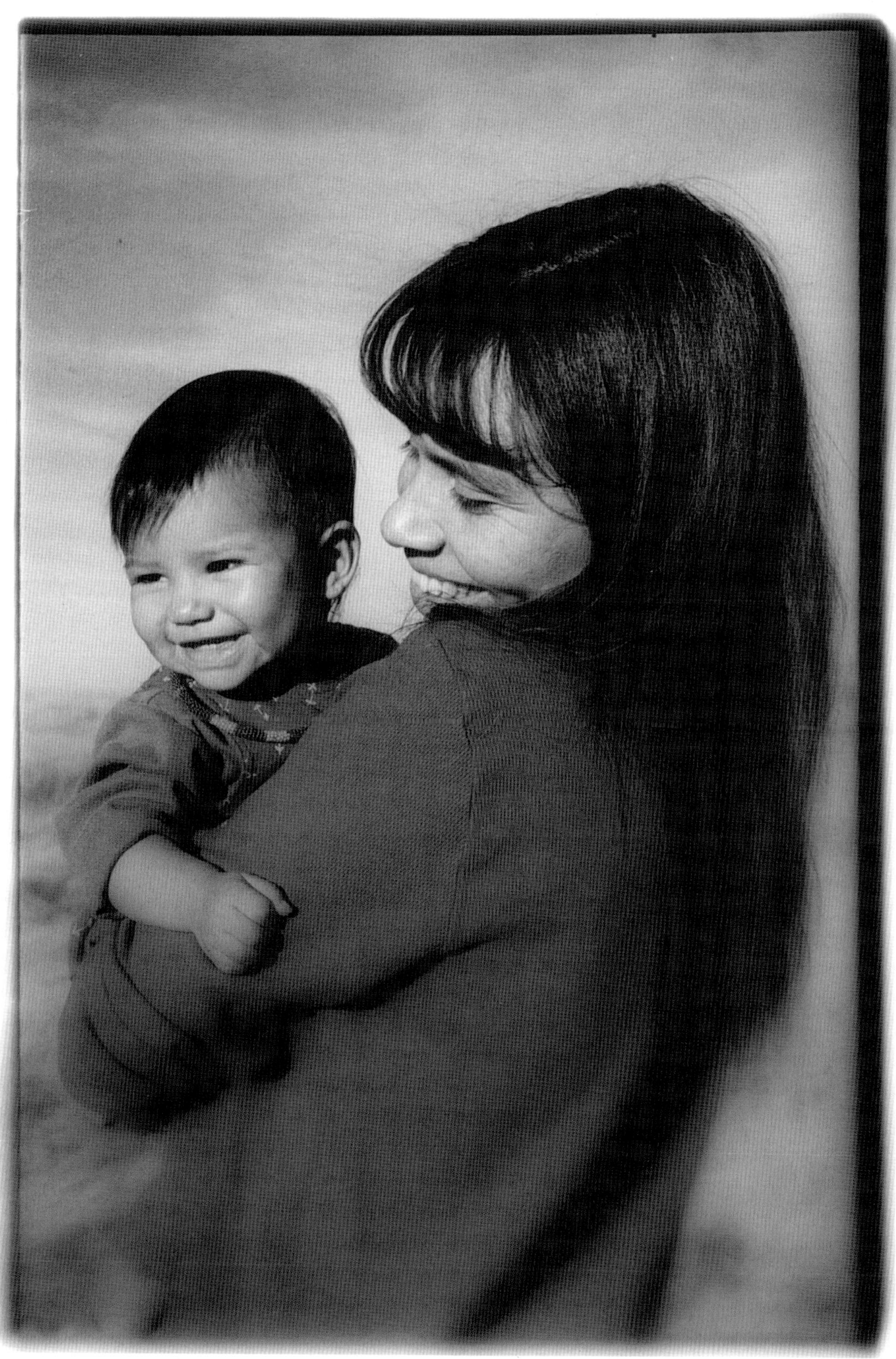

Lori holding Shahiyela.

Ingrid's Menominee tribal name was *O'Peqtaw-Metamoh*, which means 'Flying Eagle Woman'. In talking to individuals across the country, the thing that everyone remembers with loving affection was Ingrid's vivacious and infectious laughter. You could be talking with her or you could be clear across the room from her, but wherever you were you could feel her laughter and for a brief moment it filled your soul.

We sat talking one evening, about a month before she left for Colombia that last time. I was eight months pregnant. All night long she filled the rustic cabin with her laughter. My unborn daughter, Shahiyela (which means Cheyenne in our Lakota language), would start kicking inside my womb, reacting to the laughter that surrounded her. Our extended family of women and children at the Indigenous Women's Network called Ingrid 'Auntie Ing'. I teased her that Shahiyela would always recognize her laughter and that Shahiyela already knew her Auntie Ing even before she was born. Auntie Ing had her own column in *Indigenous Woman* magazine where she gave great parental advice to us all.

Later that night, Ingrid talked about her trip into the U'wa territory; it was like any other trip, she said. She was going to meet with 'the people'. It is common knowledge that Occidental Oil, an American company, is aggressively maneuvering to extract crude oil from the U'wa territory, thereby completing the genocide of the remaining two hundred U'wa people who are fighting for their remaining homelands.

Ingrid lived her life fighting for the rights of indigenous people all over the world. Her parents introduced her to indigenous politics very early in life. Ingrid watched her parents and other members of the Menominee Nation take a stand to protect their homelands from outside developers.

More than a decade before the birth of the Indigenous Rights movement, the United States Congress began a policy of terminating, relocating and assimilating Indian tribes. The Menominee tribe was terminated in the late 1950s, their former tribal lands privatized and sold for large-scale tourism development. The Menominees launched a courageous and successful struggle to regain their reservation landbase. In an interview for *Indigenous Woman* magazine, Ingrid vividly remembers, 'a lake development began on our reservation that cut up our natural lakes to form one huge man-made lake, which would be available for sale to non-Indians'. The advertisements read, 'Walk in the moccasin trails of ancient Indians'. It was Ingrid's parents' generation who defeated the notorious Legend Lake development and successfully fought for restoration.

By the early 1970s many of the young women who became politicized like Ingrid, did so because their families were wrongfully removed from their original homelands through 'Relocation' and 'Termination'. As a child Ingrid learned first-hand how US federal policy and its legally defined 'trust' responsibility was impacting her family, community and Nation. She spent much of her childhood in Chicago. The Chicano and Black Panther movements that later became known as the Civil Rights movement in America, inspired Ingrid. She said, 'There was all kinds of jelling at the same time in different camps and races of peoples so this is what you had to do, it was the right thing to do'.

And so Ingrid became a founding mother of the Indigenous Women's Network, created in 1985 to support the self-determination of indigenous women, families, communities and Nations. IWN is working to recover our history – the knowledge of who we are and where we come from – and is helping to recover ourselves. IWN's mission grew from the decades-long struggles of our elders. Nilak Butler, also a founding mother, says, 'I really see everything we are doing as an intergenerational struggle and we are just the seed planters for the generations that will be coming and we are the product of the seed that was planted before us'. Thus the experience, the teachings, and the women's courageous spirit is passed on.

I lived through the same era that inspired Ingrid. At a young age, I witnessed the uprising at Wounded Knee, when my Nation was under siege on the Pine Ridge Reservation in South Dakota. Members of the Oglala Lakota Nation called the American Indian Movement for help in investigating a corrupt tribal government, and to help the Oglalas take a stand for justice and to restore dignity in people's lives. The cry for Oglala rights resulted in a seventy-one-day occupation at Wounded Knee in 1973. During the occupation tribal members experienced first-hand federal martial law within our homelands. US government armored personnel carriers, helicopters and armed marshals behind blockades became a daily occurrence. Since that time, many other Indian women have taken a stand for the right to self-determination and sovereignty. Women began to fight for what we believed in as an inherent right to determine our own destiny and that of our future generations.

Many years later, I traveled to the remote jungles in Chiapas, Mexico, to the village of La Realidad where I saw Tzeltal, Tojolabal and Tzoztl Indian people struggling in a low intensity war. I was reminded of my own childhood on Pine Ridge. While in La Realidad, I watched armored tanks and more than one hundred soldiers pass through the small community of less than fifty families. During my stay I met with several indigenous families and comandantes (captains) of the EZLN (Zapitista Army of National Liberation). Twenty-three-year-old Comandante Benita, in a message to her sisters from the North, echoed the voices of the indigenous women I had met in Beijing, China, a couple of years earlier at the World Conference on Women. Comandante Benita said, 'I ask that you look inside yourself, look around you and the conditions in which you live and make a decision to stand up for what is rightfully yours'.

Ingrid, Nilak and all the other activist women in these pages and all over the world speak of a common purpose. They know what they believe and they know what is real for them. Tribal teachings tell these women how their people came to be. It is those sets of teachings, followed by subsequent cultural and spiritual guidance, that provides them with clear directions in life. These women recognize the relations among all living things and the responsibility to live in accordance with the natural laws given to us by the Creator. As women we understand this responsibility to care for our Mother Earth, because in caring for her we are caring for future generations and ourselves.

Our sister Ingrid left us many gifts. She was a mother, a daughter, a sister and Auntie Ing. Shortly after my Shahiyela was born, Ingrid crossed over to the spirit world. I am reminded of our own Lakota creation story. I am at peace knowing Ingrid's spirit passed Shahiyela's. Ingrid was reborn into that sacred place in the stars, and her journey through the Big Dipper, our place of origin, began again.

We celebrate women like Ingrid and the generation of women who came before her, who fought with dignity in their struggle to live the laws the Creator gave each individual. In Ingrid's name I share this story with you and thank you for sharing this moment; this call for pause. My daughter, and her daughter, and many other young women who follow in the footsteps of their Ancestors before them will forever carry on the struggle with that same dignity. Their voices too, will be strong!

Lori Pourier (Maka Citomini Omani Win) has served as the Executive Director of the Indigenous Women's Network. While retaining a position on the board of directors of the Indigenous Women's Network, she is presently the Executive Director of the First People's Fund.

"*We* talk about *'our'* sovereignty, but instead of being *only* a human concept *'our'* must be inclusive of all *Creation's* sovereignty. Sovereignty is *not a right* and responsibility reserved for all *human beings*. Sovereignty is an *integral component* within the rest of Creation and *belongs* to all components of that *Creation*. We *cannot* forget that."

Ingrid Washinawatok.

About SERLE CHAPMAN

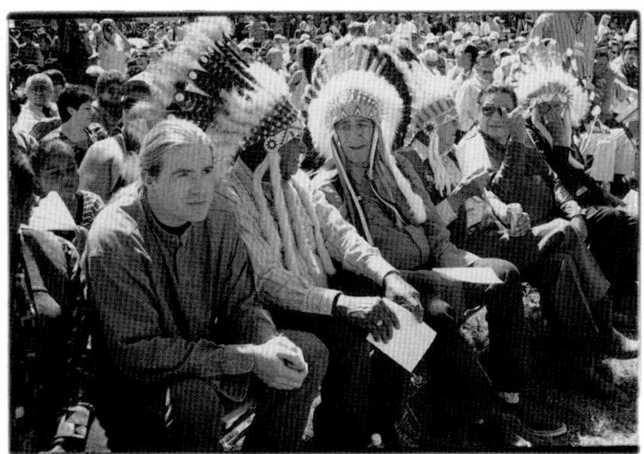

Pine Ridge, July 7, 1999: *Serle waiting for President Clinton with traditional chiefs and elders of the Oglala Lakota Nation, including Gerald One Feather, Oliver Red Cloud, Spencer Weston, Isaac White Face and Vincent Black Feather.*

Serle Chapman's first book, *The Trail of Many Spirits*, received a 1996 Book of the Year accolade in Europe and his second, *Of Earth and Elders: Visions and Voices from Native America*, achieved both outstanding mainstream reviews and approval in the Native community. Chapman's work has frequently been highlighted on national TV and radio and one of the world's premiere arts complexes, London's Barbican Center, described him in their *Written America* series as 'a critically acclaimed writer and one of the world's leading photographers'. His photography is on permanent display in various museums and visitor centers in North and Central America, including the Biosphere Reserve in Mexico. In the capacity of both author and photographer, Chapman's work has appeared in numerous national and international publications, including *The Sunday Times*, *The Guardian/Observer*, *The Daily Express*, *The Mail on Sunday*, *The Navajo Times*, *Indian Country Today*, *The Lakota Times*, *Aboriginal Voices* and various US city and statewide newspapers such as *The Denver Post* and *The Rapid City Journal*. His work for the Inter-Tribal Bison Cooperative featured in *Audubon Magazine* and he has been recognized in both *The Washington Post* and *Le Monde*. His first US royalties from *The Trail of Many Spirits* were donated to the Headstart program located in Martin on the Pine Ridge Indian Reservation, and his author royalty from *Of Earth and Elders* was committed to the American Indian College Fund. Chapman has undertaken extensive public speaking itineraries in the US and UK, and since 1996 he has led cultural awareness tours on reservations in the Northern Plains and the Southwest. Following the publication of *Of Earth and Elders* and his associated activities, Chapman received a letter of commendation from Nelson Mandela.

For further information about Serle Chapman's work visit
www.gonativeamerica.com

Serle Chapman used a standard Canon EOS 500 for all of the photography in *We, The People*.

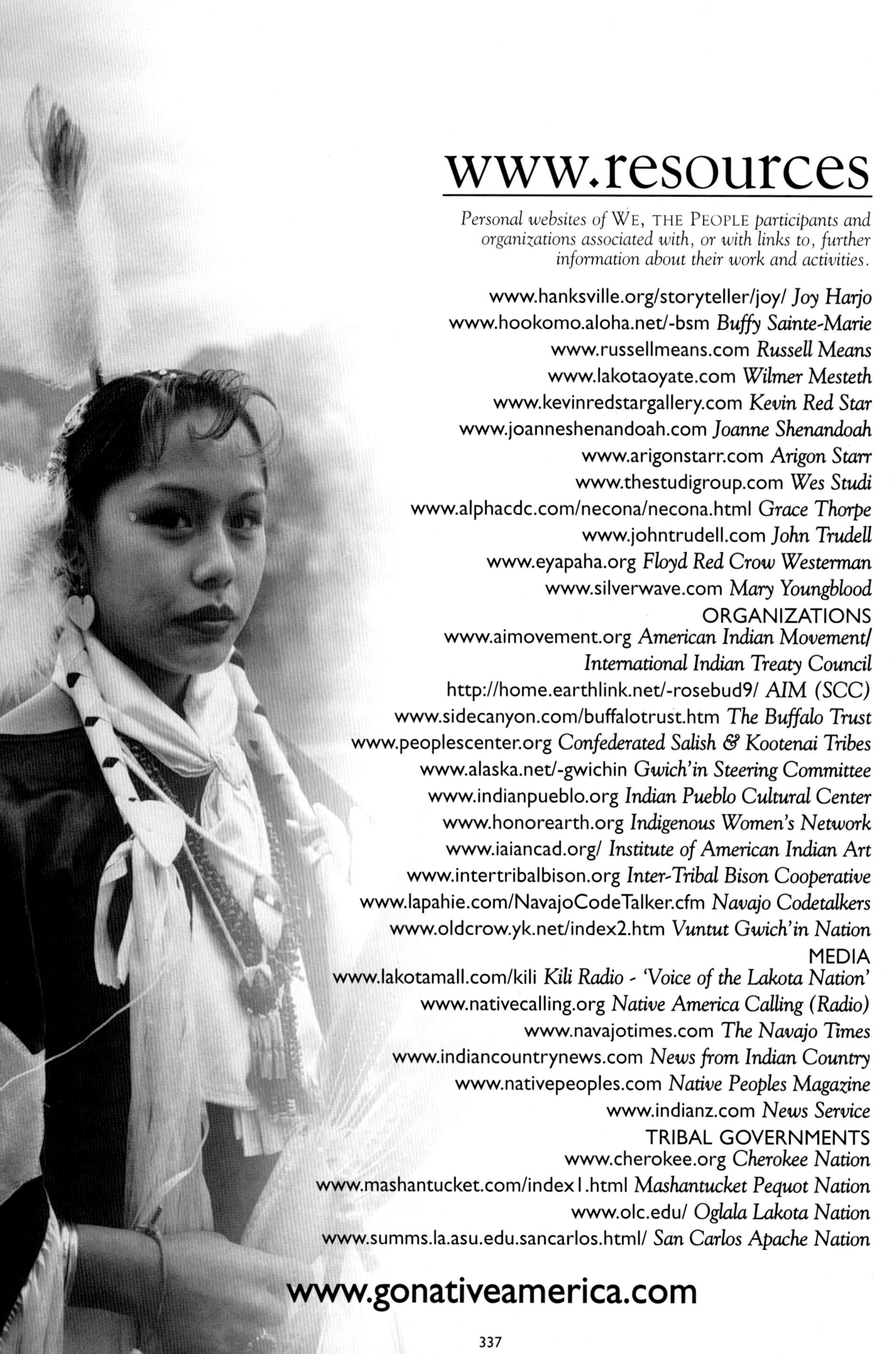

www.resources

Personal websites of WE, THE PEOPLE *participants and organizations associated with, or with links to, further information about their work and activities.*

www.hanksville.org/storyteller/joy/ *Joy Harjo*
www.hookomo.aloha.net/-bsm *Buffy Sainte-Marie*
www.russellmeans.com *Russell Means*
www.lakotaoyate.com *Wilmer Mesteth*
www.kevinredstargallery.com *Kevin Red Star*
www.joanneshenandoah.com *Joanne Shenandoah*
www.arigonstarr.com *Arigon Starr*
www.thestudigroup.com *Wes Studi*
www.alphacdc.com/necona/necona.html *Grace Thorpe*
www.johntrudell.com *John Trudell*
www.eyapaha.org *Floyd Red Crow Westerman*
www.silverwave.com *Mary Youngblood*

ORGANIZATIONS

www.aimovement.org *American Indian Movement/ International Indian Treaty Council*
http://home.earthlink.net/-rosebud9/ *AIM (SCC)*
www.sidecanyon.com/buffalotrust.htm *The Buffalo Trust*
www.peoplescenter.org *Confederated Salish & Kootenai Tribes*
www.alaska.net/-gwichin *Gwich'in Steering Committee*
www.indianpueblo.org *Indian Pueblo Cultural Center*
www.honorearth.org *Indigenous Women's Network*
www.iaiancad.org/ *Institute of American Indian Art*
www.intertribalbison.org *Inter-Tribal Bison Cooperative*
www.lapahie.com/NavajoCodeTalker.cfm *Navajo Codetalkers*
www.oldcrow.yk.net/index2.htm *Vuntut Gwich'in Nation*

MEDIA

www.lakotamall.com/kili *Kili Radio - 'Voice of the Lakota Nation'*
www.nativecalling.org *Native America Calling (Radio)*
www.navajotimes.com *The Navajo Times*
www.indiancountrynews.com *News from Indian Country*
www.nativepeoples.com *Native Peoples Magazine*
www.indianz.com *News Service*

TRIBAL GOVERNMENTS

www.cherokee.org *Cherokee Nation*
www.mashantucket.com/index1.html *Mashantucket Pequot Nation*
www.olc.edu/ *Oglala Lakota Nation*
www.summs.la.asu.edu.sancarlos.html/ *San Carlos Apache Nation*

www.gonativeamerica.com

American Indian College Fund

In 1989, the tribal college presidents launched the American Indian College Fund to raise needed private-sector funds for the thirty-two tribal colleges and their students and to increase the public's awareness of the tribal colleges.

The American Indian College Fund has spent more than a decade helping to increase enrollment and improve retention rates by providing funds for scholarships to thousands of American Indian students and raising support for other tribal college developmental needs. The American Indian College Fund, through its public education initiatives and national advertising campaign, also has brought the tribal college movement to a wider audience.

Tribal colleges provide accredited academics and personal attention in an atmosphere that rebuilds, reinforces, and explores traditional tribal cultures. For approximately 26,000 students representing 250 different tribes, their Native culture is made the center of the curriculum where studies include Native language and history, as well as biology and computer science courses. The American Indian College Fund works to ensure that the tribal colleges and Indian students have the opportunities to build upon their successes and improve the lives of Indian people and Indian communities.

Tribal colleges are succeeding in a unified mission to provide opportunities to Indian people through education, cultural preservation, and their ability to offer such vital community services as libraries, business centers, tribal archives and childcare centers. In addition to *We, the People*, The American Indian College Fund also received royalties from Serle Chapman's prior publication, *Of Earth and Elders – Visions and Voices from Native America*, and those royalties turned into scholarships for tribal college students, just as they will from this book.

To learn more about the American Indian College Fund, visit our website at **www.collegefund.org**

Educating the mind and spirit

For Annie Mae.

'But what is denied actually does exist and eventually comes to the surface, just as any truth will eventually surface despite acts to hide it.'

JOY HARJO